100
Questions and Answers

Advanced Accounting

Prepared by

CHART FOULKS LYNCH

HOLT, RINEHART AND WINSTON

LONDON · NEW YORK · SYDNEY · TORONTO

Holt, Rinehart and Winston Ltd: 1 St Anne's Road,
Eastbourne, East Sussex BN21 3UN

British Library Cataloguing in Publication Data

100 questions and answers on advanced accounting.
1. Accounting
I. Chart Foulks Lynch
657 HF5635

ISBN: 0-03-910503-2

Printed in Great Britain by A. Wheaton & Co. Ltd., Exeter

Last digit is print no: 9 8 7 6 5 4 3 2 1

ACKNOWLEDGEMENTS

We wish to thank the following bodies for permission to use questions from their examination papers:

Institute of Chartered Accountants in England and Wales
Association of Certified Accountants
Institute of Cost and Management Accountants

INTRODUCTION

A book full of questions and answers could be the single most important purchase that you as a student make in preparing for your examination.

Having experienced similar questions before sitting down to the real thing will give you a tremendous advantage. Having actually answered say, fifty questions on the same topics as those to be examined must give you a good chance of meeting the ambiguities, peculiarities of terminology and downright catches that crop up in any paper.

In this book we have drawn questions from the main accounting bodies but we have not individually identified them as to source or date. The reasons we hope are obvious. Almost all the questions could have been posed by any of the accounting bodies concerned—standards are very similar and style and emphasis vary only slightly. Also, due to changing legislation we have adapted many questions to cater for the *Finance Act 1983* and *Companies Act 1981*, for instance, and it would not be fair to attribute credit or blame in these circumstances.

Dates can be misleading as students try to discern trends. These trends can best be identified from the students' own magazines, newsletters and journals. The questions we have selected generally will be examined, albeit in some disguise, on many future occasions.

The book itself is divided into main subject areas to help you select relevant questions. If you have time, treat it as a workbook—if not, use it as a final topping-up exercise.

We hope it helps to bring you examination success.

EXAMINATION TECHNIQUE

Sensible preparation and excellent examination technique will help you succeed in (if not enjoy) your forthcoming examinations.

Contained in the following few pages are some guidelines to smooth your path through the fast approaching ordeal.

Part 1—The Build-up

This vital time must concentrate on full and structured revision. There is no escape from hard work, but for optimum benefit there are some rules:

Plan your revision time

(a) Write down your revision plan, giving yourself plenty of time to revise each subject in full.
(b) Don't concentrate so much on your weak subjects that you ignore your strong ones.
(c) Do lots of questions against the clock to build up your speed. A very large proportion of candidates who fail an exam do so because they run out of time, not because they lack the basic knowledge.

Plan your leisure also

(a) Work done after midnight or when you are tired is counterproductive. You will not be able to concentrate and you will make mistakes.
(b) If you have time off work to study, try to keep to roughly similar office hours plus say 7.00–9.00 in the evening. Work Saturdays but have a break on Sunday.

Stick to your plan

(a) Despite your plan there is a great temptation to spend too much time on one subject. Don't.
(b) Beware the dreaded tipsters. Tipsters don't know, they can only guess, and with a wide syllabus, concentrating on one or two topics is very dangerous.

The day before

(a) Relax as much as possible. If you haven't done enough work by now you won't have enough time to make up the difference. The only work you *must* do is ensuring you know where and when you are taking the exams and checking train and bus timetables to ensure you get there in good time.

(b) Do what you like doing—play the harp, pore over your stamp collection. If your hobby is drinking, *don't!*
(c) Overhaul your equipment. New calculator batteries and some spares, plenty of sharp pencils and full pens, are all essential.
(d) Go to bed early.

The aim is to rest so that you are on top form next morning. You will appreciate this when you turn up at the examination hall and encounter in the foyer the haggard faced and bleary eyed who are frantically borrowing pencil sharpeners. If they are tired before they start, think what they will feel like after the first two papers.

Part 2—In the Examination Room

This is the point at which you undergo a metamorphosis into a ruthless 'mark grubber'. Any examiner's report invariably will refer to at least half of the points listed below, and students, when reading of such basic errors, vow that they would never have been so stupid. This vow generally lasts until the moment they enter the examination room!

Attend to detail

'Topping and tailing' should be practised on all possible occasions. Underlining headings, using £ signs, dates and so on, all help to pick up any presentation and discretion marks available.

Don't annoy the examiner

Submit your questions in the right order. Don't use words like 'obviously' and 'of course' too often. Don't be critical of any specific question or the paper in general.

Examiners are only human (we think) and such behaviour is bound to upset them. You cannot afford to waste even half a mark when your career is at stake, so play the game by their rules and change the system afterwards if you feel strongly about it.

Workings

Refer specifically to workings and put them in order, clearly labelled. Don't allow the examiner merely to stumble on them by accident.

Remember, random jottings around a page will not attract as many marks as a carefully sequenced set of workings, even if the same information is present. You will be expected to order your thoughts and present information/reports when qualified, so the examiners have a right to expect similar treatment now.

Answer the question

There are many faults under this heading:

(i) Overkill—seeing a particular word in the question and writing all there is to know about that subject. It may have nothing much to do with the real question you have been asked.

(ii) Woods and trees—being unable to identify the major mark-carrying areas, or possibly devoting fifteen minutes to part (c) of a question carrying only 3 marks while writing only a few lines on part (a) carrying, say, 12 marks.

(iii) Not reading the question. A question may ask for a report or a letter, but some students nevertheless steadfastly produce essays or lists or anything but the required format.

(iv) Rewriting the question! Many students believe (mistakenly) that they can, in effect, alter the emphasis of a question, or even change it completely. Only answer the specific question set.

What I meant to say was . . .

You cannot stand at the examiner's shoulder and explain the real meaning of your script or terminology. Say what you mean and leave nothing to chance. Communication is a two way process. You have first to absorb and understand what is being asked. But having got the message you must then formulate your answer in as understandable a way as possible. Both parts are equally fundamental.

Arrange your answer in a logical sequence

Spending a few moments jotting down the main points of your answer and assembling them in a logical order will pay handsome dividends. After all, jottings on a narrative question are the equivalent of ordinary figure workings for a computational problem.

Treat the examiner as an intelligent layman

You must not assume the examiner knows certain things. He probably does, but you haven't proved to him that you do if you leave such matters out altogether.

You will probably feel less self-conscious in explaining carefully the way in which a bad debts account works if you assume that the examiner is an intelligent layman.

But, remember also that, since the examiner is most definitely not a layman, he will not tolerate wrong statements. Don't bluff!

Use of abbreviations

Using abbreviations like confetti can cause problems, particularly where non-standard abbreviations are thrown in for good measure. CCA,

I/REV, MCT, SSAP are acceptable (but not many people know that G.I.N. means goods inwards note).

If you do use initials, always put the full meaning in on the first occasion (followed by its abbreviation).

Check whether answer is reasonable

Whenever you produce an answer to a computational question spend a few seconds asking yourself whether the solution arrived at is sensible. It is so easy to press the wrong calculator button and you must give yourself every chance of picking up these silly errors.

Answer all questions

You have 180 minutes to try for 100 marks and therefore can allocate 1.8 minutes for each mark on the paper.

Don't overrun your time on each question as you are far more likely to pick up the first five marks of a new question than the last five marks of an earlier one.

1. Don't panic—two or three deep breaths as soon as you sit down will help calm you.
   Try to ensure you are not caught out by some unexpected event. To this end find out what types of examination paper are used and check which rates and allowances you are to be provided with.
2. You are only trying to pass the paper, not (necessarily) achieve 100%. There *will* be things you don't know so don't leave the examination room after the first exam in a black depression simply because you failed to deal fully with parts 3(a) and 4(c) of a paper.
3. Remember the three R's. Perhaps the best piece of advice we can give is to obey the three *R*'s *in the following order*:
   Read
   Reflect
   Write!

   Good luck with your examinations.

CONTENTS

?

Questions

QUESTION A1

The following extracts have been taken from N. Gineer Ltd's published profit and loss account for the year ended 31 March 19–0.

Historic costs:

	£000
Net profit before extraordinary items	2,653
Extraordinary items (note 5)	1,678
Net profit	4,331

Note 5 Extraordinary items	
Surplus on disposal of properties (after tax £1,032,601 and bank interest £507,586)	*2,441*
Provision against listed investments	*(763)*
	1,678

The report of the directors stated that a freehold property developed at a total cost of £3,560,998 had been sold for the sum of £7,035,000 under a contract completed on 1 April 19–0 and that the profit had been included in the profit and loss account as an extraordinary item.

Current costs:

	£000
Profit after taxation	998
Extraordinary items	1,678

The note in the accounting policy for fixed assets stated, 'The current replacement cost of fixed assets is calculated by using appropriate published indices to adjust the historical cost except for freehold and long leasehold properties within the United Kingdom where a professional valuation at 31 March 19–0 has been made and incorporated in the accounts.'

You are required to:

(*a*) *define and explain the term "extraordinary item"* (*5 marks*), *and*
(*b*) *comment on the treatment of these particular extraordinary items.* (*15 marks*).

(*20 marks*)

QUESTION A2. COALVILLE LTD

Coalville Ltd own plant and machinery with an expected useful life of 8 years. The plant was purchased in Jan. 19–1. You are provided with the following index numbers.

	Plant Cost Index	*Retail Price Index*
1 Jan. 19–1	120	100
1 Jan. 19–5	280	180
Average 19–5	360	200
31 Dec. 19–5	440	220

The plant cost £80,000 when purchased.
You are required to show the fixed asset note for the year ended 31 Dec. 19–5 using the following conventions:

(*a*) *Historical cost accounting.*
(*b*) *Current purchasing power accounting.*
(*c*) *Current cost accounting charging depreciation based upon the closing value to the business.*
(*d*) *Current cost accounting charging depreciation based upon the average value to the business.*

(*15 marks*)

QUESTION A3. UPPINGHAM LTD

Uppingham Ltd buy and sell sprocket–flanges. During the 3 months ended 31 Mar. 19–6 the company enter into the following transactions:

1 Jan. 19–6	Buy 500 units costing £750
31 Jan. 19–6	Sell 400 units for £2,000 and replace them with units costing £1,400
28 Feb. 19–6	Sell 200 units for £1,000. Buy 50 units costing £200
31 Mar. 19–6	Sell 200 units for £1,100. Buy 100 units costing £500.

The retail price index during the period was as follows:

1 Jan. 19–6	200
31 Jan. 19–6	220
28 Feb. 19–6	230
31 Mar. 19–6	240

You are required to prepare trading accounts using the following conventions.

(*a*) *Historical cost accounting* (*F.I.F.O.*)
(*b*) *Current purchasing power accounting*
(*c*) *Current cost accounting*

(*17 marks*)

QUESTION A4. SOUTHPORT MANUFACTURING CO. LTD

General Background

Southport Manufacturing Co. Ltd specialises in the manufacture of electronic components. The Financial Accountant has produced a draft set of accounts for the year ended 31 Dec. 19–8, prepared on the usual historical cost principles. The company has decided for the first time to prepare a summary of results and financial position using current cost accounting techniques.

Case study requirement

The accountant has asked you to prepare the necessary statements which the company intends to present to the shareholders, following the recommendation of SSAP 16. Make your workings to the nearest £1,000. Give comparative figures for the balance sheet.

Information given

(a) *Trading and profit and loss account for the year ended 31 Dec. 19–8*

	£000	*£000*
Sales		800,000
Opening stock	52,000	
Purchases	640,000	
	692,000	
Closing stock	72,000	620,000
Gross profit		180,000
Depreciation	42,000	
General expenses (including interest of £15.3m)	31,800	73,800
Net profit before taxation		106,200
Corporation tax		51,000
Net profit after taxation		55,200
Interim dividend (paid 30.6.–8)	10,000	
Final dividend (proposed)	20,000	30,000
Retained profit for the year		25,200

(b) *Balance Sheets as at 31.12.–7 and 31.12.–8*

Capital employed

	31.12.–7 *£000*	31.12.–8 *£000*
Ordinary shares of £1 each, authorised issued and fully paid	150,000	150,000
General revenue reserve	80,500	105,700
5% Debenture stock	200,000	200,000
	430,500	455,700

Represented by

	£000	*£000*	*£000*	*£000*
Fixed assets (Note 1)		320,000		358,000
Current assets (Note 2)	230,000		291,500	
Less current liabilities (Note 3)	119,500	110,500	193,800	97,700
		430,500		455,700

(c) *Information relating to the above accounts*

	31.12.–7 *£000*	31.12.–8 *£000*
1. Fixed assets—Plant and machinery		
Cost	400,000	480,000
Aggregate depreciation	80,000	122,000
	320,000	358,000

The company acquired several additional items of machinery on 30.9.–8 and the assets held at 31.12.–7 were originally acquired on 1.1.–6. The company's depreciation policy is to provide for depreciation at a rate of 10% pa on a straight line basis.

	31.12.–7 *£000*	31.12.–8 *£000*
2. Current assets		
Stock	52,000	72,000
Debtors	170,000	218,000
Cash	8,000	1,500
	230,000	291,500

	31.12.–7	31.12.–8
	£000	*£000*
3. Current liabilities		
Creditors	63,500	122,800
Final dividend	15,000	20,000
Corporation tax	41,000	51,000
	119,500	193,800

4. Profit and loss account items
   (i) Assume that sales, purchases and expenses have occurred at an even rate during the year.
   (ii) Assume that in each of the two years, the stock held at the end of the year was originally acquired three months before the year end.
   (iii) Assume that the debtors and creditors at the year end arose evenly over the last three months of the year.

(d) *Index numbers*

You are provided with the following index numbers for the company's assets and the Retail Price Index.

	Plant and Machinery	Stock	R.P.I.
31.12.–4	100 (base year)		
31.12.–5	105		
31.12.–6	110		
30.9.–7	114	140	
1.1.–8	115	145	178
31.3.–8	117	150	
Average 19–8	120	160	190
30.9.–8	122	170	195
31.12.–8	125	180	199

(*40 marks*)

QUESTION A5. REEFLY PLC

Reefly Plc wishes to prepare current cost accounts in accordance with *SSAP 16*. The accounting year ending 31 Dec. 19–10, would be the first year in which the company prepared such inflation adjusted accounts. The company's Profit and Loss account and Balance Sheet prepared on a historic cost basis are given below:

Profit and Loss Account for year ending 31 Dec. 19–10

	£000	£000
Sales		1,000
Less: Opening stock	300	
Purchases	900	
	1,200	
Closing stock	500	
		700
		300
Depreciation	90	
Interest payable	50	
		140
		160
Less: Corporation Tax		80
		80
Dividend paid		40
Retained profit for the year		40

Summarised Balance Sheet (in £000) as at*:*

	31.12.–9	31.12.–10
Plant and Machinery		
Cost	700	1,100
Accumulated Depreciation	230	320
	470	780
Current Assets		
Stock	300	500
Debtors	150	250
Cash	200	50
	1,120	1,580
Shareholders' Funds		
Ordinary Share capital	200	300
Revenue reserves	300	340
Loan stock	400	600
Taxation	100	112
Current Liabilities		
Creditors	120	228
	1,120	1,580

The following information is available:

The Plant and Machinery was purchased on 1.1.–5 for £300,000
on 1.1.–8 for £400,000
and on 30.6.–10 for £400,000
it is all being depreciated at 10% pa on a straight line basis. The annual depreciation charge in the Profit and Loss Account is to be based on average asset values, for current cost accounting purposes. The additional Loan stock of £200,000 and equity shares of £100,000 were issued on 30 Jun. 19–10. Both issues were for cash.

The specific price indices relevant to the company are as follows:

	Plant and Machinery	*Stock, Debtors and Creditors*
1.1.–5	110	
1.1.–8	150	
30.11.–9	195	120
31.12.–9	200	125
Average for 19–10	218	140
31.5.–10	—	140
30.6.–10	220	142
30.11.–10	240	156
31.12.–10	242	160

The company has a seasonal stock problem. As the Balance Sheets show the stock at the beginning of the year was £300,000 and at the end of the year £500,000. The stock levels did however rise steadily to a peak of £800,000 on 30 Jun. 19–10, and then steadily fell to the level on 31 Dec. 19–10. The company wishes to allow for this seasonal fluctuation of stock in its current cost accounts.

You can assume price levels, both for plant and machinery and for items in stock have risen steadily over the year. Stock is held on average for one month. You can further assume that the cash balance does not fluctuate in line with working capital items.

You are informed that the Monetary Working Capital adjustment for 19–10 is £7,257. This amount is to be deducted from the historic cost operating profit.

Required:

Prepare the Current Cost Profit and Loss account for the year ending 31 Dec. 19–10, and the Current Cost Balance Sheet as at 31 Dec. 19–10 for Reefly Plc. These accounts should be prepared in accordance with SSAP 16.
(40 marks)

QUESTION A6 Y LTD

The five year financial record of Y Ltd as presented in the published accounts prepared on the historical cost basis is shown below.

	Year ended 31 Dec. (£m)				
	19–10	*19–9*	*19–8*	*19–7*	*19–6*
Capital employed					
Capital and reserves	631	499	421	377	323
Loans	149	29	34	33	35
	780	528	455	410	358
Fixed assets	764	460	326	297	268
Net current assets—stock	10	15	25	24	26
—net monetary assets	6	53	104	89	64
	780	528	455	410	358
Profit after taxation	152	78	44	54	37

The indices which represent the price changes appropriate to the particular assets held by the company and the general price index over the years were:

	Year ended 31 Dec.				
	19–10	*19–9*	*19–8*	*19–7*	*19–6*
Beginning of year					
General prices	188	168	146	117	100
Fixed assets	165	144	121	110	100
Stocks, other current assets and current liabilities	180	160	140	120	100
Average during year					
General prices	197	182	157	135	108
Fixed assets	172	154	133	116	105
Stocks, other current assets and current liabilities	190	170	150	130	110
End of year					
General prices	204	188	168	146	117
Fixed assets	180	165	144	121	110
Stocks, other current assets and current liabilities	200	180	160	140	120

You are required to:

(a) present a revised five year financial record which reflects the application of inflation or current cost accounting principles insofar as the data provided permits, explaining any calculations you make, and

(14 marks)

(*b*) *comment on three significant differences between this new record and the original data.*

(*6 marks*)
(*Total 20 marks*)

QUESTION A7. CHELSEA RETAILERS PLC

The current assets and current liabilities of Chelsea Retailers plc. at the beginning and end of the year to 31 Dec. 19–10 are summarised below.

	Opening		*Closing*	
	£000	*£000*	*£000*	*£000*
Current assets				
Stock	54		75	
Debtors	40		50	
Cash	21		15	
	—	115	—	140
Less: Current liabilities				
Trade creditors	50		60	
Bank overdraft	30		50	
	—	80	—	110
Net current assets		35		30

The bank overdraft is considered a permanent source of finance. Stock at the end of each year represents purchases made evenly during the preceding three months. Debtors represent sales in the preceding two months.

The monthly index of stock prices and the general price index was:

		Stock Price Index	*General Price Index*
19–9	Oct.	115	162
	Nov.	117	164
	Dec.	118	167
19–10	Jan.	120	170
	Feb.	124	174
	Mar.	126	178
	Apr.	129	175
	May	132	176
	Jun.	132	177
	Jul.	134	179
	Aug.	134	180
	Sep.	135	181
	Oct.	138	182
	Nov.	140	184
	Dec.	141	186
	Average for Year	132	177

You are required to:

(*a*) *explain the purpose of the monetary working capital adjustment,* (*3 marks*)

(*b*) *calculate the monetary working capital adjustment in accordance with SSAP 16 by reference to the data given above (work to the nearest £100), and* (*4 marks*)

(*c*) *explain briefly why some authorities do not consider that a monetary working capital adjustment is necessary,* (*3 marks*)

(*Total 10 marks*)

QUESTION A8. ASSET LTD

Set out below is information relating to Asset Ltd.

(1) *Fixed assets*

	1.1.19–8		*31.12.19–8*	
	Cost	*Depcn*	*Cost*	*Depcn*
	£	£	£	£
Acquisition date				
19–2	300	180	300	210
19–4	400	160	400	200
19–6	200	40	—	—
	900	380	700	410

(2) P & L a/c—Depreciation charge £70
Profit on disposal of fixed asset £100

(3) Sale proceeds on sale of fixed asset £260

(4) *Index Nos.*

19–2	100
19–4	130
19–6	160
1.1.19–8	200
Average 19–8	210
31.12.19–8	220

Show the relevant amounts in the current cost reserve relating to fixed assets. Compute the current cost depreciation charge for the year on the year-end values of the fixed assets.

(*8 marks*)

QUESTION A9

Set out below are data relating to two identical pieces of plant. The company is preparing accounts for the year ended 31.12.–5.

	Item A	*Item B*
Age of plant at 31.12.–5	7 years	2 years
	£	£
H Cost	1,500	3,200
H Depreciation at 31.12.–4	900	320

The total expected life of these assets was 10 years.

A decision has been made at 31.12.–5 that these asset lives are too conservative and that the total expected life is 15 years.

The gross current replacement costs of each of the assets at 31.12.–4 and 31.12.–5 were £5,000 and £6,000. This is the first year in which C.C. accounts are being prepared.

You are required to show:

(*a*) *How these assets will be shown in the H.C. and C.C. accounts including comparative figures.*
(*b*) *The H.C. and C.C. depreciation charges for the year* (*compute the C.C. depreciation charge on the year end values of the fixed assets*).
(*c*) *The revaluation amounts of item A and item B during the year for inclusion in the current cost reserve.*

(*8 marks*)

QUESTION A10

Assume the same data as in Question A9 with the only difference that this is *not* the first year for which C.C. accounts are being prepared.

You are required to show:

(*a*) *How these assets will be shown in the H.C. and C.C. accounts including comparative figures.*
(*b*) *The H.C. and C.C. depreciation charges for the year* (*compute the C.C. depreciation charge on the year end values of the fixed assets*).
(*c*) *The revaluation amounts of item A and item B during the year for inclusion in the current cost reserve.*

(*10 marks*)

QUESTION A11

An item of plant is shown in the H.C. accounts as at 31.12.–4 as follows:

	£
Cost	100,000
Depreciation (10% pa) (on cost)	50,000
	50,000

The company is preparing H.C. accounts and supplementary C.C. accounts for the year ended 31.12.–5.

The following information is available:

1. Replacement price of an equivalent machine is £300,000.
2. Estimates of future net cash flows from the continued use of the machine in each year and realisable values are:

	Net cash flows	*Realisable value*
	£	£
31.12.–5		60,000
31.12.–6	40,000	35,000
31.12.–7	25,000	15,000
31.12.–8	15,000	*Nil*
31.12.–9	—	*Nil*

Show the amount at which the asset will be stated in the H.C. accounts and C.C. accounts at 13.12.–5 and the amount in the C.C. reserve relating to the asset (ignore C.C. depreciation charge for the year) and you are required to revise the remaining useful life of the asset for the H.C. accounts based upon the future cash flows.

(*10 marks*)

QUESTION A12. UK BANK LTD

The H.C. balance sheets as at 30.9.–9 and 30.9.–8 for UK Bank Ltd are:

	30.9.–9	30.9.–8
	£m	*£m*
ASSETS		
Liquid assets		
Bank notes and balances with the Bank of England	700	800
Money at call and short notice	5,000	4,500
Customers' accounts		
Advances less provisions	20,000	19,200
Trade investments	100	90
Premises and equipment	800	750
	26,600	25,340
Ordinary shareholders' funds		
Share capital	240	240
Reserves	1,260	920
Loan capital	700	600
Current, deposit and other accounts	24,000	23,200
Other liabilities		
Creditors	100	80
Taxation	300	300
	26,600	25,340

Notes:

(1) The H.C. profit and loss account for the year ended 30.9.–9 was:

	£m
Profit	640
Taxation	300
	340

(2) Interest on loan capital of £65m was charged in arriving at H.C. profit.
(3) The following current cost information is relevant:

C.C. Valuations of:	*30.9.–9*	*30.9.–8*
	£m	*£m*
Trade investments	180	160
Premises and equipment	1,200	1,100

(4) The depreciation adjustment has been computed as £40m.

(5) The UK index of retail prices for relevant dates is:

	£
At 30.9.–8	438
At 30.9.–9	488
Average for year ended 30.9.–9	460

This is the fourth year supplementary C.C. accounts have been prepared. The opening reserves at 1.10.–8 comprise:

	£m	*£m*
Profits		720
Current cost reserve of which:		
Realised	200	
Unrealised	420	
	—	620
		1,340

Prepare:

(*a*) *A supplementary profit and loss account under SSAP 16.*
(*b*) *The current cost reserve under SSAP 16.*
(*c*) *A supplementary profit and loss account following the Hyde Guidelines.*
(*d*) *A supplementary profit and loss account applying the gearing proportion to all holding gains* (*the Godley-Cripps method*).

(*30 marks*)

QUESTION A13. CHIPPING NORTON LTD

Chipping Norton Ltd is a manufacturing company which has been in existence for many years. You are presented at 31st Dec. 19–9 with the following balance sheets prepared on a historical cost basis.

	At 31.12.19–8		*At 31.12.19–9*	
	£000	*£000*	*£000*	*£000*
Freehold Land and Buildings		800		929
Plant and Machinery		370		479.5
		1,170		1,408.5
Stock	220		620	
Debtors	230		300	
Cash	175		340	
		625		1,260
		1,795		2,668.5
Dividend		—	100	
Creditors	270		320.5	
Taxation	100		120	
		370		540.5
		1,425		2,128
Ordinary shares of 10p each		700		1,000
Share premium		—		150
Revenue Reserves		245		504
10% Debentures		450		450
Deferred Taxation		30		24
		1,425		2,128

The profit and loss account for the year ended 31st Dec. 19–9 showed the following.

	£000
Profit before taxation	473
Taxation	114
Profit after tax	359
Dividends	100
Retained	259

You are supplied with the following information

(1) Interest payable during the year amounted to £42,500.
(2) The freehold land cost £400,000 many years ago.
Additional land was acquired on 30th June 19–9 at a cost of £40,000. The land was professionally valued at 31st Dec. 19–8 at a figure of £450,000 and at 31st Dec. 19–9 at a figure of £540,000. No depreciation is provided on the land.

(3) The freehold buildings held at 31st Dec. 19–8 had cost £500,000 several years ago. An additional factory costing £100,000 was purchased on 30th June 19–9. A professional valuation of the buildings at 31st Dec. 19–8 showed their value to be £520,000. Their estimated value at 31st Dec. 19–9 was £602,000, including £99,000 on the new factory. Depreciation is provided at 2% per annum on cost. No change has been made with regard to the estimate of their remaining useful life. Compute the current cost depreciation charge to profit and loss account on the year end valuation.

The net book value of the land and buildings is made up as follows:

	31.12.–8	*31.12.–9*
	£000	*£000*
Cost	900	1,040
Accumulated depreciation	100	111
	800	929

(4) The net book value of the plant and machinery is made up as follows:

	31.12.–8	*31.12.–9*
	£000	*£000*
Cost	520	690
Accumulated depreciation	150	210.5
	370	479.5

Depreciation is provided at 10% per annum on cost. There were no disposals during the year. The additional plant was purchased on 30th June 19–9. A price index for the type of machines used by the company gives the following. Compute the current cost depreciation charge to profit and loss account at the year end valuations.

Index at date of acquisition of original machines	132
At 31.12.19–8	209
At 30.6.19–9	216
At 31.12.19–9	220

(5) A price index for the type of stock held by the company gives the following

At 31.12.19–8	179
Average for 19–9	204
At 31.12.19–9	230

The stock at each year end was purchased shortly before the end of the year.

(6) Deferred tax is accounted for based on SSAP 15.

You are required:

(*a*) *To prepare a supplementary statement for Chipping Norton Ltd in accordance with SSAP 16.*

(*25 marks*)

(*b*) *Discuss the results obtained in* (*a*)

(*5 marks*)

(*Total 30 marks*)

QUESTION A14

The recently issued consolidated balance sheet and profit and loss account of a public company, prepared on an historical cost basis, are summarised below.

	30 Sep. 1980 £m	30 Sep. 1979 £m
Consolidated balance sheet		
Capital and reserves	631	499
Loans	149	29
	780	528
Fixed assets		
Cost	1,016	590
Depreciation	232	130
Net	784	460
Current assets		
Stocks	502	304
Debtors	332	211
Liquid funds for day to day use	25	23
	859	538
Current liabilities		
Creditors	405	208
Taxation	20	15
Overdraft	418	234
Dividends	20	13
	863	470
Net current assets/(liabilities)	(4)	68
	780	528

Consolidated profit and loss account for year to 30 Sep. 1980

	£m
Turnover—Home	1,246
Export	532
	1,778
Trading profit	303
Depreciation (the same rate on all fixed assets)	102
Profit before interest	201
Interest	13
	188
Taxation	30
Profit after taxation	158
Ordinary dividends	26
Retained profit	132

The directors have asked you to prepare current cost accounts in accordance with SSAP16. A loan of £120m was raised halfway through the year. The cost of sales adjustment for 1980 has been calculated as £21m and the monetary working capital adjustment as £9m. (Both are debits to Profit and Loss Account.) There have been no sales of fixed assets during the last five years and those held at the beginning of the year represent purchases of £100m, 130m, 150m, 210m in 1976, 1977, 1978 and 1979 respectively, spread equally throughout each year. They have been depreciated at 10% pa including the year of purchase. The stocks at the year end represent purchases made at the year end (50%) and equally over the year (50%), and similarly for trade creditors. The age analysis for debtors showed that 75% represented year end sales and 25% equally over the year. The indices which represent the price changes experienced by the particular assets held by the company and the general price index over the years were:

		Year ended 30 Sep.				
		1980	*1979*	*1978*	*1977*	*1976*
Beginning of year	Fixed assets	165	144	121	110	100
	Stocks	180	160	140	120	100
	Other current assets and liabilities	180	160	140	120	100
	General prices	188	168	146	117	100
Average during year	Fixed assets	172	154	133	116	105
	Stocks	190	170	150	130	110
	Other current assets and liabilities	190	170	150	130	110
	General prices	197	182	157	135	108
End of year	Fixed assets	180	165	144	121	110
	Stocks	200	180	160	140	120
	Other current assets and liabilities	200	180	160	140	120
	General prices	204	188	168	146	117

You are required to:

(*a*) *Calculate the depreciation adjustment for 1980 (based upon average value of fixed assets).*

(*10 marks*)

(*b*) *Calculate the gearing adjustment for 1980.*

(*10 marks*)

(*c*) *Present the current cost reserve account.*

(*10 marks*)
(*Total 30 marks*)

QUESTION A15

Shown below is the group profit and loss account (current cost basis) for a public quoted company, together with related notes.
Profit and loss account for the year ended 31 Dec. 1980.

1979	*1979 restated in 1980 £s*		*1980*
£ million	*£ million*		*£ million*
5,368	6,334	Sales	5,715
374	441	Trading profit before financing costs and taxation (Note 5)	119
(8)	(9)	Interest and other financial items	(46)
(80)	(94)	As in historical costs accounts	(110)
72	85	Gearing adjustment (Note 6)	64
366	432	Profit before taxation	73
(123)	(145)	Taxation	(123)
(20)	(24)	Minority interests	(11)
223	263	Profit (loss) attributable to parent company	(61)
(16)	(19)	Extraordinary items	(173)
207	244	Profit (loss) attributable to parent company after extraordinary items	(234)
(134)	(158)	Dividends	(101)
73	86	Profit (loss) retained for year	(335)

Note 5

Current cost adjustment reduced the historical cost trading profit as shown below:

	1980	*1979 restated in 1980 £s*	*1979*
	£ million	*£ million*	*£ million*
Trading profit–historical cost accounts	358	787	667
Cost of sales	(109)	(164)	(139)
Monetary working capital	(3)	(70)	(59)
Supplementary depreciation	(165)	(148)	(125)
Indexation of government grants	38	36	30
Trading profit-current cost accounts	119	441	374
The amount of depreciation charged and government grants credited in the current cost accounts were:			
Depreciation	456	440	373
Government grants	59	58	49

Note 6 Gearing adjustment

Under SSAP 16 the gearing adjustment in respect of fixed assets is related to the charge for supplementary depreciation (after making allowance for the difference between historical and CCA asset lives). The adjustment thus excludes revaluation surpluses not yet treated as realised. The company believes that this results in mis-stating the amount by which the interests of the equity stockholders have been affected by loan and other external financing, the interest on which has been charged against profits.

Under the company's method, the gearing adjustment represents the total holding gains less losses for the year on assets effectively financed by borrowings less cash; the exchange gains on the non sterling part of these net borrowings are then added to the adjustment.

The cost of interest and other financial items calculated in accordance with the company's method would be:

	1980	*1979 restated in 1980 £s*	*1979*
	£ million	*£ million*	*£ million*
As in historical cost accounts	(110]	(94)	(80)
Gearing adjustment	86	117	99
Exchange gains on financial items	118	81	69
The company's method	94	104	88

You are required to:

(*a*) *explain the second column of figures, the one that is headed 1979 restated in 1980 £'s,*

(*3 marks*)

(*b*) *comment upon the three figures given for sales,*

(*3 marks*)

(*c*) *explain the entry in Note 5 "indexation of government grants",*

(*4 marks*)

(*d*) *explain and comment upon the phrase in Note 6 "the charge for supplementary depreciation (after making allowance for the difference between historical and CCA asset lives)"*

(*4 marks*)

(*e*) *explain and comment upon the statement in Note 6 "excludes revaluation surpluses not yet treated as realised"*

(*4 marks*)

(*f*) *comment upon the difference between the gearing adjustment in the accounts and that preferred by the company, and*

(*3 marks*)

(*g*) *comment upon the three figures given for dividends.*

(*3 marks*)
(*24 marks*)

QUESTION B1. CHEDDAR LTD

Cheddar Ltd is a highly profitable company. At 31 Dec. 19–5 the accounts WDV of fixed assets ranking for capital allowances exceeds tax WDV by £1,750,000, but the company has hitherto not provided for deferred tax.

The company has produced a budget indicating likely capital expenditure over the next few years:

Year	*Expenditure on plant (=FYA)*	*Forecast total depreciation charge*
	£000	*£000*
Actual 19–5	1,500	1,200
Forecast 19–6	1,600	1,400
Forecast 19–7	1,750	1,600
Forecast 19–8	1,100	1,670

Forecast 19–9 onwards—FYAs are likely to be well in excess of depreciation.

Show the deferred tax charges for 19–5 to 19–8 following the requirements of SSAP 15, and the provisions required in the balance sheet for 19–4 to 19–8, assuming that there are no other timing differences to be considered and the corporation tax is 50%.

(*5 marks*)

QUESTION B2. CHESHIRE LTD

At 31 Dec. 19–0 the written-down value of fixed assets ranking for capital allowances exceeds tax WDV by £1,400,000. Cheshire has not previously provided for deferred tax. Actual and anticipated expenditure is as follows:

Year	*Expenditure on plant (=FYA)*	*Depreciation*
	£000	*£000*
Actual 19–0	1,500	1,200
Forecast 19–1	1,100	1,670
Forecast 19–2	1,600	1,400
Forecast 19–3	1,750	1,600
Forecast 19–4 and after—FYA always in excess of depreciation		

Show the deferred tax charges for 19–0 to 19–3 following the requirements of SSAP 15, and the provisions required in the balance sheet, assuming that there are no other timing differences to be considered and the corporation tax rate is 50%. Identify separately the amount to be treated as a prior year adjustment in 19–0.

(*8 marks*)

QUESTION B3. OFFSET LTD

At 31 Dec. 19–0, the accounts NBV of plant exceeds the tax WDV by £2,890,000. Offset Ltd has previously provided for deferred tax under *SSAP 11*. Actual and anticipated timing differences are as follows:

Year	*Capital allowances minus depreciation*
	£000
Actual 19–1	110
Forecast 19–2	152
Forecast 19–3	290
Forecast 19–4	(204)
Forecast 19–5	10
Forecast 19–6	(312)
Forecast 19–7 originating exceed reversing in all years	

Show extracts from the accounts relating to deferred tax for the year ended 31.12.–1 following the requirement of SSAP 15. Corporation tax is 50%. Comparatives should be shown where information allows.

(*Total 8 marks*)

QUESTION B4. HUCKLEBERRY LTD

Huckleberry Ltd is a manufacturing company which commenced trading 10 years ago. It has not previously maintained a deferred taxation account. Owing to the issue of *SSAP 15* the directors have decided to reconsider the accounting policy on deferred tax.

They have provided you with the following information:

(a) During the year ended 31 Dec. 19–7 the company revalued a freehold property at £950,000. The company intends to incorporate this revaluation in its final accounts, but there is no intention to dispose of the property in the foreseeable future. The property was originally acquired in 19–1 at a cost of £700,000.

(b) Additions to plant and machinery during 19–7 amounted to a cost of £196,750 but there were no disposals. Depreciation provided on plant has been calculated at £133,000. 100% FYAs are attributable to all plant expenditure.

(c) In the three years ended 31 Dec. 19–6, the company has obtained IBAs amounting to £384,400. Writing down allowances at 4% of the cost of the industrial buildings are available. The buildings are depreciated at 2% of cost. The cost of the buildings totals £620,000.

(d) At the end of 19–6 the book written down value of plant and machinery amounted to £643,500 compared with a tax written down value of £141,000. All assets in this total are entitled to a writing down allowance of 25%.

(e) Forecasts made by the company, based upon current revenue law, show that the following changes in timing differences are expected in the next four years.

	Excess of plant allowances over depreciation
	£
19–8	45,000
19–9	(20,000)
19–10	(50,000)
19–11	10,000

Thereafter net originating timing differences are expected. The IBAs available are as per note (c). Corporation tax is at 52%.

You are required to:

(*a*) *draft the relevant extract from accounting policies for the year ended 31 Dec. 19–7;*

(*3 marks*)

(*b*) *draft the relevant notes and extracts from the accounts relating to the taxation matters above.*

(*10 marks*)
(*Total 13 marks*)

QUESTION C1. LESSEE LTD

On 31 Dec. 19–0 a company leases a machine with an expected useful life of four years on conditions which transfer substantially all the risks and rewards of ownership to the company. The cost of the machine is £50,000 and the lease is for four years. A rental of £4,291 is payable at the end of each quarter, so that the total lease payments will be 16 × £4,291 = £68,656.

The company depreciates plant of this kind over a period of four years by the straight line method. Finance charges are to be apportioned over the four years as follows:

	£
Year to 31 Dec. 19–1	7,435
Year to 31 Dec. 19–2	5,783
Year to 31 Dec. 19–3	3,850
Year to 31 Dec. 19–4	1,588
	18,656

This allocation is based on the use of an implicit interest rate of 16% as a discounting factor.

Indicate the way in which the machine and the lease liability will appear in the company's balance sheet in the years 31 Dec. 19–0 to 31 Dec. 19–4.
(8 marks)

QUESTION C2

After much discussion about leases a UK exposure draft has arrived. However, the FASB issued a standard some time ago and the IASC issued their exposure draft in 1980. Both recognise that some lease arrangements are equivalent to a sale and purchase.

Kingsway Ltd obtained the benefit of the use of plant costing £100,000 on 1 Jul. 19–0. This plant is expected to have a useful life of 5 years. The payments to be made under the non-cancellable financial lease are 5 annual payments of £30,000 commencing on 1 Jul. 19–0. The summarised balance sheet of Kingsway Ltd on 1 Jul. 19–0, excluding anything in respect of the lease arrangement was:

	£		£
Share capital and reserves	200,000	Fixed assets	125,000
		Current assets	225,000
Current liabilities	150,000		
	350,000		350,000

The estimated profit for the year to 30 Jun. 19–1 after tax would have been £50,000 without the use of the new plant. The use of new plant is expected to increase trading profits after lease payments but before depreciation and tax by £40,000 pa. Assume a corporation tax rate of 40%.

You are required to:

(*a*) *show how the leasing transaction would be reflected in the balance sheet on* 30 *Jun.* 19–1, *on the assumptions that:*

(*i*) *the leasing arrangement is shown by way of note;*
(*ii*) *the leasing arrangement is capitalised,* (*use the "rule of 78" for interest purposes*),

(*8 marks*)

(*b*) *calculate the return for the year ended 30 Jun. 19–1 on the shareholders' funds at the beginning of that year under the same two assumptions, and*
(*4 marks*)

(*c*) *comment briefly on the alleged necessity for a standard on this topic.*
(*3 marks*)
(*Total 15 marks*)

QUESTION C3

Steelparts Ltd has entered into an agreement with a finance company, to lease a machine for a four year period. Under the terms of the agreement, the machine is to be made available to Steelparts Ltd on 1 Jan. 19–1, when an immediate payment of £15,000 has to be made, followed by seven semi annual payments of an equivalent amount.

The fair market price of the machine on 1 Jan. 19–1 is £96,000. The estimated life of such machines is four years. Steelparts Ltd can borrow money from the bank at a rate of 18% pa. The company has a policy of depreciating the machines of this type that it owns over a four year period on a straight line basis.

Required:

(*a*) *What are the key factors that differentiate a finance lease from an operating lease?*

(*3 marks*)

(*b*) *If this lease is to be capitalised show how the above transaction will be recorded in the Profit and Loss Account and the Balance Sheet of Steelparts Ltd during the first two years of the lease agreement. Show such entries under both of the following different set of assumptions:*

(*i*) *the lessee wishes to allocate the interest charge based on the 'actuarial method'. The implicit rate of interest is 7% per six months,*

(*ii*) *the lessee wishes to allocate the interest charge based on the Rule of 78 (sum of digits) method*

Give details of the method being followed.

(*14 marks*)
(*Total 17 marks*)

QUESTION C4

The Accounting Standards Committee first considered the proposed exposure draft on leasing in 1978. Some of the proposals which have been considered include:

(1) Leases which are equivalent to the purchase of an asset (financial leases) should be capitalised in financial statements prepared by lessees and depreciated over their useful lives.
(2) Future lease rentals for financial leases which extend for more than one year beyond the balance sheet date should be disclosed separately for each of the next five years and in one sum thereafter.
(3) Lessors should account for financial leases as if they were equivalent to a loan of money. The finance charge should therefore be allocated over the period of the lease to give a constant rate of return on funds employed, and correspondingly lessees should account for the finance charge on a similar basis.

You are required to apply these proposals to the following case.

The Hard Up Manufacturing Company Ltd whose year end is 31 Dec. has acquired two items of machinery on leases, the terms of which would mean that they should be treated as financial leases.

Item A 10 annual instalments of £10,000 each, the first payable on 1 Jan. 19–6. The machine was completely installed and first operated on 1 Jan. 19–6 and its purchase price on that date was £80,000. The machine has an estimated useful life of 10 years at the end of which it will be of no value.

Item B 10 annual instalments of £15,000 each, the first payable on 1 Jan. 19–8. The machine was completely installed and first operated on

1 Jan. 19–8 and its purchase price on that date was £117,000. This machine has an estimated useful life of 12 years at the end of which it will be of no value.

The finance charges should be allocated over the period of the lease on the sum of digits method.

The basic calculation of this allocation is shown below:

Item A

Sum the years 1 + 2 + 3 + 4 + 5 + 6 + 7 + 8 + 9 + 10 = 55
Allocate finance charge £20,000 (being £100,000 – £80,000) to each year.

		Finance charge	*Total payment*	*Capital repayment*
		£	£	£
19–6	10/55 × 20,000 =	3,636	10,000	6,364
19–7	9/55	3,273	10,000	6,727
19–8	8/55	2,909	10,000	7,091
19–9	7/55	2,545	10,000	7,455
19–10	6/55	2,182	10,000	7,818
19–11	5/55	1,818	10,000	8,182
19–12	4/55	1,454	10,000	8,546
19–13	3/55	1,091	10,000	8,909
19–14	2/55	727	10,000	9,273
19–15	1/55	365	10,000	9,635
		20,000		80,000

Item B

Sum the years 1 + 2 + 3 + 4 + 5 + 6 + 7 + 8 + 9 + 10 = 55
Allocate finance charges £33,000 (being £150,000 – £117,000) to each year.

		Finance charge	*Total payment*	*Capital repayment*
		£	£	£
19–8	10/55 × 33,000 =	6,000	15,000	9,000
19–9	9/55	5,400	15,000	9,600
19–10	8/55	4,800	15,000	10,200
19–11	7/55	4,200	15,000	10,800
19–12	6/55	3,600	15,000	11,400
19–13	5/55	3,000	15,000	12,000
19–14	4/55	2,400	15,000	12,600
19–15	3/55	1,800	15,000	13,200
19–16	2/55	1,200	15,000	13,800
19–17	1/55	600	15,000	14,400
		33,000		117,000

You are required to:

(*a*) *state briefly the terms that would make a lease a finance lease,* (*4 marks*)

(*b*) *calculate and state the charge to the profit and loss account for 19–9 and 19–10 if lease payments are charged thereto,* (*2 marks*)

(*c*) *calculate and state the charge to profit and loss account for 19–9 and 19–10 if these leases are treated as financial leases and capitalised using the sum of the digits method for the finance charges,* (*4 marks*)

(*d*) *show how items A and B would be incorporated in the balance sheet, and notes thereto, at 31 Dec. 19–10, if capitalised,* (*5 marks*)

(*e*) *comment on the necessity for the consideration of this topic and possible reasons for the delay in publishing the proposed standard.* (*5 marks*)

Ignore taxation.

(*Total 20 marks*)

QUESTION C5

Part (*1*)

Rowlf Ltd is a large quoted company engaged in the manufacture of food products. The following extracts are taken from its financial statements for the year ended 31 Dec. 19–7.

Accounting policies—leased plant and vehicles

An amount equivalent to the cost of certain leased plant and vehicles is included under fixed assets and depreciated in accordance with the group's normal rates, which ensure that such amount is written off within the terms of the leases.

Outstanding lease instalments, excluding interest, are shown under *other liabilities*. Interest is charged to profit and loss account by annual instalments over the terms of the primary leases.

Consolidated balance sheet—other sources of finance

Other liabilities (note 13)	£8,885,000

Notes to the accounts

	£000
Note *13—other liabilities*	
Capital portion of outstanding lease and hire purchase payments on plant and vehicles payable 19–8/19–9	11,139
Less: Amounts payable within twelve months included in creditors	2,254
	8,885

You are required to:

(*a*) *distinguish between operating leases and finance* (*or capital*) *leases,*
(*6 marks*)

(*b*) *describe, and state the case for, the accounting treatment followed by Rowlf Ltd.*
(*8 marks*)
(*Total 14 marks*)

Part (*2*)

Sam Ltd has entered into a finance lease in respect of a crane. The terms of the lease are:

(a) Three year primary period with a quarterly rent payable in advance of £2,500, i.e. total payments of £30,000.
(b) Ten year secondary period at a nominal rent (which can be ignored for the purposes of this question).

The cost of a new crane, if purchased outright, would be £25,000.

Its estimated useful life is six years with a nil scrap value. Sam Ltd uses the straight line basis of depreciation for plant.

You are required to:

(*a*) *compute the charge to the profit and loss account using the traditional* (*expensing*) *approach, indicating the minimum legal requirements for disclosure,*
(*3 marks*)

(*b*) *compute the charge in the profit and loss account, assuming the leasing commitment is capitalised, using:*

(*i*) *the sum of the digits approach, spreading the interest charge over* 12 *quarters,*
(*3 marks*)

(*ii*) *using the actuarial approach* (*the present value of a periodic payment of £1 a period for 11 periods at $3\frac{1}{2}$% per period is £9*),
(*6 marks*)

(*c*) *show the relevant entries in the balance sheet for the first year, using the actuarial method.*
(*4 marks*)
(*Total 16 marks*)

QUESTION D1. TEXAS, BLACK AND GOLD

Texas Ltd, Black Ltd and Gold Ltd are three companies in the oil and mineral exploration business. They agree to set up a fourth company Bonanza Ltd in order to participate in oil exploration in the North Sea.

Bonanza Ltd is formed with an authorized share capital of 600 shares of £1,000 each. The three parent companies each purchase 200 shares for cash. During the first year of operations the following transactions take place:

(a) Bonanza Ltd pays £500,000 to various governments in order to purchase the licences required to operate in the North Sea. The licences run for five years.
(b) The company begins exploration and development work in four areas. The following exploration and development costs are incurred:

	£
Area one	400,000
Area two	330,000
Area three	50,000
Area four	60,000

(c) By the end of the first year the following results have been achieved:

Area one—Fully explored; 45,000 barrels discovered.
Area two—Fully explored; 220,000 barrels of which 120,000 barrels have been extracted and sold at £5 per barrel, incurring production costs of £1 per barrel.
Area three—Fully explored; no reserves discovered.
Area four—Exploration continuing. No reserves yet discovered.

At the end of the first year the board of directors meets to consider the accounting policies which it should adopt in preparing the annual accounts.

(i) Mr Wayne, who is also a director of Texas Ltd wishes the company to adopt *Successful Efforts Accounting*.
Under this method exploration and development costs are carried forward in the balance sheet if in that area, the value of the reserves discovered, covered the cost incurred.
(ii) Mr Red, who is also a director of Black Ltd, wishes the company to adopt *Full Cost Accounting*.
This method is similar to successful efforts accounting except that the right to carry forward such expenditure is based upon all of the operations of the company, rather than the one particular area in which the oil was discovered.
(iii) Mr Adair, who is also a director of Gold Ltd, suggests that the company should adopt *Reserve Recognition Accounting*.
Under this method revenue is recognised when the reserves are discovered rather than when the oil is sold. Exploration and development expenditure is not carried forward. Instead the balance sheet shows reserves of oil not yet extracted, at its valuation to the business.

You are required to:

(*a*) *prepare revenue accounts and balance sheets for the current year for each of the three methods described above. Assume that the selling price and production cost of the oil will remain constant in the future and that all companies amortise the licence cost in equal amounts over its term. All calculations should be made to the nearest £000,*

(*16 marks*)

(*b*) *state briefly, giving appropriate reasons, which method you consider would be most suitable for the purpose of:*

(*i*) *internal reporting; and*
(*ii*) *external reporting.*

(*6 marks*)
(*Total 22 marks*)

QUESTION D2. OLDAGE CONCERN LTD

Accounting for pension costs

(a) Distinguish between externally funded and internally financed schemes.

(*3 marks*)

(b) Benefits to be charged in the profit and loss account should be calculated using an actuarial method. Two possible methods are available.

(i) A discontinuance basis that values pension liabilities at the amount required to meet the rights to future benefits which present members have built up by service to date based on their current pensionable salary; or

(ii) An accrued benefit basis where it is assumed that the pension scheme will continue in existence and new members will be admitted. Pension liabilities are valued by reference to net benefits to which present members will be entitled on retirement rather than that to which they are currently entitled.

State with your reasons which you would consider to be most appropriate as a method of accounting for pension costs in the light of SSAP 2.

(*6 marks*)

(c) Explain why it would be considered unsatisfactory for pension costs to be accounted for either by making provision for pension benefits only at the date of retirement of the employee or by charging the profit and loss account with pension payments as they are made.

(*2 marks*)

(d) State to what extent you consider that an employer's arbitrary right to suspend or reduce his obligations towards a pension scheme should be taken into account when determining the appropriate accounting treatment.

(*2 marks*)

(e) State what you would consider in each case to be the most suitable accounting treatment when an actuarial valuation reveals a material surplus or deficiency as a result of:

(i) Actual events not coinciding with the assumptions used by the actuary when he made his last valuation.
(ii) Changes occurring in actuarial assumptions for future experience.
(iii) An improvement in pension benefits to current pensioners in excess of those provided for in the rules of the scheme.

(*6 marks*)

(f) Funding a pension scheme is a matter of providing sufficient assets to discharge pension obligations as they become due. An employer may make payments to an externally funded scheme in advance of or in arrears of recognising in the profit and loss account the appropriate annual cost assessed by the actuary.

Oldage Concern Ltd operated an externally funded pension scheme. At 31 Dec. 19–9 amounts paid to the trustees exceed amounts charged in the company's profit and loss account and deducted from employees' salaries by £25,000. *Explain how this would be reflected in the balance sheet of Oldage Concern Ltd.*

(*5 marks*)
(*Total 24 marks*)

QUESTION D3.
POST BALANCE SHEET EVENTS AND CONTINGENCIES

SSAP 17 accounting for post balance sheet events:

(a) What is a post balance sheet event in the context of this standard?
(b) What is the difference between an 'adjusting event' and 'non-adjusting event'?

(*4 marks*)

SSAP18 accounting for contingencies:

(c) What is a 'contingency' in the context of the standard?

(*4 marks*)
(*Total 8 marks*)

QUESTION D4

The following extracts are from the accounting policies section of two different annual reports:

Depreciation of fixed assets
Fixed assets are depreciated on a straight-line basis at annual rates of 2 to 20% of cost, depending on the class of asset. Expenditure on tools, dies, jigs and moulds is written off to revenue. Investment and regional grants in respect of each year's capital expenditure are included with the reserves on the balance sheet and credited to profit and loss account over a period of 12 years.

Depreciation
No depreciation is provided on freehold properties or properties held on leases with fifty years and over to run at the balance sheet date. Properties held on leases of less than fifty years are amortised over the unexpired term. All other fixed assets are depreciated over their estimated useful lives.

You are required to:

(*a*) *comment upon the two accounting policies quoted above*
(*5 marks*)

(*b*) *discuss the purpose(s) of the depreciation charge in the profit and loss account,*
(*5 marks*)

(*c*) *explain the necessity for an accounting standard on the topic of depreciation,*
(*5 marks*)

(*d*) *describe the requirements of the standard on depreciation (SSAP 12).*
(*5 marks*)
(*Total 20 marks*)

QUESTION D5

Technological Components Ltd manufactures components for sale. It uses advanced machinery with an estimated useful life of four years. As the technology is continually improving it has adopted the reducing balance method for depreciation at a rate of 50% pa.

On 1 Jan. 19–6 the company took delivery of machine K, costing £200,000 which was estimated to produce up to 500,000 components pa for four years, after which it would be sold for £10,000.

On 30 Sep. 19–8 it was announed in the trade press that a replacement for machine K was now available at a cost of £100,000 which could produce at twice the rate of the old one. The directors decided that this was a 'modern equivalent asset' and are considering revaluing the old machine K. The new machine would last four years and be worth £5,000 at that date.

You are required to:

(*a*) *show the effect of the purchase of K in the accounts for the year ended 31 Dec. 19–7,*

(*4 marks*)

(*b*) *calculate the new value to be placed on the old machine for the accounts for the year ended 31 Dec. 19–8,*

(*5 marks*)

(*c*) *present the asset and depreciation accounts for the year end 31 Dec. 19–8 if the new value is used in the accounts,*

(*4 marks*)

(*d*) *present the appropriate disclosure in accordance with SSAP 12, assuming the depreciation item is material.*

(*5 marks*)
(*Total 18 marks*)

QUESTION D6

(a) *SSAP 13* is the accounting standard dealing with research and development. It was issued in Dec. 1977 after two exposure drafts. ED14 (Jan. 1975) and ED17 (Apr. 1976), on the same subject.

You are required to:

(*i*) *Define the three broad categories of activity covered by the term 'research and development' in SSAP 13,*

(*5 marks*)

(*ii*) *state how the standard says these three categories of expenditure should be treated in the annual accounts,*

(*3 marks*)

(*iii*) *describe and explain the major difference between ED14 and ED17.*

(*2 marks*)

and

(b) *SSAP 15* is the accounting standard dealing with deferred taxation.

You are required to:

(*i*) *describe the five main categories of timing differences dealt with in SSAP 15,*

(*4 marks*)

(*ii*) *state the criteria which must be met before 'it will be reasonable to assume that timing differences will not reverse and tax liabilities will therefore not crystallise',*

(*3 marks*)

(*iii*) *Describe how 'deferred taxation' should be shown in the balance sheet and the notes thereto.*

(*3 marks*)
(*Total 20 marks*)

QUESTION D7

ED30 'Accounting for goodwill' was published by the Accounting Standards Committee in Oct. 1982

You are required to explain and discuss:

(*a*) *the reasons why accounting for goodwill is a problem area,*
(*b*) *the merits and demerits of the alternative accounting treatments available for goodwill.*

Note:

A discussion of the item 'Goodwill arising on consolidation' in group accounts is not required.

(*18 marks*)

QUESTION D8

SSAP 17 and *SSAP 18* deal with accounting for post balance sheet events and contingencies respectively.

In eight companies whose year ends were 31 Dec. 19–1, the financial statements were approved by their respective directors on 15 Mar. 19–2. During 19–2, the following material events take place:

(1) Alpha Ltd sold a major property which was included in the balance sheet at £100,000 and for which contracts had been exchanged on 15 Dec. 19–1. The sale was completed on 15 Feb. 19–2 at a price of £250,000.
(2) On 28 Jan. 19–2, a wholly owned subsidiary of Beta Ltd paid a dividend of £300,000 in respect of its own year ended on 31 Dec. 19–1.
(3) On 28 Feb. 19–2 the mail order activities of Gamma Ltd, a retail trading group, were shut down with closure costs amounting to £2.5 million.

(4) On 1 Apr. 19–2 the discovery of sand under Delta Ltd's major civil engineering contract site causes the costs of the contract to increase by 25% for which there would be no corresponding recovery from the customer.

(5) A fire on 2 Jan. 19–2 completely destroyed a manufacturing plant of Epsilon Ltd. It was expected that the loss of £10 million would be fully covered by insurance.

(6) A damages claim of £8 million for breach of patent had been served on Phi Ltd prior to the year end. It is the directors' opinion, backed by considered legal advice, that the claim will ultimately prove to be without foundation but that it will still involve the expenditure of considerable legal fees.

(7) The movement in a foreign exchange rate of 8% between 1 Jan. 19–2 and 1 Mar. 19–2 has resulted in Kappa Ltd's foreign assets being reduced by £1.3 million.

(8) An actuarial valuation of Lambda Ltd's pension fund on 1 Feb. 19–2 revealed that it was under funded by £800,000. The company paid this amount over to the pension fund trustees on 31 Mar. 19–2.

You are required to state, with reasons, how each of the above items numbered (1) to (8) should be dealt with in the financial statements of the various companies for the year ended 31 Dec. 19–1. You are not required to draft the relevant notes to the financial statements.

(16 marks)

QUESTION E1

Stock and work-in-progress at 31 Mar. 19–7 has been valued in accordance with Statement of Standard Accounting Practice No. 9. The effect of the adjustment to the basis of stock and work-in-progress valuation at 31 Mar. 19–6 was not significant. The basis of valuation is the lower of cost and net realisable value, due allowance being made for obsolete and slow-moving items. In the case of products manufactured by companies in the Group, stock and work-in-progress consists of direct materials and labour costs and all other expenditure which has been incurred in the normal course of business and which is attributable to bringing these products to their present location and condition.

The above extract from *accounting policies* is typical of many that have appeared. A company adopting such an accounting policy manufactures engineering components and assembles some of these into production lines at the customers' premises.

At 31 Mar. 19–7 there were two items of finished stock and one item of work-in-progress. The item in progress is in connection with a long-term project commenced in Nov. 19–6 (Project X). The contracted price of Project X is £190,000. Half of the manufactured parts for Project X have been completed, delivered to the site and successfully assembled. The following information is also available.

	Manufacturing £	*Assembly on location (excluding all manufacturing costs)* £
Total expenditure for the year ended 31 Mar. 19–7:		
Direct material	300,000	—
Direct labour	250,000	100,000
Overheads	250,000	10,000
Direct costs of finished stock at 31 Mar. 19–7:		
Item 1 Direct material	20,000	
Direct labour	10,000	
Item 2 Direct material	15,000	
Direct labour	5,000	
Direct costs of work-in-progress to 31 Mar. 19–7:		
Direct material	25,000	
Direct labour	20,000	15,000
Estimated total costs of Project X:		
Direct material	50,000	
Direct labour	50,000	30,000

You are required to:

(*a*) *show how the finished stock and work-in-progress might be included in the balance sheet at 31 Mar. 19–7 together with any supporting notes you feel would be necessary,*

(*18 marks*)

(*b*) *explain why SSAP 9 was required and what it seeks to achieve.*

(*7 marks*)

(*Total 25 marks*)

QUESTION E2. STOCK VALUATION

A company processes and sells a single product. Purchases of raw material during the year were made at a regular rate of 1,000 tons at the beginning of each week. The price was £100 per ton on 1 Jan. 19–8 and was increased to £150 per ton on 1 Jul. 19–8 and remained constant from then until the end of the year, 31 Dec. 19–8. In addition to this price a customs duty of £10 per ton was paid throughout the year, and transport from the docks to the factory cost £20 per ton.

Variable costs of processing were £25 per ton—there was capacity to process 1,500 tons per week and the fixed production costs for all levels of activity up to this capacity level were £30,000 per week. One ton of raw material is processed into one ton of finished product and sold, at a delivered price of £240 per ton, by a sales force whose cost was fixed at £3,000 per week. Average delivery costs to customers were £7.50 per ton.

At the beginning of the year there were no stocks and at the end of the year there was 5,000 tons of raw material and 2,000 tons of finished product. It is expected that the costs and prices current at 31 Dec. 19–8 will continue during 19–9.

You are required to:

(*a*) *draft an accounting policy statement on stock for the company to include in its annual accounts,*

(*4 marks*)

(*b*) *calculate the value of stock at 31 Dec. 19–8 on a basis acceptable under SSAP 9,*

(*7 marks*)

(*c*) *calculate the value of raw material stock on a LIFO basis,*

(*2 marks*)

(*d*) *comment upon the relative merits of FIFO, any other bases recognised under SSAP 9 for valuing stock, and LIFO.*

(*6 marks*)

(*Total 19 marks*)

QUESTION E3. BYRON LTD

Byron Ltd building contractors, commenced trading on 1 Jan. 19–6. You are provided with the following information:

(a) Trial balance at 31 Dec. 19–6:

	£	£
Ordinary share capital:		
320,000 shares at 25p each		80,000
Plant and machinery, at cost	40,000	
Vehicles, at cost	25,000	
Furniture and fixtures, at cost	7,000	
Sales, including progress payments invoiced		526,000
Debtors	53,000	
Creditors		34,000
Balance at bank	7,000	
Contract costs:		
Wages	230,000	
Materials	107,000	
Plant hire	8,000	
Direct expenses	19,000	
Plant running expenses	39,000	
Administrative expenses:		
Salaries	58,000	
Office and administration	21,000	
Auditors' remuneration	2,000	
Directors' remuneration	20,000	
Bank charges	4,000	
	640,000	640,000

(b) At 31 Dec. 19–6, there were three contracts (Nos. 13, 17 and 21) uncompleted. All other contracts had been completed before the year end at a profit, and none had any retentions outstanding.

(c) Details of the uncompleted contracts were as follows:

	Contract Nos.		
	13	*17*	*21*
	£	£	£
Cost	26,000	31,200	15,300
Value of work certified	37,000	26,000	16,000
Less: Retentions	3,700	2,600	1,600
Sales value to date	33,300	23,400	14,400
Progress payments invoiced at 31 Dec. 19–6	30,000	19,200	12,000
Progress payments received at 31 Dec. 19–6	25,000	16,000	10,000
Estimate of final cost	32,000	36,000	50,000
Sales value	40,000	29,000	60,000

Estimate of final cost includes allowance for contingencies and provision for warranty work.

(d) The value for accounts purposes of materials and stores not allocated to any particular contract at 31 Dec. 19–6 was £5,000.

(e) Depreciation on a straight line basis is to be provided at the following rates pa:

Plant, machinery and vehicles	25%
Furniture and fixtures	10%

You are required to:

(*a*) *prepare a statement showing how profits or losses on uncompleted contracts may be calculated,*

(*6 marks*)

(*b*) *state any specific and general assumptions that you consider important as regards part* (*a*),

(*5 marks*)

(*c*) *prepare a detailed trading and profit and loss account for the year ended 31 Dec. 19–6,*

(*6 marks*)

(*d*) *draft the section of the accounting policies regarding long-term contract work-in-progress,*

(*2 marks*)

(*e*) *draft the notes to the balance sheet regarding work-in-progress required to comply with statement of standard accounting practice number 9* (*stock and work-in-progress*).

(*3 marks*)
(*Total 22 marks*)

QUESTION F1

Recently there has been discussion of the 'equity' method of accounting for an investor company's equity interest in the shares of another company. One of the contentious points is whether this method should be used in the preparation of group accounts only, or also for the accounting records of the investor company.

M Ltd bought 75,000 shares out of the issued 100,000 shares of £1 in P Ltd on 1 Jan. 19–0 for £3 per share payable in cash. At this date the share capital and reserves of P Ltd totalled £225,000 after including the assets at a fair value. During the year to 31 Dec. 19–0 the profit after all charges and tax was £60,000, and a dividend of £30,000 was paid before the year-end.

M Ltd bought 200,000 shares out of the issued share capital of 800,000 shares of £1 of R Ltd on 1 Apr. 19–0 for £300,000 payable in cash. On 25 Apr. 19–0, the sales director of M Ltd was appointed a director of R Ltd. He attended and participated at the subsequent meetings of the board. R Ltd had profits after tax for the year ended 31 Dec. 19–0 of £250,000 and a first and final dividend of £100,000 was paid in respect of these profits on 30 Dec. 19–0.

You are required to:

(*a*) *present the journal entries to show how these transactions would be dealt with if they were included in the accounts of M Ltd using:*

(*i*) *the traditional cost method; and*
(*ii*) *the equity method*

(*10 marks*)

and

(*b*) *compare (using appropriate figures from the data provided) these two methods in relation to the adjustments required in the subsequent preparation of consolidated accounts in respect of:*

(*i*) *a subsidiary company; and*
(*ii*) *an associated company.*

(*10 marks*)
(*Total 20 marks*)

QUESTION F2. ATLANTIC AND CROSSING

The balance sheets of Atlantic Ltd and Crossing Ltd at 31 Jan. 19–6 were as follows:

	Atlantic Ltd	*Crossing Ltd*
	£000	*£000*
Issued share capital:		
Ordinary shares of £1	500	100
Share premium account	200	—
Revenue reserves	450	240
8% debenture stock	120	—
Disposal of shares (90,000 shares)	360	—
	1,630	340
Fixed assets	810	290
Shares in Crossing Ltd (90,000 shares)	300	—
Net current assets	520	50
	1,630	340

(1) Atlantic Ltd acquired 90,000 ordinary shares in Crossing Ltd on 1 Feb. 19–2 when the reserves of Crossing Ltd amounted to £180,000. The acquisition had been financed by the issue of 100,000 shares in Atlantic Ltd valued at £3 per share.

(2) On 1 Jun. 19–5 Atlantic Ltd sold all its shares in Crossing Ltd to a merchant bank for proceeds of £360,000. The reserves of the two companies at 31 Jan. 19–5 were as follows:

Atlantic £350,000; Crossing £210,000.

You are required to prepare:

(*a*) *the consolidated balance sheet at 31 Jan. 19–6; and*

(*b*) *the consolidated profit and loss account for the year ended 31 Jan. 19–6 in so far as information permits.*
Assume profits accrue evenly on a time basis.
Assume no dividends were paid or proposed during the year, and that Atlantic's results include those of a wholly owned non-trading subsidiary.

(*15 marks*)

Atlantic and Crossing part 2

Assume the same situation as in F2 but Atlantic sell 10,000 shares for £40,000. Net current assets of Atlantic at the end of the year are £200,000.

(*20 marks*)

Atlantic and Crossing part 3

Assume the same situation as in F2 but that Atlantic sell 45,000 shares for £240,000. Net current assets of Atlantic at the end of the year are £400,000 and Crossing is to be treated as an associated company from 1 June. 19–5.

(*20 marks*)

QUESTION F3. HIYO, SILVER AND AWAY

The draft profit and loss accounts of Hiyo Ltd, Silver Ltd and Away Ltd for the year ended 31 Dec. 19–8 are as follows:

	Hiyo Ltd	*Silver Ltd*	*Away Ltd*
	£000	*£000*	*£000*
Turnover	8,000	6,000	4,800
Profit before tax	1,020	480	360
Taxation	400	180	144
	620	300	216
Dividends paid (31 Mar. 19–8)	100	90	
Dividends proposed	240	120	60
Retained profits	280	90	156
Balances at 1 Jan. 19–8	600	300	200
Balances at 31 Dec. 19–8	880	390	356

Hiyo acquired 400,000 shares in Away Ltd several years ago when the reserves of Away Ltd were £50,000. Hiyo Ltd sold 175,000 shares in Away Ltd for £345,000 on 30 Sep. 19–8. The proceeds were credited to the cost of investment account.

Hiyo acquired 600,000 shares in Silver Ltd on 1 Sep. 19–8 for £1,000,000.

The balance sheets of the companies were as follows:

	Hiyo Ltd	*Silver Ltd*	*Away Ltd*
	£000	*£000*	*£000*
Ordinary shares of £1 each	1,000	800	500
Reserves	880	390	356
Dividends payable	240	120	60
	2,120	1,310	916
Sundry assets	868	1,310	916
Dividends receivable	117	—	—
Cost of investment in Silver Ltd	1,000	—	—
Cost of investment in Away Ltd	135	—	—
	2,120	1,310	916

Requirements:

(*a*) *State the requirements of SSAP 14 for dealing with the partial disposal of the shares of Away Ltd.*

(*4 marks*)

(*b*) *What date should be used for the effective date of an acquisition or disposal of a subsidiary?*

(*2 marks*)

(*c*) *Prepare a consolidated balance sheet, a consolidated profit and loss account and a statement of movement on reserves for the Hiyo Group. Assume that profits accrue evenly over the period. Ignore tax on the disposal of the shares. Assume that the company follows the proposals of SSAP 14 and SSAP 1 (revised). Make calculations to the nearest £100.*

(*23 marks*)

(*d*) *State the possible reasons for the revision of SSAP 1 and the main difference between the accounting treatment in the revised and the original SSAP.*

(*6 marks*)
(*Total 35 marks*)

QUESTION F4. METROPOLIS LTD

Metropolis Ltd is a holding company with five subsidiaries. The balance sheets of the six companies at 31 Dec. 19–5 are given below:

	Metropolis	*Euston*	*Marylebone*	*Pancras*	*Waterloo*	*Victoria*
	£	£	£	£	£	£
Share capital	100,000	50,000	40,000	30,000	20,000	2
Reserves	320,000	30,000	88,000	12,000	8,000	—
Current liabilities	160,000	20,000	15,000	8,000	16,000	—
Inter-company accounts	18,002	32,000	6,000	4,000	—	—
	598,002	132,000	149,000	54,000	44,000	2
Fixed assets	390,000	108,000	128,000	21,000	19,000	—
Current assets	36,000	24,000	21,000	25,000	13,000	—
Cost of investment	132,002	—	—	—	—	—
Inter-company accounts	40,000	—	—	8,000	12,000	2
	598,002	132,000	149,000	54,000	44,000	2

Profit and Loss Accounts for the year ended 31.12.–5 are:

	Metropolis	*Euston*	*Marylebone (estimate)*	*Pancras*	*Waterloo*
	£	£	£	£	£
Profit	140,000	46,000	—	20,000	12,000
Tax	30,000	20,000	—	10,000	6,000
	110,000	26,000	—	10,000	6,000
Dividends paid					
Preference					1,000
Ordinary	40,000	20,000	—	6,000*	3,000
Retained for year	70,000	6,000	NIL	4,000	2,000
Res b'f	250,000	24,000	88,000	8,000	6,000
Res c'f	320,000	30,000	88,000	12,000	8,000

*Paid 30.6.19–5

You are given the following information regarding the subsidiaries:

1. Euston Ltd is an insurance company. Metropolis purchased 80% of the shares of Euston when the reserves of Euston were £20,000. Due to the significantly different type of business in which Euston is engaged, the directors of Metropolis have decided not to consolidate the results of this company.
2. Marylebone Ltd operates in the country of Utopia. On 1 Jul. 19–5 a civil war in Utopia forced the management representatives of Metropolis to leave the country. The balance sheet and profit figures given above are based upon estimates. The country of Utopia is now governed by a new regime backed by the US government. Metropolis purchased 60% of the shares of Marylebone several years ago when the reserves of Marylebone were £10,000.
3. Metropolis purchased 75% of the shares in Pancras in Oct. 19–5 when the reserves were £10,000. Under the terms of the agreement Metropolis agreed to sell those shares to nationals of the country in which Pancras operates for a sum still to be agreed. The planned date of sale is Oct. 19–6.
4. The share capital of Waterloo is divided equally between preference and ordinary shares. All shares have voting rights. Metropolis purchased 60% of the ordinary shares of Waterloo when the reserves of Waterloo were £5,000. Metropolis is unable to control the composition of the board of directors of Waterloo but does have two representatives on the board of directors of that company.
5. Metropolis owns both shares in Victoria Ltd which has not yet commenced trading.

   The cost of investment account is made up as follows:

	£
Euston	58,000
Marylebone	33,000
Pancras	31,000
Waterloo	10,000
Victoria	2
	132,002

Inter-company accounts are all for current items, and are made up as follows:

1. Metropolis owes £8,000 to Pancras, £10,000 to Waterloo and £2 to Victoria.
2. Metropolis is owed £32,000 from Euston and £4,000 from both Marylebone and Pancras.
3. Marleybone owes £2,000 to Waterloo.

6. All subsidiaries were consolidated with the parent company in last years accounts.

You are required to produce a group balance sheet and profit and loss account of Metropolis, together with supporting notes. So far as the above information allows.

(*30 marks*)

QUESTION F5. SSAP 14

In Sep. 1978, the *Accounting Standards Committee* issued SSAP *14* 'Group Accounts'. The following question relates to this standard.

(*1*) *The standard requires a holding company to prepare group accounts in the form of a single set of consolidated financial statements. What do you understand by the term 'consolidated financial statements'? What other forms of group accounts are there?*

(*4 marks*)

(*2*) *Under what circumstances should a subsidiary be excluded from consolidation under the standard?*

(*4 marks*)

(*3*) *You are the accountant of Carrington Ltd and you are responsible for the consolidation of the results of Carrington and its subsidiaries. Explain how you would deal with the following problems relating to certain subsidiaries*:

(*a*) *Victoria Ltd is incorporated and operates in Central Africa. There are exchange control restrictions which prevent the distribution of some of the profits of this subsidiary.*

(*b*) *London Low Level Ltd is incorporated in a South American country and is required under the law of that country to produce accounts ending on 31 Dec. each year. The group's year-end is 31 Mar.*
(*c*) *London High Level Ltd is incorporated in a European country and, in order to benefit from full tax relief, writes off a high proportion of the cost of fixed assets when acquired.*
(*d*) *Manvers Ltd is an insurance company, an activity which is significantly different from that of the rest of the group.*
(*e*) *Midland Ltd is a new subsidiary acquired during the year.*

(*15 marks*)
(*Total 23 marks*)

QUESTION G1

H Ltd acquired a 60% interest in the share capital of S Ltd when the reserves of S Ltd were $20,000.

Balance sheets at 31.12.–2 are:

	H Ltd	*S Ltd*
	£	$
Ordinary share capital	10,000	10,000
Reserves	15,000	50,000
	25,000	60,000
Fixed assets—Cost	43,000	120,000
—Depn	(10,000)	(40,000)
	33,000	80,000
Investment in S	8,000	
Debtors	20,000	30,000
Creditors	(20,000)	(10,000)
Loan	(16,000)	(40,000)
	25,000	60,000

Profit and loss accounts for the year ended 31.12.–2 were

	H Ltd	*S Ltd*
	£	*$*
Profit before depreciation	8,000	18,000
Depreciation	2,000	8,000
	6,000	10,000
Tax	2,000	4,000
Retained profit	4,000	6,000

NOTES:

1. The fixed assets were acquired by S prior to its takeover by H Ltd. There were no additions or disposals of fixed assets by the group during the year.
2. Exchange rates to £1

At acquisition	31.12.–1	31.12.–2
$4.0	$2.7	$2.4

Average of year ended 31.12–2 $2.6

You are required to produce the group accounts for the year ended 31.12.–2 (i.e. balance sheet, profit and loss account, statement of reserves and notes) insofar as the information allows.

(*18 marks*)

QUESTION G2

H Ltd acquired a 60% interest in the share capital of S Ltd when the reserves of S Ltd were $20,000. The cost of the investment was £8,000.

The balance sheet of S Ltd at 31.12.–2 is:

	$
Ordinary share capital	10,000
Reserves	50,000
	60,000

		$
Fixed assets—Cost		120,000
	Dep'n	40,000
		80,000
Debtors		30,000
Creditors		(10,000)
Loan		(40,000)
		60,000

(1) The fixed assets were acquired by S prior to its takeover by H Ltd. The depreciation charged for the year ended 31.12.–2 was $8,000.
(2) Exchange rates to £1:

At acquisition	31.12.–1	31.12.–2
$4.0	$2.7	$2.4

Average for year ended 31.12.–2 $2.6.

S Ltd P & L a/c for the year ended 31.12.–2 was:

	$
Profit before depreciation	18,000
Dep'n	8,000
	10,000
Tax	4,000
Retained profit	6,000

You are required to show the relevant amounts in relation to S Ltd that would be included in the consolidated accounts for the year ended 31.12.–2 (ignoring comparative figures). Translate S Ltd using the temporal method.
(20 marks)

QUESTION G3. TOWERS AND MANUEL

Towers Ltd (a UK company) acquired 80% of the ordinary share capital of Manuel Ltd when the retained profits of Manuel were 30,000 pesetas (P). At that date the rate of exchange was P4 = £1. Manuel's fixed assets were subsequently acquired when the exchange rate was P3.5 = £1. You are provided with the following summarised balance sheets as at 31 Dec. 19–7:

(1)

		Towers		*Manuel*
		£000		*P000*
Ordinary share capital		800.00		400.00
Retained profits		564,00		279.00
Long-term loans (obtained locally)		120.00		80.00
		1,484.00		759.00
Fixed assets—cost		1,400.00		700.00
less depreciation		510.00		210.00
		890.00		490.00
Investment in Manuel (at cost)		105.00		—
Trade investment (at cost)		—		45.00
Stock	156.00		151.00	
Debtors	632.00		73.00	
Dividend receivable from Manuel	5.33		—	
Current account—Towers	—		139.00	
Cash	29.67		4.00	
	823.00		367.00	
Creditors	211.44		125.00	
Current account—Manuel	52.56		—	
Proposed dividends	70.00		18.00	
	334.00		143.00	
		489.00		224.00
		1,484.00		759.00

(2) Summarised profit and loss accounts for the year ended 31 Dec. 19–7

		Towers	*Manuel*
		£000	*P000*
Sales—external		2,710.82	1,347.00
—inter-company		—	422.00
		2,710.82	1,769.00
Cost of sales (including £162,780 inter-company purchases from Manuel)		2,033.10	1,411.00
Gross profit		677.72	358.00
Translation differences:			
19–6 dividend from Manuel		0.18	
		677.54	358.00
Dividends from Manuel			
Received (interim)	3.69		
Receivable (final)	5.33	9.02	—
		686.56	358.00
Sundry expenses	104.56		(131.00)
Depreciation	140.00	(244.56)	(70.00)
Profit before taxation		442.00	157.0
Taxation		(198.00)	(68.0)
Profit after taxation		244.00	89.0
Dividends			
Interim—paid	40.00		(12.0)
Final—proposed	70.00		(18.0)
		110.00	
Retained profit		134.00	59.0
Balance carried forward		564.00	279.0
Balance carried forward		564.00	279.0

(3) Exchange rates during the year were as follows:

1.1. –7	P 2.4	=£1
31.1. –7	P 2.425	=£1
28.2. –7	P 2.450	=£1
31.3. –7	P 2.475	=£1
30.4. –7	P 2.500	=£1
31.5. –7	P 2.525	=£1

30.6. –7	P 2.550	=£1
31.7. –7	P 2.575	=£1
31.8. –7	P 2.600	=£1
30.9. –7	P 2.625	=£1
31.10.–7	P 2.650	=£1
30.11.–7	P 2.675	=£1
31.12.–7	P 2.700	=£1
Average rate	P 2.550	=£1

(4) (i) Manuel's trade investment consists of quoted equity shares. They were acquired on 31.3.–7 and since acquisition their market value has increased considerably. No income was received from this investment during the current year.
(ii) Manuel's interim dividend was paid on 31.8.–7

(5) Additional information regarding items in the accounts:

(i) Dividend income of Towers:

£000

$$\text{Interim } 80\% \times \frac{\text{P } 12{,}000}{2.600} = 3.69$$

$$\text{Final } 80\% \times \frac{\text{P } 18{,}000}{2.700} = 5.33$$

9.02

(ii) Current accounts

	In books of Manuel P000	*Rate*	*In books of Towers £000*
Sales invoices to Towers			
31.3.–7	92	2.475	37.17
30.6.–7	122	2.550	47.84
30.9.–7	69	2.625	26.29
31.12.–7	139	2.700	51.48
	422		162.78
Cash received by Manuel			
30.4.–7	(92)	2,500	(36.80)
31.7.–7	(122)	2.575	(47.38)
31.10.–7	(69)	2.650	(26.04)
	139		52.56

The inter company sales are contracted in the vendor's books

(iii) Translation differences—books of Towers

	£000
(a) Difference on receipt of 19–6 final dividend from Manuel	
Debtor at 31.12.–6	5.40
Cash actually received (date of receipt 28.2.–7)	
$80\% \times \frac{\text{P } 16{,}000}{2.450}$	5.22
Therefore translation loss	(0.18)

(iv) All inter-company transfers are at cost.

You are required to prepare consolidated financial statements in accordance with SSAP20. All calculations are to be made to the nearest £10. Translate profit and loss items at average rate

(*25 marks*)

QUESTION G4. ELTERWATER

Santana is a trading company operating in Gnomeland. The currency in Gnomeland is the Gnome (G). The results of the company for the current trading year have been as follows:

Summarised profit and loss account for the year ended 31 Dec. 19–9

	G000	G000
Sales		607
Cost of sales		420
Gross profit		187
Sundry expenses	43	
Depreciation	34	
Taxation	50	127
		60
Proposed dividend for the year		25
Retained profit		35
Reserves brought forward		202
Reserves carried forward		237

Summarised balance sheet at 31 December 19–9	*G000*
Ordinary share capital	400
Reserves	237
Proposed dividend	25
Sundry creditors	69
	731
Fixed assets—cost	962
—depreciation	388
	574
Stock	76
Debtors	59
Cash	22
	731

Elterwater Ltd (a UK holding company with several subsidiaries) acquired a 30% holding in the above company. The investment cost £36,000 and at the date of acquisition (in 19–5) the reserves of Santana amounted to G49,000. The investment is regarded as an associated company investment. The accounting policy of the group is to use the closing rate method of currency translation, in accordance with SSAP 20 (profits and loss translated at average rate). You are provided with the following additional information:

(1) As regards Santana, there have been no additions to or disposals of fixed assets other than in 19–6, and the share capital of the company has remained unchanged since incorporation.
(2) The relevant exchange rates with Gnomes and £(sterling) were as follows:

(i) At the date of acquisition of the shares in 19–5	4.3 G = £1
(ii) At the date of acquisition of the fixed assets in 19–6	4.0 G = £1
(iii) At 31.12.–8	3.6 G = £1
(iv) Average rate for 19–9	3.2 G = £1
(v) At 31.12.–9	2.8 G = £1

You are required to show how the results of Santana for the current year would be reflected in the final accounts of the Elterwater Group. All calculations should be made to the nearest £100.

(*23 marks*)

QUESTION G5. MOORGATE PRODUCTIONS LTD AND TROPICAL ISLANDS DEVELOPMENTS LTD

Summarised accounts for the year ended 31 Oct. 19–9 of Moorgate Productions Limited and its subsidiary Tropical Islands Developments Limited are given below:

	Moorgate *£000*	*Tropical* *N000*
Share capital		
Authorised shares of £1/N1 each	75,000	25,000
Issued ordinary	73,000	20,000
Reserves	81,734	65,230
Loans	120,236	200,000
Current liabilities		
Trade creditors	81,579	45,698
Taxation	48,247	20,232
Dividend	13,021	10,000
	417,817	361,160
Fixed assets (net)	261,287	220,000
Shares in Tropical	2,400	—
Current assets		
Stock	67,246	52,734
Debtors	85,173	60,596
Cash	1,711	27,830
	417,817	361,160
Turnover	672,436	547,634
Cost of Sales	470,705	410,857
	201,731	136,777
Administrative and distribution costs	125,956	95,017
Profit before taxation	75,775	41,760
Taxation	40,000	20,232
Dividends payable	13,021	10,000
Retained	22,754	11,528

The subsidiary was formed by Moorgate Productions in 19–1 when the rate of exchange was N5 = £1. The local loan was obtained when the rate of exchange was N4 = £1. In 19–2 when the net book value per ordinary share was N2.50, 40% of the ordinary share capital was sold to local residents at N3.00 per share and the resulting surplus included in the reserves of Moorgate. Fixed assets totalling N440^{m} were acquired 8 years ago when the exchange rate was N3.00 to the £1, and a further N440^{m} 7 years ago when the rate was N2.20 to the £1. The rate at 31 Oct 19–9 was N2.00 to the £1, and at 31 Oct. 19–8 was N2.10 to the £1.

The accounting policies of the group follow SSAP 20 (using average rate to translate the profit and loss account).

You are required to prepare consolidated accounts for the group for the year ended 31 *Oct. 19–9 on the usual basis in a form consistent with best practice as far as the given information permits.*

(*20 marks*)

QUESTION H1. AVARICIOUS PLC

It has been accounced that Avaricious Plc, a quoted company, has undertaken to purchase the whole of the issued share capital of Parochial Ltd, a private company carrying on business as wholesalers and retailers of wines and spirits. The following are extracts from the accountants' report on Parochial Ltd.

Profit and Loss Accounts

Year ended 31 Mar	Note	19–4	19–5	19–6	19–7	19–8
		£000	*£000*	*£000*	*£000*	*£000*
Sales		5,157	6,489	8,651	13,026	18,042
Cost of sales	1	5,013	6,299	8,375	12,647	17,520
		144	190	276	379	522
Interest on bank deposits		—	11	6	29	78
Profit before taxation		144	201	282	408	600
Taxation	2	55	106	125	223	306
Profit after taxation		89	95	157	185	294
Dividends—ordinary		27	17	22	15	20
Retained profits for year		62	78	135	170	274

Notes:

1. Cost of sales is stated after charging:

	19–4	19–5	19–6	19–7	19–8
Depreciation	11	13	23	25	29
Directors' remuneration	57	52	59	77	80
Finance charges	5	6	17	3	4

2. Taxation comprises:

	19–4	19–5	19–6	19–7	19–8
	£000	*£000*	*£000*	*£000*	*£000*
Corporation tax	55	—	—	13	—
Deferred taxation	—	106	125	202	310
Prior year adjustments	—	—	—	2	(4)
Advance corporation tax written off	—	—	—	6	—
	55	106	125	223	306

Statement of Net Assets at 31 Mar. 19–8

	Note	*£000*	*£000*
Fixed assets	1		1,430
Investments			18
Current assets			
Stock		3,256	
Debtors		348	
Cash		4	
		3,608	
Current liabilities			
Creditors		2,378	
Loans		68	
Bank overdraft		617	
		3,063	
Net current assets			545
Deferred taxation	2		(696)
Net assets at 31 Mar. 19–8			1,297

Notes:

1. Fixed Assets

	At cost	*Aggregate depreciation*	*Net book value*
	£000	*£000*	*£000*
Freehold land and buildings			
Warehouses, etc.	241	—	241
Retail outlets	1,032	—	1,032
	1,273	—	1,273
Short leasehold property	58	14	44
Plant and motor vehicles	200	87	113
	1,531	101	1,430

2. Deferred taxation

The balance at 31 Mar. 19–8 comprises:	*£000*
Capital allowances	1,335
Unutilised losses arising from stock relief claims	(606)
Advance corporation tax	(33)
	696

The liability to tax in respect of capital gains rolled over, not included above, is estimated at £5,500.

Two companies which are considered to be in the same line of business as Parochial Ltd are quoted and the most recent data from the Financial Times relating to them is shown below:

19–8					Div.		Yield	
High	Low	Stock	Price	+ or −	net	Cover	Gross	P/E
$117\frac{1}{2}$	87	Company K 50p	103	+2	4.25	3.5	6.3	6.9
390	225	Company L 10p	340	−1	4.4	4.8	2.0	16.2

You are required:

(*a*) *to calculate for Parochial Ltd the dividend per share and cover, assuming that there are 400,000 shares of £1 each in issue;*

(*4 marks*)

(*b*) *with the disclosed information to estimate, and justify, a value for Parochial Ltd; and*

(*15 marks*)

(*c*) *to state, and explain the necessity for, three additional topics you would expect to find dealt with in the accountants' report.*

(*6 marks*)
(*Total 25 marks*)

QUESTION H2. HURD PLC

(Assume CT 50%; ACT 30/70ths)

(i) The following information is available for Hurd Plc:

(a) *Issued Capital*		£
Ordinary share capital (50p shares)		300,000
$6\frac{1}{2}$% Preference capital (£1 shares)		200,000
(b) *Profit and Loss Account—year 19.10*	£	£
Profit before tax		146,000
Corporation tax		73,000
Profit after tax		73,000
Extraordinary items (less tax)		20,000
		93,000
Dividends paid and proposed		
Ordinary	48,750	
Preference	13,000	
		61,750
Retained profit		£31,250
The shares are quoted:		
Ordinary		150p
Preference		60p

You are required to compute

(*a*) *earnings per share*
(*b*) *dividend yield on* (*i*) *ordinary shares*
(*ii*) *preference shares*
(*c*) *dividend cover on ordinary shares*
(*d*) *price/earnings ratio*
(*e*) *market capitalisation of company.*

(ii) *Summarise the factors which affect the required dividend yield on a minority holding of ordinary shares in a private company*

(iii) Jim is considering an investment in ordinary shares in Welcome Plc. The £1 shares are currently quoted at 250p and the current dividend is 25p per share. The investor intends to hold the shares for 3 years and requires an overall return from the investment of not less than 12%. *What must be the minimum quoted share price at the end of year 3 if he is to achieve his objective, assuming the company continues to pay the same rate of ordinary dividend? (Ignore taxation)*

(iv) Goldie is considering an investment in 9% loan stock in Welcome Plc at £75 per £100 of stock. The stock is redeemable at par at the end of 6 years. *He wishes to know the yield to redemption:*

(a) on a simple (non-discounted) basis
(b) on a discounted basis.
(Ignore taxation) *(14 marks)*

QUESTION H3. HOMES PLC AND GARDENS PLC

Homes Plc and Gardens Plc are two quoted companies and the following are summaries of their balance sheets as on 31 Dec. 19–11

Homes Plc	*£000*	*Gardens Plc*	*£000*
Issued and fully paid share capital:		Issued and fully paid share capital:	
12 m ordinary shares of £1 each	12,000	4 m ordinary shares of 25 p each	1,000
1 m 6% preference shares of £1 each	1,000	8 m 'A' (non-voting) ordinary shares of 25 p each	2,000
		1 m 8% preference shares of £1 each	1,000
	13,000		4,000
Reserves	17,000	Reserves	7,000
	30,000		11,000
Represented by sundry assets	30,000	Represented by sundry assets	11,000

The profit and loss accounts of the two companies for the year ended on 31 Dec. 19–11 show the following:

	Homes Plc	*Gardens Plc*
Profit before taxation	£6,000,000	£1,100,000
Corporation tax	£2,940,000	£420,000
Preference dividend	6%	8%
Ordinary dividend	12%	16%

Homes Plc proposes, on 1 Jul. 19–12, to make an offer to acquire the entire share capital of Gardens Plc and, in conjunction with its advisers, obtains the following information:

1. On 30 Jun. 19–12 the market prices of the shares of the two companies were:

	Homes Plc	*Gardens Plc*
Ordinary	400p	40p
'A' ordinary	—	35p
Preference	75p	100p

2. The market assessment of the value attaching to the voting rights of the ordinary shares of Gardens Plc was fair and reasonable.
3. That an increase in the rate of the ordinary dividend of Homes Plc was not anticipated for the years 19–12 and 19–13.

Homes decides to make its offer to the shareholders of Gardens Plc on the following basis (based on Homes Plc quoted prices at 30 Jun. 19–12):

(1) 8% preference shares:
 6% preference shares sufficient to increase income by 5%.

(2) Ordinary shares:
 Ordinary shares, valuing the Gardens Plc shares on a price/earnings ratio of 75% of that applying to its own shares, based on the results of 19–11 and the share price on 30 Jun. 19–12.

(3) 'A' ordinary shares:
 Ordinary shares on the basis as in 2 suitably modified so as to maintain the differential revealed by the market prices referred to above.

(4) Ordinary shares and 'A' ordinary shares:
 8% Unsecured Loan Stock 19–19/24 at par sufficient to make up five-sixths of the loss in income arising from the share exchange based on the 19–11 dividends paid by the companies.

You are required to compute the terms of the offer to be made.

Assume ACT at 30/70. (*20 marks*)

QUESTION H4. STRANGHUM LTD

The two members of Stranghum Ltd require valuations of their share-holdings. Stanghum Ltd trades as builders' merchants. The Balance Sheet of the company at 31 Mar. 19–0 is summarised below:

	£	£	£
Fixed assets, at cost, less depreciation:			
Freehold buildings		100,000	
Fixtures and equipment		15,000	
Delivery vans		5,000	
			120,000
Goodwill			50,000
Net current assets:			
Stocks		150,000	
Trade debtors		130,000	
Balance with bank		18,000	
		298,000	
Trade creditors	110,000		
Current taxation	44,154		
Proposed dividend (net)	30,000		
		184,154	
			113,846
Deferred asset (Act recoverable)			16,154
			300,000
Represented by:			
Ordinary shares of £1 each:			
190,000 held by Maxus		190,000	
10,000 held by Minus		10,000	
			200,000
Revenue reserves: Brought forward			95,000
Balance for year			5,000
			300,000

During the 5 years ended 31 Mar. 19–0 the trade profits and appropriations have been consistent and are expected to continue at the present levels. Profits for the year ended 31 Mar. 19–0 were:

		£	£
Trading profit			90,000
Less: Directors' remuneration:	Maxus	15,000	
	Minus	3,000	
	Others	2,000	
			20,000
			70,000
Corporation tax			35,000
			35,000
Dividend			30,000
Profit for year			5,000

You ascertain that:

(1) the freehold buildings have been revalued at £160,000 and could command a rent of £14,000 pa for use in the company's trade,
(2) a company engaged in a similar trade, but of much larger size, is shown in the issue of the *Financial Times* dated 31 Mar. 19–0 as having a price/earnings ratio of 8 and a dividend yield of 10% pa,
(3) a return of 16% (after tax) on capital employed would be regarded as acceptable in this type of industry,
(4) Maxus could be effectively replaced by someone earning £7,000 pa,
(5) depreciation and profits shown in the accounts accord closely with the comparative figures in the tax computations, and
(6) take-over proposals or public issues are not under discussion.

You are required to write a report, supported by figures, giving your opinion of the values, as on 31 Mar. 19–0 of the shares in Stranghum Ltd held by (a) Maxus and (b) Minus. The two holdings are to be offered separately to independent buyers.

You can make whatever assumptions you consider relevant but you should ignore the possible impact on the valuations of income tax, capital transfer tax and tax on capital gains. Assume the rate of corporation tax to be 50%.

(20 marks)

QUESTION H5. GRAPES LTD

The directors of Grapes Ltd, clients of yours, have informed you that they are contemplating the acquisition of the entire share capital of Pip Ltd.

Although they are aware of three methods of valuing shares:

(1) Assets
(2) Price/earning ratio
(3) Gross dividend yield

they are inexperienced and have requested further explanation.

You are required to write a letter advising them briefly on:

(*a*) *each of these methods, and*
(*b*) *the propriety of each method in relation to a 100% acquisition.*

(*20 marks*)

QUESTION H6 FRAIL PLC

You are asked by the board of Frail Plc to report upon their proposal to make an offer for the ordinary stock of Hale Plc. Your views are sought as to whether the value of their offer of eleven £1 shares and two 4½% cumulative preference £1 shares for every five ordinary shares in Hale Plc could be improved on without putting existing shareholders of Frail Plc to any disadvantage, and whether the offer is fair as it stands to shareholders of Hale Plc. In addition to the information listed below in respect of each of the companies you are told that immediate post-merger economies will reduce overheads and management costs of Hale Plc by £52,000 pa; and that with the aid of additional capital and management expertise available from Frail Plc a rate of growth in the profits of Hale Plc materially in excess of that expected from the Frail Group should be obtained.

Frail Plc

1. *Capital structure*

   1,000,000 4½% cumulative preference shares of £1 issued; 2,000,000 authorised.
   10,000,000 ordinary shares of £1 issued; 15,000,000 authorised.

2. *Finances*

   (a) Surplus cash on deposit at 6%—£200,000.
   (b) Quoted investments held in addition to subsidiary and associated company holdings, amount to £2,000,000 providing an average yield of 6%—all franked income.

3. *Market values, dividends, etc.*

   (a) Middle market quotation for preference shares—50p.
   (b) Middle quotation for ordinary shares—150p.
   (c) Dividend rate on ordinary shares—6%.
   (d) PE ratio at 150p—10.

Hale Plc

1. *Summarised profit and loss account—year ended 31 Mar. 19–8*

	£	£
Trading profit		1,920,000
After charging: Rent of warehouse	12,000	
Depreciation	110,000	
Gross debenture interest		120,000
Pre-tax profits		1,800,000
Corporation tax		900,000
Available for ordinary dividend		900,000
Gross dividend payable on ordinary capital		225,000
Profits retained		675,000

2. *Capital structure*

   1,500,000 ordinary shares of £1 each authorised and issued. £2,000,000 6% debenture stock 19.20/.25 in issue.

3. *Finances*

   No surplus liquid funds are available.

4. *Warehouse premises*

   A break in the lease occurs in May 19–9 and the lessors have indicated that they are willing to sell the freehold to Hale Plc for £150,000. If the lease is continued the rent will rise to £15,000 pa.

5. *Market value, dividend, etc.*

   (a) Middle market quotation for ordinary shares—£3.
   (b) Dividend rate on ordinary shares—15%.

You are required to draft a letter to the board of Frail Plc giving your views on the matter remitted to you.
Note: You are not required to advise on the amount of increased bid.
Assume ACT at 30/70, CT at 50%.

(*25 marks*)

QUESTION H7. JAMES LTD AND CHARLES LTD

Two brothers James and Charles had worked for a number of years in a firm manufacturing swoozling rods. They decided that they would both leave, and set up separate companies to wholesale and retail these rods.

On 1 July 19–1 James formed a company, James Ltd, in which he had, with his wife, 100% of the share capital and he commenced trading in Birmingham. Charles formed a company on a similar basis, Charles Ltd, and commenced trading in London on the same date.

Both companies were successful and it was agreed that, with effect from 1 July 19–3 a holding company Jamchar Ltd would be formed to take over the shares in both the companies.

It was agreed that the accounts of James Ltd for the two years ended 30 June 19–3, should be adjusted, as necessary, so as to conform to the accounting policies and conventions used by Charles Ltd.

Jamchar Ltd would then issue securities to the shareholders in James Ltd and Charles Ltd on the following basis:

(a) £1 of 9% loan stock 19–33 for every £1 of net assets owned by each company, and
(b) £1 ordinary shares based on a two-year purchase of the profits after taxation. These profits are to be the average profits of the two years, with the second year being weighted on the 2:1 basis. The accounts for the two years ended 30 Jun. 19–3 showed:

Balance sheets at 30 Jun.

	James Ltd		*Charles Ltd*	
	19–2	*19–3*	*19–2*	*19–3*
	£	£	£	£
Fixed assets:				
Furniture, etc.	12,000	12,000	16,000	16,000
Less: Aggregate depreciation	1,200	2,400	2,400	4,800
	10,800	9,600	13,600	11,200
Quoted investments (at market value)	—	—	—	30,000
Current assets:				
Stock at cost	26,000	34,500	29,000	35,200
Debtors	29,250	42,400	32,400	43,200
Quoted investments at cost (market value £14,000)	—	10,000	—	—
Cash at bank	1,000	—	3,500	—
	56,250	86,900	64,900	78,400
	67,050	96,500	78,500	119,600

	James Ltd		*Charles Ltd*	
	19–2	*19–3*	*19–2*	*19–3*
	£	£	£	£
Share capital:				
£1 ordinary shares fully paid	20,000	20,000	25,000	25,000
Reserves:				
Profit and loss	12,800	27,000	13,900	30,200
Unrealised appreciation in investments	—	—	—	8,000
Current liabilities:				
Creditors	26,050	30,700	30,000	34,200
Bank overdrawn	—	8,000	—	10,500
Taxation	8,200	10,800	9,600	11,700
	34,250	49,500	39,600	56,400
	67,050	96,500	78,500	119,600

The following information is obtained:

(a) Both companies purchase the rods from the same supplier, who sells on a fixed price list. James Ltd and Charles Ltd themselves apply a 50% uplift on cost, to calculate their own selling prices. The supplier's price list showed:

Swoozling Rods

1 July 19–1—£10 each
1 June 19–2—£11 each
1 May 19–3—£12 each

The number of rods purchased and sold in the periods after the price increases were:

	James Ltd		*Charles Ltd*	
	Purchased	*Sold*	*Purchased*	*Sold*
1 June to 30 June 19–2	1,000	800	1,200	900
1 May to 30 June 19–3	1,500	1,000	2,900	2,500

(b) Stock. James Ltd calculates the cost price of stock on the 'first in, first out' basis, whilst Charles Ltd used the 'last in, first out' basis.

(c) Depreciation in both companies is provided on the straight-line method. There has been no material change in the fixed assets since 1 Jul. 19–1, when the companies commenced trading. The fixed assets of the two companies are of a similar nature.

(d) James Ltd deducts 1% from gross trade debtors, as a general provision against doubtful debts.

(e) Debtors comprise:

	James Ltd		*Charles Ltd*	
	19–2	*19–3*	*19–2*	*19–3*
	£	£	£	£
Trade debtors	24,750	39,600	32,000	42,500
Prepaid expenses	500	800	400	700
Advertising (see note)	4,000	2,000	—	—
	29,250	42,400	32,400	43,200

Note: James Ltd carried out an extensive advertising campaign when commencing to trade, and decided to write off this expense equally over three years. Charles Ltd incurred similar expenditure which was, however, written off as incurred.

(f) It is agreed by all parties that the directors' remuneration paid by Charles Ltd is on a strictly commercial basis, whereas that paid by James Ltd contains a 'distribution of profit' element of £3,000 in each year.

(g) The net profits, including the investment income, after provision for corporation tax were:

James Ltd		*Charles Ltd*	
19–2	*19–3*	*19–2*	*19–3*
£	£	£	£
12,800	14,200	13,900	16,300

You are required:

(*a*) *to calculate the terms of the offer to be made to James Ltd and Charles Ltd by Jamchar Ltd, showing your working schedules*; *and*

(*b*) *to prepare the balance sheet of Jamchar Ltd after the transaction has been completed* (*N.B. a consolidated balance sheet is not required*).

Note: *Ignore VAT and formation costs of new company, and do not make any corporation tax adjustments consequent upon any of your workings.*

(*30 marks*)

QUESTION H8. WALNUT CASTINGS LTD

You have been approached by the board of Walnut Castings Ltd to advise them on an offer of £2.50 per share which they propose to make for the whole of the ordinary share capital of Cashew Industrials Ltd.

Both companies have been engaged for some years in the manufacture of light engineering products for the export market. Audited accounts of Cashew Industrials Ltd have been produced to you and contain the following details.

Balance sheet at 31 Mar. 19–4

	£	£
Property at cost		87,500
Plant and machinery, at cost	52,500	
Less: Aggregate depreciation	12,000	
		40,500
		128,000
Current assets (mainly stock and debtors)	149,000	
Less: Current liabilities	48,450	
		100,550
		228,550
Loan on property		22,050
		206,500
Share capital—		
Authorised, issued and fully paid:		
100,000 ordinary shares of £1 each		100,000
50,000 6% redeemable preference shares of £1 each, redeemable in 19.25		50,000
		150,000
Reserves		56,500
		206,500

Profit and loss account for the year ended 31 Mar. 19–4

	£	£
Profit, after all charges except taxation		49,000
Corporation tax		24,500
		24,500
Preference dividend	3,000	
Ordinary dividend	10,500	
		13,500
Retained		11,000

You have obtained the following additional information:

(1) It is the intention of the directors of Walnut Castings Ltd that their company should, through the acquisition of its whole issued capital, purchase Cashew Industrials Ltd as a going concern, and thereafter sell half of its property as being surplus to requirements. The market value of the whole property, all of which was acquired on commencement of trading, is £120,000, and the part due to be sold £60,000.
(2) The value of all other assets and liabilities is estimated to be their book value. The loan on the property, which was taken out on 31 Jan. 19–4 bears interest at 10% pa and is repayable in 19–14 or earlier at the discretion of the company.
(3) Preference shareholders are entitled to a premium of 25p per share on redemption, and have no voting rights. All preference dividends to date have been paid when due.
(4) Profits before taxation and ordinary dividends paid since commencement of trading have been as follows:

		Profits	*Ordinary dividend*
		£	%
Year to 31 Mar.	19–0	25,600	8
	19–1	28,000	9
	19–2	43,100	10
	19–3	45,600	10
	19–4	49,000	10.5

(5) On acquisition, one of the directors of Cashew Industrials Ltd will retire. This will result in a saving in directors' remuneration of £7,500 pa. In addition, further economies envisaged will result in a reduction of overheads estimated at £2,500 pa.

You are required to draft a letter to the directors of Walnut Castings Ltd giving your opinion as to whether their proposed offer for the ordinary share capital in Cashew Industrials Ltd is reasonable and showing how your conclusions have been reached.

(*25 marks*)

QUESTION H9. ENGINEERING PRODUCTS LTD

Engineering Products Ltd is a family business which has proved successful. Existing shareholders are planning to sell some of their shares to the public by way of an offer for sale. The directors have examined quoted companies making similar products and have decided that Machine Components Plc provides a relevant comparison.

Summarised information relating to Machine Components Plc (adjusted to reflect the current tax law) over the last five years includes:

Earnings per share	—current	3.00p
	—average 19–10–19–14	2.00p
Price per share	—current	24.00p
	—range 19–10–19–14	10.00–40.00p
Dividend per share	—current	1.50p
	—average 19–10–19–14	1.20p
Book value of net assets per share–19–14		20.00p

Summarised financial data for Engineering Products Ltd includes:

Balance sheet as on 31 Dec. 19–14

	£
Authorised and issued share capital 5,000,000 shares of 10p each	500,000
Accumulated reserves	600,000
Long-term loans	400,000
	1,500,000
Fixed assets at cost, less depreciation	1,000,000
Net current assets	500,000
	1,500,000

Profit and loss accounts 19–10 to 19–14

	19–10 £	*19–11* £	*19–12* £	*19–13* £	*19–14* £
Profit after tax	150,000	175,000	200,000	200,000	225,000
Dividend	50,000	50,000	50,000	100,000	100,000
Retention	100,000	125,000	150,000	100,000	125,000

You ascertain that:

(1) There has been no change in the issued share capital:

(2) The fixed assets include land which cost £50,000 and has recently been revalued by professional experts at £150,000 in its current use and at £250,000 as housing land.

(3) It is expected that planning permission for the change of use will be obtained and that alternative premises can be obtained at an inclusive rent of £15,000 pa.

You are required to:

(*a*) *calculate information in respect of Engineering Products Ltd similar to that relating to Machine Components Plc;*
(*b*) *recommend a price range for the sale of 2 million shares to the public, clearly indicating the factors that you have used in arriving at your recommendation; and*
(*c*) *explain briefly how (or if) and why (or why not) your recommendation would change if a sale to a single buyer of 3 million shares was being considered.*

Assume ACT at 30/70. Ignore capital gains tax and development land tax.
(*20 marks*)

QUESTION H10. MASSIVE CO. LTD

Massive Co. Ltd was incorporated on 1 July 19–15 for the purpose of acquiring North Ltd, South Ltd and West Ltd.

The balance sheets of these companies as at 30 June 19–15 are as follows:

	North Ltd	*South Ltd*	*West Ltd*
	£	£	£
Tangible fixed assets— at cost less depreciation	500,000	400,000	300,000
Goodwill		60,000	
Other assets	200,000	280,000	85,000
	700,000	740,000	385,000
Liabilities	80,000	130,000	35,000
Issued ordinary share capital—shares of £1 each	400,000	500,000	250,000
Issued 10% loan stock	70,000		40,000
Unappropriated profits	150,000	110,000	60,000
	700,000	740,000	385,000
Average annual profits before loan interest (July 19–10 to June 19–15 inclusive)	90,000	120,000	50,000
Professional valuation of tangible fixed assets on 30 Jun. 19–15	620,000	480,000	360,000

(1) The directors in their negotiations agreed: (i) the recorded goodwill of South Ltd is valueless; (ii) the 'other assets' of North Ltd are worth £35,000; (iii) the valuation of 30 June 19–15 in respect of tangible fixed assets should be accepted; (iv) these adjustments are to be made by the individual companies before the completion of the acquisition.

(2) The acquisition agreement provides for the issue of 12% unsecured loan stock to the value of the net assets of companies North Ltd, South Ltd and West Ltd, and for the issuance of £1 nominal value ordinary shares for the capitalised average profits of each acquired company in excess of net assets contributed. The capitalisation rate is established at 10%.

You are required to:

(*a*) *calculate the amounts of Massive Co. Ltd's loan stock and ordinary shares to be issued to the shareholders of North Ltd, South Ltd and West Ltd;*

(*b*) *calculate the effect of the scheme on a holding of* 1,000 *shares in South Ltd if the profits before loan interest of Massive Co. Ltd for the year ended 30 June 19–16 are* (*i*) *£520,000*;

(*ii*) *£230,000* (*ignore taxation*); *and*

(*c*) *suggest an alternative scheme explaining why it would be preferable.*

(*25 marks*)

QUESTION H11. CRUMBLE LTD

The directors of Crumble Ltd—a private company—have decided that it is likely they will have to sell the company in the near future. They intend adopting a positive approach to this by seeking out prospective purchasers. Prior to doing this they wish you to put a value on an ordinary share in the company using the methods which a prospective purchaser might apply.

You are required to make this valuation using the undernoted information—no more than six valuations are required—commenting briefly on each method adopted, and showing clearly how you have arrived at your answers.

Crumble Ltd

Summary position as at most recent balance sheet date

					Net book value
Capital:	£	£	Fixed assets:	£	£
Share capital			Land/buildings		500,000
200,000 £1			Plant/equipment		275,000
ordinary shares		200,000	Motor vehicles		55,000
Reserves		595,000			
		795,000			830,000
Loan (Secured on land/buildings)		150,000			
Current liabilities:			Current assets:		
Taxation	45,000		Cash	15,000	
Other creditors			Debtors	145,000	
and accruals	135,000		Stock	133,000	
		180,000			293,000
					1,123,000
			Preliminary expenses		2,000
		1,125,000			1,125,000

Crumble Ltd—profit/dividend record

The profit record after tax and interest but before dividends over the last five years has been as follows:

Year	
Year 1	£80,000
2	£75,000
3	£95,000
4	£80,000
5	£85,000

The annual dividend has been £30,000 (gross) for the last ten years. The operating budget shows that the estimated after tax profit for the next twelve months will be £85,000 and thereafter it is estimated that this will increase by 5% pa over the next four years.

In light of recent developments in the field of financial reporting the company has had its fixed assets valued by an independent expert whose report discloses:

Land/buildings	£610,000
Plant/equipment	£288,000
Motor vehicles	£102,000

A study of three public companies in the same market as Crumble Ltd shows that the average dividend yield and price earnings ratio of these over the last three years has been:

	Company 1		*Company 2*		*Company 3*	
	Dividend Yield %	*PE Ratio*	*Dividend Yield %*	*PE Ratio*	*Dividend Yield %*	*PE Ratio*
Year 1	17.0	8.00	17.0	8.50	16.5	9.00
2	17.0	8.00	15.0	9.00	17.0	10.00
3	17.0	9.00	18.0	10.00	17.5	11.50
Average	17.0	8.33	16.7	9.17	17.0	10.17

One director has indicated that in conversation with colleagues in other larger companies they have said that for acquisition purposes their after tax cost of capital is now 17½%. The estimated cash flows of the company after taking into consideration taxation and capital expenditure over the next five years in order to achieve/and as a result of, the five year profit plan, are as follows:

Year 1	£100,000
2	£120,000
3	£140,000
4	£10,000
5	£150,000

Another director has commented, however, that in the past they only used 17½% to measure their profitability on an investment not backed by tangible assets as opposed to only 12½% for the net tangible assets.

P/V of £1 discounted at:

	17½%		*15%*		*12½%*
Year 1	0.85	Year 1	0.87	Year 1	0.89
2	0.72	2	0.76	2	0.79
3	0.62	3	0.66	3	0.70
4	0.52	4	0.57	4	0.62
5	0.45	5	0.50	5	0.56

(*30 marks*)

QUESTION H12

The following information has been extracted from the most recent public accounts and stock exchange listings of a public company.

You are required to analyse this from the point of view of a potential investor in the ordinary shares.

For this purpose you can assume that a reasonable estimate of next year's profit after taxation will be £33,500 and that there is a 0.5 probability that there will be no increase in the ordinary share dividend and a 0.5 probability that the increase will be 10%.

Summary information extracted from the most recent profit and loss account

	£	£
Profit before taxation		63,000
Less: Taxation		32,760
		30,240
Extraordinary profits		1,420
		31,660
Less: Net dividend on preference shares	3,960	
Net dividend on ordinary shares	17,820	
		21,780
		9,880

Share and loan stock

	Number	*Nominal value*	*Market value*
Ordinary shares	360,000	25p	125p
Preference shares	75,000	100p	58p
11% convertible loan stock (19–15/20)	240,000	100p	80p

The loan stock becomes convertible in 19–12 on terms of 1 ordinary share for each £2.00 of loan stock.

(*25 marks*)

QUESTION H13. CLAYBORN LTD

Clayborn Ltd, a manufacturer of glass bottles, owns 40% of a bottling plant in Nigeria. The other 60% is owned by a local Nigerian company. Sales are at present 1 million naira pa. Last year they were 0.75 million naira (N), and for each of the next five years they are expected to increase by an extra 0.25 million naira. The variable costs are at present 75% of sales and are expected to maintain this relationship with sales. Fixed costs are N100,000 pa and included in this is a depreciation charge of N50,000. The plant is estimated to have another five years of useful life, which is also the remaining depreciable life. It has not yet been decided what will happen after year five. Fixed costs are not expected to increase over this five year period.

To finance the increased sales, the working capital needs to be increased each year. It is estimated that the working capital needs each year are equal to 20% of sales. This working capital can be financed from internally generated funds.

The current exchange rate between the Naira and pound sterling is N2 = £1, but this rate is expected to change with the pound becoming progressively stronger against the naira. It is forecast that with the passing of each year it will require an extra N0.20 to purchase £1. That is, at the end of year 1, N2.20 = £1, at the end of year 2, N2.40 = £1 and so on.

Corporation tax is at 30% in Nigeria and 52% in the UK. UK tax is payable only on dividends which are distributed by the Nigerian company to its UK shareholder. You may assume tax is paid in the year in which the profits are earned.

At the moment the subsidiary is prevented by Nigerian law from making any remittances to the UK, but it is thought this piece of legislation will only remain in effect for two more years and after that future dividends will be able to be distributed, as will the two years arrears of dividends. Depreciation cannot be repatriated.

The company has a policy of distributing 50% of available profits as dividends. Funds which are not distributed and which are not used for financing working capital will be retained within the company and can be invested to earn 10% net of tax.

The Nigerian partner in the venture have offered to buy out Clayborn's born's 40% share, and have offered an immediate payment of N150,000 in cash. The Ministry of Finance in Nigeria has indicated this amount could immediately be remitted to the UK should the sale go through.

The assets in Nigeria are of a very specialist kind, and even if Clayborn could influence a decision on whether or not to close down the business in Nigeria immediately and realise the assets, the funds so obtained by Clayborn would be much less than the offer that has been made by the partner.

Ignore the tax paid in the UK on dividends received from Nigeria and on the sale of the investment.

You are required to advise Clayborn on whether to accept the offer or whether to maintain its shareholding in the Nigerian company for at least another five years. Clayborn believe that their after tax cost of capital on such investment in the UK is 15%.

(*25 marks*)

QUESTION H14. LAFAYETTE LTD

The directors of Lafayette Ltd, a medium sized private company, have been approached by a large public company which is interested in purchasing their business. The directors of Lafayette Ltd have indicated they would like to receive cash for their shares which is acceptable to the prospective purchaser. They have been asked by the public company to state the price at which they would be willing to sell. You have been asked to advise Lafayette Ltd.

Extracts from the last set of published accounts for Lafayette Ltd for 19–2 are given below:

	£
Profit before interest and tax	6,000,000
Interest	1,000,000
Profits before tax	5,000,000
Taxation	2,000,000
Profits after tax	3,000,000
Extraordinary item	500,000
	3,500,000
Dividends paid: Preference	200,000
Ordinary	1,000,000
Profits retained	2,300,000

Balance sheet as at 31 Dec. 19–2

	£000		*£000*
Ordinary shares (£1 par)	20,000	Goodwill	5,000
5% preference shares (£1 par)	4,000	Freehold property	10,000
		Plant and machinery	20,000
Reserves	10,000	Investments	5,000
Debentures	10,000	Stock	3,000
		Debtors	6,000
Creditors	6,000	Cash	1,000
	50,000		50,000

For the year ending 31 Dec. 19–0, the profits before interest and tax were £10 million, and in the year ending 31 Dec. 19–1 they were £8 million. The basic rate of income tax is currently 30%. The owners of the preference shares have found a financial institution who will buy at a price of £0.40 per preference share. They are willing to sell at this price.

You are asked to take the following factors into account in calculating a value per share:

(a) The prospective purchaser has agreed to purchase the debentures at a price of £75 per £100 stock.
(b) It has been ascertained that the current rental value of the freehold property is £1.5 million pa, and that this could be sold to a financial institution on the basis of offering an 8% return to the freeholder.

(c) The investments owned by Lafayette have a current market value of £7.5 million.

(d) There is an amount of £1 million shown in the 19–2 debtors figure which is now thought to be irrecoverable.

Two companies in the same business as Lafayette Ltd are quoted on the stock market, however both are slightly bigger in size than Lafayette. The most recent financial data relating to the companies is given below:

	Par value of shares £	*Market price per share* £	*P/E ratio*	*Net dividend per share* £	*Times covered*	*Yield gross %*
X	1.00	3.50	11.3	0.12	2.6	4.9
Y	0.50	1.25	8.2	0.04	3.8	4.1

Required:

The directors of Lafayette Ltd are naturally interested in obtaining the highest price possible for their shares. You are asked, based on the following valuation methods:

(*i*) *the net asset value;*
(*ii*) *the price earnings ratio;*
(*iii*) *the dividend yield;*

(*a*) *to determine the highest possible asking price for the shares that can be justified on the basis of the available information. You are required to explain to the directors how you have arrived at the alternative prices;* (*16 marks*)

(*b*) *to advise the directors on the lowest price at which they should be willing to sell.*

(*4 marks*)
(*Total 20 marks*)

QUESTION H15. BARRINGTON PLC AND HUNT PLC

Barrington Plc and Hunt Plc are both manufacturers of similar products. Their summarised profit and loss accounts and balance sheets for the year just ended are as follows:

Profit and loss accounts for the year ended 30 Nov. 19–9

	Barrington Plc	*Hunt Plc*
	£	£
Sales revenue	90,000	18,000
Less: Operating expenses	86,000	17,200
Net profit	4,000	800
Dividends	2,000	800
Added to reserves	2,000	Nil

Balance sheets as on 30 Nov. 19–9

Fixed assets, less depreciation	30,000	5,000
Net current assets	10,000	1,000
	40,000	6,000
Represented by:		
Share capital—ordinary shares of £1 each:		
Authorised	15,000	15,000
Issued	5,000	2,500
Reserves	35,000	3,500
	40,000	6,000

On 30 Nov. each company paid the dividend for the year ended on that date. The current (1 Dec. 19–9) market value of Barrington Plc's ordinary shares is £4.20 per share. For a number of years, the directors of Barrington Plc have followed a policy of retaining and reinvesting one half of the company's net profits. This policy has resulted in both net profits and dividends growing at a compound rate of 5% pa. This pattern is expected to continue indefinitely.

Hunt Plc earned a constant level of profit for many years and is expected to continue to do so. Its directors have recently adopted a policy of distributing all net profits as ordinary dividends and intend to continue this policy in the future. The current (1 Dec. 19–9) market value of Hunt Plc's ordinary shares is £2.00 per share.

The directors of Barrington Plc are now considering whether to submit a bid for the entire share capital of Hunt Plc. They believe that, if the bid succeeded, the combined net profit would increase immediately by £1,200,000 pa. Some of the fixed assets at present owned by Hunt Plc would no longer be required, and could be sold immediately for £1,000,000.

The directors of Barrington Plc also believe that the takeover would result in a reduction in the company's risk, as perceived by shareholders and the stock market, and that, in consequence, the annual return required by shareholders in Barrington would fall by 1%.

The directors of Barrington Plc would continue their present policy of retaining and reinvesting one half of net profits and believe that this policy would result in a future compound rate of growth for both the dividends and net profits of the enlarged company of 5% pa.

You are required to:

(*a*) *calculate the following, on the basis of the information given in the question:*

(*i*) *the* maximum *price that Barrington Plc should be prepared to pay for the entire share capital of Hunt Plc; and*

(*ii*) *the* minimum *price that the ordinary shareholders in Hunt Plc should be willing to accept for their shares.*

(*12 marks*)

(*b*) *assuming that the takover price is agreed at the figure you have calculated in* (*a*) (*ii*) *above, and that the price is to be paid by a new issue of ordinary shares in Barrington Plc having identical rights to the shares already issued by Barrington Plc, calculate the total number of new shares in Barrington Plc which will be issued in return for the entire ordinary share capital of Hunt Plc and demonstrate that the entire benefit from the takeover will accrue to the present shareholders of Barrington Plc.*

(*6 marks*)

(*c*) *discuss briefly any other factors that the directors and shareholders of both companies might consider in assessing the desirability of the proposed takeover.*

(*7 marks*)

Ignore taxation.

(*Total 25 marks*)

QUESTION H16. MR CANARIO

Your client, Mr Canario, is considering purchasing the consultancy practice of Mr Puskas, whose latest balance sheet as on 31 Dec. 19–9 as follows:

Capital account	£	£	*Fixed assets*	£	£
Balance at 1 Jan. 19–9		62,000	Freehold premises, at cost		50,000
Net profit for the year		18,200	Office equipment, at cost	6,400	
			Less: Depreciation	1,600	
		80,200			4,800
Drawings		20,000			
			Motor car, at cost	7,600	
Balance at 31 dec. 19–9		60,200	*Less:* Depreciation	3,800	
					3,800
					58,600
Current liabilities			*Current assets*		
Accrued expenses	800		Debtors		7,600
Bank overdraft	5,200				
		6,000			
		66,200			66,200

Mr Canario estimates that the current values of Mr Puskas' fixed assets are:

	Replacement cost	*Realisable value*
	£	£
Freehold premises	80,000	76,000
Office equipment	7,600	2,000
Motor car	4,600	3,000

In addition to the fixed assets, Mr Canario would take over the current assets and liabilities. He believes that £1,000 of the debtors are irrecoverable.

Mr Puskas' net profits for the past five years have been as follows:

Year ended 31 Dec. 19–5	19,000
19–6	15,800
19–7	18,600
19–8	16,400
19–9	18,200

Mr Canario has recently inherited £200,000, which is earning an annual rate of interest of 10%. If he buys Mr Puskas' business he will pay for it out of this inheritance. Mr Canario is employed at an annual salary of £8,000, and would probably relinquish his employment in order to run the business.

You are required to draft a report to Mr Canario advising him, on the basis of the above information, how much he might offer for Mr Puskas' business—a substantial part of your report should be devoted to a discussion of both the relevance of alternative methods of valuation and also the additional information which you think would be useful before a final decision is made.
Ignore taxation.

(*20 marks*)

QUESTION N1. RESTART LTD

(a) The balance sheet of Restart Ltd at 30 Sep. 19–7 was as follows:

	£	£
Share capital		
Authorised		700,000
Issued		
320,000 8% Cumulative preference shares of £1 fully paid		320,000
320,000 Ordinary shares of £1 each, 75p paid	240,000	
Less: Profit and loss account (Debit balance)	220,000	
		20,000
Loans from directors		30,000
Current liabilities		
Bank overdraft	104,000	
Sundry creditors	220,000	
		324,000
		694,000
Fixed assets		
Freehold properties (cost)		70,000
Plant and machinery (written down book value)		120,000
Patents and trade marks		34,000
		224,000
Investment in subsidiary company		
—Shares at cost	120,000	
—Current account	42,000	
		162,000
Current assets		
Stock	124,000	
Debtors	160,000	
		284,000
Other debit balance		
—Deferred revenue expenditure		24,000
		694,000

Note to Balance Sheet: Preference dividends are in arrears amounting to £25,600.

A scheme for reconstruction was duly approved with effect from 1 Oct. 19–7 under the following conditions:

(a) The unpaid capital on the ordinary shares will be called up.
(b) The arrears of preference dividend will be cancelled and each preference shareholder will accept a reduction of 25p per share. The dividend rate on the new preference shares is to be raised to 10%.
(c) The ordinary shareholders will accept a reduction of 75p on each share held.
(d) Patents and trade marks are to be reduced to £24,000; a provision for doubtful debts of £30,000 is to be created; £50,000 is to be written off plant and machinery and £20,000 off shares in subsidiary.
(e) Freehold properties are professionally valued and are to be written up to £190,000.
(f) Deferred revenue expenditure is to be eliminated.
(g) The directors agree to take ordinary shares at the new par value of 25p each in settlement of the loans outstanding.
(h) The debit balance on profit and loss account is to be eliminated.
(i) New capital is issued for cash and is fully paid, as follows:
    (*i*) Each ordinary shareholder (including those to the directors for their loans) to take up two new ordinary shares for every one held.
    (*ii*) Each preference shareholder to take up one new preference share for every four held.

The resolution for the reduction of capital, provided for the restoration of the authorised capital to £700,000. The group profit attributable to shareholders is expected to be £60,000 without the additional capital raised and £100,000 with additional capital.

Assuming all these transactions were completed on 1 Oct. 19–7. You are required:

(*a*) *to show the necessary ledger entries to effect the above, including a capital reduction account, and*
(*b*) *the balance sheet of the company after the reconstruction,*
(*c*) *show how the £60,000 expected profit would be split between the interested parties assuming there was no reconstruction and how the £100,000 would be split after the reconstruction.*

Ignore taxation.

(*25 marks*)

QUESTION N2

The summarised balance sheet of Rejuvenated (19–10) Ltd and of Rejuvenated (19–4) Ltd from which it has recently emerged by way of a reorganisation are shown below.

	Rejuvenated (19–4) £000	*Rejuvenated (19–10) £000*
Fixed assets	2,450	1,800
Current assets		
Stock	1,300	900
Work in progress	1,300	700
Debtors	400	350
	5,450	3,750
Share capital		
Ordinary shares of £1	1,000	200
Deferred shares of 5p	—	100
5% Preference shares of £1	1,000	—
8% Preference shares of £1	—	500
Reserves	350	50
15% Loan 19–22	—	1,000
10% Loan 19–12	1,000	—
Current liabilities		
Trade creditors	1,250	1,250
Overdraft	850	650
	5,450	3,750

The changes in share capital reflect the writing-off of 90% of the ordinary share capital; the issue for cash of £100,000 of deferred shares at par to the existing ordinary shareholders; the writing-off of 50% of the preference share capital and the increase in the rate of interest from 5% to 8%; the issue for cash of 50,000 ordinary shares at par to the existing preference shareholders.

The debenture holders agreed to redate their loan from 19–12 to 19–22 in consideration for the increase in the rate of interest from 10% to 15%. They also purchased 50,000 ordinary shares at par.

The assets in the balance sheet of Rejuvenated (19–10) reflect up to date valuations on a going concern basis.

It is expected that the profit available for payment of interest and dividends in the following year will amount to £300,000, and would have been available whether or not the new company had been reorganised.

The deferred shares do not participate in any dividend in any year until a dividend of 20% has been paid on the ordinary shares. Thereafter they rank equally with the ordinary shares on a 'per share' basis.

You are required to:

(*a*) *show how the £300,000 available would have been paid to the interested parties if Rejuvenated (19–4) had survived,*
(*4 marks*)

(*b*) *show how the £300,000 available would be distributed by Rejuvenated (19–10),*
(*4 marks*)

(*c*) *calculate and state the amounts available to the original interested parties of Rejuvenated (19–4) following the reorganisation,*
(*5 marks*)

(*d*) *calculate one gearing ratio reflecting the capital position and one gearing ratio reflecting the income position, for both companies.*
(*4 marks*)

Ignore all taxation matters when answering this question. No credit will be given for reflecting current taxation legislation.
(*Total 17 marks*)

QUESTION N3

The Shires Property Construction Company Ltd found itself in financial difficulty. The following is a trial balance at 31 Dec. 19–9. Extracted from the books of the company.

	£
Land	156,000
Building (net)	27,246
Equipment (net)	10,754
Goodwill	60,000
Investment in shares, quoted	27,000
Stock and work in progress	120,247
Debtors	70,692
Profit and loss account	39,821
	511,760
Ordinary shares of £1 each	200,000
5% Cumulative preferred shares of £1 each	70,000
8% Debenture 19–12	80,000
Interest payable on debenture	12,800
Trade creditors	96,247
Loans from directors	16,000
Banks overdraft	36,713
	511,760

The authorised share capital is 200,000 ordinary shares of £1 each and 100,000 5% cumulative preferred shares of £1 each.

During a meeting of shareholders and directors, it was decided to carry out a scheme of internal reconstruction. The following scheme has been agreed.

(1) Each ordinary share is to be redesignated as a share of 25p.
(2) The existing 70,000 preference shares are to be exchanged for a new issue of 35,000 8% cumulative preference shares of £1 each and £140,000 ordinary shares of 25p each.
(3) The ordinary shareholders are to accept a reduction in the nominal value of their shares from £1 to 25p, and subscribe for a new issue on the basis of 1 for 1 at a price of 30p per share.
(4) The Debenture holders are to accept 20,000 ordinary shares of 25p in lieu of the interest payable. The interest rate is to be increased to $9\frac{1}{2}$%. A further £9,000 of this $9\frac{1}{2}$% Debenture is to be issued and taken up by the existing holders at £90 per £100.
(5) £6,000 of directors loan is to be cancelled. The balance is to be settled by issue of 10,000 ordinary shares of 25p each.
(6) Goodwill and the profit and loss account balance are to be written off.
(7) The investment in shares is to be sold at the current market price of £60,000.
(8) The bank overdraft is to be repaid.
(9) £46,000 is to be paid to trade creditors now and the balance at quarterly intervals.
(10) 10% of the debtors are to be written off.
(11) The remaining assets were professionally valued and should be included in the books and accounts as follows:

Land	£90,000
Building	80,000
Equipment	10,000
Stock and work in progress	50,000

(12) It is expected that due to changed conditions and new management, operating profits will be earned at the rate of £50,000 pa after depreciation but before interest and tax. Due to losses brought forward and capital allowances it is unlikely that any tax liability will arise until 19–17.

You are required to:

(*a*) *show the necessary journal entries including cash, to effect the reconstruction scheme*

(*10 marks*)

(*b*) *prepare the balance sheet of the company immediately after the reconstruction*

(*4 marks*)

(*c*) *show how the anticipated operating profit will be divided amongst the interested parties before and after the reconstruction*

(*4 marks*)

(*d*) *comment on the capital structure of the company subsequent to reconstruction.*

(*2 marks*)
(*Total 20 marks*)

QUESTION N4

On 1 Jan. 19–10 Heavy Plc acquired 80% of the ordinary shares of Small Ltd. In consideration it issued two of its own ordinary shares for every one share of Small Ltd. The shares of Heavy Plc are quoted on the Stock Exchange, and the price of a share was on 1 Dec. 19–9, £0.80, on 1 Jan. 19–10 £1.00 and on 8 Jan. 19–10 £0.75.

At the time of acquisition the fixed assets of Small Ltd were valued at £200,000 above their book value, and the stocks and debtors at £100,000 less than their book value.

The summarised balance sheets of the two companies as at 31 Dec. 19–9 are as below:

	Heavy Plc £000	*Small Ltd £000*
Ordinary shares: Heavy Plc—of 50p		
Small Ltd—of £1	500	200
Long term borrowing	100	200
Current liabilities	200	200
	£800	£600
Fixed assets	500	400
Current assets	300	200
	£800	£600

Required:

(*a*) *Using the 'acquisition' method, show the consolidated balance sheet of Heavy Plc following the acquisition.*

(*8 marks*)

(*b*) *There is disagreement as to the period of time over which goodwill arising from consolidation should be written off. The EEC approach is that normally goodwill should be written off over a period not exceeding five years. An alternative approach, one that has considerable support in the UK, is that it should be written off over the useful economic life of the assets concerned. Discuss the arguments for and against the alternative approaches.*

(6 marks)

(*c*) *There is also disagreement on the correct method of accounting for mergers and acquisitions. The exposure draft issued on the subject in the UK proposed that the so called 'merger' method of accounting, the pooling of interests, should be allowed in certain cases. Give details of the features of merger accounting that differentiate it from the alternative 'acquisition' method.*

(6 marks)
(Total 20 marks)

QUESTION N5

The summarised Balance Sheet of Down Ltd at 31 Aug. 19.15 was as follows:

Authorised and Issued Capital		£	*Fixed Assets*		£
50,000 6% cumulative preference shares of £1 each		50,000	Goodwill at cost		12,000
100,000 ordinary shares of £1 each		100,000	Patents at cost		5,000
			Land & buildings at cost		45,000
		150,000	Plant and equipment at cost less depreciation		42,000
Less: Profit and loss account		45,000	Investment in an associated company		15,000
		105,000			119,000
5% Debentures (secured on land and buildings)	25,000		*Current Assets*		
			Stock	37,500	
			Debtors	44,750	82,250
Add: Accrued interest	1,250				
		26,250			
Current Liabilities			*Deferred Revenue Expenditure*		
Bank overdraft		28,000	Sales promotion		
Creditors		42,500	expenditure		12,500
Directors' loans		12,000			
		£213,750			£213,750

Note: (i) Dividends on the preference shares are three years in arrear;
(ii) There is a contingent liability for damages relating to the infringement of patent rights amounting to £1,500.

A capital reduction scheme, duly approved by the company and confirmed by the Court, contained the following provisions:

(a) The preference shares to be reduced to 85p each and the ordinary shares to 20p each, and the resulting shares to be then converted into preference and ordinary stock respectively and consolidated into units of £1. The authorised capital to be restored to £50,000 6% cumulative preference stock and £100,000 ordinary stock. The preference shareholders waive two-thirds of the dividend arrears and receive ordinary stock for the balance.
(b) All intangible assets are to be written off, and obsolete stock of £15,500 together with bad debts of £9,750 are also to be eliminated.
(c) The contingent liability materialised at £1,200.
(d) The shares in the associated company were sold for £42,450.
(e) The debenture holders agreed to take over one of the company's properties (book value £14,000) at a price of £16,250 in satisfaction of the accrued interest and in part satisfaction of the debentures. They also agreed to provide £8,000 on a second 12% debenture secured by a floating charge.
(f) The directors of the company agree to take up £40,000 ordinary stock at par, the loan accounts to be offset against the money due.
(g) The costs of the reconstruction were £2,000.

You are required to:

(*a*) *set out the Capital Reduction Account, giving effect to the above matters, and*
(*b*) *set out the revised balance sheet after all transactions have been carried through.*

Ignore taxation

(*18 marks*)

QUESTION N6

The following is the balance sheet of Harvey Ltd at 31 Mar. 19–12. In spite of a succession of losses over the past three years, it is anticipated that the company will be able to trade profitably in the future. It is therefore proposed that a scheme of capital reduction should be devised and submitted to the creditors and to the Court for approval.

Balance Sheet at 31 Mar. 19.12

Capital employed		*Authorised*	*Issued and fully paid*
Share Capital		£	£
Ordinary £1 shares		£200,000	100,000
6% preference shares of £1 each		50,000	50,000
		£250,000	150,000
Reserves			
Share premium account			10,000
			160,000
Less: Profit and loss account		59,300	
Formation expenses		2,450	
Deferred revenue expenditure—advertising		7,800	69,550
			90,450
5% debentures (secured on freehold)			40,000
			£130,450

Represented by		*Book values*		*Estimated values*
Fixed assets (at cost less depreciation)	£	£	£	£
Freehold			60,000	80,000
Plant and machinery			38,000	17,000
Goodwill			20,000	—
			118,000	
Current assets				
Stock		62,000		49,000
Quoted investments		10,000		17,500
Debtors		28,500		21,000
Bills receivable		4,000		3,000
Cash		50		
		104,550		
Less: Current liabilities				
Creditors	48,700			
Debenture interest 6 months	1,000			
Bank overdraft	42,400			
		92,100		
			12,450	
			130,450	

Notes to accounts

(a) The preference dividend is in arrears for three years amounting to £9,000.
(b) There is a contingent liability in respect of bills discounted amounting to £1,800.

The following information is also available:

(a) The preference shareholders are entitled to priority of dividend and to repayment of capital in a winding up. There is no entitlement to dividends not declared at the date of winding up.
(b) The debenture holders may appoint a receiver where the interest is in arrear for more than 3 months after the due date of payment (which is half yearly 30 Sep; 31 Mar.).
(c) The bank requires a substantial reduction in the overdraft if it is to agree to any scheme of capital reduction.
(d) The estimated costs of the scheme are £1,200.
(e) The discounted bills were dishonoured on 30 Apr. 19.12.
(f) The creditors include £4,700 which would be preferential in a winding up.
(g) All the directors have substantial service agreements until 19.16. All the ordinary share capital is owned by the directors.

As financial advisers to the company you are required to put forward, in the form of a report to the directors, a scheme of capital reduction which is likely to be acceptable to the creditors, members and to the Court.
Your answer should include as a working the Capital Reduction Account, and as part of the report, the balance sheet as it would appear after your proposals have been put into effect.
You may make any assumptions which you consider necessary.

(25 marks)

QUESTION N7

Shatterhopes Ltd is a company which has suffered a significant reversal of fortune in recent years. The balance sheet of the company at 30 Sep. 19–07 is set out below:

Fixed Assets	*Cost*	*Dep'n*	
	£	£	£
Land and buildings	40,000		40,000
Plant	36,315	19,284	17,031
Fixtures and fittings	3,855	1,225	2,630
	£80,170	£20,509	59,661
Goodwill			20,000
Quoted investment (at cost)			45,000
Current Assets			
Stock		40,166	
Debtors		35,802	
Deferred development expenditure		15,000	
		£90,968	
Less: Current Liabilities			
Bank overdraft		15,209	
Trade creditors		63,420	
Directors' loans		10,000	
		£88,629	
Net current assets			2,339
			£127,000

Represented by
Share Capital

	Authorised	*Issued and fully paid*
	£	£
Ordinary shares of £1 each	100,000	80,000
7% Cumulative preference shares of £1 each	40,000	40,000
	£140,000	120,000
Reserves		
Profit and Loss Account		(27,200)
		92,800
7% Debentures	30,000	
Accrued interest	4,200	
		34,200
		£127,000

The directors of the company have sought your advice in drafting a scheme of reorganisation to be submitted to the Court for approval. The following information is relevant:

(i) The preference dividend is three years in arrears.
(ii) The debentures are secured on the freehold buildings, the entire debenture being held by the Lendem Bank Ltd. The bank has requested that the arrears of debenture interest be paid at once, but have intimated that they might be prepared to lend the company a further £10,000 in view of the increased value of the collateral, provided the interest rate on the additional and the existing loan is increased to 10%
(iii) The company banks with the Southern Bank Ltd. The bank has demanded that the overdraft be repaid immediately.
(iv) The directors have agreed to waive half the loans owed to them.
(v) The land and buildings have been valued at £55,000, quoted investments at £50,000, stock at £24,000, and plant at £16,000.
(vi) It is estimated that 10% of debtors may prove to be doubtful.

You are required to prepare a report to the Board of Directors of Shatterhopes Ltd:

(*a*) *suggesting a scheme of reorganisation which you feel would be acceptable to all parties concerned. This report should contain a balance sheet of Shatterhopes Ltd, after the reorganisation,*
(*b*) *commenting briefly on the financial position of Shatterhopes Ltd consequent upon the reorganisation.*

(*25 marks*)

QUESTION N8

On 1 July 19–06 Convertit Plc, a quoted company had the following issued share and loan capital.

10,000,000	25p ordinary shares (fully paid)
2,000,000	£1 8% redeemable preference shares (fully paid)
£1,500,000	9% convertible loan stock 19–06/19–07

Share premium account stands at £560,000.

The following information is relevant:

(a) The preference shares are redeemable on or before 1 July 19–06 at a premium of 10%; the redemption to be settled as to one half in cash and one half by the issue of 25p ordinary shares at their mid-market price on the day of redemption.

(b) 9% loan stock is convertible between 1 Jan. 19–06 and 30 June 19–07 into 25p ordinary shares on such terms as will provide loan stock holders with a premium of 8% based on the mid-market price of the shares on the day of conversion.
(c) In respect of both preference shares and loan stock any fractional allotments resulting from the redemption or conversion are to be sold at the mid-market value and the proceeds distributed to the share or stock holders pro rata.

On 1 July 19–06 all the preference shares were redeemed and all the loan stock was converted in accordance with the terms. Fractional allotments of 5,000 ordinary shares arose in respect of the issue to preference shareholders and 3,000 in respect of loan stock holders and these were sold on 1 July.

The mid-market price quoted for the 25p ordinary shares was 80p on 1 July 19–06 and this gave rise to a dividend yield of 6.96% twice covered.

The company's projected accounts for the year ended 30 June 19–07 show an anticipated increase in profit after taxation by 30% over the previous years (based on the existing capital structure). The directors indicate that they intend to pay dividends for that year in such manner as will exactly maintain the present dividend cover.

Corporation tax is at 52% and income tax at 30%.

You are required:

(*a*) *to prepare journal entries reflecting the capital reorganisation on 1 July 19–07,*
(*b*) *to calculate the effect of the reorganisation on a holder of 1,000 ordinary shares on 1 July 19–06 if the forecast profits for the next year are realised and the present P/E ratio of the company's ordinary shares is expected to remain constant.*

(*20 marks*)

QUESTION P1.

The following information related to the audited consolidated accounts of Life & Line Ltd, (a shipping company) and its subsidiaries.

	Years ended 31 December				
	19.00	*19.01*	*19.02*	*19.03*	*19.04*
Group Turnover	16,081	18,049	21,364	29,425	32,869
Group Profit before taxation	4,041	5,495	8,915	12,642	12,590
After charging:					
Depreciation (Note 1)	7,021	7,819	7,986	7,762	8,308
Provisions for surveys	1,652	1,084	1,552	1,780	1,170
Redundancy payments	123	173	38	—	222
Interest payable	2,095	3,500	4,200	4,900	6,500
Directors' emoluments	36	39	42	46	53
After crediting:					
Profit on sale of short term investments	—	310	94	—	—
Taxation	1,541	2,095	3,311	5,123	5,390
Group profit after tax (in 19–04 before extraordinary items)	2,500	3,400	5,604	7,519	7,200
Extraordinary items					
Net profit on sale of ships					740
Provision for reduction in value of trade investments					(4,169)
Profit after extraordinary items					3,71
Dividends	2,300	2,300	4,200	5,100	5,100
	(10%)	(10%)	(12%)	(14%)	(14%)
Retained Profit added to reserves	200	1,100	1,404	2,419	(1,329)
Amounts (charged) or credited direct to reserves during 19–00 to 19–03 were as follows:					
Net profit (loss) on sale of ships	972	934	(458)	(1,172)	
Net profit on sale of investments	140	26			
Provision for reduction in value of trade investments		(1,500)		(239)	
Provision for surveys					
Set aside from Profit and Loss Account	1,652	1,084	1,552	1,780	1,170
Expenditure during year	1,531	1,325	1,317	1,289	2,057

Notes:

1. Following a review of group depreciation policy changes have been made to the bases of charging depreciation. The expected lives of most categories of fixed assets have been reassessed and rates of depreciation applied in future adjusted. The depreciation charge for the year to 31 Dec. 19–04 is £0.9 m less than it would have been had the above changes not been made. Depreciation is calculated on a straight line basis.

Ships are depreciated at the rate which will write down their book value to their estimated residual value over the balance of their assumed lives: the assumed life of offshore oil rig servicing vessels is 10 years, of container ships, tankers and oil/bulk/ore carriers is 15 years and of other ships is 20 years.

If the new policy had been operated in earlier years the depreciation charge would have been reduced by the following amounts—19.00 £0.75 m, 19.01 £0.25 m, 19.02 £1.0 m, 19.03 £1.1 m.

The provision for surveys represents annual amounts set aside for refits and repairs to pass periodical insurance surveys. The amount expended represents costs of surveys incurred in the respective years.

The consolidated balance sheet of Life and Line Ltd as on 31 Dec. 19–04 was:

		£000	
	Cost	*Depreciation*	*Net*
Fixed Assets			
Ships	346,805	158,032	188,773
Ships under construction	20,582	—	20,582
Properties	28,021	4,404	23,617
Plant and equipment	20,213	5,617	14,596
	415,621	168,053	247,568
Trade Investments (Directors' valuation £23 m)			22,635
Stocks and work in progress			23,105
Debtors			42,081
Cash and deposits			27,020
			362,409
Issued share capital			36,428
Reserves			166,265
Interest of minority shareholders			10,840
Investment grants			18,433
Debentures and loans (repayable within 5 years)			69,717
Creditors			42,860
Bank overdraft			4,025
Taxation			8,741
Dividend			5,100
			362,409

You are required to draft the accountants' report for inclusion in a prospectus in as much conformity with best practice and the requirements of the Stock Exchange as the information given will allow. Ignore any requirement to produce funds flow statements.

(*30 marks*)

QUESTION P2

You have been asked to act as a reporting accountant in connection with an Issue of shares to the public by a company, X Ltd, of which you are not the auditor. The last audited accounts of the company were made up to 31 Dec. 19–04. During the course of your examination you have ascertained the following information:

1. In the year to 31 Dec. 19–01, the whole issued share capital of Y Ltd was acquired by the issue to the vendors of 200,000 ordinary shares of £1 each fully paid.
2. Goodwill of £100,000 as shown in the balance sheet of X Ltd as at 31 Dec. 19–02 has been written off since that date at the rate of 20% per annum on the straight-line basis.
3. In the year to 31 Dec. 19–00, one of the factories of X Ltd was sold, resulting in a profit, which was credited to reserves, of £120,000. In the same year, an additional unit was purchased to replace this factory, and it was decided that the corporation tax arising on the profit should be deferred under the 'roll-over' provisions.
4. As a result of the change in factory premises, plant and machinery owned by X Ltd was moved to the new unit at a cost of £65,000. This amount was debited to works overhead in the year in which the move took place.
5. During the period under review, the following professional fees were debited to the profit and loss account of X Ltd:

	£
Re valuation of company properties	5,500
Re trade mark protection	3,200
Re debt collection	7,800

6. From time to time, certain directors of X Ltd made interest-free loans to the company in order that the overdraft limit be not exceeded. In the year to 31 Dec. 19–04, the bank raised this limit by £100,000 in order to ensure that the company had sufficient working capital, and the directors loans were repaid.
7. Until 31 Dec. 19–02, government grants in respect of the purchase of fixed assets were credited to reserves. Since that date, it has been the policy of X Ltd to deduct grants received from the cost of acquisition of the assets.
8. As at 31 Dec. 19–04, an amount of £16,000 was apparently due to X Ltd in respect of a repayment of value added tax. In verifying this asset, you ascertain that the turnover figure for that year included £45,000, being value added tax on taxable outputs, and that works overhead had been debited with £12,500 of tax charged on company cars.

Required:

State, giving your reasons, what action (if any) you would take on these points in preparing your report.

Note: You may assume that all figures contained in the question are material. *(15 marks)*

QUESTION P3. DIONYSUS LTD

Dionysus Ltd is seeking a Stock Exchange quotation. The following profit and loss accounts are to form the basis of the information to be included in the Accountants' Report.

Profit and Loss Accounts for the years ended 31 Dec.

	19–01	*19–02*	*19–03*	*19–04*	*19–05*
	£000	*£000*	*£000*	*£000*	*£000*
Turnover	450	600	720	1,200	1,350
Profit before tax	37	60	68	82	95
After charging					
Depreciation	15	12	19	25	21
Audit	5	5	6	7	10
Directors	25	27	30	30	35
Loss on sequestration of assets abroad			25		
	45	44	80	62	66
After crediting					
Investment income	10	9	—	—	—
Profit on sale of freehold		15			
	10	24	—	—	—
Share of associated company profit			27	30	32
Total profit before tax	37	60	95	112	127
Corporation tax					
Group	8	12	22	27	35
Deferred tax	—	—	14	13	10
Associated company	—	—	13	15	16
	8	12	49	55	61
Profit after tax	29	48	46	57	66
Dividends	15	25	20	20	40
Retained profit for year	14	23	26	37	26
Retained profit b/f	83	94	134	198	235
Provision for deferred taxation	—	—	(38)	—	—
Under/overprovision for tax	(3)	2	—	—	—
Change in basis of stock valuation	—	15	—	—	—
Associated company	—	—	76	—	—
	80	111	172	198	235
Retained profit c/f	94	134	198	235	261

(a) Changes of accounting policy have occurred as follows:

(i) In 19–03 when the results of an associated company were incorporated for the first time. The adjustment of £76,000 includes amounts relating to:

19–02	£24,000 less tax £12,000 = £12,000
19–01	£22,000 less tax £11,000 = £11,000

Investment income in 19–01 and 19–02 relates to dividends received from the associated company.

(ii) In 19–03 when deferred taxation was provided for the first time. The adjustment of £38,000 includes amounts relating to:

19–02	Operating profit	£5,000
	Chargeable gain rolled over	£4,000
19–01	Operating profit	£7,000

(iii) In 19–02 the basis of stock valuation was changed from prime cost to factory cost. The proportion of overheads relating to stock at 31 Dec. 19–01 was £15,000 and at 1 Jan. 19–01 would have been £11,000.

(b) Tax relief of £10,000 relating to the loss on sequestration of assets abroad has been taken into account in the tax charge for 19–03.

You are required:

to prepare the statement of adjustments for submission to the Stock Exchange and the summary of profits for inclusion in the accountants' report.

(*20 marks*)

QUESTION P4

The following are the balance sheets of A Ltd and B Ltd.

	A £000	*B* £000		*A* £000	*B* £000
Share capital (£1 ordinary shares)	100	80	Sundry net assets	170	110
Reserves	70	30			
	170	110		170	110

Unrecorded goodwill is A—£20,000, B—£5,000. Assets are valued in excess of their book values by A—£10,000, B—£5,000.

Neither A Ltd nor B Ltd wish to revalue assets nor raise goodwill accounts in their separate balance sheets.

(a) A Ltd acquires the total share capital of B Ltd by an issue of its shares. *Compute the offer terms by reference to the net asset values of the two companies. Required: the balance sheet of A Ltd after the acquisition, and the consolidated balance sheet, following acquisition accounting principles.*
(b) A new company C Ltd is formed to acquire the shares of A Ltd and B Ltd by the issue of 200,000 ordinary £1 shares. *Required: the balance sheet of C Ltd and the consolidated balance sheet after the acquisitions, following acquisition accounting principles.*
(c) Facts as in (a) above, but merger principles are applied.
(d) Facts as in (b) above, but merger principles are applied, and C Ltd to record the sundry net assets at their revalued amounts, but no goodwill is to be recorded.
(e) Facts as in (d) above, but due to synergetic processes the total assets of C Ltd are worth 10% more than their separate valuations prior to merger. Calculate the share exchange terms if the synergy is to be apportioned on an equitable basis.

(*14 marks*)

QUESTION P5

Sellit Plc, a supermarket chain with city stores, has been trying to extend into surburban areas, but has had difficulty in obtaining suitable sites. Go Plc a fast growing company operating large surburban stores has planning permission for further stores, but is finding difficulty in obtaining suitable finance for its expansion programme. Both companies are quoted on the Stock Exchange.

The directors have agreed in principle on an amalgamation to be effected by Sellit Plc making a bid in ordinary shares for all the issued ordinary shares of Go Plc. No bid would be made for the loan stock of Go Plc. As an independent accountant, you have been asked to prepare a report setting out the terms which you feel would be acceptable to the shareholders of each company.

The latest accounts are summarised as follows:

Balance Sheets at 31 Dec. 19–04

		Sellit Plc		*Go Plc*
	£000	*£000*	*£000*	*£000*
Fixed assets at cost less depreciation:				
Land and buildings		17,100		3,520
Equipment and fittings		7,200		2,000
Motor vehicles		4,000		1,500
		28,300		7,020
Current assets:				
Stocks	16,215		3,325	
Debtors	1,650		1,700	
Cash and deposits	10,000		2,150	
		27,865		7,175
		56,165		14,195
Less: Current liabilities				
Bank overdraft	—		1,000	
Creditors	16,810		4,960	
Current taxation	1,400		680	
Dividends	1,400		170	
		19,610		6,810
		36,555		7,385
Less: Corporation tax payable 1 Jan. 19–06		5,260		1,630
Net assets (subject to unsecured loan, Go Plc)		£31,295		£5,755
Representing:				
5% unsecured loan 19–20		—		600
Ordinary shares of 25p fully paid	7,000		1,700	
Capital reserves	8,050		1,590	
Accumulated revenue	16,245		1,865	
		31,295		5,155
		£31,295		£5,755

Profit and Loss Accounts for the year ended 31 Dec. 19–04

		Sellit Plc *£000*		*Go Plc* *£000*
Sales		170,000		70,000
Trading profit		12,000		4,000
Interest		500		50
		12,500		4,050
Less: Depreciation	2,255		720	
Interest on—overdraft	—		100	
—loans	—		30	
Rentals	100		70	
		2,355		920
		10,145		3,130
Taxation		5,260		1,630
		4,885		1,500
Dividends		2,100		340
Retained		2,785		1,160

Additional information:

1. During the last five years the earnings per share of Sellit Plc have grown at the rate of 15% per annum, and those of Go Plc at the rate of 20% per annum.
2. Profits before tax in 19–05 are expected to be at about the same level as in 19–04.
3. After the amalgamation, Sellit Plc expects to pay the same proportion of its earnings in dividends as at present.
4. The fixed assets have been revalued as follows:

	Sellit Plc *£000*	*Go Plc* *£000*
Land and buildings	24,100	5,300
Equipment and fittings	8,000	2,300
Motor vehicles	4,200	1,400

These values should be taken into account in fixing the terms, and will be incorporated in the accounts in the future.

5. The latest share prices and the 'highs' and 'lows' for the last twelve months are as follows:

	Sellit Plc	*Go Plc*
Current	70p	76p
High	142p	160p
Low	60p	55p

You are required:

(*a*) *to write a report to the directors of Sellit Plc giving your opinion of the values of the shares for the amalgamation scheme and the basis of exchange,*

(*15 marks*)

(*b*) *to prepare the consolidated balance sheet assuming the scheme was implemented on 1 Jan. 19–05, and that acquisition accounting has to be used because the scheme is not approved by the members of Sellit Plc,*

(*10 marks*)

(*c*) *state* briefly *the effect on the balance sheet if merger accounting principles were applied.*

(*5 marks*)

(*Total 30 marks*)

QUESTION P6

The summarised Balance Sheet of Hope Ltd at 30 Jun. 19–05 was as follows:

		£000
Capital employed		
Share capital issued and fully paid—		
2,940,000 shares of 25p each		735
Reserves		900
		1,635
Represented by:		
Fixed assets		540
Current assets	1,695	
Less: Current liabilities	600	1,095
		1,635

At that date the company acquired the whole issued share capital of Prey Ltd by the issue of 480,000 new ordinary shares at the days market price of 80p.

Prey Ltd's Balance Sheet just prior to acquisition was:

		£000
Capital employed		
Share capital issued and fully paid—		
60,000 shares of £1 each		60
Reserves		150
		210
Represented by		
Fixed assets		120
Current assets	165	
Less: Current liabilities	75	90
		210

The fair value of the fixed assets is £210,000.

You are required to:

(*a*) *discuss the various methods which have been proposed for the treatment of goodwill in the accounts,*

(*b*) *explain and illustrate two possible methods of reflecting this transaction in the consolidated balance sheet of the group, and to comment on their relative advantages and weaknesses.*

(*18 marks*)

QUESTION P7

Oldfashioned Plc has recently appointed a new chairman and the board has now been asked to consider a merger with Sixties Plc, a company well established in a new growth area. There is agreement to merge on the basis of the following data for liabilities, assets and expected future profits.

	Estimated accounts to 30 Sep. 19–9	
	Old fashioned	*Sixties*
	£	£
Ordinary share capital fully paid shares of 50p	2,000,000	400,000
Reserves and unappropriated profits	1,500,000	600,000
10% Debentures, 19–25/29	4,000,000	3,000,000
8% Convertible unsecured loan stock	1,000,000	2,000,000
	£8,500,000	£6,000,000
Fixed assets, at valuation by same valuer on same basis	6,000,000	5,500,000
Net current assets	2,500,000	500,000
	£8,500,000	£6,000,000
Estimated profits after all expenses and taxation for year to 30 Sep. 19–9	1,000,000	800,000
	Forecast for future profits for companies continuing independently	
year to 30 Sep. 19–10 (assuming interest on convertible unsecured loan stock up to 31 Mar. 19–10)	1,000,000	1,000,000
year to 30 Sep. 19–11	900,000	1,200,000
year to 30 Sep. 19–12	800,000	1,600,000

While no benefits from the merger are expected in the year to 30 Sep. 19–10 the following year will see an extra £400,000 profits after tax and the year to 30 Sep. 19–12 an extra £600,000 after tax.

The convertible unsecured loan stocks are convertible into ordinary shares at the option of the shareholders, that of Oldfashioned Plc on the basis of 1 ordinary share for each £1 of stock, that of Sixties Plc on the basis of 2 ordinary shares for each £1 of stock.

It has been proposed that the two companies should merge on the basis of one new 50p share in a new company, Eighties Plc, for one Oldfashioned share or one Sixties share. The whole of the convertible loan stock of both companies was expected to be converted into ordinary shares on 31 Mar. 19–10 and it was proposed that the merger should take place, after this conversion, on 1 Apr. 19–10 with effect from 1 Oct. 19–9.

You are required to:

(*a*) *Show the earnings per share calculations and the resulting disclosure which would be included with the 19–9 accounts of Oldfashioned Plc and Sixties Plc.*

(*6 marks*)

(*b*) *Calculate the earnings per share for the year ended 30 Sep. 19–10 of Eighties Plc on the proposed basis for the merger, assuming the estimated profits are obtained.*

(*3 marks*)

(*c*) *Present a pro forma balance sheet of the Eighties Group as of 1 Oct. 19–9.*

(*i*) *on the acquisition accounting basis, and*
(*ii*) *the merger accounting basis.*

(*8 marks*)

(*d*) *What conditions are necessary for a business combination to be accounted for as a merger?*

(*5 marks*)

(*e*) *What justification is there for merger accounting?*

(*8 marks*)
(*Total 30 marks*)

QUESTION P8

Expanding Plc has an authorised capital of £2 million. Already in issue are 500,000 7% Cumulative Preference shares of £1 and 1,000,000 ordinary shares of 75p each. It published a prospectus in connection with issuing the remainder of its authorised capital, as ordinary shares at a price of £1.25.

25p per share was payable on application (due by October 1981), the balance of the nominal value upon allotment and the final balance on or before 31 Dec. 1981.

£3 million was received with properly completed application forms and all applications were scaled down pro rata with the excess money being applied first towards the amount due on allotment and any further excess being returned.

By 31 Dec. 1981 all amounts due had been received.

You are required to:

(*a*) *present the journal entries (including cash) recording all aspects detailed above in connection with the share issue and,*

(*8 marks*)

(*b*) *explain the main matters to which attention should be directed in the preparation of a published profit forecast*

(*10 marks*)
(*18 marks*)

QUESTION P9

Combined Engineering Plc, a holding company, makes up financial statements to 31 Jul. During 19–1, the group experienced difficult trading conditions which have strained its finances and its bankers have applied pressure on the directors for a substantial reduction in borrowings. Trading has been particularly bad in the wholly owned subsidiary, Rex Garages Ltd, engaged in the motor trade. The directors therefore resolved early in 19–2 to dispose of Rex Garages Ltd.

Management accounts drawn up at 30 Apr. 19–2 showed the following:

		Parent *£000*		*Res* *£000*
Fixed assets:				
Properties		3,646		1,352
Plant and machinery		4,201		462
Vehicles		2,948		437
		10,795		2,251
Shares in subsidiaries at cost (includes £500,000 re Rex)		1,550		—
Loans to subsidiaries (includes £1,000,000 re Rex)		2,000		—
Current assets:				
Stocks	12,529		3,368	
Debtors and prepayments	11,620		1,675	
Cash	25		8	
	24,174		5,051	
Current liabilities				
Trade creditors and accruals	11,206		1,486	
Bank overdraft	17,483		1,817	
	28,689		3,303	
Net current (liabilities)/assets		(4,515)		1,748
		9,830		3,999
Share capital		2,000		500
Reserves		2,830		499
Loan capital		5,000		3,000
		9,830		3,999

In early May 19–2 the following plan of action, relating to Rex, was agreed:

(1) Certain properties with a book value of £950,000 will be sold to a third party for £1.2 m. The sale proceeds will be used to repay the loans of £750,000 secured on these properties and the balance used to reduce the loan of £1 m from the holding company (included in Rex's loan capital).

(2) The three group executives concerned with the management of Rex will be declared redundant. Under their contracts of employment they will be entitled to £150,000 each which will be paid to them in cash and borne by Combined Engineering Plc.

(3) The same three will purchase Rex at net asset value as shown in the 30 Apr. 19–2 management accounts after the adjustments for the properties to be sold and after further adjustments referred to below.

(4) The remaining property is to be written down by £100,000. This will necessitate a repayment of £150,000 of the third party loan secured thereon. This sum will be advanced temporarily by Combined Engineering Plc.

(5) Subsequently the loan from Combined Engineering Plc, including the temporary advance, will be repaid. To raise the necessary finance for this, sufficient new car stocks will be sold off to the trade at a discount of 30% on the cost price used in 30 Apr. 19–2 management figures.

(6) The three executives will acquire Rex's shares using their compensation for redundancy augmented by personal borrowing.

(7) Management Venture Capital Ltd, an independent company, will advance £600,000 loan capital which will be used to reduce Rex's bank overdraft.

(8) The consideration for the Rex shares will be paid in cash by 31 Jul. 19–2.

You are required to produce the pro forma balance sheets of Combined Engineering Plc and Rex Garages Ltd at 31 Jul. 19–2 assuming that the above transactions duly take place and that both companies break even in trading between 30 Apr. 19–2 and that date.

Ignore taxation.

(*18 marks*)

QUESTION P10. CAPITAL REORGANISATION

The following statements are based on extracts from two recently published circulars to holders of shares or loan stock in publicly quoted companies.

(1) *The proposal*
It is proposed that the Company issues £178,326,900 nominal of 12% Capital Notes 1986 to shareholders on the register on 11 February 1977. The detailed procedure for the issue of Capital Notes, which involves a prior scrip issue of fully paid Capital Shares followed by their cancellation, is set out in Appendix A and will effectively result in Capital Notes being received by the Ordinary Shareholders on the following basis:

$32\frac{1}{2}$p nominal of Capital Notes	*in respect of*	*each Ordinary Share of 25p of the Company*

The Capital Notes will be issued in units of £100 and application will be made for a listing for the Capital Notes on The Stock Exchange. Any fractions of £100 nominal of Capital Notes will not be allotted to the persons who would otherwise be entitled thereto but will be aggregated and sold on their behalf and the net proceeds distributed to them in accordance with their entitlements.

Appendix A

Procedure Proposed for Issue of Capital Notes

The first step will be to increase the capital of the Company by creating a new class of Capital Shares. The Capital Shares will then be issued to the Ordinary Shareholders credited as fully paid by capitalising £178,326,900 out of the amount of £263,398,007 currently standing to the credit of the share premium account. The share capital will then, subject to confirmation of the Court, be reduced back to its original level by cancelling the newly created Capital Shares and, in consideration of their cancellation, issuing Capital Notes to the shareholders in their place. The result of completing this procedure will be to leave the shareholders with the same number of Ordinary Shares of 25p each as they previously held together with a number of Capital Notes of £100 each and/or cash realised for their fractional entitlements.

The fractional holdings of Capital Notes totalled £3 million and were sold for net proceeds of £2.7 million. The documents also showed that current net dividend totalled 3.595p per share and the market price was 160p per share.

(2) *It was announced to the press today that the company is making an offer of new ordinary shares of 25p each in exchange for the cancellation of the whole of the outstanding 7.5 per cent Convertible Unsecured Loan Stock 1984/89 (the Stock).*

The offer
At the request of the company and on its behalf we hereby offer (*the offer*), on and subject to the terms and conditions set out in this document, new ordinary shares of 25p each, credited as fully paid (*the new ordinary shares*) in exchange for the cancellation of the whole of the outstanding Stock, on the following basis:

For each £100 nominal of the Stock 115 new ordinary shares and so in proportion for any greater or less nominal amount of the Stock.

The stock
The nominal amount of the Stock outstanding is £8,117,700. The Trust Instruments contain provisions (inter alia) to the following effect:

1. Interest
   Interest on the Stock at the rate of 7.5 per cent per annum (subject to income tax) is payable by equal half-yearly instalments on 6th January and 6th July in each year.
2. Conversion
   In any of the 7 years 1977 to 1983, both inclusive, each Stockholder shall have the right to convert (in amounts or multiples of £1) all or any of his Stock into fully paid ordinary share capital of the company on the following basis:

   £23.2862 in nominal amount of ordinary share capital for every £100 nominal Stock and pro rata for any other amount of Stock.

The document also showed that the current net dividends totalled 4.493p per share and the latest market quotations were 67p per ordinary share and £70 per £100 nominal of stock.

Assume that all the necessary resolutions and Court approvals were obtained.

You are required to:

(*a*) *prepare journal entries to record these events in the records of the respective companies and*

(*17 marks*)

(*b*) *calculate the effect of these proposals on the individual personal holder of either 100 shares or £100 of CULS. Ignore capital gains tax and assume that the market prices of existing securities will not change and that the Capital Notes will be quoted at par.*

(*8 marks*)

(*Assume the rate of ACT is 35/65*) (*25 marks*)

QUESTION Q1.

(a) *Why is it invariably necessary for a company's accounts to be adjusted prior to their inclusion in the accountant's report in a prospectus?*

(b) *Mention two instances in which such adjustments may be necessary.*

(*c*) *Draw up a check list of matters required by the Stock Exchange to be covered by an accountant's report in a prospectus to be issued by a private company seeking a public quotation for its shares.*

(*18 marks*)

QUESTION Q2

Your client, Windfall Ltd, has asked you to report on a profit forecast which it is preparing in connection with its application for the admission of its securities for a listing on the Stock Exchange.

You are required to state the main points which you would wish to consider in carrying out your examination of the accounting policies and calculations for the profit forecast and the procedures followed by the company for its preparation.

(*15 marks*)

QUESTION Q3

Questions (a) to (g) below relate to the Stock Exchange requirements contained in the 'Admission of Securities to Listing' (The 'Yellow Book').

(*a*) *A Ltd is an unlisted company in the process of making an offer for sale. The accountants' report contained in the prospectus covers the five years to 31 Mar. 19–8. On the 14 May 19–8, A Ltd acquired an 80% equity interest in an unlisted company, B Ltd. What information must be contained in the accountants' report in respect of B Ltd?*

(*b*) *What are the basic duties of the reporting accountant in relation to a profit forecast contained in the prospectus of an unlisted company?*

(*c*) *On admission to listing, a company is required to enter into a Listing Agreement with the Stock Exchange.*

(*i*) *What is the overall effect of this on the company?*
(*ii*) *What formalities need to be undertaken by the company?*
(*iii*) *What does the Listing Agreement require as regards the publication of half-yearly or interim reports?*
(*iv*) *What minimum information is required as a result of* (*iii*) (*above*)?

(*d*) *What minimum proportion of issued equity share capital must be in public hands?*

(*e*) *What is a class I transaction? When is an accountants' report required in a class I circular?*

(*f*) *What is the attitude of the Stock Exchange to qualified accountants' reports in the following situations:*

(*i*) *an unlisted company wishing to make an offer for sale.*
(*ii*) *the acquisition by a listed company of a material* (*class I*) *unlisted company whose accounts have been qualified?*

(*g*) *You are the reporting accountant involved in the proposed offer for sale by E Ltd. The original stock sheets for the earlier years of the five-year summary have either been mislaid or destroyed. What steps should you take?*

(*h*) *What is the City Code, to what companies does it apply, on what basis is it observed and how is it enforced?*

(*i*) *Where the City Code applies to a company:*

(*i*) *To what standard of care should all issued documents be drafted?*
(*ii*) *What legal liabilities may arise if mis-statements should occur?*
(*iii*) *Indicate whether the company's auditor can properly decline to report on any profit forecast involved in offer documents?*

(*25 marks*)

QUESTION R1. BAFFLE LTD

You are given below the balance sheets of Baffle Ltd, and its subsidiary, New Ltd, at 31 Jul. 19–6 and 19–7.

	£000	*£000*
Share capital (£1 ordinary)	2,000	2,700
Reserves	3,400	4,700
Debenture stock	1,200	1,700
Minority interests	—	700
Creditors	1,100	2,400
	7,700	12,200
Fixed assets	5,100	9,070
Goodwill	—	200
Stock	1,100	1,500
Debtors	900	1,700
Cash	600	(270)
	7,700	12,200

Baffle Ltd acquired 75% of the 1,000 ordinary shares of New Ltd on 17 Nov. 19–6. At that date the assets of New Ltd were:

	£000
Fixed assets	2,500
Stock	300
Debtors	400
Cash	500
Liabilities of New Ltd were:	
Debenture stock	500
Creditors	800

There were no disposals of fixed assets during the year. Group depreciation charged during the year was £1,950,000. No dividends are proposed but interim dividends paid during the year were:

Baffle Ltd.	£450,000
New Ltd.	£200,000

These dividends were paid on 1 Jul. 19–7. Baffle Ltd paid £2,000,000 to acquire the shares in New Ltd. This was made up of an issue of shares valued at £1,750,000 plus £250,000 of cash. The share premium is included in reserves. All other reserves are revenue.

You are required to produce a consolidated statement of source and application of funds together with supporting notes.

(*25 marks*)

QUESTION R2. GREAT EASTERN LTD

Great Eastern Ltd bought 80% of the ordinary shares of Yare Ltd several years ago when the reserves of Yare were £20,000. You are given below extracts from the balance sheets and profit and loss accounts for the two years ended 31 Dec. 19–7 and 19–8.

	Great Eastern		*Yare*	
	19–7	*19–8*	*19–7*	*19–8*
Ordinary shares	60,000	80,000	30,000	30,000
20% Preference shares	—	—	25,000	25,000
Share premium	12,000	17,000	—	—
Revenue reserves	90,000	114,600	41,000	43,000
Loan stock	50,000	55,000	10,000	10,000
Creditors	29,000	31,000	18,000	17,000
Taxation	18,000	20,000	3,000	8,000
Bank overdraft	2,000	—	6,000	18,000
Dividends	10,000	5,000	10,000	12,000
	271,000	322,600	143,000	163,000
Fixed assets	168,000	190,000	109,000	120,000
Stock	22,000	29,000	26,000	24,000
Debtors	30,000	45,000	8,000	19,000
Dividends	8,000	9,600	—	—
Cash	—	6,000	—	—
Cost of investment	43,000	43,000	—	—
	271,000	322,600	143,000	163,000

	Great Eastern		*Yare*	
	19–7	*19–8*	*19–7*	*19–8*
Profits before the following items:	78,000	91,000	40,000	54,000
Dividends received	8,000	9,600	—	—
Depreciation	30,000	38,000	20,000	24,000
Taxation	21,000	23,000	8,000	11,000
Preference dividends paid	—	—	5,000	5,000
Ordinary dividends paid	15,000	10,000	—	—
Ordinary dividends proposed	10,000	5,000	10,000	12,000
Retained profit	10,000	24,600	(3,000)	2,000

There were no disposals of fixed assets during the year.

You are required to prepare a consolidated statement of source and application of funds for the year ended 31 Dec. 19–8.

(*22 marks*)

QUESTION R3. SPIXWORTH PLC

The following information relates to Spixworth Plc, a public company, for the year ended 30 Jun. 19–8.

	£000
Turnover	31,311
Purchases (stocks adjusted)	7,192
Wages	8,306
Salaries	2,941
Depreciation	1,056
Pension contributions	840
Directors' remuneration	36
Transfer to Plant Replacement Reserve	300
Debenture Interest Paid (gross)	120
Dividends Paid and Proposed	900
Corporation Tax—y.e. 30.6.19–8 (including associate 100,000)	2,600
Other direct overheads	3,520
Other indirect overheads	2,106
Revenue reserves as at 1.7.19–7	69,471
Group retained profit for the year (including associate)	1,657

Included, where relevant, in the above figures are amounts relating to Spax Ltd, a subsidiary of Spixworth in which Spixworth has 60% of the ordinary share capital and 30% of the preference shares.

Spax Ltd P & L A/c for the year ended 30 Jun. 19–8 was:

	£
Profit	50,000
Taxation	15,000
	35,000
Dividends paid/payable	
Preferential	10,000
	25,000
Ordinary	15,000
	10,000

Pix Ltd is treated as an associated company of Spixworth Plc. Spixworth has a 40% interest in the ordinary share capital.

Pix Ltd P & L A/c for the year ended 30 Jun. 19–8 was:

	£
Trading profit	500,000
Investment income	50,000
	550,000
Taxation	100,000
	450,000
Ordinary dividends	100,000
Retained profit for year	350,000

(*a*) *You are required to prepare a value added statement on the lines suggested in the Corporate Report.*

(*14 marks*)

(*b*) '*The maintenance of short-term profit is not the sole aim of modern business enterprises although by making the profit figure the keynote figure of financial reports, users are encouraged to believe that it is the sole aim.*'

To what extent do you consider the above statement to be true in relation to companies and their published reports in modern times? Discuss briefly three other objectives of economic entities and how these objectives might be recognised in their published reports.

(*8 marks*)
(*Total 22 marks*)

QUESTION R4

The Duncan Manufacturing Co. have asked you to prepare a Value Added Statement suitable to be presented in the Report to Employees. You are given the following selection of figures taken from the company's annual accounts, some of which will be needed in the Value Added Statement.

	£000
Sales during year (net of VAT)	1,200
Opening stocks of raw material	200
Closing stocks of raw material	500
Royalties received	50
Purchase of raw materials during year	800
Opening creditors	150
Closing creditors	250
VAT collected	180
Opening debtors	400
Closing debtors	600
Wages net—paid to employees	200
PAYE	50
Pensions paid	50
Corporation Tax (P & L A/c)	165
Taxation due, opening balance sheet	300
Taxation due, closing balance sheet	200
Dividends paid during year	65
Depreciation charge (P & L A/c)	100
Purchase of fixed assets	800
Associated companies earnings	100
Dividends received from associated companies	50
Increase in Bank borrowings	200
Interest paid during year	120
Earnings retained (as per P & L A/c of Duncan Manufacturing Co.)	100
Accumulated depreciation	1,075

Required:

(*a*) *Prepare a Value Added Statement for the Duncan Manufacturing Co. based on the figures given.* (*10 marks*)

(*b*) *Write a report for the Managing Director explaining your treatment of two controversial aspects of such Value Added Statements. The two areas causing concern are:*

(*i*) *whether depreciation should be treated as a distribution of value added or as an external cost, and*

(*ii*) *whether the various forms of taxation should be treated as an external cost, distribution of value added, or whether the firm should just be regarded as a collecting agent for the government.* (*10 marks*)

(*Total 20 marks*)

QUESTION R5. SAUCES LTD

The following accounts of a company have been prepared for the year ended 30 Sep. 19–6.

	19–6		*19–5*	
Balance sheet	*£m*	*£m*	*£m*	*£m*
Share capital		273.3		266.5
Share premium		71.9		45.6
Reserves		412.3		350.6
Deferred tax		132.9		116.6
Long-term indebtedness		478.8		360.0
		1,369.2		1,139.3
Represented by:				
Property plant and equipment		782.9		695.7
Pre production expenditure		53.5		40.8
Exploration and development		4.8		10.0
Associated companies		101.8		86.1
Current assets:				
Stock	314.6		243.2	
Debtors	247.5		221.0	
Bank	301.2		259.1	
	863.3		723.3	
Deduct current liabilities:				
Creditors	261.0		240.0	
Short-term indebtedness	94.8		72.8	
Tax	68.2		93.9	
Dividend	13.1		9.9	
	437.1		416.6	
		426.2		306.7
		1,369.2		1,139.3

Profit and loss account	*19–6* £m	£m	*19–5* £m	£m
Sales revenue		1,184.0		
Operating profit		92.8		
Share of profit of associated companies		6.0		
Interest receivable		26.4		
		125.2		
Deduct interest payable		37.9		
Profit before tax		87.3		
Tax on profit for year (incl. £16.3 for deferred tax)		48.7		
Net profit after tax before extraordinary items		38.6		
Extraordinary items		22.3		
Net profit after tax and extraordinary items		60.9		
Dividends paid and proposed				
Preference	0.4		(0.4)	
Ordinary				
Interim paid	6.3		(4.1)	
Final proposed	6.6		(5.6)	
		13.3		
Retained:				
By company	46.0			
By associates	1.6			
		47.6		

During the year 27,200,000 ordinary shares of 25p were issued at a premium of £1 per share under a rights issue made to ordinary shareholders. The expenses of the issue, amounting to £900,000 were charged against the share premium account.

The investment in associated companies was revalued during the year providing a surplus over book value of £14.1 million. There was no additional investment.

Operating profit is after charging depreciation on property, plant and equipment of £77.1 million, preproduction expenditure of £8.6 million and exploration and development costs of £22.2 million.

You are required to:

(*a*) *Prepare a statement of source and application of funds for the year ended 30 Sep. 19–6 in a form consistent with best practice as far as the given information permits, and*

(*15 marks*)

(*b*) *Briefly discuss the reasons for an accounting standard on this topic.*

(*5 marks*)

(*Total: 20 marks*)

QUESTION R6. FURNITURE AND CHAIRS

The following summarised accounts have been prepared by Furniture Ltd and its subsidiary Chairs Ltd for the years ended 31 May 19–9 and 19–8.

	Furniture Ltd		*Chairs Ltd*	
	19–9	*19–8*	*19–9*	*19–8*
Balance sheet at 31 May	£000	£000	£000	£000
Issued ordinary share capital	6,000	4,000	550	500
Issued preference share capital	3,000	3,000	400	400
Retained profits	2,490	2,000	117	100
10% Debentures	5,000	4,000	1,000	500
Trade creditors	600	400	300	250
Current taxation	1,695	1,446	127	60
Proposed dividend	600	500	55	—
Overdraft	—	—	1,392	1,304
	19,385	15,346	3,941	3,114
Land and buildings	2,500	2,000	700	600
Plant and machinery	9,500	8,000	1,000	800
Investment in Chairs Ltd at cost	440	400	—	—
Stock and work in progress	750	600	600	400
Debtors	2,500	2,000	1,500	1,250
ACT recoverable	546	497	41	14
Cash and bank balances	3,149	1,849	100	50
	19,385	15,346	3,941	3,114

	Furniture Ltd		*Chairs Ltd*	
	19–9	*19–8*	*19–9*	*19–8*
	£000	*£000*	*£000*	*£000*
Profit and loss account for year to 31 May				
Trading profit for the year	3,500	3,000	300	150
Debenture interest	500	400	100	50
Taxation (treated as current taxation)	1,400	1,200	100	60
Dividends paid				
Ordinary	300	300	—	—
Preference	210	210	28	28
Dividends proposed, ordinary	600	500	55	—
Retained	490	390	17	12
The trading profit for the year is stated after charging depreciation of	1,000	800	150	100

Furniture Ltd acquired the ordinary shares of Chairs Ltd. on two dates; 400,000 of £1 each on 31 Jan. 19–0 for £400,000 and 40,000 of £1 each for £40,000 on 31 Jan. 19–9 on the occasion of a right's issue to all ordinary shareholders. Neither company sold any fixed assets during the year.

You are required to:

(*a*) *Prepare a consolidated statement of source and application of group funds for the year ended 31 May 19–9.*

(*19 marks*)

(*b*) *State what difference it would make to the statement if Furniture Ltd had acquired its holding of 400,000 ordinary shares on 1 Jun. 19–8 instead of on 31 Jan. 19–0.*

(*7 marks*)
(*Total 26 marks*)

QUESTION R7

Halsall Ltd is a well-established family company which makes up its accounts to the 31 Oct. each year. On 1 Jul. 19–8 it acquired 85% of the ordinary share capital of Ormskirk Ltd. The details of the acquisition were as follows:

(a) *Assets and liabilities of Ormskirk Ltd at 1.7.–8*

	£	£
Plant and machinery at cost		165,000
Accumulated depreciation at 1.7.–8		81,250
		83,750
Stock	20,000	
Debtors	16,500	
Cash	2,700	
		39,200
		122,950
Creditors	21,050	
Corporation tax	17,400	
		38,450
Net assets		84,500

(b) Purchase consideration (85% holding)

£1 ordinary shares (premium of 50p per share)	37,500
Cash	50,000

You are provided with the following financial statements:

Consolidated profit and loss account for the year ended 31 Oct. 19–8

	£	£
Profit before tax (after charging depreciation)		267,420
Corporation tax		122,500
Profit after tax		144,920
Minority shareholders' interest		4,320
		140,600
Dividends—paid	12,500	
—proposed	32,500	
		45,000
Retained profit		95,600

Balance sheets (summarised)

	Halsall Ltd *31.10.7*	*Consolidated balance sheet* *31.10.–8*
	£	£
Ordinary share capital	75,000	100,000
Share premium	—	12,500
Revenue reserves	141,225	236,825
Minority interest	—	16,995
Creditors	19,600	50,070
Corporation tax	49,700	139,900
Proposed dividend	25,000	32,500
	310,525	588,790
Plant and machinery—cost	320,000	671,000
—depreciation	(191,297)	(313,247)
Goodwill on consolidation	—	15,675
Stock	53,600	116,800
Debtors	41,722	62,400
Cash	86,500	36,162
	310,525	588,790

The following additional information is provided:

1. *Corporation tax*

	£
Balance at 1.11.–7	49,700
Acquisition of Ormskirk	17,400
Provided during year	122,500
Paid during year	(49,700)
Balance at 31.10.–8	139,900

2. *Plant and machinery*

	Cost	*Depreciation*
	£	£
Balances at 1.11.–7	320,000	191,297
Acquisition of Ormskirk	165,000	81,250
Additions	186,000	—
Depreciation provided	—	40,700
Balances at 31.10.–8	671,000	313,247

	£
3. *Goodwill on consolidation*	
Purchase consideration—acquisition of Ormskirk Ltd	87,500
Attributable net assets (85% × £84,500)	71,825
Goodwill arising on acquisition	15,675

4. Profit before tax (£267,420) includes only those profits of Ormskirk Ltd which have arisen since acquisition.

You are required to:

(*a*) *Prepare a statement of source and application of funds, for the year ended 31 Oct. 19–8, showing the effects of acquiring Ormskirk Ltd on the separate assets and liabilities of the group.*

(*17 marks*)

(*b*) *Indicate and quantify the items which would change if the statement was intended to show the effect of the acquisition as a separate item (the net outlay approach).*

(*5 marks*)

(*c*) *Discuss briefly which of the two approaches you consider more informative from the viewpoint of a shareholder in Halsall Ltd.*

(*4 marks*)
(*Total 26 marks*)

QUESTION R8

You are provided with the following information regarding the Grasmere group of companies.

1. The consolidated profit and loss account for the year ended 31 Dec. 19–8 is as follows:

	£000	*£000*
Turnover		4,168
Profit before tax		468
Share of profits of associated company		63
		531
Corporation tax (including £27,000 relating to associated company)		250
		281
Minority shareholders' interest		8
		273
Dividends—paid	50	
—proposed	70	
		120
Retained profit		153
Holding company	102	
Subsidiary	27	
Associated company	24	
	153	

2. Profit before tax is arrived at after charging:

	£
Debenture interest	44,000
Wages and salaries	487,000
Depreciation	155,000

3. Grasmere Ltd has only one subsidiary, Easedale Ltd and one associated company, Tarn Ltd. Both of these investments have been held for many years.

4. Abbreviated profit and loss account details of Easedale Ltd (Grasmere has a 90% interest) are:

	£000	£000
Profit after tax		80
Dividends—paid	20	
—proposed	30	
	—	50
Retained profit		30

5. Abbreviated profit and loss account details of Tarn Ltd are:

	£000
Profit before tax	210
Tax	90
	120
Dividend paid	40
Retained	80

Grasmere has a 30% interest in Tarn Ltd.

You are required to:

(*a*) *Define, briefly, the term value-added.* (*2 marks*)

(*b*) *Prepare a value-added statement for the Grasmere Ltd group in a form you consider suitable for publication.* (*14 marks*)

(*c*) *Discuss briefly your treatment of the following two items, indicating whether you consider there are any acceptable alternative methods of presentation.*

(*i*) *Minority interest* (*4 marks*)

(*ii*) *Associated company* (*3 marks*)

(*Total 23 marks*)

QUESTION R9. ACCOUNTING RATIOS

The following is an extract from *Accountancy*, Mar. 1977, p. 50:

Take profit before tax divided by current liabilities; current assets as a proportion of total liabilities; current liabilities as a proportion of total tangible assets: take into account the no-credit interval; mix them in the right proportions and you can tell whether a company will go bust.

The no-credit interval is defined as (current assets − current liabilities) ÷ (operating costs excluding depreciation).

The following are the summarised accounts of Go-go Products Ltd and Numerous Inventions Ltd for the years ended 30 Apr. 19–7 and 19–6.

	Go-go Products		*Numerous Inventions*	
	19–7	*19–6*	*19–7*	*19–6*
	£	£	£	£
Turnover	30,067	25,417	9,734	8,044
Costs: Depreciation	311	284	331	195
Other	28,356	24,198	8,313	6,571
Profit before tax	1,400	935	1,090	1,278
	30,067	25,417	9,734	8,044
Intangible assets	918	937	—	—
Fixed assets	4,644	5,228	1,950	1,530
Stock	6,243	6,773	986	1,257
Debtors	4,042	4,580	3,234	2,236
Bank	516	184	2,578	1,366
	16,363	17,702	8,748	6,389
Creditors	5,261	5,144	1,297	972
Current taxation	312	379	483	321
Short-term borrowing	2,357	4,447	2,577	1,174
Long-term loans	1,409	1,168	55	38
Capital and reserves	7,024	6,564	4,336	3,884
	16,363	17,702	8,748	6,389

You are required to:

(*a*) *Calculate three of the stated factors for the two companies and two others you consider relevant to their going-concern status.*

(*15 marks*)

(*b*) *Compare the two companies stating clearly which of your calculated ratios have moved in an unfavourable direction, and*

(*5 marks*)

(*c*) *Describe and discuss the limitations of ratio analysis as a predictor of failure.*

(*5 marks*)
(*Total 25 marks*)

QUESTION R10. HYDRA PLC

Hydra Plc had the following capital structure:

	£
Ordinary shares of 25p fully paid	800,000
8% £1 preference shares	150,000

On 31 Mar. 19–8, Hydra Plc made a 1 for 5 rights issue at 60p per share. The following additional information is provided:

(i) the market price of the ordinary shares on the last day of quotation cum rights was 80p

(ii) the profits after tax but before preference dividend in the last two years were:

Year ending	30.9.–7	£465,000
	30.9.–8	£612,000

You are required to:

(*a*) *define earnings per share*

(*3 marks*)

(*b*) *calculate the earnings per share for the current year, together with the comparative*

(*7 marks*)

(*c*) *state how the information would be disclosed in the published accounts*

(*4 marks*)

(*d*) *state the three circumstances specified in SSAP 3* (*earnings per share*) *where the fully diluted earnings per share has to be shown in addition to the basic earnings per share*

(*6 marks*)

(*e*) *indicate problem areas in the measurement and comparison of earnings per share which have arisen as a result of recent standards and exposure drafts*

(*5 marks*)
(*Total 25 marks*)

QUESTION R11

The following extracts are taken from a takeover offer document by which S. Pearson & Son Ltd offered to acquire the whole of the fully paid capital not already owned of Madame Tussaud's Ltd.

Letter from Lazard Brothers & Co Ltd

To the members of Madame Tussaud's:

25 Jan. 1978

Dear Sir or Madam

NEW AND RECOMMENDED OFFER TO ACQUIRE YOUR SHARES

It was announced to the press on 18 Jan. 1978, that the boards of Pearsons and Madame Tussaud's had reached agreement on the terms of a new offer to be made on behalf of Pearsons for the Madame Tussaud's shares. A letter from the Chairman of Madame Tussaud's is printed on the previous two pages and forms part of this document.

(1) *The new offer*

On behalf of Pearsons we now offer to acquire, on the terms and conditions set out in this document, all the Madame Tussaud's shares on the following basis:

for each Madame Tussaud's share	65p in cash (*the new cash offer*)
	OR
	65p nominal of a new $10\frac{1}{2}\%$ partly convertible unsecured loan stock 1993/98 of Pearsons (*the convertible alternative*)

Holders of Madame Tussaud's shares will be entitled to receive and retain the final dividend for the year ended 31 Dec. 1977 of 2.025p net per Madame Tussaud's share which the directors of Madame Tussaud's have stated they intended to propose for payment. It is intended that this dividend will be paid on 4 Apr. 1978 to holders of Madame Tussaud's shares entitled thereto who are on the register on 8 Feb. 1978. The Madame Tussaud's shares are to be acquired free from all liens, charges and encumbrances and, except as aforesaid, together with all rights now or hereafter attach thereto, including the right to all dividends and other distributions hereafter declared, made or paid.

Particulars of the Pearson convertible are set out in Appendix I on pages 8 to 12 from which you will see that interest thereon is payable half-yearly on 30 Jun. and 31 Dec. The first payment of interest in respect of the period from the date the new offer becomes unconditional as to acceptances will be made on 30 Jun. 1978. The Pearson convertible will be convertible as to £50 nominal of stock out of every £100 nominal of stock at a price of 220p per Pearsons ordinary share of 25p in any of the years 1981 to 1987.

Fractions of £1 nominal of the Pearson convertible failing to be issued under the convertible alternative will not be allotted but will be aggregated and sold and the net proceeds of sale distributed proportionately among the holders of Madame Tussaud's shares entitled thereto, except that no payment of less than £1 will be made, such payments being aggregated and retained for the benefit of Pearsons.

Additional terms of the new offer are set out in Appendix II on pages 13 and 14.

You are provided with the following additional information:

(a) The middle market quotation of Madame Tussaud's shares on 21 Nov. 1977 (the day preceding the announcement of the original offer) was 30½p.

(b) The following extract is taken from a letter by Cazenove & Co:

We write to confirm that it is our opinion that if the 10½% partly convertible unsecured loan stock 1993/98 of S. Pearson & Son Ltd, to be issued in connection with the offer for the ordinary stock of Madame Tussaud's Ltd, were listed on the Stock Exchange today, it would command a price of approximately £98%.

This opinion is made in the light of market conditions prevailing at the date of this letter and taking into account the middle market quotation of 193p for the ordinary shares of 25p each of S. Pearson & Son Ltd, based on the Stock Exchange Daily Official List for 23 Jan. 1978.

(c) The forecast dividend of Madame Tussaud's shares for the year ending 31 Dec. 1978 is 4.833p (inclusive of tax credit).

(d) Middle market Stock Exchange quotations for Madame Tussaud's shares have been as follows:

1977	*Madame Tussaud's*
31 Jan.	18p
28 Feb.	18p
31 Mar.	20p xd
29 Apr.	21½p
31 May	24p
30 Jun.	22p
29 Jul.	24½p
31 Aug.	26p xd
30 Sep.	30½p xd
31 Oct.	32½p
21 Nov.	30½p
30 Nov.	51½p
30 Dec.	58p
1978	
17 Jan.	59½p

You are required to:

(*a*) *Calculate the benefits of accepting the new cash offer.*

(*3 marks*)

(*b*) *Calculate the benefits (including income) of accepting the convertible alternative.*

(*6 marks*)
(*Total 9 marks*)

QUESTION R12

Summarised balance sheet, profit and loss account and statement of source and application of funds for Northern Manufacturing Plc follow:

	31 Dec.	
	19–9	*19–8*
	£000	*£000*
Balance sheet		
Fixed assets	1,900	1,400
Current assets:		
Stocks	1,000	600
Debtors	800	500
Cash	—	40
	3,700	2,540
Share capital:		
Ordinary shares of £1	1,000	600
Reserves	600	300
Convertible 8% loan	500	500
12% loan repayable 10 years hence	600	600
Current liabilities:		
Trade creditors	700	350
Overdraft	300	190
	3,700	2,540

	31 Dec. 19–9 £000	31 Dec. 19–8 £000
Profit and loss account		
Turnover	7,000	5,000
Trading profit, before depreciation	800	500
Depreciation	600	400
Advance corporation tax paid and written off	60	33
Dividends paid, as interim and only one for year	140	67
Retained	—	—
Statement of source and application of funds		
Profit before taxation and depreciation	800	500
Share issues	700	—
Increase in creditors	350	100
	1,850	600
Purchase of plant	1,100	200
Dividends paid	140	67
Advance corporation tax paid and written off	60	33
Increase in debtors	300	100
Increase in stock	400	200
	2,000	600
Increase (decrease) in net bank and cash balance	(150)	—

The overdraft has been renewed every three months since 10 years ago. Since that time the maximum overdraft each year has varied between £750,000 and £250,000.

The 8% loan is convertible into ordinary shares at the rate of 1 ordinary share for each £1 of loan stock on 31 Dec. 19–15.

There was an issue of new shares to existing shareholders on the basis of four new shares for every six held at a full market price of £1.75 each on 1 May 19–9.

The 19–9 accounts were published on 31 May 19–10 and since that date the share price has fluctuated between £2 and £1.10. The current price is £1.80.

No taxation is provided as planned expansion of activities indicates that none will be payable in the foreseeable future.

You are required to:

(*a*) *calculate earnings per share as disclosed in the accounts of 19–8 and 19–9;*

(*5 marks*)

(*b*) *calculate the current PE ratio and the range of the ratio since 31 May 19–10;*

(*4 marks*)

(*c*) *calculate three ratios based on the accounts of 19–8 and 19–9 appropriate to an assessment of the liquidity of the company;*

(*5 marks*)

and

(*d*) *comment on the liquidity position of the company at 31 Dec. 19–9.*

(*6 marks*)

(*Total 20 marks*)

QUESTION R13

The following extracts have been taken from a notice sent to the holders of the 10% Convertible Unsecured Loan Stock 1991/96 of a company.

Final opportunity to convert into ordinary shares

Holders of the 10% Convertible Unsecured Loan Stock 1991/96 of the company ('Loan Stock') are reminded that by giving notice on or between 20 Feb. and 19 Mar. 1979 they have the right to convert (on 19 Mar. 1979 and in amounts or multiples of £1) all or any of their Loan Stock into fully paid Ordinary Share Capital of the company. The basis of conversion is 50p in nominal amount of Ordinary Share Capital for every 83.2p in nominal amount of Loan Stock and *pro rata* for any other amount of Loan Stock converted.

The forthcoming conversion period between 20 Feb. and 19 Mar. is the last opportunity for Stockholders to convert their Loan Stock into Ordinary Shares. Conversion rights not exercised by 19 Mar. 1979 will lapse.

Interest and dividends

Interest on Loan Stock converted will cease from 1 Oct. 1978. The Ordinary Shares allotted upon conversion will rank *pari passu* in all respects with the Ordinary Shares of the company in issue on 19 Mar. 1979 except that they will not carry the right to the final dividend of 2.6p net per share recommended in respect of the year ended 30 Sep. 1978, which is expected to be paid on 24 Apr. 1979. They will otherwise rank in full for all dividends hereafter declared or paid, including all dividends in respect of the year commencing 1 Oct. 1978. Interest on Loan Stock not converted will continue to be paid half-yearly on 31 Mar. and 30 Sep.

Information provided included:

Market value of ordinary shares of 50p on the latest practicable date before the printing of this document (98p)

Maximum permissible dividend for year ending 30 Sep. 1978, per ordinary share (4.6p net)

Market value of 10% unsecured loan stock 1991/96 without any conversion rights excluding accrued interest per £100 stock as estimated on the basis of redemption yields for comparable stocks by two brokers £81.27.

The basic rate of income tax is 33%.

You are required to:

(*a*) *calculate the effects of conversion on capital and income values of the loan stock holder based on conversion of £832 of loan stock;* (*10 marks*)

(*b*) *state the additional information you would expect to find in the letter to stockholders;* (*4 marks*)

(*c*) *prepare the journal entries to record in the company's books the conversion of £16,640,000 of convertible loan stock;* (*5 marks*)

and

(*d*) *comment on the suggestion of some financial writers that if the market values indicate that conversion is beneficial then the company should convert for all stockholders, whether or not they apply for conversion.* (*4 marks*)

(*Total 23 marks*)

QUESTION R14. TOR LTD

Tor Ltd is a private company in the petroleum industry. It is currently planning an expansion programme which requires additional capital. One method of achieving this is for the company to be taken over by a larger group, which would inject cash into the business.

You are an adviser to a diversified trading group which is contemplating a takeover bid and you have obtained the following summarised data:

Historic cost profit and loss account

	Year ended	
	31 Dec. 19–2	*31 Dec. 19–1*
	£000	*£000*
Sales	2,591	1,774
Cost of sales	1,320	1,130
Operating expenses	447	382
Interest:		
Short-term loans	23	11
Long-term loans	25	23
	1,815	1,546

		Year ended 31 Dec. 19–2		31 Dec. 19–1
		£000		*£000*
Profit before taxation		776		228
Taxation		(226)		(58)
		550		170
Minority interest		(22)		(7)
		528		163
Extraordinary items		(34)		105
		494		268
Dividends:				
Preference	(14)		(14)	
Ordinary	(90)	(104)	(70)	(84)
		390		184
Current cost profit before taxation		311		76

Source and application of funds statement

	31 Dec. 19–2		*31 Dec. 19–1*	
	£000	*£000*	*£000*	*£000*
Sources:				
Funds generated from trading		912		404
Long-term loans		20		40
Sales of fixed assets		13		41
Issue of share capital		297		—
		1,242		485
Applications:				
Purchases of fixed assets	(910)		(270)	
Dividends	(94)		(82)	
Taxation	(102)		(78)	
		(1,106)		(430)
		136		55
Represented by:				
Increase in working capital	142		75	
Decrease in cash and bank	(6)		(20)	
		136		55

Historic cost balance sheet

	31 Dec. 19–2		31 Dec. 19–1	
	£000	£000	£000	£000
Fixed assets		2,302		1,493
Goodwill		420		420
Current assets:				
Stocks	554		388	
Debtors and debit balances	330		191	
Cash and bank	2		8	
	886		587	
Current liabilities:				
Creditors and credit balances	(306)		(201)	
Short-term loans	(130)		(70)	
Taxation	(204)		(62)	
Dividends	(40)		(30)	
	680		363	
		206		224
Assets employed		2,928		2,137
Represented by:				
Share capital				
Ordinary shares		1,130		1,030
Preference shares		140		140
Reserves		1,265		678
Minority interest		119		97
Long-term loans		178		158
Deferred grants		96		34
Funds employed		2,928		2,137
Current cost assets employed		4,146		2,942

Required:

Prepare a report examining the performance and position of the company for submission to your Board of Directors who wish to consider making the takeover bid, incorporating current cost data where available.

(15 marks)

QUESTION R15

The following data relate to Unsatiable Appetites Plc for the two years ended 31 Dec. 19–9.

	19–8	*19–9*
	£	£
Trading profit before tax	67,220	103,580
Taxation (Marginal rate 52%)	27,630	35,760
Profit after taxation	39,590	67,820
Dividends		
Preference paid 31 Dec.	(5,400)	(5,400)
Ordinary paid 14 Sept.	(19,250)	(14,000)
proposed	(9,625)	(16,000)
Retained	5,315	32,420

At 1 Jan. 19–8 the issued share capital consisted of 160,000 ordinary shares of 50p each and 100,000 5.4% cumulative preference shares of £1 each.

On 1 Apr. 19–8 a bonus issue was made on the basis of one new ordinary share for every four held.

On 1 Oct. 19–8 options were granted to the senior executives to subscribe for a total of 100,000 ordinary shares at the current market price of 75p each. These options were exercisable on the 1 Dec. 19–9, 19–10 or 19–11.

An investment of £100 $2\frac{1}{2}$% consolidated stock would have given a gross yield of:

16% on 1 Jan. 19–8, 15% on 1 Dec. 19–8
14% on 1 Jan. 19–9, 13% on 1 Dec. 19–9

On 1 Jan. 19–9 a previously announced rights issue of ordinary shares was taken up by all eligible shareholders. The basis was one for four at 60p per share and the market price on the last day of dealing, cum rights, was 70p.

On 1 July 19–9 the company issued £300,000 of a 15% convertible debenture. The terms of conversion were one ordinary share for each £1 of the debenture exercisable on the 31 Dec. of any year up to and including 19–25. Interest was payable each year on 30 Jun. and 31 Dec.

On 1 Dec. 19–9 20,400 ordinary shares were issued on the exercise of the executives share options.

You are required to:

(*a*) *explain the purpose of presenting the earnings per share statistic in the annual accounts and*

(*4 marks*)

(*b*) *calculate the earnings per share figures that will be disclosed in the published accounts for the year ended 31 Dec. 19–9 (the published explanatory note is not required but clear working notes are expected).*
(*16 marks*)
(*Total 20 marks*)

QUESTION R16

Shown below are two statements from the published accounts of quoted companies. First an added value statement from company A, and then a statement called 'application of group sales revenue' from company B.

Company A Added value statement

	19–8	*19–7*
	£000	*£000*
Bought-in materials and services	253,375	217,637
Taxation to governments	2,763	3,324
Interest on loans £6,935,000 (19–7 £4,275,000) and dividends to shareholders £3,164,000 (19–7 £3,091,000)	10,099	7,366
Wages, pensions and benefits to employees	100,711	87,574
Depreciation and retentions	7,906	11,089
Total added value	121,479	109,353
Total income generated—sales and other income	374,854	326,990

Company B Application of group sales revenue

	19–9 £m	*% to total*	*19–8 £m*	*% to total*
During the year ended 31 March 19–9 the Group sales revenue was applied in the following ways:-				
To suppliers of merchandise and services	1,423.0	69.6	1,259.7	69.7
For the benefit of employees				
Salaries (including welfare staff)	164.6		144.6	
Deductions for income tax and national insurance	33.0		27.9	
	131.6		116.7	
Pension schemes	28.1		22.9	
Employees' profit sharing schemes	3.2		3.1	
Welfare and staff amenities—excluding related staff salaries of £5.2 million (last year £4.6 million)	7.9		7.6	
	170.8	8.4	150.3	8.3
To central and local government				
United Kingdom	304.4		262.9	
Overseas	6.9		10.9	
	311.3	15.2	273.8	15.1
To the providers of group capital				
Interest on loan capital and overdrafts	15.8		12.0	
Income tax deducted	1.0		1.0	
	14.8		11.0	
Dividends to shareholders of the company	49.7		44.4	
	64.5	3.2	55.4	3.1
c/f	1,969.6	96.4	1,739.2	96.2

		19–9 £m	% to total	*19–8* £m	% to total
	b/f	1,969.6	96.4	1,739.2	96.2
For the replacement of assets and the expansion of the business					
Depreciation		19.1		15.4	
Deferred taxation		3.6		3.7	
Retained profits, after adjusting for minority interests		50.9		50.0	
		73.6	3.6	69.1	3.8
Group sales revenue, including sales taxes		2,043.2	100.0	1,808.3	100.0

You are required to:

(*a*) *explain and comment briefly, with reasons, on the following aspects of these statements*:

(*i*) *the differences and similarities between the concept of added value and that of application of group sales revenue*

(*4 marks*)

(*ii*) *the different view taken by the two companies on the calculation of the amounts allocated to employees*

(*4 marks*)

(*iii*) *the different view taken by the two companies on the calculation of the amounts allocated to providers of capital*

(*4 marks*)

(*b*) *analyse, compare and comment upon the information provided by the statements of added value and application of group sales revenue*

(*6 marks*)

(*18 marks*)

QUESTION R17. NEW IDEAS PLC

The summarised accounts of New Ideas Plc are shown below:

Balance Sheet on
30 Apr. 19–6

	£000	*19–5* *£000*
Fixed assets (net)	6,401	2,519
Current assets		
Stock	25,426	20,231
Debtors	21,856	20,264
Balance at bank	2,917	6,094
	56,600	49,108
	£	*£*
Ordinary shares of 50p	5,000	5,000
Revenue reserves	14,763	12,263
Deferred taxation	5,433	3,267
Loans		
10% Debenture 19–15/19–19	10,000	10,000
Current liabilities		
Creditors	18,762	16,431
Taxation	1,642	1,247
Dividends	1,000	900
	56,600	49,108

Results for the year ended
30 Apr. 19–6

	£000	*19–5* *£000*
Sales	264,626	220,393
Trading profit	9,380	8,362
Interest payable	1,000	1,000
Taxation	4,380	3,642
Dividend	1,500	1,400

(1) The ordinary shares are quoted at £1.20

(2) New Ideas Plc requires £16 million for an investment project and is considering one of the following:

(i) the issue to shareholders of £16 million 10% Convertible (£1 for 1 share) Debentures 19–10 at par,

(ii) a rights issue at 80p, or

(iii) the sale in the market of £16 million 13% Debentures 19–10/19–20 at par.

You are required to:

(*a*) *calculate from the balance sheet and results:*

(*i*) *two ratios particularly significant to creditors,*
(*ii*) *two ratios particularly significant to management, and*
(*iii*) *two ratios particularly significant to shareholders,*

(*b*) *comment briefly upon the change between 19–5 and 19–6 in the ratios you have calculated,*
(*c*) *calculate the immediate effect of the three schemes upon the gearing (or leverage) ratio,*
(*d*) *calculate the effect of the three schemes on the earnings per share on the assumption that the 19–6 profits from the existing assets will be maintained and that the £16 million new investment will produce £3.5 million profit before interest and tax at 50%, and*
(*e*) *briefly advise the management on the most appropriate method to use.*

(*25 marks*)

QUESTION R18. BRISTOL LTD

You are presented with the following summarised accounts and details in respect of Bristol Ltd. and its subsidiaries.

Consolidated balance sheets

	31.12.–5	*31.12.–6*
	£000	*£000*
Ordinary share capital	800.0	800.0
Revenue reserves	1115.7	1321.4
Dividends payable—holding company	105.0	120.0
—minority shareholders	15.0	18.0
Creditors	451.0	463.0
Minority interest	372.3	264.6
Bank overdraft	411.0	—
Corporation tax	506.0	352.0
	3776.0	3339.0
Fixed assets—cost	3050.0	2550.0
—depreciation	(1062.0)	(1019.0)
Goodwill on consolidation	149.0	78.0
Stock	618.0	661.0
Debtors	949.0	859.0
Cash at bank	72.0	210.0
	3776.0	3339.0

Consolidated profit and loss account for the year ended 31 Dec. 19–6

	£000
Group profit	781.5
Corporation tax	412.8
	368.7
Minority shareholders interest	67.8
	300.9
Extraordinary item—gain on disposal of shares in subsidiary	24.8
	325.7
Proposed ordinary dividend	120.0
Retained profit	205.7

Statement of revenue reserves

	£000
Balance at 1 Jan. 19–6	1115.7
Retained profit	205.7
Balance at 31 Dec. 19–6	1321.4

The following information is also provided:

(1) Bristol has for several years held 70% of the ordinary share capital of Cardiff Ltd and 60% of the ordinary share capital of Swindon Ltd.
(2) Bristol Ltd sold its entire shareholding in Swindon Ltd on 30 Sep. 19–6. The details are as follows:

	£000	£000
Proceeds of sale		320.0
Net assets		
Fixed assets—cost	500	
—depreciation	(207)	
	293	
Stock	41	
Debtors	132.8	
Cash	26.7	
	493.5	
Creditors	(59.0)	
Taxation	(60.8)	
	373.7	
Group share 60%	224.2	
Goodwill	71.0	
		295.2
Extraordinary gain		24.8

(3) Fixed assets—cost

	£000		£000
Balance b/f	3050	Disposals	500
		Balance c/d	2550
	3050		3050

(4) Fixed assets—depreciation

	£000		£000
Disposals	207	Balance b/d	1062
Balance c/d	1019	P/L account	
		—depreciation charge	164
	1226		1226

(5) Minority interest account

	£000		£000
Minority interest at disposal	149.5	Balance b/d	
Dividend paid		SC & res.	372.3
—Cardiff	15.0	Dividend	15.0
—Swindon	8.0	P/L account	67.8
Balance c/d			
SC & res.	264.6		
Dividend	18.0		
	455.1		455.1

(6) Corporation tax account

	£000		£000
Cash	506.0	Balance b/d	506.0
Disposal of Subsid.	60.8	P/L account (inc. 60.8 in respect of Swindon)	412.8
Balance c/d	352.0		
	918.8		918.8

You are required to prepare a funds flow statement for the year ended 31 Dec. 19–6, in a form suitable for publication to the shareholders, based on:

(*a*) *the detailed breakdown approach*

(*14 marks*)

(*b*) *the net outlay approach*

(*14 marks*)

(*Total 28 marks*)

Ignore ACT on dividends and tax on disposal of shares in Swindon Ltd.

Answers

ANSWER A1. N. GINEER LTD

(a) Extraordinary items are defined in SSAP 6 as being those items which derive from events or transactions outside the ordinary activities of the business and which are both material and expected not to recur frequently or regularly. They do not include items which though exceptional on account of size and incidence (and which may, therefore, require separate disclosure) derive from the ordinary activities of the business. Neither do they include prior year items merely because they relate to a prior year.

SSAP 6 is thus recognising that there are certain unusual types of gains and losses that should not be included with trading profit due to the distortion that would result but they still require disclosure somewhere in the profit and loss account rather than being transferred directly to or taken from reserves.

The classification of items as extraordinary will depend on the particular circumstances of the case—what is extraordinary in one business will not necesarily be extraordinary in another. SSAP 6 states that subject to this overriding consideration examples of extraordinary items could be the profits or losses arising from the following:

(i) The discontinuance of a significant part of the business;
(ii) The sale of an investment not acquired with the intention of resale;
(iii) Writing off intangibles, including goodwill because of unusual events or developments during the period;
(iv) The expropriation of assets.

(1) *Surplus on disposal of properties*
There are a number of contentious issues relating to this figure:

(i) *Classification of the gain*
The application of the definition from SSAP 6 to particular profits or losses often presents problems. The disposal of a fixed asset is not normally outside the ordinary activities of the business and so the surpluses or deficits on disposal would not normally be treated as extraordinary.

In this case the engineering company may be of the opinion that the disposal is akin to the sale of an investment not originally acquired for resale and that such disposals are unlikely to occur frequently. The treatment could be contrasted with, say, the treatment in the accounts of a property company which may feel that such a profit was within its normal activities. The treatment adopted in this question is quite common. The *Survey of Published Accounts 1980* showed over 50% of significant fixed asset disposals treated as extraordinary items.

(ii) *Amount of the gain*
The determination of the amount of the extraordinary item can cause problems. A general principle is that the expenses and

costs of the extraordinary transaction are matched with the revenue from the disposal to comply with SSAP 2.
The gain in the question was computed as follows:

	£000
Sale proceeds	7,035
Less: Costs (including interest)	3,561
	3,474
Less: Taxation	1,033
Extraordinary gain	2,441

SSAP 6 only mentions the need to reduce the extraordinary item by its attributable taxation. In the question, the engineering company have included the interest costs of money borrowed for the development of the project. This treatment is in line with the Appendix of SSAP 9 (para. 21). This suggests that in those infrequent circumstances where sums borrowed can be identified as financing specific long-term contracts, it may be appropriate to include such related interest in the cost of that contract work.

The current cost accounts include the same extraordinary profit as the historical costs accounts. This is unusual since the historical cost book values of fixed assets would normally be quite different from the current cost book values. In this question, however, a professional valuation of property has been incorporated into both the historical cost and current cost financial statements though it would appear that the asset disposed of was still stated at original cost.

The correct treatment of a fixed asset disposal in current cost accounts is to split the HC gain into a realised holding gain and an operating gain. If we assume a valuation on current cost principles of the asset at the date of disposal was £7m, the gain would be treated as follows:

	£000		
Sale proceeds	7,035	£35,000	Profit and loss account
Current value at date of sale	7,000		
Historic costs (including taxation)	4,594	£2,406,000	Current cost reserve

(iii) *Timing of the gain*

The date of disposal is crucial in determining the accounting period in which the gain is reported. The directors' report refers to the sale being complete on 1 Apr. 19–0. It is unclear what precisely this means.

If it means that the contract of sale was completed on that date, then the company should deal with the disposal in the following accounting period. The transaction is sufficiently important to warrant disclosure as a post-balance sheet event (to comply with SSAP 17) but it would appear to be a non-adjusting event.

If, however, the sale was agreed before 1 Apr. 19–0 it may be that the gain validly relates to the year ended 31 Mar. 19–0. It may be that the terms of sale were finalised on 1 Apr. following the professional revaluation

The Appendix to SSAP 17 gives as an example of an adjusting event 'the subsequent determination of the proceeds of the sale of assets sold before the year end'.

Once again, the case in question is far from clear.

(2) *Provision against listed investments*

The Companies Acts disclosure requirements with regard to the amount at which listed investments held as fixed assets are stated in the balance sheet are that the aggregate amount of such investments can be shown at cost or a valuation. It appears that the companies in which our engineering company has an investment are in some financial difficulty. The prudence concept in *SSAP 2* requires the recognition of losses as soon as they are anticipated and the company has decided that such a provision is extraordinary in this instance. In addition, para. 19(2) Sch. 1 CA 1981 requires that where the reduction in value of any fixed asset (including investments) is expected to be permanent, a provision for diminution in value must be made.

The writing down of investments or goodwill is recognised in SSAP 6. The standard refers to writing off goodwill due to unusual developments. It is often difficult to decide how unusual such developments should be. For example, the writing off of the investment may well be due to losses incurred by those companies. It could be argued that the purchase of listed investments always involves a risk of loss and that provided such losses derive from trading, the subsequent provision against the investments does fall within the normal activities of the business. It could be argued that if profits from dividends from these investments are 'normal' profits then it is inconsistent to treat provisions as extraordinary.

SSAP 16 requires investments to be shown at directors' valuation. Where the investment is listed and the directors' valuation is materially different from mid-market value, the basis of valuation and the reasons for the difference should be stated. Normally differences between the directors' valuation and the amount at which these investments are stated in historical cost accounts would go to the current cost reserve whether that difference is a surplus or a deficit. However, SSAP 16 also states that amounts to reduce assets from net current replacement cost to their recoverable amount should be charged to the profit and loss account. It would appear that the nature of the provision is to reduce the investments from a normal valuation to the estimated recoverable amount and thus should be charged against profits. However, the change from valuation to recoverable amount is likely to produce a different loss from that reflected in the historical cost accounts.

ANSWER A2. COALVILLE LTD

Fixed asset note

	a	*b*	*c*	*d*
	£	£	£	£
Cost/valuation at 1.1.19–5	80,000	176,000	186,666	186,666
Revaluation at 31.12.19–5	—	—	106,667	106,667
	80,000	176,000	293,333	293,333
Depreciation at 1.1.19–5	40,000	88,000	93,333	93,333
Charge for year	10,000	22,000	36,666	30,000
Revaluation	—	—	53,334	60,000
	50,000	110,000	183,333	183,333
Net book value: 31.12.–5	£30,000	£66,000	£110,000	£110,000
31.12.–4	£40,000	£88,000	£93,333	£93,333

Workings:

1. *Historical cost*

	£
Depreciation to 31.12.–4	4/8 × £80,000 = 40,000
Depreciation to 31.12.–5	5/8 × £80,000 = 50,000
Depreciation charge for year	= 10,000
WDV = Cost – Depreciation each year	

2. *CPP*

Balance sheet at 31.12.–5

	HC	*Rate*	*CPP*
	£		£
Cost	80,000	220/100	176,000
Depreciation	50,000	220/100	110,000
	30,000		66,000

Balance sheet at 31.12.–4 (comparative for 19–5)

	HC	*Rate*	*CPP*
	£		£
Cost	80,000	220/100	176,000
Depreciation	40,000	220/100	88,000
	40,000		88,000

Depreciation charge $= £10{,}000 \times \frac{220}{100} = 22{,}000$

3. *CCA*

Balance sheet at 31.12.–5

	HC	*Rate*	*CCA*
	£		£
Cost	80,000	440/120	293,333
Depreciation	50,000	440/120	183,333
	30,000		110,000

Balance sheet at 31.12.–4

	HC	*Rate*	*CCA*
	£		£
Cost	80,000	280/120	186,666
Depreciation	40,000	280/120	93,333
	40,000		93,333

Depreciation charge based on closing value $= £293{,}333 \div 8 = 36{,}666$

Depreciation charge based on average value $= \frac{£(293{,}333 + 186{,}666)}{2 \times 8} = 30{,}000$

ANSWER A3. UPPINGHAM LTD

Trading accounts for the 3 months ended 31 Mar. 19–6

(a) *Historical cost accounts*

	£	£
Sales 31 Jan.		2,000
28 Feb.		1,000
31 Mar.		1,100
		4,100
Cost of sales		
31 Jan. (4/5 × 750)	600	
28 Feb. (1/5 × 750 + 1/4 × 1,400)	500	
31 Mar. (2/4 × 1,400)	700	
		1,800
Gross profit		2,300

(b) *Current purchasing power accounting*

	£
Sales	
31 Jan. $2{,}000 \times \frac{240}{220}$	2,182
28 Feb. $1{,}000 \times \frac{240}{230}$	1,043
31 Mar.	1,100
	4,325

Cost of sales

	HC £	*Adj. to year end RPI*	*CPP* £	
Purchased 1 *Jan.*	750	$\times \frac{240}{200}$	900	
31 Jan. (3/4 × 1,400)	1,050	$\times \frac{240}{220}$	1,145	2,045
	1,800			
Gross profit				2,280

(c) *Current cost accounting*

		£
Sales (as for historical cost)		4,100
Cost of sales		
31 Jan.	1,400	
28 Feb. $\left(\frac{200}{50} \times 200\right)$	800	
31 Mar. $\left(\frac{200}{100} \times 500\right)$	1,000	
		3,200
Gross profit		900

ANSWER A4. SOUTHPORT MANUFACTURING CO. LTD

Current Cost Profit and Loss Account for the year ended 31 Dec. 19–8

	£000	£000
Turnover		800,000
Profit before interest and taxation as in the historical cost accounts		121,500
Less: Current cost adjustments		
Cost of sales	11,664	
Depreciation	5,739	
Monetary working capital	21,239	
		38,642
Current cost operating profit		82,858
Gearing adjustment	17,019	
Interest payable	(15,300)	
		1,719
Current cost profit before taxation		84,577
Taxation		51,000
Current cost profit attributable to shareholders		33,577
Dividends		30,000
Current cost profit retained		3,577

Current cost earnings per share 22.4p

Current Cost Balance Sheet at 31 Dec.

19–7 £000	19–7 £000		19–8 £000	19–8 £000
		Assets employed		
	350,476	Fixed assets (note 3)		413,251
		Net current assets:		
53,857		Stock	76,235	
106,500		Monetary working capital	95,200	
160,357		Total working capital	171,435	
(15,000)		Proposed dividends	(20,000)	
(33,000)		Other current liabilities (net)	(49,500)	
	112,357			101,935
	462,833			515,186

19–7 £000	19–7 £000		19–8 £000	19–8 £000
		Financed by:		
		Share capital and reserves		
150,000		Share capital	150,000	
32,333		Current cost reserves (note 2)	81,109	
80,500		Retained profit	84,077	
	262,833			315,186
	200,000	5% Debenture stock		200,000
	462,833			515,186

Notes to current cost accounts

Note 1

A. *General description of current cost accounts*

The current cost accounts have been prepared in compliance with SSAP 16. The current cost system, whilst not a system of accounting for general inflation allows for price changes specific to the business when reporting assets employed and profits thereon.

The *current cost operating profit* is the surplus (before interest and taxation) arising from the ordinary activities of the business in the period. It is determined after allowing for the impact of price changes on the funds needed to maintain the productive assets of the business (the net operating assets) but does not take into account the way in which these assets are financed.

This result is achieved by making adjustments to trading profit before interest calculated on the historical cost basis. These adjustments are described in sections B and C below.

The *current cost profit attributable to shareholders* is the surplus allowing for the impact of price changes on the funds needed to maintain only their proportion of the net operating assets. It is shown after interest, taxation and the gearing adjustment described in Section D below.

In the *balance sheet* fixed assets and stocks are included at their current cost (net of depreciation on fixed assets).

Corresponding amounts for previous period are shown in values relating to last year, without further adjustment. This is the first year for which the company has prepared current cost accounts and corresponding figures are not shown in the profit and loss account since they are not readily available.

B. *Fixed assets and depreciation*

The gross current cost of fixed assets has been derived as follows: Plant and specialised buildings have been restated using appropriate Government indices applied to the historical costs. Asset lives have been reviewed upon the introduction of current cost accounting and the existing asset lives were found to be adequate. Total depreciation charged in the CC profit and loss account represents the average current cost of the proportion of fixed assets consumed in the period. The depreciation adjustment is the difference between the depreciation charge in the HC and CC accounts.

C. *Working capital*

This includes stocks (including work in progress) and trade debtors less trade creditors.

In order to allow for the impact of price changes on working capital, two adjustments are made to the operating costs calculated on the historical cost basis, one on stock and the other on monetary working capital. The adjustments are based on movements in price indices issued by the Government Statistical Service. These indices reflect closely the changes in input prices experienced by the company.

D. *The gearing adjustment*

A proportion, called the gearing proportion, of the net operating assets of the business is financed by borrowing. As the obligation to repay borrowing is fixed in monetary amounts, irrespective of price changes on the proportion of assets so financed, it is unnecessary to provide for the impact of price changes on these assets when determining the current cost profit attributable to shareholders. Thus, the gearing adjustment has been applied which abates the current cost operating adjustments by the average gearing proportion in the year.

E. *Other accounting policies*

Except as set out above the policies used in the current cost accounts are the same as those used in the historical cost accounts.

Note 2

Current cost reserve

	£000	*£000*	*£000*
Balance at 1 Jan. 19–8			32,333
Revaluation surpluses reflecting price changes			
—Plant and machinery (24,775 + 5,739)	30,514		
—Stocks and work in progress (2,378 + 11,664)	14,042		
		44,556	
—Monetary working capital adjustment		21,239	
—Gearing adjustment		(17,019)	
			48,776
Balance at 31 Dec. 19–8			81,109
of which = realised			21,623
unrealised (4,235 + 55,251)			59,486
			81,109

Note 3

Fixed assets

	31 Dec. 19–8			*19–7*
	Gross CRC	*Depn.*	*Net CRC*	*Net CRC*
	£000	*£000*	*£000*	*£000*
Plant and machinery	558,157	144,906	413,251	350,476

Workings

1. *Cost of sales adjustment*

	HC £000	*Index adjustment*	*CC £000*	*Difference £000*
Opening stock	52,000 ×	$\frac{160}{140}$	59,428	7,428
Closing stock	72,000 ×	$\frac{160}{170}$	67,764	4,236
				11,664

2. *Depreciation adjustment*

	HC £000	*Index adjustment*	*CC* £000	*Difference* £000
Charge for year: —on assets owned all year	40,000 ×	$\frac{120}{105}$	45,714	5,714
—on purchased during year	2,000 ×	$\frac{(122 + 125) \div 2}{122}$	2,025	25
	42,000		47,739	5,739

3. *Monetary working capital adjustment*

	HC £000	*Index adjustment*	*CC* £000	*Difference* £000
Opening debtors	170,000			
Less: Creditors	63,500			
	106,500 ×	$\frac{160}{(140 + 145) \div 2}$	119,579	13,079
Closing debtors	218,000			
Less: Creditors	122,800			
	95,200 ×	$\frac{160}{(170 + 180) \div 2}$	87,040	8,160
				21,239

4. *Gearing adjustment*

(a) *Shareholders' interest at current cost*

	19–7 £000	19–8 £000
Per HC accounts		
—Share capital	150,000	150,000
—General revenue reserve	80,500	105,700
—Proposed dividend	15,000	20,000
c/fwd	245,500	275,700
Add: Increases in year end value of non-monetary assets when restated from HC to CC		

	£000	*19–7* *£000*		*£000*	19–8 *£000*
c/fwd		245,500			275,700
—Stock					
—HC	52,000			72,000	
—CC × $\frac{145}{140}$	53,857		× $\frac{180}{170}$	76,235	
	———	1,857		———	4,235
—Fixed assets (NBV) Bought 1.1.–6					
—HC	320,000			280,000	
—CC × $\frac{115}{105}$	350,476		× $\frac{125}{105}$	333,333	
	———	30,476		———	53,333
Bought 30.9.–8					
—HC	—			78,000	
—CC	—		× $\frac{125}{122}$	79,918	
	———	—		———	1,918
		277,833			335,186

$$\text{Average } \frac{277{,}833 + 335{,}186}{2} = £306{,}510{,}000$$

(b) *Net borrowings*

	19–7 *£000*	19–8 *£000*
Debentures	200,000	200,000
Corporation tax	41,000	51,000
	241,000	251,000
Less: Cash	8,000	1,500
	233,000	249,500

Average £241,250,000

(c) *Gearing adjustment*

$$\frac{241{,}250}{241{,}250 + 306{,}510} \times (11{,}664 + 5{,}739 + 21{,}239) = £17{,}019{,}000$$

5. *Current cost EPS*

$$\frac{33{,}577{,}000}{150{,}000{,}000} = 22.4\text{p}$$

6. *Current cost reserve*

	19–7	*19–8*	*Increase/ (decrease)*
	£000	*£000*	*£000*
Unrealised surpluses on non-monetary assets held at year end			
—Stock	1,857	4,235	2,378
—Fixed assets	30,476	55,251	24,775
CC P + L adjustments to date			
—cost of sales	—	11,664	11,664
—depreciation		5,739	5,739
—monetary working capital		21,239	21,239
—gearing adjustment		(17,019)	(17,019)
	32,333	81,109	48,776

7. *Retained profit*

	19–7	*19–8*
	£000	*£000*
Per HC accounts	80,500	105,700
Less: CC P + L adjustments to date	—	
—cost of sales	—	(11,664)
—depreciation	—	(5,739)
—monetary working capital	—	(21,239)
—gearing	—	17,019
	80,500	84,077

8. *Gross value of fixed assets at 31.12.–8*

	HC	*Index adjustment*	*CC*
	£000		*£000*
Bought 1.1.–6	400,000	× 125/105	476,190
Bought 30.9.–8	80,000	× 125/122	81,967
	480,000		558,157

ANSWER A5. REEFLY PLC

Current cost profit and loss account for the year ended 31 Dec. 19–20

	£	£
Profit before interest and taxation as in the historical cost accounts		210,000
Less: Current cost adjustments:		
Cost of sales	149,776	
Depreciation	48,588	
Monetary working	7,257	
		205,621
Current cost operating profit		4,379
Gearing adjustment	72,980	
Interest payable	50,000	
		22,980
Current cost profit before taxation		27,354
Taxation		80,000
Current cost loss attributable to shareholders		(52,641)
Dividends		40,000
Current cost loss to reserves		(92,641)

Current cost balance sheet as at 31 Dec. 19–10

Notes

Net operating assets

	£	£
Fixed assets		1,133,733
Working capital:		
Stock	512,821	
Debtors	250,000	
Creditors	(228,000)	
		534,821
		1,668,554

Net borrowings:		
Loan stock	600,000	
Taxation	112,000	
Cash	(50,000)	
		662,000
Shareholders' funds:		
Ordinary share capital	300,000	
1 Current cost reserve	499,730	
2 Revenue reserves	206,824	
		1,006,554
		1,668,554

Notes to accounts

1. *Current cost reserves*

	£	£
Balance at 1.1.80		241,894
Revaluation surpluses reflecting price changes:		
Plant	172,927	
Stocks	150,097	
		323,024
		564,918
MWCA	7,257	
Gearing adjustment	(72,445)	
		65,188
Balance at 31.12.80		499,730

of which—Realised £133,176
Unrealised £366,554

2. *Revenue reserves*

Balance at 1.1.80	300,000
Loss for year	(93,176)
Balance at 31.12.80	206,824

Workings:

1. *COSA*

	Stock	*Relevant index numbers*	*Average*
1 Jan. 1980	300,000	120 (30.11.79)	1.1 to 30.6

$$\frac{142 + 125}{2} = 133.5$$

	Stock	*Relevant index numbers*	*Average*
30 Jun. 19–10	800,000	140	1.7. to 31.12 $\frac{142+160}{2}=151$
31 Dec. 19–10	500,000	156 (30.11.–10)	

(a) COSA (1 Jan. to 30 Jun.)

$$=£(800{,}000-300{,}000)-£800{,}000\times\frac{133.5}{140}-£300{,}000\times\frac{133.5}{120}$$
$$=£500{,}000-£(762{,}857-333{,}750)$$
$$=+£70{,}893.$$

(b) COSA (30 Jun. to 31 Dec.)

$$=£(500{,}000-800{,}000)-£500{,}000\times\frac{151}{156}-£800{,}000\times\frac{151}{140}$$
$$=-£300{,}000-£(483{,}974-862{,}857)$$
$$=-£300{,}000-£(-378{,}883)$$
$$=+£78{,}883$$

The overall cost of sales adjustment is therefore £70,893 + £78,883 = £149,776.

2. *Balance sheet stock values*

	31.12.–9 £	*31.12.–10* £	*To CC reserve* £
$£300{,}000\times\frac{125}{120}$	312,500		12,500
$£500{,}000\times\frac{160}{156}$		512,821	12,821

3. *Depreciation adjustment*

Plant acquired	*HC dep'n charge* £	*Adjustment*	*CC dep'n charge* £
1.1.–5	30,000	$\frac{218}{110}$ =	59,455
1.1.–8	40,000	$\frac{218}{150}$ =	58,133
30.6.–10	20,000	$\frac{(220+242)\div 2}{220}$ =	21,000
	90,000		138,588
			90,000
			48,588

4. *Acq. date*

Balance sheet plant values

		Opening			*Closing*		
		NBV £	*Adj.*	*CC NBV* £	*NBV* £	*Adj.*	*CC NBV* £
1.1.–5	Cost	300,000					
	Dep'n $\frac{5}{10}$	(150,000)					
		150,000	$\frac{200}{110}$	272,727	120,000	$\frac{242}{110}$	264,000
1.1.–8	Cost	400,000					
	Dep'n $\frac{2}{10}$	(80,000)					
		320,000	$\frac{200}{150}$	426,667	280,000	$\frac{242}{150}$	451,733
30.6.–10	Cost				400,000		
	Dep'n 5%				(20,000)		
					380,000	$\frac{242}{220}$	418,000
Total NBV		470,000		699,394	780,000		1,133,733
				470,000			780,000
To CC reserve				229,394			353,733

5. *Current cost reserve*

	Unrealised holding gains *Plant*	*Stock*	*Realised holding gains*
	£	£	£
At 1.1.–10	229,394(W4)	12,500(W2)	
COSA			149,776
MWCA			7,257
DA	(48,588)		48,588
			205,621
Gearing			(72,980)
Net movement in UHG	172,927	321	
At 31.12.–10	353,733(W4)	12,821(W2)	132,641

6. *Gearing adjustment*

(a) *Average net borrowings*

	31.12.–9	*31.12.–10*
	£	£
Taxation	100,000	112,000
Loan stock	400,000	600,000
	500,000	712,000
Less: Cash	200,000	50,000
	300,000	662,000
Average for year		481,000

(b) *Average shareholders' funds*

	31.12.–9	*31.12.–10*
	£	£
Per HC balance sheet: share capital	200,000	300,000
Revenue reserves	300,000	340,000
Revaluations: plant	229,394	353,733
Stock (W5)	12,500	12,821
	741,894	1,006,554
Average for year		874,224

(c) *Gearing adjustment*

$$£\frac{481,000}{874,224 + 481,000} \times 205,621 \quad \begin{matrix}\text{(CC adjustments)} \\ \text{(W5)}\end{matrix} = £72,980$$

ANSWER A6. Y LTD

(a) *Five year financial record*

Year ended 31 Dec. (19–10£m)

	19–10	*19–9*	*19–8*	*19–7*	*19–6*
Profit after taxation	152	85	53	75	64
Fixed assets	764	499	396	415	467
Working capital	16	74	157	158	157
	780	573	553	573	624
Loans	149	31	41	46	61
Capital and reserves	631	542	512	527	563

Assumptions

(i) The requirement to present a revised record only *in so far as the data provided permits* has been ignored. Nothing can be done unless assumptions are made about the data.

(ii) All fixed assets and working capital arose on the last day of each accounting period. This is clearly nonsense but if the fixed assets have very short lives and stock turnover is high this may not be a very material distortion.

(iii) Given assumption (ii) the net assets per the question are already stated in current cost terms (i.e. at current values).

Method of computation

All figures for years prior to 19–10 have been uplifted by movement in the general price index between the relevant year end and 31 Dec. 19–10.
The calculation is:

$$\text{Item} \times \frac{\text{Index at } \mathit{31} \text{ Dec. } \mathit{19\text{–}10}}{\text{Index at date at which it appears in balance sheet}}$$

(b) The five year financial record of the company in historical cost terms seems to show two major pieces of information:

(i) The company had experienced a steady growth in its profits and a steady growth in the size of the business as indicated by the fixed asset trend.

(ii) There was a great expansion in capacity in the year ended 19–10 with additional loans of £120m and a very large reduction in net monetary assets. In fact the size of the reduction in net monetary assets from the year ended 31 Dec. 19–8 to the year ended 31 Dec. 19–10 would seem to indicate that the amount in net monetary assets up to 19–8 was largely surplus cash rather than necessary working capital.

The restatement of the financial data to a common unit of currency has produced some significant differences from the historical cost data but those differences relate to point (i) above rather than point (ii). They still show the very real additional investment made by the company in 19–10 in its fixed assets.

Three significant differences are:

(1) Profit after taxation: Profits did not increase in real terms from 19–6 to 19–8 but it remains clear that profits made in 19–10 are very impressive when compared to the previous years' profit.

(2) Fixed assets: Investment in fixed assets in fact declined over the period of 19–6 to 19–8 with the real amount of investment in fixed assets only being returned to in 19–9.

(3) Financing of the business: The real investment by third parties in the business declined quite markedly in the period 19–6 to 19–9, presumably due to the high level of net monetary assets in this period. The view that the amount of net monetary assets in those years represented surplus cash is reinforced by the CPP data as that data in the years 19–6 to 19–8 shows the constant level of working capital which would explain the real decline in the loans. The historical cost data in this same period gives the impression that although the amount of net monetary assets was increasing no attempt was made to reduce the borrowings outstanding.

The uplift of a company's historical cost data and preferably its current cost data to current year end money values does show clearly whether the company has satisfied the most critical test of its performance, i.e. has it maintained the real level of sales, profit, dividend and investment in assets over time?

ANSWER A7. CHELSEA RETAILERS PLC

(a) The monetary working capital adjustment is an attempt to reflect both:

(i) The inflationary cost of maintaining the value of the monetary assets included in working capital.

(ii) The contribution to the financing of the inflationary increases in monetary and non-monetary trading assets made by monetary liabilities included in working capital.

The adjustment is best viewed as an extension of the principles and need for the cost of sales adjustment. The cost of sales adjustment is a recognition of the need to reserve historical cost profits to maintain the physical capacity of an enterprise to invest in stock. The MWCA extends this principle to other elements of working capital.

For example, a business which sells goods on credit terms will, in a period of rising costs, need to retain funds to finance a higher monetary value of both stocks and debtors in order to maintain its capacity to sell stock units to customers on credit terms. In contrast, a business which buys goods from suppliers on credit terms will be able to obtain some of the finance to purchase stock at higher prices from those suppliers who are willing to increase the amount of credit for that business.

(b) Items to be included in MWC:
Debtors
Cash (represents money in tills of the retail company)
Trade creditors
It is assumed that the averaging method can be applied solely by reference to opening and closing balance sheet figures, i.e. working capital has moved steadily throughout the period.

Form of calculation

$$\left(\begin{matrix}\text{Opening}\\ \text{MWC}\end{matrix} \times \frac{\text{Representative index no. for period}}{\text{Index no. at typical transaction date}}\right) - \begin{matrix}\text{Opening}\\ \text{MWC}\end{matrix} = \text{Part of MWCA}$$

Workings are in £000.

Creditors

Assume that they arise over same period as stocks (three months). Stock price index is appropriate and indices relate to price levels ruling during the month.

$$50 - \left(50 \times \frac{132}{\left[\frac{115 + 117 + 118}{3}\right]}\right) = (6{,}571.4)$$

$$\left(60 \times \frac{132}{\left[\frac{138 + 140 + 141}{3}\right]}\right) - 60 = (3{,}293.6)$$

$$\underline{\underline{(9{,}865.0)}}$$

Debtors

Assume stock price index is appropriate.

$$\left(40 \times \frac{132}{\left[\frac{117 + 118}{2}\right]}\right) - 40 = 4{,}936.2$$

$$50 - \left(50 \times \frac{132}{\left[\frac{140 + 141}{2}\right]}\right) = 3{,}024.9$$

$$\underline{\underline{7{,}961.1}}$$

Cash

Assume stock price index is appropriate. Balance sheet date is transaction date.

$$\left(21 \times \frac{132}{\left[\frac{118 + 120}{2}\right]}\right) - 21 = 2{,}294.1$$

$$15 - \left(15 \times \frac{132}{141^*}\right) = \quad 957.4$$

$$\underline{\underline{3{,}251.5}}$$

*Index for Jan. 19–1 also required but not given in the question.

$$\frac{\text{MWCA } (9{,}865.0) + 7{,}961.1}{+ 3{,}251.5} = \underline{\underline{1{,}347.6}}$$

$$\text{MWCA} = \underline{\underline{£1{,}347{,}600}}$$

(c) There are a number of reasons why some authorities do not believe that a monetary working capital adjustment is necessary.

(i) In the view of the Sandilands Committee (para. 537) no gains or losses on monetary items should be recognised in CCA, since the accounts are drawn up in monetary units (pounds) not units of purchasing power. The approach in the Sandilands Report was to eliminate holding gains on non-monetary assets from the profit and loss account on the grounds that adjustments for stock and fixed assets alone provided a comprehensive system of accounting for inflation.

(ii) Some authorities argue that the monetary working capital adjustment confuses profitability with liquidity. The inclusion of liabilities in monetary working capital provides a CCA 'gain' not supported by a tangible asset. It may encourage too great a reliance by companies on short-term finance.

(iii) Some accept that monetary assets form an essential part of operating capability but reject the notion that creditors can reduce the company's need, except in the short-term, to finance such assets from within.

(iv) Some accept the principle that liabilities reduce the need for internal financing but reject the split made in SSAP 16 between the MWCA and the gearing adjustment. The split of monetary items between working capital and others is rejected as arbitrary in many cases.

(v) Some argue that any gain or loss on monetary items is related not to the specific costs of goods purchased and sold but instead to the fall in the value of money itself which is more accurately reflected by the use of a general index such as the RPI.

ANSWER A8. FIXED ASSET VALUES AND CURRENT COST DEPRECIATION

Asset acquired	*At 1.1.19–8*				*Depreciation charge for year*			*At 31.12.19–8*			
	HC amounts	*Factor*	*GCRC*	*Accum. depn.*	*HC*	*Factor*	*CC*	*HC Amounts*	*Factor*	*GCRC*	*Accum. depn.*
	£		£	£	£		£		£		£
19–2	300	200/100	600			220/100		300	220/100	660	462
	(180)			360	30		66	(210)			
19–4	400	200/130	615			220/130		400	220/130	677	338
	(160)			246	40		68	(200)			
19–6	200	200/160	250								
	(40)			50	Nil		Nil				
	900		1,465	656	70		134	700		1,337	800
	(380)		(656)					(410)		(800)	
NBV	520		809					290		537	

Current cost reserve

	Unrealised holding gain	Realised holding gain
	£	£
Opening balance (809–520)	289	
Additional depreciation (134–70)	(64)	64
Adjustment redisposal of fixed asset (note 1)	(40)	40
Revaluation (note 2)	62	
Closing balance (537–290)	247	104

Note 1

Adjustment to disposal of fixed asset

CC Profit	£
Sale proceeds	260
Less: CC NBV at date of sale (assume beginning of year value) (250–50)	200
	60

Additional adjustment 100–60 = 40

Note 2

Gross revaluation of assets	Opening GRC	Closing GRC	
	£	£	£
re: 19–2 acq.	600	660	60
re: 19–4 acq.	615	677	62
			122

Restatement of prior years' depreciation (Backlog depreciation)

re: 19–2 acq. $\left(180 \times \frac{220}{100}\right) - 360 = 36$

re: 19–4 acq. $\left(160 \times \frac{220}{130}\right) - 246 = 24$ — 60

Net revaluation 62

ANSWER A9.

(a) *H.C. Accounts*
Fixed assets

31.12.–4		*31.12.–5*
£		£
4,700	Cost	4,700
1,220	Depreciation	1,493
3,480		3,207

C.C. Accounts
Fixed assets

10,000	Gross CRC	12,000
2,333	Depreciation	3,600
7,667		8,400

(b) P + L Account Depreciation charge

Per HC Accounts (W1)	273
Additional charge to reflect current costs (800 – 273) (W2)	527

(c) Current cost reserve (W3)

	Unrealised holding gains *Items A*	*Item B*	*Realised holding gains*
	£	£	£
At beginning of year	2,400	1,787	
Additional depreciation	(333)	(194)	527
Revaluation during year	600	933	
At end of year	2,667	2,526	527

Workings:

1. *H.C. depreciation*

	Item A	*Item B*
	£	£
NBV at 31.12.–4	600	2,880
Remaining useful life	9 years	14 years
Charge for year	67	206

2. *C.C. depreciation*

	£	£
On year-end values	6000	6,000
Proportion of asset consumed in year $\frac{1}{15}$	400	400

3. *Valuation of assets*

		Item A		*Item B*
		£		£
At 31.12.–4 GCRC		5,000		5,000
Accumulated depreciation	$\frac{6}{15}$	2,000	$\frac{1}{15}$	333
C.C. NBV		3,000		4,667
At 31.12.–5 GCRC		6,000		6,000
Accumulated depreciation	$\frac{7}{15}$	2,800	$\frac{2}{15}$	800
C.C. NBV		3,200		5,200

ANSWER A10.

(a) *H.C. Accounts*

Fixed assets	*31.12.–4*		*31.12.–5*
	£		£
	4,700	Cost	4,700
	1,220	Depreciation	1,493
	3,480		3,207

C.C. Accounts

Fixed assets			
	10,000	Gross GRC	12,000
	3,500	Depreciation	3,600
	6,500		8,400

(b) *P & L accounts depreciation charge*

Per H.C. accounts (W1) £273

Per C.C. accounts	
Additional charge to reflect current costs £(800 – 273) (W2)	527
Less: Overprovision in prior years (W4)	(1,167)
	(640)

(c) *Current cost reserve*

	Unrealised holding gains Item A £	Item B £	*Realised holding loss*
At beginning of year (W3)	1,400	1,620	
Overprovision of depreciation (W4)	1,000	167	(1,167)
Additional depreciation (W2)	(333)	(194)	527
Revaluation during year	600	933	
	2,667	2,526	(640)

Workings:

		Item A		*Item B*
1. *H.C. depreciation*				
NBV at 31.12.–4		600		2,880
Remaining useful life		9 years		14 years
Charge for year		67		206
2. *C.C. depreciation*		£		£
On year-end values		6,000		6,000
Proportion of asset consumed in year $\frac{1}{15}$		400		400
3. *Valuation of assets*				
At 31.12.–4 GCRC		5,000		5,000
Accumulated depreciation	$\frac{6}{10}$	3,000	$\frac{1}{10}$	500
C.C. NBV		2,000		4,500
At 31.12.–5 GCRC		6,000		6,000
Accumulated depreciation	$\frac{7}{15}$	2,800	$\frac{2}{15}$	800
C.C. NBV		3,200		5,200
4. *Restatement of accumulated depreciation at 31.12.–4*				
was:	$\frac{6}{10}$	3,000	$\frac{1}{10}$	500
restated to:	$\frac{6}{15}$	2,000	$\frac{1}{15}$	333
Overprovision in prior years		1,000		167

The guidance notes to *SSAP 16* regard the re-assessment of asset lives as a change in the assets service potential. Changes in NBV arising from such change should go through the P & L account.

ANSWER A11. EXTRACTS FROM BALANCE SHEETS AS AT 31.12.–5

	H.C.		*C.C.*
	£		£
Cost	100,000		
Depreciation	62,500		
	37,500	Recoverable amount	80,000

The amount in the CC reserve relating to the asset (ignoring the CC depreciation charge) at 31.12.–5 represents an unrealised holding gain of £(80,000 − 37,500) = £42,500

Workings:

1. *Recoverable amount as at 31.12.–5*

If the plant is sold on:	*31.12.–5*	*31.12.–6*	*31.12.–7*	*31.12.–8*
	£	£	£	£
Realisable value	60,000	35,000	15,000	Nil
Operating cash flows:				
31.12.–6		40,000	40,000	40,000
31.12.–7			25,000	25,000
31.12.–8				15,000
Total cash flows	60,000	75,000	80,000	80,000

∴ £80,000 gives the best cash recoverable, so is the recoverable amount.

2. *H.C. NBV at 31.12.–5*

NBV at 31.12.–4 £50,000

Remaining useful life at 31.12.–4 = 4 years (from estimates of future cash flows)

∴ Per *SSAP 12* depreciate NBV of asset over new estimate of remaining useful life.

Depreciation charge for year to 31.12.–5 $\frac{50,000}{4} = £12,500$

3. *Net current replacement cost*

Gross CRC at 31.12.–5 = £300,000

C.C. accumulated depreciation:

Estimated life of asset = 5 years (per H.C. depreciation at 31.12.–4)
+ 4 years (see working 2)

Life of asset expired at 31.12.–5 = 6 years

∴ $\frac{6}{9} \times 300,000 = 200,000$

Net CRC = £100,000

As this is above recoverable amount (working 1)

Value to the business of asset = £80,000

ANSWER A12. UK BANK LTD

(a) *Supplementary C.C. P & L account for the year ended 30.9.–9*

	(*a*) SSAP 16 £m	(*c*) Hyde £m	(*d*) Godley Cripps £m
Profit before interest and taxation as per historical cost accounts	705	705	705
Less: Adjustments to reflect current cost depreciation adjustment	40	40	40
MWCA	153		153
	193		193
Current cost operating profit	512	665	512
Adjustment for net monetary assets		(53)	
Gearing	67		88
Interest payable	(65)	(65)	(65)
	2	(118)	23
Current cost profit attributable to shareholders	514	547	535
Taxation	300	300	300
	214	247	235

(b) *Current cost reserve for the year ended 30.9.–9*

	£m	£m	£m
Opening balance			620
Revaluation surpluses reflecting price changes:			
Premises and equipment	90		
Trade investments	10		
		100	
Monetary working capital adjustment		153	
Gearing adjustment		(67)	
			186
Closing balance			806
Of which: Realised			326
Unrealised			480
			806

Workings:

1. *MWCA*

(a) MWC includes all items necessarily tied up in the day to day running of the business.

	30.9.–9	*30.9.–8*
	£m	*£m*
Monetary assets:		
Liquid assets	5,700	5,300
Customers' accounts	20,000	19,200
	25,700	24,500
Monetary liabilities:		
Current, deposit and other accounts	24,000	23,200
Creditors	100	80
	24,100	23,280
Net MWC	1,600	1,220

(b) Calculation
Assume averaging method is appropriate and can be computed by change in RPI.
Restate opening and closing MWC to average prices and eliminate volume change:

		£m
	$1{,}220 \times \frac{460 - 438}{438} =$	61.28
	$1{,}600 \times \frac{488 - 460}{488} =$	91.80
MWCA		153.08

2. *Gearing proportion*

(a) Average net borrowings

	30.9.–9	*30.9.–8*
	£m	*£m*
Loan capital	700	600
Taxation	300	300
	1,000	900
Average	£950m	

(b) Average shareholders' funds

	30.9.–9		*30.9.–8*
	£m		*£m*
Share capital	240		240
H.C. reserves	1,260		920
Revaluations:			
Trade investment			
£(180 – 100)	80	£(160 – 90)	70
Premises £(1,200 – 800)	400	£(1,100 – 750)	350
	1,980		1,580
Average		£1,780m	

(c) Adjustment

$$\frac{\text{Average net borrowings}}{\text{Average shareholders' funds and}} \times \text{C.C. adjustments}$$

Average net borrowings

$$\frac{950}{950 + 1{,}780} \times £m(40 + 153) = £67.16m$$

3. *Current cost reserve*

	Unrealised holding gains		*Realised holding gains*
	Trade investments	*Premises*	
	£m	*£m*	*£m*
Opening balances	70	350	200
C.C. adjustments			
MWCA			153
Depreciation adjustment		(40)	40
Gearing			(67)
Net movement in unrealised holding gains	10	90	
Closing balances	80	400	326

4. *Hyde adjustment*

(a) Only one adjustment is made for all monetary items.
As monetary assets exceed monetary liabilities a charge should be made to reflect an increase in net monetary assets needed to maintain the scale of operation. The Hyde guidelines suggested that this should be calculated by multiplying the net balances of

monetary assets by the percentage change in an appropriate index during the accounting period.

(b) Average net monetary assets

	30.9.–9	*30.9.–8*
	£m	*£m*
Net MWC assets (working 1)	1,600	1,220
Less: Net borrowings (working 2a)	1,000	900
Average	600	320

(c) Charge $460 \times \frac{488 - 438}{438} = £52.51\text{m}$

5. *Godley Cripps*

This adjustment recognises that the external financing of the net operating assets of the company produces a gain to shareholders of part of all holding gains recognised during the accounting period. Total holding gains recognised during the year:

	£m
MWCA	153
Net movement in unrealised holding gains	
Trade investments	10
Premises	90
	253

The depreciation adjustment is not included as to do so would be double counting. It represents the realisation of unrealised gains already accounted for (i.e. last year's revaluations £350m and this year's revaluations £90m).

The gearing *proportion* is computed as per *SSAP 16.*

$$\frac{\text{Average net borrowings}}{\text{Average shareholders' funds and Average net borrowings}} \times \text{Holding gains}$$

$$\frac{950}{950 + 1{,}780} \times £253\text{m} = £88\text{m}$$

ANSWER A13. CHIPPING NORTON LTD

(a) *Current cost statement of profit for the year ended 31 Dec. 19–9*

	£000	£000
Profit before taxation and interest as given in the historical cost accounts		515.5
Less: current cost adjustments		
Cost of sales (note 1)	100.8	
Depreciation (note 2)	37.7	
Monetary working capital (note 3)	(7.9)	130.6
Current cost operating profit		384.9
Interest payable	42.5	
Gearing adjustment (note 4)	(20.6)	21.9
Current cost profit before taxation		363.0
Taxation		114.0
Current cost profit attributable to shareholders		249.0
Dividends		100.0
Current cost profit retained		149.0
Current cost earnings per share (note 5)		2.9p

Current cost balance sheet as at 31 Dec. 19–9

	£000	£000
Fixed assets (note 6)		1,836.5
Net Current assets		
Stock	620	
Debtors less creditors	(20.5)	
Other net current assets	120	719.5
		2,556.0
Capital and reserves		£000
Share capital		1,000
Reserves (note 7)		1,082
		2,082
Debentures		450
Deferred taxation		24
		2,556

Notes to the current cost statement of profit

1. The cost of sales adjustment represents the difference between the actual cost of goods sold and their replacement cost at the date of sale. Replacement cost has been calculated by an averaging method using the UK widget cost index.
2. The depreciation adjustment represents the additional depreciation required if the provision were to be based upon the year end replacement cost of the fixed assets used in the business during the year. In the case of freehold land and buildings replacement cost has been calculated by means of a professional valuation carried out by Messrs Corinth and Co. Chartered Valuers. The replacement cost of plant has been calculated using the National Association of Widget Machine Tool Manufacturers price index.
3. The monetary working capital adjustment represents the proportion of additional replacement costs of goods sold which is financed by the excess of creditors over debtors and thus is not borne by the shareholders of the company.
4. The gearing adjustment ascribes part of the burden of the cost of sales adjustment plus the depreciation adjustment less the monetary working capital adjustment to the borrowings of the company. It is based on the proportion of the company's operating assets which is financed by borrowings less cash. In calculating the company's operating assets, the fixed assets of the company have been valued on a current cost basis.
5. The current cost earnings per share is based upon the current cost profits after tax of 249,000 divided by the average 8,500,000 shares in issue during the year.

	£000	£000
6. Fixed assets		
Land at valuation		540
Buildings at valuation		602
Plant and machinery		
Gross replacement cost	1,039.8	
Less: depreciation	345.3	694.5
		1,836.5

7. Reserves		
Share premium—issue during year		150
Revenue Reserves		
At 1st January	245	
Profit retained	149	
		394
Current cost reserve (note 8)		538
		1,082

	£000
8. Current cost reserve	
Balance at 1st January	385.8
Surplus on revaluations	
Fixed assets	79.9
Stock	100.8
	566.5
MWCA	7.9
	558.6
Gearing adjustment	20.6
Balance at 31 Dec.	538.0
of which: Realised 110,000	
Unrealised 428,000	

(b) *Comments on the statement*

As might be expected the statement shows that the company's profit using a CCA basis is considerably lower than that using the historical cost convention. The profit after tax has fallen by over 30% from its historical cost figure of £359,000 to its CCA figure of £249,000.

The depreciation adjustment has reduced the profit by over £35,000. Taking into account the high level of fixed assets which the company owns, this is possibly less than might at first have been expected. The reasons for this are:

(i) The company owns substantial freehold land which is not depreciated.
(ii) The freehold buildings attract only a low rate of depreciation.
(iii) The replacement price of the plant has increased by only 5.3% (from 209 to 220) during the year.

The cost of sales adjustment is considerably higher than the depreciation adjustment due largely to the rapid increase in stock prices of over 28% during the year (from 179 to 230). Only a small proportion of this has been credited in the monetary working capital adjustment reflecting the small excess of creditors over debtors.

The gearing adjustment has reduced the total inflation adjustments by about 15%. This is relatively low and reflects:

(i) The low gearing of the company.
(ii) The significant effect of adding the holding gains on the fixed assets to the shareholders funds.

In other words the vast majority of the extra replacement costs have had to be borne by shareholders.

One final point to consider is where the management and shareholders go from here! The shareholders have to consider whether the statement is relevant for their decisions. If not, it seems pointless producing such a statement. Management also presumably should gain some knowledge from the statement. Does it imply that profits of £110,000 (£130,600 – £20,600) should be retained in the business for higher replacement costs? It may be that management will take some note of the statement but the actual link between:

(i) the *SSAP 16* statements; and
(ii) management policy

may be impossible to determine.

Workings

(1) *Cost of sales adjustment*

	£
(a) Restate opening stock in mid year prices	
$£220{,}000 \times \frac{204}{179} =$	250,726
(b) Restate closing stock in mid year prices	
$£620{,}000 \times \frac{204}{230} =$	549,913
(c) Calculate difference in stock valuations	
Historical cost (620,000 – 220,000)	400,000
CCA (549,913 – 250,726)	299,187
Cost of sales adjustment	100,813

(2) *Depreciation adjustment*
(a) *Calculation of historical cost depreciation*

	£	£
Buildings		
2% × £500,000		10,000
2% × 6/12 × £100,000		1,000
		11,000
Plant		
10% × £520,000	52,000	
10% × 6/12 × £170,000	8,500	60,500
Total		71,500

(b) *Calculation of current cost depreciation*

(i) *Buildings*
Depreciation charge is based on number of years useful life at the end of the year.
Old buildings
The accumulated depreciation on buildings at 31.12.–8 is £100,000. This represents 10 years depreciation. At 31.12.–9 there are presumably 39 years of useful life remaining (since no change has been made in estimated useful life). ∴ current cost depreciation on old buildings is 1/39 × (602,000 – 99,000) i.e. *£12,897.*
New buildings
These were acquired halfway through year so remaining useful life is $49\frac{1}{2}$ years. ∴ current cost depreciation is

$$\frac{£99{,}000}{49.5} \times 6/12 \text{ i.e. } £1{,}000.$$

(ii) *Old plant and machinery*

$$\text{Replacement cost: at 31.12.–9 } £170{,}000 \times \frac{220}{216} = £173{,}148$$

∴ Current cost depreciation
= 10% × £866,667 = *£86,667*

(iii) *New plant and machinery*

$$\text{Replacement cost: at 31.12.–9 } £170{,}000 \times \frac{220}{216} = £173{,}148$$

Current cost depreciation
= 10% × 6/12 × 173,148 = *£8,657*

(iv) *Summary of current cost depreciation*

	£
Old buildings	12,897
New buildings	1,000
Old plant	86,667
New plant	8,657
	109,221

Depreciation adjustment	£
Current cost depreciation	109,221
Historical cost depreciation	71,500
∴ Depreciation adjustment	37,721

(3) *Monetary working capital adjustment*

Assume balance sheet dates can be taken as typical transaction dates.

	£
(a) Restate opening net creditors in mid-year prices $£40{,}000 \times \frac{204}{179}$	45,587
(b) Restate closing net creditors in mid-year prices $£20{,}500 \times \frac{204}{230}$	18,183
(c) If prices were constant the decrease in creditors would be 45,587 – 18,183	27,404
(d) The historical cost accounts show a decrease of 40,000 – 20,500	19,500
MWCA	7,904

(4) *Gearing adjustment*

(a) *Net borrowings*

	31.12.–8		*31.12.–9*
	£000		£000
Debentures	450.0		450.0
Deferred taxation	30.0		24.0
Taxation	100.0		120.0
	580.0		594.0
Less: Cash	175.0		340.0
	405.0		254.0
Average		329.5	

(b) *Revaluation of assets on a CCA basis*

	31.12.–8	*31.12.–9*
	£	£
(i) *Freehold land*		
Valuation	450,000	540,000
Historical cost	400,000	440,000
Current cost reserve	50,000	100,000

	31.12.–8 £	*31.12.–9* £
(ii) *Freehold buildings*		
Valuation	520,000	602,000
Historical cost WDV		
(800 – 400)	400,000	
(929 – 440)		489,000
Current cost reserve	120,000	113,000

(iii) *Plant and machinery*

CCA WDV £370,000 × $\frac{209}{132}$	585,833	
Original assets:		
(370,000 – 52,000) × $\frac{220}{132}$		530,000
New assets:		
(170,000 – 8,500) × $\frac{220}{216}$		164,491
	585,833	694,491
HCA – WDV	370,000	479,500
Current cost reserve	215,833	214,991

(c) *Shareholders' interest*

	19–8 *£000*	*19–9* *£000*
Per HC accounts:		
Ord. share capital	700.0	1,000.0
Share premium	—	150.0
Revenue reserves	245.0	504.0
Proposed dividend		100.0
	945.0	1,754.0
Add: Increases in net book value of balance sheet assets —CC & HC		
Freehold land	50.0	100.0
Freehold buildings	120.0	113.0
Plant and machinery	215.8	215.0
	1,330.8	2,182.0

$$\text{Average } \frac{1{,}330.8 + 2{,}182.0}{2} = 1{,}756.4$$

(d) *Adjustment*

$$\frac{329.5}{329.5 + 1{,}756.4} \times (100.8 + 37.7 - 7.9) = 20.6$$

(5) Current cost reserve

	Unrealised holding gains Fixed assets	Stock	*Realised holding gains*
	£000		*£000*
Opening revaluations (see below)	385.8	—	
C.O.S.A.			100.8
MWCA			(7.9)
Depreciation adjustment	(37.7)		37.7
Gearing			(20.6)
Revaluations (bal. fig.)	79.9	—	
Closing revaluations (see below)	428.0	—	110.0

	19–8	*19–9*
	£000	*£000*
Increase in net valuation of assets at balance sheet date:		
Freehold land	50.0	100.0
Freehold buildings	120.0	113.0
Plant and machinery	215.8	215.0
	385.8	428.0

(6) Plant and machinery—Fixed Asset Disclosure

H.C. Amounts at *31.12.–9*		Index Adjustment	C.C. Amounts
	£000		*£000*
Original assets			
Cost	520	$\frac{220}{132}$	866.7
Depcn	202		336.7
	318		530.0

	£000	Index Adjustment	C.C. Amounts £000
New Assets			
Cost	170	220 / 216	173.1
Depcn	8.5		8.6
	161.5		164.5

ANSWER A14.

(a) *Depreciation adjustment*

Analysis of HC depreciation

Amount relating to assets acquired:

	10% of cost *£m*	*Uplift to reflect current costs*	*£m*
1976	10	$\frac{172}{105}$	16.38
1977	13	$\frac{172}{116}$	19.27
1978	15	$\frac{172}{133}$	19.40
1979	21	$\frac{172}{154}$	23.45
1980	43	—	43.00
	102		121.50

Depreciation adjustment = £121.5 – £102.0
= £19.5 million

(b) *Gearing adjustment*

$$\frac{\text{Average net borrowings}}{\text{Average net operating assets}} \times \text{additional adjustments made to reflect current costs}$$

$$\frac{432.5}{1{,}163.56} + (21\text{m} + 9\text{m} + 19.5\text{m}) = \underline{\underline{18.4\text{m}}}$$

Workings

(i) *Net borrowings*

	At 30.9.79	*At 30.9.80*
Loan	29	149
Taxation	15	20
Overdraft	234	418
	278	587

= 432.5

(ii) *Current cost values of fixed assets*

At 30.9.79

Year of purchase	*Cost £m*	*Depn £m*	*NBV £m*	*Uplift to currents values*	*CCA NBV £m*
1976	100	40	60	$\times \frac{165}{105}$	= 94.29
1977	130	39	91	$\times \frac{165}{116}$	= 129.44
1978	150	30	120	$\times \frac{165}{133}$	= 148.87
1979	210	21	189	$\times \frac{165}{154}$	= 202.50
			460		575.10

At 30.9.80

Year of purchase		*NBV £m*	*Uplift to current values*	*CCA NBV £m*
1976		50	$\times \frac{180}{105}$	= 85.71
1977		78	$\times \frac{180}{116}$	= 121.03
1978		105	$\times \frac{180}{133}$	= 142.11
1979		168	$\times \frac{180}{154}$	= 196.36
1980	426 × 90%	383*	$\times \frac{180}{172}$	= 400.81
		784		946.02

* balancing figure.

(iii) *Current cost value of stock*

At 30.9.79	*£m*	*At 30.9.80*	*£m*
Date of purchase:			
At year end	152		251
Remainder at average 31.3.79	152	Remainder at average 30.3.80	251
	304		502

CCA stock			
At year end	152		251
$152 \times \frac{180}{170}$	161	$251 \times \frac{200}{190}$	264
	313		515

(iv) *Net operating assets*

	30.9.79	*30.9.80*
	£m	*£m*
Fixed assets (working (ii))	575.1	946.02
Stock (working (iii))	313	515
MWC debtors	211	332
Liquid funds	23	25
Creditors	(208)	(405)
	914.1	1,413.02
Average	1,163.56	

(c) *Current cost reserve*

	£m	*£m*
Opening balance:		
Stocks (313 – 304)	9.0	
Fixed assets (575.1 – 460)	115.1	
		124.1
Revaluations during year.		
Fixed assets (946.02 – 784) + 19.5 – 115.1	66.42	
Stock (515 – 502) + 21 – 9	25.00	
MWCA	9.00	
		100.42
Less: Gearing adjustment		18.4
		82.02
		206.12

Comprising:

Year end revaluations:	
Fixed assets (946.02 – 784)	162.02
Stock	13.00
	175.02
Current cost profit and loss adjustments (21 + 9 + 19.5 – 18.4)	31.10
	206.12

ANSWER A15

(a) The second column of figures represents the comparative figures for 1979 multiplied by a constant factor in order to provide a more useful comparison between 1979 and 1980. The constant factor will reflect the increase in the general level of prices from 1979 to 1980 and thus takes account of the decline in the purchasing power of the pound which may render comparatives misleading unless restated. The increase in the general level of prices is likely to be measured by using the Retail Price Index.

(b) The first figure of sales of £5,368 million shows the original money amount of sales revenue in 1979. The second figure of £6,334 million shows what the equivalent of the 1979 sales would be when expressed in 1980 pounds, (i.e. after taking into account the decline in the purchasing power of money). The third figure of £5,715 million shows the money amount of sales revenue for 1980.

A comparison of the figures shows that although sales have risen in money terms between 1979 and 1980, in real terms they have fallen.

(c) SSAP 4 requires that grants relating to fixed assets should be credited to revenue over the expected useful life of the asset. Under CCA the charge for depreciation is based on the gross replacement cost of fixed assets. Thus, where replacement costs have risen, additional depreciation will need to be charged in the current cost accounts compared to the historical cost accounts. However, where government grants would still be available on a fixed asset whose replacement cost has risen, the increased replacement cost would lead to an increased grant giving an increased credit to revenue in respect of grants. Thus, 'indexation of government grants' reflects the additional credit for government grants to reflect the increased replacement costs of fixed assets in the current cost accounts. It has the effect of offsetting to an extent the additional depreciation charge on the replacement cost of fixed assets.

(d) The 'charge for supplementary depreciation' means the additional charge for depreciation in the current cost accounts (where the charge is based on the replacement cost of fixed assets) compared to the historical cost accounts (where the charge is based on the historical cost of fixed assets).

'After making allowance for the difference between historical and CCA asset lives' means that the company is charging depreciation on its fixed assets over different expected useful lives for CCA purposes from those lives used in the historical cost accounts.

This difference in expected useful lives has probably arisen because the company has adopted conservative asset lives in its historical cost accounts but less conservative, (i.e. more realistic) lives in its current cost accounts. This approach could be supported on the grounds that there is a range of possible lives and the company has simply chosen different lives within the possible range to apply under the different accounting conventions.

However, it does seem potentially confusing to users of the financial statements to use different lives and the approach could be criticised on these grounds.

(e) Rises in the value to the business of fixed assets are normally realised only over a period of years as the assets are depreciated. The revaluation surpluses realised in any period are represented by the depreciation adjustment (where a surplus is realised by consumption of the asset) and the disposal of fixed asset adjustment (where a surplus is realised by selling the asset). Since in calculating the gearing adjustment, the gearing proportion is applied only to the current cost operating adjustments (including the depreciation adjustment and disposal of fixed asset adjustment referred to above) it only reflects realised revaluation surpluses and takes into account unrealised surpluses which, to the extent they are financed by net borrowing, accrue to the shareholders. Thus, the gearing adjustment 'excludes revaluation surpluses not yet treated as realised'.

This reflects the long standing convention that unrealised capital value increases are not included as part of the annual profit.

(f) The gearing adjustment in the accounts reflects the convention that unrealised capital value increases are not included as part of the annual profit. The treatment thus follows the fundamental accounting concept of prudence and this is why it is the method required by *SSAP 16.*

The gearing adjustment preferred by the company reflects the benefits of borrowing by reference to revaluation surpluses *arising* during the period and not simply those *realised* during the period (which may have arisen in previous periods). Many people would agree that this approach is a better reflection of the benefits of borrowing since the *SSAP 16* method uses the gearing ratio for the *current* period while the additional depreciation will in part relate to changes in asset values which have arisen in *earlier* periods.

Despite this argument it was decided that, on balance, the *SSAP 16* approach was preferable to the alternative of introducing a major unrealised element into the gearing adjustment. *SSAP 16* does however permit alternative methods of calculation to be shown by way of note.

(g) The three figures for dividends show that the dividend pay out has fallen by £33 million in money terms and by £57 million in real terms measured in 1980 pounds. Additionally, it can be seen that the dividend was covered 1.66 times in 1979 (based on current cost profit attributable to the parent company before extraordinary items) whilst it was uncovered in 1980 since losses were made.

ANSWER B1. CHEDDAR LTD

Timing differences

	Originating/Reversing
	£000
Actual 19–5	300
Forecast 19–6	200
Forecast 19–7	150
Forecast 19–8	(570)
After	net originating only in any one year

Balance sheet provisions required at 31 Dec. each year
(To cover expected future net reversals).

19–4 50% × (570 − (300 + 200 + 150))	= Nil
19–5 50% × (570 − (200 + 150))	= £110,000
19–6 50% × (570 − 150)	= £210,000
19–7 50% × (570)	= £285,000
19–8 Nil	

P & L charge for each year ended 31 Dec.
(Difference between opening and closing balance sheet provision)

19–5 110 − 0	= £110,000 Dr.
19–6 210 − 110	= £100,000 Dr.
19–7 285 − 210	= £ 75,000 Dr.
19–8 0 − 285	= £285,000 Cr.

ANSWER B2. CHESHIRE LTD

Timing differences

	Originating/Reversing
	£000
19–0	300
19–1	(570)
19–2	200
19–3	150
19–4 and after	originating exceed reversing in all years

Provisions required
(To cover net future reversals)

19–3 Nil	
19–2 Nil	
19–1 Nil	
19–0 50% × £570	= £285,000

P & L charge
(Differences between opening and closing provision required)

19–0 285 – 0	= £285,000 Dr.
19–1 0 – 285	= £285,000 Cr.
19–2 Nil	
19–3 Nil	

Amount of 19–0 charge to be adjusted as prior year adjustment

	£
Amount to be set aside at end of 19–0	285
Maximum amount which can be deemed to relate to timing differences arising in 19–0 – 50% × 300	150
	135

ANSWER B3. OFFSET LTD

Extracts from accounts relating to deferred taxation

Accounting policy

The policy of accounting for deferred taxation has been changed this year to comply with the recently introduced standard *SSAP 15*. Provision is made for timing differences between treatment of certain items for taxation and accounting purposes except that no provision is made where it can be reasonably foreseen that such deferred tax will not be payable in the future.

The comparative figures have been adjusted to reflect this policy.

Balance sheet as at 31.12.–1

31.12.–0 *£000*		31.12.–1 *£000*
	Provisions for liabilities and charges	
—	Deferred taxation (note 14)	32

Notes to accounts

14. Deferred taxation

	£000
Balance at 1.1.–1	1,445
Prior year adjustment transferred to reserves	(1,445)
Charge for the year in the profit and loss account	32
	32

The potential amount of deferred tax for all timing differences is set out below:

	–1 Full Potential liability	Provision made	–0 Full Potential liability	Provision made
Tax deferred by reason of:	*£000*	*£000*	*£000*	*£000*
accelerated capital allowances	1,500	32	1,445	—

Taxation in charge in profit and loss account 31.12.–1

	£000
UK corporation tax	X
Deferred taxation	32

The full potential deferred tax charge is £55,000 solely relating to capital allowances.

Reserves

	–1	–0
At 1 Jan. as previously stated	X	X
Add: Deferred tax prior year adjustment	1,445	X
At 1 Jan. re-stated	X	X

Workings

1. *Full provision*

	31.12.–0 *£000*	*Movements in year* *£000*	*31.12.–1* *£000*
Timing differences on:			
Plant 2,890 × 50%	1,445	(110) × 50% (55)	1,500
of which SSAP 15 liability	Nil		(64 × 50%) 32 (working 2)
giving			
1. Profit and loss account charge		(32 – Nil) 32	
2. Prior year adjustment	1,445		

2. *SSAP 15 liability at 31.12.–1 and at 31.12.–0*

Net future timing differences and their reversal:

		Cumulative forecasts	
		19–0	*19–1*
19–1	110	110	N/A
19–2	152	262	152
19–3	290	552	442
19–4	(204)	348	238
19–5	10	358	248
19–6	(312)	46	(64)
Reversal to be accounted for		Nil	(64)

ANSWER B4. HUCKLEBERRY LTD

(a) *Extract from accounting policies—deferred taxation*

Deferred tax

Deferred tax is provided in respect of the tax effects arising from all timing differences of material amount to the extent that it is probable that a liability will crystallise.

(b) *Extract from final accounts*

(i) *Analysis of potential liability for deferred taxation*

No provision has been made for deferred tax. The amount of unprovided defered tax is as follows:

	31.12.–7 *Full potential liability* £	*30.12.–8* *Full potential liability* £
Accelerated tax allowances on plant and industrial buildings	499,772	441,844
Revaluation of property	75,000	—
	574,772	441,844

Working 1—Net reversals are not expected hence deferred taxation need not be provided.

	IBAs	*Plant allowances*	*Net*	*Cumulative*
	£	£	£	£
19–8	12,400	45,000	57,400	57,400
19–9	12,400	(20,000)	(7,600)	49,800
19–10	12,400	(50,000)	(37,600)	12,200
19–11	12,400	10,000	22,400	34,600

In year 19–8, however, tax on £45,200 of timing differences will need to be provided in order to cover the net reversals of £7,600 and £37,600 occurring in 19–9 and 19–10.

Working 2—calculation of contingent liability in respect of deferred taxation

Deferred Tax Account

	At 1.1.–7 Timing differences	*Opening balance*	*Movements during year*	*Gross*	*Net*	*At 31.12.–7 Closing balance*
	£	£		£	£	£
Plant						
A/cs NBV	643,500		CAs	232,000*		
Tax WDV	141,000		Depcn	133,000		
	502,500 × 52%	261,300		99,000 × 52%	51,480	312,780
IBs						
A/c NBV (620,000 – 37,200)	582,800		CAs	24,800		
Tax WDV (620,000 – 384,400)	235,600		Depcn	12,400		
	347,200 × 52%	180,544		12,400 × 52%	6,448	186,992
		441,844			57,928	499,772
SSAP 15 Provision made		Nil			Nil	Nil

*(25% × £141,000) + £196,750 = £232,000

Deferred tax on revaluation of property is:

30% × £(950,000 – 700,000) = £75,000

ANSWER C1. LESSEE LTD

(1) The machine will be included in leased plant and be shown as follows:

	In the accounts for year ended 31.12.–0	31.12.–1	31.12.–2	31.12.–3	31.12.–4
	£	£	£	£	£
Cost	50,000	50,000	50,000	50,000	50,000
Depreciation	—	12,500	25,000	37,500	50,000
Written down value	50,000	37,500	25,000	12,500	—

(2) The liability can be shown in one of two ways:

(a) *Creditors: Amounts falling due within one year:*
Obligation under finance lease:

	In the accounts for year ended				
	31.12.–0	*31.12.–1*	*31.12.–2*	*31.12.–3*	*31.12.–4*
	£	£	£	£	£
Minimum lease payments	17,164	17,164	17,164	17,164	—
Future finance charges	7,435	5,783	3,850	1,588	—
Net liability	9,729	11,381	13,314	15,576	—

Creditors: Amounts falling due after more than one year:

Obligation under finance lease:

	In the accounts for year ended				
	31.12.–0	*31.12.–1*	*31.12.–2*	*31.12.–3*	*31.12.–4*
	£	£	£	£	£
Minimum lease payments	51,492	34,328	17,164	—	—
Future finance charges	11,221	5,438	1,588	—	—
Net liability	40,271	28,890	15,576	—	—

OR

(b) *Creditors: Amounts falling due within one year:*

Obligation under finance lease:

	In the accounts for year ended				
	31.12.–0	*31.12.–1*	*31.12.–2*	*31.12.–3*	*31.12.–4*
	£	£	£	£	£
Net present value of minimum lease payments discounted at 16%	50,000	40,271	28,890	15,576	—
Deferred liability	40,271	28,890	15,576	—	—
Current liability	9,729	11,381	13,314	15,576	—

Creditors: Amounts falling due after more than one year:

Obligation under finance lease:

	In the accounts for year ended				
	31.12.–0	*31.12.–1*	*31.12.–2*	*31.12.–3*	*31.12.–4*
	£	£	£	£	£
Deferred liability (see above)	40,271	28,890	15,576	—	—

Note:
ED29—Accounting for leases and hire purchase contracts requires the total of minimum lease payments to be disclosed, showing future finance charges being separately deducted. Thus only method (a) above complies with *ED29.*

(3) A note to the accounts would disclose the following:

Future minimum lease rentals to which the company is committed under a finance lease are:

	In the accounts for year ended				
	31.12.–0	*31.12.–1*	*31.12.–2*	*31.12.–3*	*31.12.–4*
	£	£	£	£	£
Year ending 31 Dec.					
19–1	17,164	—	—	—	—
19–2	17,164	17,164	—	—	—
19–3	17,164	17,164	17,164	—	—
19–4	17,164	17,164	17,164	17,164	—
	68,656	51,492	34,328	17,164	—
Less: Finance charges allocated to future periods	18,656	11,221	5,438	1,588	—
	50,000	40,271	28,890	15,576	

ANSWER C2

(a) *Effect of leasing transaction on balance sheet as at 30 Jun. 19–1*
Under (i) there would be no amounts shown relating to the transaction in the balance sheet, but the note would show that at 1 Jul. 19–0

the company entered into a four-year non-cancellable financial lease. Sums payable under the terms of this lease at 30 Jun. 19–1 are £120,000 including £30,000 payable within one year.

Under (ii) the difference from the balance sheet under (i) would be:

Working

Working		£
3	Fixed assets	80,000
2	Creditors: Amounts falling due within one year	15,000
4	Capital and reserves	(10,000)
2	Creditors: Amounts falling due after more than one year	75,000

(b) *Return on shareholders' funds*

Working		*(i)*	*(ii)*
4	Post-taxation profit for year / Shareholders' funds at 1 Jul. 19-0	$\frac{74,000}{200,000} \times 100$	$\frac{64,000}{200,000} \times 100$
		= 37%	= 32%

(c) If leases are written off against profits as the rent payments fall due and disclosure is restricted to that required by the *Companies Acts* the following problems arise:

Profit and loss account

(i) No distinction is made between the usage (depreciation) of the asset and the cost of finance (interest).

(ii) The charge for a year, the annual rent, does not necessarily equate to the aggregate of the usage (exhausted capital cost) plus the cost of finance. This is particularly so where the primary lease period (when the bulk of the rent is paid) is much shorter than the useful life of the asset.

Balance sheet

(i) The source of lease finance does not appear on the balance sheet.

(ii) The leased assets (which may be very material) do not appear as fixed assets on the balance sheet.

The effect of this is to make evaluation of the lessees' accounts very difficult, e.g. gearing. In many cases it is little short of misrepresentation.

Financial leases are very popular and growing. They are attractive for corporation tax purposes as the lessor retains the legal ownership of the asset (and can, therefore, obtain 100% first year allowances) and the lessee is able to charge the rent to the P & L a/c (and can, deduct it as a Sch.DI expense). They cannot be ignored by accountants.

A general principle of good accountancy is that accounts should display the substance of a transaction in preference to its legal nature. The substance is that the lessee has acquired a fixed asset which he is paying for over an extended period. The accounts should reflect this fact. However, this good accounting practice will not tend to be followed by companies until a standard is issued because lessees like to have *off balance sheet finance* which gives an apparently lower (better) loan to equity ratio (gearing) than is the true position.

Workings

1. *Spreading of interest using 'rule of 78'*

Period over which payments are being made is four years. First payment on 1 Jul. 19–0, effectively a deposit.

	£
Interest charge:	
Total payments 5 × £30,000	150,000
Capital cost	100,000
	50,000

Allocation year ended 30 Jun:

19–1 $\frac{4}{10} \times £50,000 = £20,000$

19–2 $\frac{3}{10} \times £50,000 = £15,000$

19–3 $\frac{2}{10} \times £50,000 = £10,000$

19–4 $\frac{1}{10} \times £50,000 = £5,000$

2. *Capital sum outstanding*

	Balance b/f	*Repayment*	*Interest*	*Balance c/f*	
	£	£	£	£	
1.7.–0	100,000	(30,000)	20,000	90,000	30.6.–1
1.7.–1	90,000	(30,000)	15,000	75,000	30.6.–2
1.7.–2	75,000	(30,000)	10,000	55,000	30.6.–3
1.7.–3	55,000	(30,000)	5,000	30,000	30.6.–4
1.7.–4	30,000	(30,000)			

At 30 Jun. 19–1:

Current liability = £90,000 – £75,000 = £15,000
Deferred liability = £75,000

3. *Addition to fixed asset*

	£
Cost	100,000
Depreciation 1/5 × £100,000	20,000
	80,000

4. *Profit for the year*

	(a) (i)	(a) (ii)
	£	£
Existing profit	50,000	50,000
Additional profit after taxation		
60% × £40,000	24,000	24,000
Add: Back lease payments		30,000
Less: Depreciation		(20,000)
Finance charge		(20,000)
	74,000	64,000

Deferred taxation consequences under (a) (ii) have been ignored.

ANSWER C3. STEELPARTS LTD

(a) The terms operating lease and finance lease are defined in *ED 29 Accounting for leases and hire purchase contracts.*
A finance lease is a lease that transfers substantially all the risks and rewards of ownership of an asset to the lessee. Normally a lease will be treated as a finance lease if the present value of the lease payments is equal to 90% or more of the cash price of the leased asset: *para. 12 ED 29.* In practice a finance lease provides a similar situation to where a business purchases an asset and obtains a loan to finance the acquisition.
An operating lease is a lease other than a finance lease: *para. 14 ED 29.* The commercial substance of an operating lease is similar to that which exists where a business rents an asset.

(b) (i) *Actuarial method*
Balance sheet extract for years ending:

Notes	*31.12.–1*	*31.12.–2*
	£	£
2. (a) Fixed assets		
Tangible assets		
Leased machine under finance lease	72,000	48,000
3. (b) Creditors: Amounts falling due within one year		
Obligation under finance lease (working 3)	22,112	25,316
4. (c) Creditors: Amounts falling due after more than one year		
Obligation under finance lease (working 3)	39,575	14,259

Profit and loss account extract for years ending

	31.12.–1	*31.12.–2*
	£	£
(a) Depreciation charge	24,000	24,000
(b) Finance charge under finance lease (working 2)	10,687	7,888

Notes to the accounts (required by ED 29: Accounting for leases and hire purchase contracts)

1. *Accounting policies note*

An amount equivalent to the cost of certain machinery leased under a finance lease is included in fixed assets and depreciated in accordance with the company's normal rates.

Outstanding lease instalments, excluding interest are shown under creditors. Interest is charged to profit and loss account by half-annual instalments over the term of the finance lease.

2. *Tangible fixed assets*

	19–1	*19–2*
	£	£
Leased machine at cost	96,000	96,000
Less: Accumulated depreciation ($\frac{1}{4} \times$ 96,000 pa)	24,000	48,000
	72,000	48,000

3. *Creditors: Amounts falling due within one year*

	19–1	*19–2*
	£	£
Obligation under finance lease:		
Minimum lease payments	30,000	30,000
Future finance charges	7,888	4,684
	22,112	25,316

4. *Creditors: Amounts falling due after more than one year*

	19–1	*19–2*
	£	£
Obligation under finance lease:		
Minimum lease payments	45,000	15,000
Future finance charges	5,425	741
	39,575	14,259

5. *Leasing commitments*

The future minimum lease payments to which the company is committed as at 31 Dec. 19–1 under a finance lease are as follows:

Year ending 31 Dec.	
	£
19–2	30,000
19–3	30,000
19–4	15,000
	75,000
Less: Finance charges allocated to future periods (7,888 + 5,425)	13,313
	61,687

NB: A similar note would appear in the 19–2 accounts but with the lease payments of £30,000 for 19–2 deleted and future finance charges reduced to £5,425.

Workings:

1. *Interest rate implicit in lease*

	£
Fair value of leased asset	96,000
Less: First payment (effectively a deposit)	15,000
Present value of lease payments	81,000

$$\text{Cumulative discount factor} = \frac{81,000}{15,000} = 5.4$$

From annuity tables, a cumulative discount factor of 5.4 in respect of equal payments made over 7 periods indicates an interest rate of approximately 7% per period. Here, the period between payments is six months, therefore the interest rate is 7% per half year.

2. *Interest (actuarial method)*

Half-year	*Capital*	*Interest 7%*	*Sub-total*	*Cash*	*Balance*
	£	£	£	£	£
1	81,000	5,670	86,670	15,000	71,670
2	71,670	5,017	76,687	15,000	61,687
		10,687			
3	61,687	4,318	66,005	15,000	51,005
4	51,005	3,570	54,575	15,000	39,575
		7,888			
5	39,575	2,770	42,345	15,000	27,345
6	27,345	1,914	29,259	15,000	14,259
		4,684			
7	14,259	741	15,000	15,000	Nil

3. *Creditors*

	19–1	*19–2*
	£	£
Capital outstanding at end of year	61,687	39,575
Less: Capital outstanding at end of next year	39,575	14,259
Capital repayable within one year	22,112	25,316

(b) (ii) *Sum of digits method*

Balance sheet extract for years ending

	31.12.–1	*31.12.–2*
	£	£
(a) Fixed assets		
Tangible assets		
Leased machine under finance lease (as in (i))	72,000	48,000
(b) Creditors: Amounts falling due within one year		
Obligation under finance lease (working 2)	22,285	25,715
(c) Creditors: Amounts falling due after more than one year		
Obligation under finance lease (working 3)	39,858	14,143

Profit and loss account extract for years ending:

	31.12.–1	*31.12.–2*
	£	£
(a) Depreciation charge (as in (i))	24,000	24,000
(b) Finance charge under finance lease (working 1)	11,143	7,715

NB: In order to comply with ED 29, notes to the accounts similar to those given under the actuarial method will be required.

Workings

1. *Interest* (*Sum of digits method*)

Interest charge:

	£
Total payments 8 × £15,000	120,000
Capital cost	96,000
	24,000

Period over which payments are being made is 7 half-years. The first payment on 1 Jan. 19–1 is effectively a deposit.

Half-year

		£
1	7/28 × £24,000	6,000
2	6/28 × £24,000	5,143
		11,143

		£
3	5/28 × £24,000	4,286
4	4/28 × £24,000	3,429
		7,715
5	3/28 × £24,000	2,571
6	2/28 × £24,000	1,714
		4,285
7	1/28 × £24,000	857

2. *Creditors: Amounts falling due within one year*

	19–1	*19–2*
	£	£
Minimum lease payments	30,000	30,000
Future finance charges	7,715	4,285
	22,285	25,715

3. *Creditors: Amounts falling due after more than one year*

	19–1	*19–2*
	£	£
Minimum lease payments	45,000	15,000
Future finance charges	5,142	857
	39,858	14,143

ANSWER C4. THE HARD UP MANUFACTURING CO LTD

(a) *Finance leases*

A finance lease is defined in ED 29: as *a lease that transfers substantially all the risks and rewards of ownership of an asset to the lessee.*

The exposure draft then goes on to look at what is meant by a transfer of risks and rewards. *It should be presumed that such a transfer of risks and rewards occurs if at the start of a lease the present value of the minimum lease payments, including any initial payment, amounts to substantially all (normally 90% or more) of the fair value of the leased asset to the lessor at the start of the lease: para. 12 ED 29.*

If the above test is satisfied, then the lease will normally be treated as a finance lease. However, the test is not conclusive, as the presumption that the lease should be classified as a finance lease may be rebutted if it can be shown that the lease does not in fact transfer substantially all the risks and rewards of ownership to the lessee.

In practice, the following criteria may be used to distinguish finance leases from operating leases:

	Finance lease	*Operating lease*
(1)	One lease exists for the whole useful life of the asset.	The lease period is less than the useful life of the asset. The lessor relies on subsequent leasing or eventual sale of the asset to cover his capital outlay and show a profit.
(2)	The lessor does not usually deal directly in this type of asset.	The lessor may very well carry on a trade in this type of asset.
(3)	The lessor does not retain the risks or rewards of ownership.	The lessor is normally responsible for repairs and maintenance.
(4)	The lease agreement cannot be cancelled. The lessee has a liability for all payments.	The lease can sometimes be cancelled at short notice.
(5)	The substance of the transaction is the purchase of the asset by the lessee financed by a loan from the lessor.	the substance of the transaction is the short-term rental of an asset.

(b) *Charge to profit and loss account—payday basis*

Lease payments written off as they are incurred:

Year ended 31 Dec.	*19–9*	*19–10*
	£	£
Item A	10,000	10,000
Item B	15,000	15,000
	25,000	25,000

(c) *Charge to profit and loss account—loan basis*

Lease payments treated as part capital part loan interest

Years ended 31 Dec.	*19–9*	*19–10*
	£	£
Depreciation:		
Item A—£80,000/10	8,000	8,000
Item B—£117,000/12	9,750	9,750
	17,750	17,750

	19–9	*19–10*
	£	£
Loan interest:		
Item A—per question	2,545	2,182
Item B—per question	5,400	4,800
	7,945	6,982
Totals	25,695	24,732

Note: It is assumed that the terms of the lease for item B include a secondary lease period for negligible rental which brings the full term of the lease to at least 12 years.

(d) *Balance sheets*

(i) Accounting policy note: *SSAP 2:*
The capital element of leased asset repayments is treated as a separate category within fixed assets. Depreciation of fixed assets is consistent with the normal company policy.

(ii) Fixed assets:

	19–9	*19–10*
	£	£
Leased machinery:		
Cost (working (i))	197,000	197,000
Depreciation (working (ii))	51,500	69,250
Net book value	145,500	127,750

(iii) Creditors: Amounts falling due within one year:
Obligations under finance leases

	19–9	*19–10*
	£	£
Minimum lease payments	25,000	25,000
Less: Future finance charges	6,982	6,018
	18,018	18,982

(iv) Creditors: Amounts falling due after more than one year:
Obligations under finance leases

	19–9	*19–10*
	£	£
Minimum lease payments	155,000	130,000
Less: Future finance charges	22,255	16,237
	132,745	113,763

The following would be disclosed in a note:
Details of creditors not wholly repayable within five years:

	19–9	*19–10*
	£	£
Net liability for lease rentals payable in annual instalments	150,763	132,745
Less: Amounts due within one year	18,018	18,982
	132,745	113,763
Instalments of lease rentals not payable within five years	51,035	28,200

(v) A note to the accounts would disclose the following:
The future minimum lease payments to which the company is committed as at 31 Dec. 19–10 under finance leases are as follows:

Year ending 31 Dec.	£
19–11	25,000
19–12	25,000
19–13	25,000
19–14	25,000
19–15	25,000
19–16 and after	30,000
	155,000
Less: Finance charges allocated to future periods	22,255
	132,745

Workings:

	19–9		*19–10*
	£		£
(i) Cost: Item A	80,000		80,000
Item B	117,000		117,000
	197,000		197,000
(ii) Depreciation:			
Item A (4 × £8,000)	32,000	(5 × £8,000)	40,000
Item B (2 × £9,750)	19,500	(3 × £9,750)	29,250
	51,500		69,250

(iii) Future finance charges

Year	*Item A*	*Item B*	*19–9*	*19–10*
	£	£	£	£
19–10	2,182	4,800	6,982	—
19–11	1,818	4,200	6,018	6,018
19–12	1,454	3,600	5,054	5,054
19–13	1,091	3,000	4,091	4,091
19–14	727	2,400	3,127	3,127
19–15	365	1,800	2,165	2,165
19–16		1,200	1,200	1,200
19–17		600	600	600
Total finance charges			29,237	22,255
Less: Payable within one year			6,982	6,018
Payable after more than one year			22,255	16,237

(e) *Treatment of financial lease*

If leases are written off against profits as the rent payments fall due and disclosure is restricted to that required by the *Companies Acts* the following problems arise:

Profit and loss account:

(i) No distinction is made between the usage (depreciation) of the asset and the cost of finance (interest).

(ii) The charge for a year, the annual rent, does not necessarily equate to the aggregate of the usage (exhausted capital cost) plus the cost of finance. This is particularly so where the primary lease period (when the bulk of the rent is paid) is much shorter than the useful life of the asset.

Balance sheet:

(i) The source of lease finance does not appear on the balance sheet.

(ii) The leased assets (which may be very material) do not appear as fixed assets on the balance sheet.

The effect of this is to make evaluation of the lessees' accounts very difficult, e.g. gearing. In many cases it is little short of misrepresentation.

Financial leases are very popular and growing. They are attractive for corporation tax purposes as the lessor retains the legal ownership of the asset (and can therefore obtain 100% first year allowances) and the lessee is able to charge the rent to the P & L a/c (and can therefore deduct it as a Sch.DI expense). The right to claim first year allowances for financial lessors of private cars has been stopped for contracts entered into after Jun. 1979: s.14 F(No. 2) A 1979 and the granting of first year allowances on other leased assets has been somewhat restricted by ss.64 to 73 FA1980, but such allowances will usually be available for machinery and plant leased for the purposes of a trade. They cannot be ignored by accountants.

A general principle of good accountancy is that accounts should display the substance of a transaction in preference to its legal nature. The substance is that the lessee has acquired a fixed asset which he is paying for over an extended period. The accounts should reflect this fact. This should be mandatory but the publication of ED 29: Accounting for leases and hire purchase contracts was delayed because:

(i) Lessees like to have *off balance sheet finance* which gives an apparently lower (better) loan to equity ratio (gearing) than is the true position.

(ii) Both lessors and lessees fear that the capitalisation of financial lease fixed assets in the lessees' balance sheet will quickly lead to the withdrawal of first year allowances from the lessor.

ANSWER C5

Part (1)

(a) The terms operating lease and finance lease are defined in *ED 29: Accounting for leases and hire purchase contracts.* A finance lease is a lease that transfers substantially all the risks and rewards of ownership of an asset to the lessee. Normally a lease will be treated as a finance lease if the present value of the lease payments is equal to 90% or more of the cash price of the leased asset: *para.12 ED 29.* An operating lease is a lease other than a finance lease: *para.14 ED 29.*

They may be further distinguished as follows:

	Operating lease	*Finance lease*
(1)	The lease period is less than the useful life of the asset. The lessor relies on subsequent leasing or eventual sale of the asset to cover his capital outlay and show a profit.	One lease exists for the whole useful life of the asset and rentals receivable are sufficient to recoup capital outlay and show a profit.
(2)	The lessor may very well carry on a trade in this type of asset.	The lessor does not usually deal directly in this type of asset.
(3)	The lessor is normally responsible for repairs and maintenance	The lessor does not retain the risks or rewards of ownership.
(4)	The lease can sometimes be cancelled at short notice.	The lease agreement cannot be cancelled. The lessee has a liability for all payments.
(5)	The substance of the transaction is the short-term rental of an asset.	The substance of the transaction is the purchase of the asset by the lessee financed by a loan from the lessor.

(b) Rowlf Ltd has leased plant and vehicles. The terms of the lease apparently fall within the definition of a *finance lease*. Traditionally, most companies have tended to write off such premiums to profit and loss account as the premiums were paid. The Companies Act 1967 required disclosure of amounts, if material, relating to hire of plant and machinery.

Rowlf, however, has treated the transaction in a similar way to an acquisition by hire purchase. The effect is to:

(i) show plant and vehicles under fixed assets;
(ii) show amounts owing in respect of capital outstanding; and
(iii) charge depreciation and interest to profit and loss account.

The arguments in favour of this treatment are as follows:

(1) The lessee (Rowlf Ltd) has decided to acquire the property rights (not the legal title) to the use of the plant and vehicles. Finance leasing may therefore be regarded as an alternative to other forms of finance such as hire purchase. If accounting is based on the substance of the transaction rather than the legal form, then the balance sheet should show the respective asset (plant) and liability (obligation to pay future rentals to the finance company).
(2) The above accounting treatment will make it easier to determine return on capital employed for the company. *Off-balance sheet financing* (the traditional approach to finance leases) makes interpretation and comparability of accounts difficult and sometimes impossible (if only the minimum information required by law is disclosed).
(3) Rowlf's accounting treatment also makes borrowing ratios (including gearing) more meaningful. Unless finance leases are capitalised by lessees, there is a danger that borrowing ratios will be distorted. This point came up in the Department of Trade report on Court Line (see *Accountancy* May 1978, p, 95), where at 30 Sep. 1973, the Court Line group's off-balance sheet finance in respect of non-cancellable leasing commitments totalled approximately £40 million.
(4) It complies with ED 29: Accounting for leases and hire purchase contracts.

Part (2)

(*a*) The charge to profit and loss account for each of the first three years would be £10,000.

(*i*) The minimum legal disclosure requirements are: *para. 53(b) Sch.1 CA 1981:*
'The amount, charged to revenue in respect of sums payable in respect of the hire of plant and machinery' and
(ii) *para. 50(5) Sch.1 CA 1981* which states;
Particulars shall also be given of any other financial commitments, which

(*a*) *have not been provided for, and*
(*b*) *are relevant to assessing the company's state of affairs.*

The minimum requirements are, therefore, to show the rentals payable (£10,000) as a note in arriving at the operating profit for the year. (In practice were this the only hire transaction involved, it is likely to be ignored as being immaterial), and to show the future minimum lease payments to which the company is committed.
The Companies Acts do not require the lessee to capitalise the leased plant, or to specifically reflect leasing commitments as a liability in the balance sheet.

(b) *Charge to profit and loss account*
(i) Sum of digits approach:

Year	*Depreciation*	*Finance charge*	*Total*
	£	£	£
1	4,167	2,692	6,859
2	4,167	1,667	5,834
3	4,166	641	4,807
4	4,167	—	4,167
5	4,167	—	4,167
6	4,166	—	4,166
	25,000	5,000	30,000

(ii) Actuarial approach:

Year	*Depreciation*	*Finance charge*	*Total*
	£	£	£
1	4,167	2,782	6,949
2	4,167	1,717	5,884
3	4,166	501	4,667
4	4,167	—	4,167
5	4,167	—	4,167
6	4,166	—	4,166
	25,000	5,000	30,000

(c) Balance sheet—first year:
Fixed assets:

	Cost	*Depreciation*		
	£	£	£	
Plant	25,000	4,167	20,833	
Creditors: Amounts falling due within one year:				
Capital payments under a leasing agreement				8,283
Creditors: Amounts falling due after more than one year:				
Capital payments under a leasing agreement				6,999

Workings—b(i) (sum of digits)

(1) Depreciation = 1/6 × £25,000 = £4,167
(2) Interest—sum of digits

$$= 1 + 2 + 3 + \ldots + 11 + 12 = \frac{12(13)}{2} = 78$$

Quarter		£	£
1	12/78 × £5,000	769	
2	11/78	705	
3	10/78	641	
4	9/78	577	
			2,692
5	8/78	513	
6	7/78	449	
7	6/78	385	
8	5/78	320	
			1,667
9	4/78	256	
10	3/78	192	
11	2/78	128	
12	1/78	65	
			641
			5,000

Working—b(ii) (actuarial method)

(1) Interest—actuarial method

Quarter	*Capital*	*Interest $3\frac{1}{2}\%$ per quarter*	*Sub total*	*Cash*	*Balance*
	£	£	£	£	£
1	22,500	787	23,287	2,500	20,787
2	20,787	728	21,515	2,500	19,015
3	19,015	666	19,681	2,500	17,181
4	17,181	601	17,782	2,500	15,282
		2,782			
5	15,282	535	15,817	2,500	13,317
6	13,317	466	13,783	2,500	11,283
7	11,283	395	11,678	2,500	9,178
8	9,178	321	9,499	2,500	6,999
		1,717			
9	6,999	245	7,244	2,500	4,744
10	4,744	166	4,910	2,500	2,410
11	2,410	90	2,500	2,500	—
		501			
Total		5,000			

(2)

Annuity (11 periods)	*Present value ($3\frac{1}{2}\%$)*
£	£
1	9
2,500	22,500

Working—(c)

	£
Capital outstanding at end of first year	15,282
Less: Capital repayable within 12 months (balancing figure)	8,283
Capital outstanding at end of second year	6,999

Note: It is assumed that the lease is entered into on the first day of the accounting period and that the payments (other than the first one) are paid on the last day of each quarter.

ANSWER D1. TEXAS, BLACK AND GOLD

(a) *Revenue accounts*

	(1) Successful efforts £000	*(2) Full cost £000*	*(3) Discovery value £000*
Sales	600	600	
Value of oil discovered			1,060
Production costs	(120)	(120)	
Exploration and development expenditure written off	(450)	(353)	(780)
Amortisation of licence	(100)	(100)	(100)
Profit (loss) on ordinary activities	(70)	27	180

Summarised balance sheets

	£000	*£000*	*£000*
Fixed assets			
Intangible assets			
Exploration and development costs	390	487	60
Licence at book value	400	400	400
	790	887	460
Current assets			
Stocks: oil reserves	—	—	580
Creditors: Amounts falling due within one year.			
Bank overdraft	(260)	(260)	(260)
Net current assets (liabilities)	(260)	(260)	320
Total assets less current liabilities	530	627	780
Capital and reserves			
Called up share capital	600	600	600
Profit and loss account	(70)	27	180
	530	627	780

(b) (i) *Suitability of methods for internal reporting*

The full cost method is not fully satisfactory for internal reporting because it deals in total with the recoverability of exploration and development expenditure whereas management must be aware of the profitability or otherwise of particular areas of exploration.

The successful efforts approach provides this information, but also gives an incomplete picture because part of the cost of a successful exploration policy is drilling in areas which in the event yield no oil. No company can hope to have success in every area and in the final analysis, a comparison must be made between all exploration costs and the net oil revenue resulting therefrom.

Reserve recognition accounting is a new method of reporting proposed by the SEC in the USA and attempts to provide this comparison. However, it requires a great deal of subjective opinion as regards (a) the quantity and (b) the valuation of discovered reserves of oil.

(ii) *Suitability of methods for external reporting*

At the present time both full cost and successful efforts are in general use. New companies tend to prefer the first and the larger established companies the second. Neither is entirely satisfactory for the reasons outlined above, the first being sometimes imprudent, the second on occasions over-conservative. Reserve recognition accounting is a form of current value accounting but is being resisted by oil companies and their auditors because of the significant estimation difficulties involved. Perhaps more important than the specific method adopted is whether sufficient details are disclosed to enable a proper assessment of the results to be made.

SSAP 13 (research and development expenditure) does not deal with the subject of exploration and development expenditure.

Workings

(1) *Cash account*

	£000		*£000*
Share capital	600	Licenses	500
Sales	600	E and D costs	840
Balance c/d	260	Production costs	120
	1,460		1,460

(2) *Income*

(i) Sales income 120,000 barrels @ £5 = £600,000

(ii) Discovery value of oil

	£
Selling price	5
Production costs	1
	4

		£000
Reserves discovered		
Area 1	45,000 @ £4	180
Area 2	220,000 @ £4	880
		1,060

(3) *Production costs*

120,000 barrels at £1 = £120,000

These should be written off as incurred.

Under the discovery value method these costs represent the difference between the sales income and the discovery value of the oil sold.

(4) *Exploration and development expenditure*

(a) *Successful efforts*

		£000
Area 1	E and D incurred	400
	Amount to be carried forward should be restricted to the NRV of the oil discovered	
	45,000 × (£5 – £1)	180
	written off	220

		£000
Area 2	E and D costs incurred	330
	Amount to be carried forward	
	$\frac{100,000}{220,000} \times £330,000$	150
	(not restricted by NRV of £400,000) written off this year	180

		£000
Area 3	No reserves found	
	All E and D written off	50

	£000
Total charge for year (220 + 180 + 50)	450

Area 4 Carried forward until area fully explored.

(b) *Full cost*

	£000
Total E and D costs incurred on areas fully explored	780
Amount to be carried forward $\frac{145,000}{265,000} \times £780,000$	427
(not restricted by NRV of 145,000 @ £4)	
Charge for the year	353

(c) *Reserve recognition accounting*

All E and D costs of areas fully explored written off

(5) *Amortisation of licence*

	£000
20% × £500,000	100

ANSWER D2. OLDAGE CONCERN LTD

Accounting for pension costs

(a) An externally funded scheme is one where benefits are provided from a separate fund held by trustees under an irrevocable deed of trust. Normally the trustees would receive regular contributions from the employer and members of the scheme and the surplus receipts over current benefits payable would be invested for the provision of future benefits. The trustees may make use of the services of an insurance company.

An internally financed scheme is one where pension benefits are paid direct by the employer to the pensioner. The employer should set up a provision in his balance sheet to meet the cost of future pension benefits. This may or may not be matched by specifically earmarked assets.

(b) Under a discontinuance basis valuation, the liability for pensions is the present value of benefits earned by employees and pensioners assuming that current employees cease to be members of the scheme at the valuation date and that pension benefits are paid to them from normal retirement age. Under an accrued benefits basis valuation, the liability for pension benefits is the present value of the benefits to which pensioners are entitled and current employees will become entitled to on retirement. Unlike the discontinuance valuation the accrued benefits valuation takes into account estimates of future salary increases and earnings on investments held by a pension scheme.

Financial statements are prepared on the basis of the *going concern* concept under *SSAP 2.* This assumes that the enterprise will continue in operational existence in the foreseeable future and that there is no necessity to liquidate or curtail significantly the level of operation. The cost of providing pension benefits should similarly be based on the going concern basis. This would require the use of the accrued benefits valuation method since only this takes into account the estimated benefits to which employees will become entitled on their retirement.

Additionally, since pension benefits are part of the remuneration package paid to employees the *matching* concept would suggest it to be appropriate to relate the cost of providing pension benefits to the salaries paid to employees in an accounting period. Under the *consistency* concept it would be reasonable for the normal cost of an employee's pension to be met by annual charges to the profit and loss account of a fixed percentage of his salary. Under the accrued benefits method the cost of providing benefits expressed as a percentage of pensionable salary should remain relatively stable over the anticipated lives of members of the scheme. This would not be the case under the discontinuance basis where the percentage cost for an employee would usually increase from year to year because of:

(i) equal rights attaching to all years service despite the different investment periods of each annual contribution; and
(ii) cost of pension benefits attributable to subsequent promotional or service increments in salary not being spread over the whole of pensionable service of members of the scheme.

The discontinuance basis might nevertheless be relevant to users of financial statements where it revealed a deficiency, since this could accrue as an immediate liability if the employer decided to close the scheme. It would also be of significance where a takeover or liquidation of the employer's business were imminent.

(c) The benefit of an employee to his employer is in the services given during the employee's working life. The accruals concept of accounting requires that the cost of providing an employee's pension should be written off over his working life by appropriate annual charges. This principle precludes *terminal funding* or *pay as you go* methods of accounting.

(d) Since financial statements are prepared on the basis of the going concern concept any provision in a pension scheme giving the employer the arbitrary right to suspend or reduce his obligations towards the scheme should be ignored for the purposes of determining the appropriate accounting treatment.

(e) (i) As an actuarial valuation is in the nature of a revision of an accounting estimate it would not be appropriate, under *SSAP 6*, to treat any part of the experienced surplus or deficiency as a prior year adjustment unless there was a fundamental error in a previous valuation.

Under normal accounting principles the surplus or deficiency would therefore be taken immediately to profit and loss account. However, since this would give rise to an erratic annual charge, and pension costs differ from most other accounting costs in that they are an assessment of a long term trend, there is an argument for spreading corrections in estimates of the cost of pension benefits over a longer period of time as the liability does not crystallise until the benefits become payable.

(ii) Changes in actuarial assumptions for future experience give rise to future costs and it is therefore appropriate to take account of these costs by adjusting the future annual charge for pension benefits.

(iii) As in (i) a prior year adjustment would be inappropriate.

Where the benefits are to be paid directly by the employer and there is no identifiable fund of assets on which to draw to pay the benefits, the employer should obviously recognise the actuarially assessed cost of them by an immediate charge to the profit and loss account, since this cost relates to retired employees whose benefit to the company ended with their retirement.

Where the benefits are to be paid from an externally funded scheme or an internally financed scheme where there is an identifiable fund of assets, there will be assets which may be drawn upon to meet the costs. If the next actuarial valuation reveals a deficiency there is a strong argument in favour of charging immediately to profit and loss any amount which relates to providing pensions to past employees. However, there are some who, even in this case, would favour spreading the cost over a number of years. This would clearly be a departure from normal accounting principles.

(f) Oldage Concern Ltd would show in its balance sheet an asset of £25,000 in respect of prepaid pension fund contributions.

ANSWER D3. POST BALANCE SHEET EVENTS AND CONTINGENCIES

(a) *Definition of a post balance sheet event*

An event, favourable or unfavourable, which occurs between the balance sheet date and the date on which the financial statements are approved by the directors.

(b) *Difference between an 'adjusting event' and a 'non-adjusting event'*

An adjusting event is a post balance sheet event which provides evidence of conditions existing at the balance sheet date and which needs to be reflected in the financial statements. Examples include subsequent information affecting provisions for bad debts and amounts received or receivable in respect of insurance claims which were in the course of negotiation at the balance sheet date.

A non-adjusting event is a post balance sheet event which concerns conditions which did not exist at the balance sheet date. It does not result in a revision of the amounts shown in the financial statements, but may need to be disclosed by way of a note to the financial statements. Examples include the issue of new share and loan capital, major changes in the composition of the company and the financial consequences of losses of fixed assets or stocks as a result of catastrophies such as fire or flood.

(c) *Definition of a 'contingency'*

A condition or situation which exists at the balance sheet date where the outcome will be confirmed only on the occurrence or non-occurrence of one or more uncertain future events.

ANSWER D4

(a) (1) Neither statement of depreciation policy gives meaningful information as to the actual rates of depreciation used. A range of 2% to 20% (Policy 1) is sufficiently wide to encompass most commonly used rates, and different rates should, therefore, be related to different assets. If fixed assets were not *depreciated over their estimated useful lives* (Policy 2), the accounts would not comply with fundamental accounting principles: *SSAP 2*, nor with *para. 18 sch.1 CA 1981.*

(2) Policy 2 does not state what method of depreciation is used.

(3) Policy 1 does not comply with *SSAP 4*, which specifically requires grants treated as deferred credits not to be shown as part of shareholders' funds. the credit should be taken to the profit and loss account on the same basis as that on which the fixed asset purchased is amortised, and in particular over the useful life of the asset.

(4) Depreciation should be allocated to accounting periods so as to charge a fair proportion to each accounting period during the expected useful life of the asset. Policy 1 may not ensure this for tools, dies, jigs and moulds.

(5) Buildings have a limited life and should be depreciated having regard to the same criteria as in the case of other fixed assets. Freehold land will not normally require a provision for depreciation. The cost or valuation figures for freehold property, therefore, need analysing between the land and building elements so that the latter may be depreciated. This does not appear to have been done by either company, although the first company may have no freehold, with long leaseholds accounting for the 2% rate.

(b) Depreciation is a measure of the wearing out, consumption or other loss of value of a fixed asset whether arising from use, effluxion of time or obsolescence through technology and market changes. The main purpose of the depreciation charge in the profit and loss account is, therefore, to allocate this depreciation as fairly as possible to the periods expected to benefit from the use of the asset. The charge is made in accordance with the accrual (or matching) concept under which revenue realised in an accounting period is compared with the costs or expenses of earning that revenue. Other reasons for the depreciation charge include (i) to keep funds in the business to provide for replacement, but this will not allow for inflation and (ii) to reduce the value of the asset in the balance sheet as the asset wears out, but this value may not equate to the market value.

(c) Financial statements are normally intended to be as helpful as possible to a wide audience, who requires as much consistency and comparability as is practicable between the financial statements of all enterprises. As soon as consistency or comparability is required between the financial statements of two or more enterprises, reasonable consistency of accounting treatment is also needed, e.g. in the depreciation of land and buildings.

The trend away from strict historical cost accounting (with, for example, the revaluation of certain assets becoming permissible) and the development of more complex corporate structures have resulted in an increase in the number of different accounting practices available to the extent that reasonable comparability has often become ineffective or impossible. It is in this context that Accounting Standards are required, not necessarily imposing uniformity but at least narrowing the choices, so as to make financial statements more helpful to users. In particular, depreciation is an important charge in most accounts and there is a need to ensure adequate disclosure of the relevant accounting policies.

Finally, there was a requirement to cover *IAS4* with a UK accounting standard.

(d) The requirements of the standard on depreciation are as follows:

(i) Provision for depreciation of fixed assets having a finite useful life should be made by allocating the cost (or revalued amount) less estimated residual value of the assets as fairly as possible to the periods expected to benefit from their use.

(ii) Where there is a revision of the estimated useful life of an asset, the unamortised cost should be charged over the revised remaining useful life.

(iii) If at any time the unamortised cost of an asset is seen to be irrecoverable in full, it should be written down immediately to the estimated recoverable amount, which should be charged over the remaining useful life.

(iv) Where there is a change from one method of depreciation to another, the unamortised cost of the asset should be written off over the remaining useful life on the new basis commencing with the period in which the change is made. The effect, if material, should be disclosed in the year of change.

(v) Where assets are revalued in the financial statements, the provision for depreciation should be based on the revalued amount and current estimate of remaining useful life, with disclosure in the year of change of the effect of revaluation, if material.

(vi) The following should be disclosed in the financial statements for each major class of depreciable assets:

(a) the depreciation methods used;
(b) the useful lives or the depreciation rates used;
(c) total depreciation allocated for the period;
(d) the gross amount of depreciable assets and the related accumulated depreciation.

(vii) The standard is applicable to financial statements of companies other than property companies, for periods starting on or after 1 Jan. 1978. The position with regard to property companies is governed by *SSAP 19: Accounting for investment properties*.

ANSWER D5. TECHNOLOGICAL COMPONENTS LTD

(a) (i) *Extract from accounting policies statement*

Depreciation
Depreciation has been calculated by reference to the expected lives of the assets concerned. The following rates of depreciation were applied:

Plant and machinery 50% reducing balance method

(ii) *Extract from balance sheet at 31 Dec. 19–7*
Included within fixed assets—plant and machinery totals:

	£
Cost	200,000
Accumulated depreciation	150,000
	50,000

(iii) *Extract from profit and loss account for the year ended 31 Dec. 19–7*
Included within total depreciation charge: £50,000

(b) Under historical cost accounting, assets are usually stated at their original or historical cost, less accumulated depreciation. However, a modification to the historical cost convention is permitted—audit reports often refer to the *historical cost concention as modified by the revaluation of certain assets.*

Such revaluations usually relate to freehold and leasehold properties although some companies occasionally incorporate revaluations of plant and machinery into their accounts.

For many items of plant and machinery, where there has been only gradual technological change, the use of suitable index numbers may provide an acceptable basis for a valuation.

However, there will be occasions where the application of index numbers to book figures will provide unrealistic results. This may occur, for example, where there has been rapid technological change. One solution in such cases is to adopt the concept of the modern equivalent asset, first put forward in *ED 18* (*Current cost accounting*) and subsequently referred to in the guidance notes to *SSAP 16* (*Current cost accounting*).

It is assumed that the valuation required is at 30 Sep. 19–8. *Para. 21 SSAP 12* (*Accounting for depreciation*) requires that where assets are revalued, depreciation after the revaluation date should be based on the revalued amount.

Calculation of valuation at 31 Dec. 19–8

The replacement for machine K has a service potential twice that of machine K:

	£	£
Current valuation of service potential of machine K if new is		
$£100{,}000 \times \dfrac{500{,}000}{1{,}000{,}000}$		50,000
Allowing for 2 years 9 months expired life on a reducing balance basis at a rate of 50%		
19–6 (12 months)	25,000	
19–7 (12 months)	12,500	
19–8 (9 months)	4,687	
		42,187
Revised valuation at 30 Sep. 19–8		7,813
Continuing with same depreciation rate:		
3 months depreciation to 31 Dec. 19–8 – 50% of £7,813 × 3/12 (It is assumed that time apportionment provides a reasonably acceptable result)		977
Written down value at 31 Dec. 19–8		6,836

At the date of valuation, 30 Sep. 19–8, it is important to ensure that £7,813 reflects a realistic value of the remaining service potential of the asset.

Tutorial note:

Strictly speaking, part (b) requires only a calculation. The explanations above are included because of the unusual nature of the situation.

(c) Fixed asset—cost or valuation account

	£		£
19–8			
Jan. 1 Balance b/f	200,000	Sep. 30 Revaluation reserve	192,187
		Dec. 31 Balance c/f	7,813
	200,000		200,000

Accumulated depreciation account

	£			£
		19–8		
Sep. 30 Revaluation reserve	168,750	Jan. 1	Balance b/f	150,000
Dec. 31 Balance c/f	977	Sep. 30	P & L a/c (depreciation)	18,750
		Dec. 31	P & L a/c (depreciation)	977
	169,727			169,727

Working

Depreciation, 9 months to 30 Sep. 19–8 = 50% × £50,000 × 9/12
= £18,750

Notes:

(i) Depreciation after 30 Sep. 19–8 is based on the revalued amount of £7,813 (*para. 21 SSAP 12*).

(ii) According to *para. 34 sch 1 CA 1981*, the deficit on revaluation of £23,437 (192,187 – 168,750) should be debited to revaluation reserve. However, best accounting practice would usually require the deficit to be debited direct to the profit and loss account, especially if this treatment can be justified as giving a more true and fair view.

(d) *Extract from statement of accounting policies*

Depreciation

The same note would be relevant as for part (a).

Profit and loss account

	£
Depreciation charge:	
Based on cost	18,750
Based on revalued amount	977
	19,727

Note to accounts

The effect of the revaluation of plant and machinery during the year is to reduce the depreciation charge by £5,273 (working 2).

Workings

(1) Deficit on revaluation of plant £192,187 – £168,750 = £23,437.

(2)

	£
Depreciation charged assuming no revaluation	
50% × £50,000	25,000
Less: Depreciation actually charged	19,727
	5,273

Balance sheet

	£
Fixed asset	
Tangible assets (see note)	6,836
Capital and reserves	
Revaluation reserve	(23,437)

Note to the accounts (comparatives ignored)

Tangible fixed assets	*Plant and machinery* £
Cost or valuation:	
Cost at 1 Jan. 19–8	200,000
Revaluation during year	192,187
Revaluation at 31 Dec. 19–8	7,813
Depreciation:	
Balance at 1 Jan. 19–8	150,000
Amount provided during year	19,727
Adjustment on revaluation during year	(168,750)
Balance at 31 Dec. 19–8	977
Net book value at 1 Jan. 19–8	50,000
Net book value at 31 Dec. 19–8	6,836

During the year ended 31 Dec. 19–8 an item of plant and machinery subject to rapid technological change was revalued by the directors on the basis of comparison with a modern equivalent asset:

Director's valuation 19–8	£7,813

The amount of plant and machinery (included above at valuation) determined according to the historical cost accounting rules is as follows:

	£
Cost	200,000
Accumulated depreciation (150,000 + 25,000)	175,000
Net book value at 31 Dec. 19–8	25,000

ANSWER D6. SSAP 13 AND 15

(a) (i) '*Research and development expenditure* means expenditure falling into one or more of the following broad categories.

(1) Pure (or basic) research: original investigation undertaken in order to gain new scientific or technical knowledge and understanding. Basic research is not primarily directed towards any specific practical aim or application;
(2) Applied research: original investigation undertaken in order to gain new scientific or technical knowledge and directed towards a specific practical aim or objective;
(3) Development: the use of scientific or technical knowledge in order to produce new or substantially improved materials, devices, products, processes, systems or services prior to the commencement of commercial production': *para. 18 SSAP 13.*

(ii) 'The cost of fixed assets acquired or constructed to provide facilities for research and development activities over a number of accounting periods should be capitalised and written off over their useful life.

Expenditure on pure and applied research (other than that referred to above) should be written off in the year of expenditure.

Development expenditure should be written off in the year of expenditure except in the circumstances given below when it may be deferred to future periods'; *paras. 19, 20, 21 SSAP 13.*

Where expenditure is carried forward on the balance sheet it should be disclosed separately and not included in current assets. Movements in the amount carried forward over the year should be disclosed and the accounting policy stated: *paras. 27, 28, 29 SSAP 13.*

Development expenditure may be carried forward if it can be related to a specific project which is technically feasible and appears commercially viable.

The anticipated future revenues must be budgeted to exceed all the costs of sales including the development costs to be carried forward.

Costs carried forward should be written off over the anticipated sales period starting with the period of commercial production.

(iii) The original exposure draft (ED 14) required all research and development costs (other than fixed assets) to be written off in the period in which they were incurred. This was neat, clear and simple to apply. However, it did breach the fundamental accounting concept of matching revenues with costs described as the *accruals* concept in *para. 14 SSAP 2.*

Following a very strong protest from the aircraft manufacturing industry where an immediate write off of all development expenditure would give rise to substantial losses and yield accounts which were probably neither true nor fair the Accounting Standards Committee withdrew ED 14 and published ED 17 which was later incorporated into *SSAP 13* described above. In certain carefully defined circumstances development expenditure may be carried forward.

(b) (i) Timing differences dealt with in *SSAP 15* arise under five main categories:

(1) short term timing differences from the use of the receipts and payments basis for taxation purposes and the accruals basis in financial statements; these differences normally reverse in the next accounting period;
(2) availability of capital allowances in taxation computations which are in excess of the related depreciation charges in financial statements;
(3) availability of stock relief is described as a timing difference in *SSAP 15.* However since the Finance Act 1981, stock relief for a company which is a going concern is never likely to be clawed back, so it is considered to be a permanent difference.
(4) revaluation surpluses on fixed assets for which a taxation charge does not arise until the gain is realised on disposal;
(5) surpluses on disposals of fixed assets which are subject to roll-over relief: *para. 6 SSAP 15.*

The quantum of each type of timing difference is calculated separately but the net charge or credit will be used to adjust the deferred taxation provision: *para. 7 SSAP 15.*

(ii) 'It will be reasonable to assume that timing differences will not reverse and tax liabilities will therefore not crystallise if, but only if, the company is a going concern and:

(1) the directors are able to foresee on reasonable evidence that no liability is likely to arise as a result of reversal of timing

differences for some considerable period (at least three years) ahead; and

(2) there is no indication that after this period the situation is likely to change so as to crystallise the liabilities': *para. 28 SSAP 15.*

(iii) Deferred taxation account balances should be shown separately in the balance sheet under 'provisions for liabilities and charges' and described as deferred taxation. They should not be shown as part of shareholders' funds. A note in the financial statements should indicate the nature and amount of the major elements of which the net balance is composed and a description of the method of calculation adopted.

Where there is a movement on the deferred taxation provision, it will be necessary to disclose the following in a note to the accounts:

(1) the balance at the beginning and end of the year,
(2) transfers to or from the provision during the year, and
(3) the source and application of the amounts transferred: *para. 46 sch. 1 CA 1981.*

Where amounts of deferred taxation arise which relate to movements on reserves (e.g. resulting from a revaluation of assets) the amounts transferred to or from deferred taxation account should be shown separately as part of such movements.

Where the value of an asset is shown by way of note on the face of or annexed to the financial statements and that value differs from the book value of the asset, the note should also show, if material, the tax implication which would result from the realisation of the asset at the balance sheet date at the stated value: *paras 37, 38 and 39 SSAP 15.*

The potential liability in respect of all timing differences should be shown by way of a note, distinguishing between the various principal categories of deferred tax and showing for each category the amount which has been provided in the accounts: *para. 33 SSAP 15.*

ANSWER D7. GOODWILL

(a) Goodwill arises when one business acquires another business as a going concern and the purchase consideration exceeds the value of the net tangible assets of the acquired business. Goodwill therefore, is different from any other type of asset. Unlike, say plant and machinery it cannot have an existence separate from the business. As the price paid for goodwill will depend upon the purchaser's expectations of future profits, goodwill is often calculated as the present value of the future super-profits of the business to be acquired. Super-profits are calculated as the excess profits over those required to provide a target rate of return on the net tangible assets.

In addition to purchased goodwill, a business may over the years generate its own goodwill, known as inherent goodwill. A cost cannot therefore be placed on such goodwill as any attempt to do so would be highly dependent on the subjective judgement of the valuer. Further the value of inherent goodwill is likely to fluctuate from year to year with the changing fortunes of the company's business.

For the above reasons only purchased goodwill is shown in a company's balance sheet.

(b) *ED30* identifies six methods of accounting for goodwill:

(i) *Carry it as an asset and write it off over a period of years through the profit and loss account*

Advantages:

(1) Treating goodwill as an asset on the balance sheet recognises the similarity in principle with other assets. Goodwill represents expenditure for a right to future profits.
(2) Writing goodwill off through the profit and loss account has the effect of matching the cost of an acquisition with the extra profits generated by that acquisition.

Disadvantages:

(1) Since non-purchased goodwill is not capitalised this method destroys comparability with other companies which have not made similar acquisitions and with other periods for the same enterprise when there is no write-off of goodwill.
(2) It is very difficult to determine the useful life of goodwill, so any period chosen for write-off will be arbitrary.

(ii) *As (i), but the write-off each year is direct to reserves*

Advantages:

(1) As advantage (1) above.
(2) Since the write-off is not through the profit and loss account comparability of profit figures is maintained with other enterprises and from year to year within the same enterprise.

Disadvantages:

(1) The process of amortisation implies that the item is an expense and therefore should be charged to the profit and loss account and not to reserves.
(2) The ASC rejects this method in *ED30*.

(iii) *Eliminate it against reserves immediately*

Advantages:

(1) Although goodwill is in principle similar to other assets it has several different characteristics. In particular, it cannot be

sold independently from the sale of the related assets and its value may disappear unpredictably due to effects outside the control of management. This method recognises the fact that it is not entirely prudent to carry such an item as an asset.
(2) The profit and loss account is not affected by the item, thus retaining comparability.

Disadvantages:

(1) The method may be excessively prudent.
(2) The write-off will form a realised loss which would restrict the distributable earnings of a company.

(iv) *Retain it as an asset with no write-off unless a permanent reduction in value becomes evident*

Advantages:

(1) This method recognises the fact that goodwill is constantly replenished by the normal operations of the business in generating further goodwill.
(2) Since the value of goodwill is maintained by normal operations its residual value will at least equal cost. Therefore following *SSAP 12* depreciation should be zero.
(3) If purchased goodwill is writen off there is effectively double counting. The profit and loss account would recognise the normal expense of generating non-purchased goodwill and in addition the expense of writing off purchased goodwill.

Disadvantages:

(1) Purchased goodwill is being constantly replaced, but it is replaced by non-purchased goodwill. Since non-purchased goodwill is not accounted for it is not valid to use it as an argument for maintaining purchased goodwill un-amortised in the balance sheet.
(2) The ASC rejects this method in *ED30.*
(3) It is contrary to the Companies Act 1981. Para. 21 Sch. 1 CA 1981 requires any goodwill treated as an asset to be written off over a period not exceeding its useful economic life.

(v) *Write it off against profits immediately*

This method is considered to be the same as method (i), except the period of write-off is nil. It therefore has the same advantages and disadvantages as that method.

(vi) *Show it as a deduction from shareholders' funds which may be amortised or carried forward indefinitely*

Advantages:

(1) This method avoids the question of the prudence of carrying goodwill as an asset.

(2) Distributable reserves do not suffer by the writing off of goodwill.

Disadvantages:

(1) The method is ambiguous. It is tantamount to writing off purchased goodwill against reserves while implying that the goodwill remains available in the form of an asset.
(2) It is rejected by the ASC in *ED30*.
(3) It is contrary to the Companies Act 1981. The balance sheet formats in Sch. 1 CA 1981 show goodwill as an intangible fixed asset, not as a deduction from reserves.

ANSWER D8. POST BALANCE SHEET EVENTS

(1) *Sale of major property*
The effect of the sale would be an adjusting event under *SSAP 17* since it relates to conditions existing at the balance sheet date. This means that the effect of the sale would be reflected by adjusting the figures in the financial statements for the year ended 31 December 19-1. The profit on disposal of £150,000 would be an extraordinary item since it (presumably) derives from an activity outside the ordinary activities of the business and it should be stated net of any attributable taxation.
(2) *Dividend from subsidiary*
This is an adjusting event since it concerns conditions existing at the balance sheet date (because the dividend was in *respect of* the year ended on 31 December 19-1). The dividend would be reflected in the holding company's own accounts as a debtor in respect of the dividend receivable and as dividend income in the profit and loss account. However, it would not affect the consolidated financial statements.
(3) *Closure of division*
If the closure was not anticipated at the year end, then it would not normally be an adjusting event. However, if it gives an indication that application of the going concern concept to the whole or a material part of the company is not appropriate, then it would give rise to changes in the amounts to be included in the financial statements. Such changes would involve restating the assets of the mail order division on a break up basis and making provision for other closure costs. The loss arising on the restatement and other costs would be reflected as an extraordinary item net of the attributable tax effect.

If the closure was not anticipated and does not give an indication that application of the going concern concept is not appropriate, then the effect of the closure should be disclosed by way of note to the financial statements since it is likely that its non-disclosure would affect the ability of users of the financial statements to reach a proper understanding of the financial position. Consideration would also need to be given as to whether fixed assets in the mail order division would require to be written down to recoverable amount under *SSAP 12* and whether stocks should be written down to net realisable value if lower than cost.

If the closure was anticipated at the year end then there would be a case for reflecting it in the financial statements by restating assets and providing for losses on closure.

(4) *Problems with long term contract*
Since the discovery was made after the financial statements were approved by the directors it is not a post balance sheet event as defined by *SSAP 17* and therefore would not be reflected in the financial statements for the year ended 31 December 19-1, although the directors may consider publishing a separate statement dealing with the matter.

(5) *Fire at manufacturing plant*
This is a non-adjusting event since the fire occurred after the year end and therefore does not concern conditions existing at the balance sheet date. However, as for (3) above, if it gives an indication that application of the going concern concept to a material part of the company is not appropriate, then the financial statements at 31 December 19-1 should be adjusted to include the insurance claim receivable of £10m in place of the plant as a fixed asset.

If this is not the case, then the event should be disclosed by way of note since it is material in reaching a proper understanding of the financial position.

(6) *Damages claim*
There is a contingency as defined by *SSAP 18* since the outcome is dependent on an uncertain future event (the outcome of a court case).

Since there is presumably a possibility that the claim will succeed (even though it is not probable), the contingent liability for the £8m claim together with possible tax implications should be disclosed by way of note to the financial statements. The note should include a statement of the nature of the contingency together with a prudent estimate of the financial effect.

If the legal fees in defence of the claim are not expected to be recovered they should be provided for at 31 December 19-1 under the prudence concept. The provision should be based on a best estimate of the amounts involved.

(7) *Movement in foreign exchange rates*
This is a non-adjusting event since it does not concern conditions existing at the balance sheet date. However, if the reduction in foreign assets is of such materiality that non-disclosure would affect the ability of users of the financial statements to reach a proper understanding of the financial position, then it should be disclosed by way of note. Before reaching a decision, the exchange rate on 15 march 19-2 (the

date the directors approved the financial statements) should be considered.

(8) *Deficiency in pension fund*

Although the valuation of the pension fund took place on 1 February 19-2, if the deficiency arose in respect of the period prior to 31 December 19-1 then it is an adjusting event. In these circumstances, the deficiency (or that part of it attributable to the period to 31 December 19-1) should be provided for in the financial statements at 31 December 19-1 in accordance with the accruals concept.

This is despite the fact that it was not funded until 31 March 19-2. The actual treatment of the deficiency in the financial statements for the year ended 31 December 19-1 will depend on the cause or causes of the deficiency. However, if it relates to normal pension costs then it should be written off against the ordinary profits before taxation for the year.

ANSWER E1

(a) *Balance sheet as at 31 Mar. 19-7*

(i) *Extract from current assets*

	£
Stocks	154,682

(ii) *Notes to balance sheet—stocks*

Work-in-progress	81,955
Finished goods	72,727
	154,682

(iii) Extract from statement of accounting policies

Stocks

Stocks and work in progress are included at the lower of cost and net realisable value. Costs include all direct costs and a proportion of production overheads.

Long-term contracts are valued in accordance with *SSAP 9* at cost plus attributable profits or cost less foreseeable losses. Profit is not taken until the outcome of the contract can be assessed with reasonable certainty. Progress payments received and receivable are deducted.

The inclusion of such profit is a departure from the statutory valuation rules for current assets but is required, and allowed by s.1 CA 1981 to enable the accounts to give a true and fair view. At the balance sheet date, stock included one long term contract valued at £81,955. This contract was not sufficiently complete to allow the outcome of the contract to be assessed with reasonable certainty. Therefore, in accordance with *SSAP 9* no profit has been taken on this contract and the departure from the statutory valuation rules, has no effect in the year ended 31 Mar. 19-7.

Tutorial note

For each balance sheet item of stock, the difference between the balance sheet amount and the replacement cost must be shown if material: para. 27 (3) sch. 1 CA 1981.

(b) Why *SSAP 9* was required:

No area of accounting has produced wider differences in practice than the computation of the amount at which stocks and work-in-progress are stated in financial accounts.
This quotation from the preface to *SSAP 9* explains the reason why a Statement of Standard Accounting Practice on the treatment of stocks and work-in-progress is so necessary. The preface explains that *SSAP 9* has three main objects.

(i) To seek to define the practices involved.
(ii) To narrow the differences and variations in those practices, and
(iii) To ensure adequate disclosure in the accounts.

Whilst no statement could ensure complete uniformity of treatment in an area of such variety, the standard does lay down the general principles to be followed in stock valuation.
For example:

(i) Stock should be valued at the lower of cost and net realisable value.
(ii) Cost should include production and other overheads which have been incurred in bringing the product or service to its present location and condition, notwithstanding that these may occur wholly or partly on a time basis.
(iii) Long-term contract work-in-progress should include an appropriate proportion of profit on the contract based upon the expected outcome on the whole contract.
(iv) Foreseeable losses on contracts should be provided for in full.

The *SSAP* has been subject to considerable criticism from chief accountants of major companies, normally on the grounds that they wish to be more cautious than the standard so far as profit-taking on work-in-progress is concerned.

Workings:

(1) *Valuation of finished stock*

Costs incurred to date

	Item 1	*Item 2*	*Total*
	£	£	£
Direct material	20,000	15,000	
Direct labour	10,000	5,000	
Overheads	13,636	9,091	
	43,636	29,091	
			72,727

Overheads have been allocated on the basis of proportion of direct costs used on each item to total direct costs incurred, i.e.

Item 1 $\frac{£30{,}000}{£550{,}000} \times 250{,}000 = £13{,}636$

Item 2 $\frac{£20{,}000}{£550{,}000} \times 250{,}000 = £9{,}091$

No information is given regarding net realisable values of items 1 and 2. It is assumed they are in excess of cost (as calculated above).

(An alternative basis of allocation of overheads would be to apportion on a percentage of direct labour basis, i.e. 100% in this case. Item 1 would then be valued at £40,000 and item 2 at £25,000.)

(2) *Valuation of work-in-progress*

		£
Costs incurred to date:		
Materials		25,000
Labour—manufacturing		20,000
		45,000
Labour—assembly		15,000
Overheads:		
Manufacturing	$\frac{£45{,}000}{£550{,}000} \times 250{,}000$	20,455
Assembly	$\frac{£15{,}000}{£100{,}000} \times 10{,}000$	1,500
Total costs to date		81,955

(On the alternative basis of allocation of overheads, manufacturing overheads would be £20,000 rather than £20,455).

Calculation of overall profitability of project X

	£	£
Contract price (assuming fixed-price contract)		190,000
Estimated total costs:		
Direct material	50,000	
Direct labour—manufacturing	50,000	
—assembly	30,000	
Overheads—manufacturing	45,455	
—assembly	3,000	
		178,455
Estimated total profit		11,545

Manufacturing overheads

	£
Manufacturing overheads to date	20,455
Direct manufacturing costs to date	45,000
Direct manufacturing—estimated total cost	100,000

Assuming overheads are related to direct costs, estimated total manufacturing overheads are

$$\frac{£100,000}{£45,000} \times £20,455, \text{ i.e. } \underline{\underline{£45,455}}$$

(If manufacturing overheads were allocated on the basis of direct labour hours, estimated total manufacturing overheads would be £50,000.)

Assembly overheads

Since these appear to be related directly to assembly labour costs, estimated total assembly overheads are:

$$\frac{£30,000}{£15,000} \times £1,500, \text{ i.e. } \underline{\underline{£3,000}}$$

It is assumed that:

(1) Contingencies, claims and rectification provisions have been taken into account.

(2) Estimates of future costs and state of contract are realistic and prudent.

(3) The basis of allocation of overheads and estimates of future overheads are reasonable having regard to the circumstances of the business.

(4) The degree of completion of project X is such that the outcome of the contract cannot be assessed with reasonable certainty and therefore that no profit will be taken in the year to 31 Mar. 19-7. (It is not clear whether project X falls within the *SSAP 9* definition of long-term contract).

Conclusion

Since there is no evidence to suggest that contract X will be unprofitable, the contract work-in-progress may be valued at cost of £81,955.

Tutorial notes

(1) The question is badly-worded and lacking information. For example, it is not clear whether project X is a long-term contract as defined by *SSAP 9*, i.e. *a contract entered into for manufacture or building of a single substantial entity or the provision of a service where the time taken to manufacture, build or provide is such that a substantial proportion of all such contract work will extend for a period exceeding one year* (*para. 22*).
Contract X commenced Nov. 19-6 and was half -completed by Mar 19-7. This makes contract X very much a borderline case.
(2) Whether or not the contract is classified as long-term, there is the problem of deciding the basis of allocation of production overheads between different items of stock.
(3) If project X is regarded as a long-term contract, should attributable profit be taken into account? The crucial point is to decide whether the outcome of the contract can be assessed with reasonable certainty as at 31 Mar. 19-7. In the absence of the type of evidence which would be required, in practice, there is a reasonable case for saying that 50% completion is not sufficiently advanced to justify the taking of profit in the year to 31 Mar. 19-7.
(4) There is no information regarding contingencies or provisions for rectification work.
(5) There is no information regarding net realisable values of items 1 and 2. Items 1 and 2 may be specific to the requirement of particular customers.
(6) In conclusion, there is a strong case to justify valuation at cost (assuming the contract is expected to be profitable overall).

ANSWER E2. STOCK VALUATION

(a) *Accounting policy for stock valuation*

Stocks are stated at the lower of cost and net realisable value; the first in first out method of valuation is used.

Cost comprises direct cost of materials, including customs duty and freight, direct labour and a due proportion of production overheads, both variable and fixed.

Net realisable value is based on expected selling price, less the estimated costs of completion, delivery and sale.

(b) *Valuation of stock on a basis acceptable under SSAP 9*

(i) Finished goods	£
At cost per ton:	
Raw materials	150
Customs duty	10
Transport from docks	20
Variable overheads	25
Fixed overheads $\frac{£30,000}{£\ 1,500}$	20
	225

Tutorial note

The difficulty in this valuation relates to the amount of fixed overheads to be included. *SSAP 9* states that this should be 'based on the normal level of activity, taking one year with another' (*para. 20*).

The question gives no guide to past or future production levels. One must decide whether it would therefore be reasonable to assume that the current operating level (less than 1,000 tons per week) is 'normal' even though capacity is 50% higher at 1,500 tons per week.

SSAP 9 states that 'the governing factor is that the cost of unused capacity should be written off in the current year' (*Appendix 1, para. 8*).

Assuming, therefore, that the 1,500 tons per week can be achieved without abnormal overtime or additional shift working, it would seem prudent to base the valuation of the fixed overhead cost at this higher level.

At net realisable value

SSAP 9 requires a valuation at the lower of cost and net realisable value (*para. 26*). In this example, net realisable value per ton comprises:

	£	£
Delivered selling price		240.00
Less: Delivery cost	7.50	
Selling costs—say $\frac{£3,000}{£1,000}$	3.00	
		10.50
		229.50

Tutorial note

The problem in this valuation is with regard to the deduction of selling costs.

Net realisable value is defined by *SSAP 9* as 'the amount at which it is expected that items of stocks and work in progress can be disposed of without creating profit or loss in the year of sale, i.e. the estimated proceeds of sale less all further costs of completion and less all costs to be incurred in marketing, selling and distributing directly related to the items in question' (*para. 5*).

The point to determine is whether costs which are fixed can directly relate to the sale of particular items. Since this is a one-product company and the stock in question is of standard quality it is only fair to assume that they can, since, presumably, while the 'sales force' are concentrating on selling the stock they will not be shifting more recent production.

Valuation for accounts

Since cost is lower than net realisable value, the finished goods should be taken at £225 per ton, giving a total of 2,000 × £225 = £450,000.

(ii) Raw materials

	£
At cost per ton:	
Raw materials	150
Customs duty	10
Transport from docks	20
	180

From the calculation of net realisable value above, it seems that these materials can be incorporated into the product at cost and still enable it to be sold at a profit (*para. 19, Appendix 1, SSAP 9*)

The cost valuation should, therefore, be used giving a total of 5,000 × £180 = £900,000.

(c) *Value of raw materials stock on a LIFO basis*

	£
At cost per ton:	
Raw materials	100
Customs duty	10
Transport	20
	130

This gives a total of £650,000. However, it is based on the assumption that the stock of raw materials at 30 Jun. was at least 5,000 tons and did not fall below that level during the second half-year of 19–8.

(d) *Relative merits of FIFO, other bases recognised under SSAP 9 for valuing stock and LIFO*

The different bases for valuing stock exist mainly because it is frequently not practicable to relate specific expenditure directly to individual items of stock and work in progress (as required for unit costing). In order to arrive at an approximation to cost it is therefore necessary to make assumptions as to the physical composition of the closing stock.

It is important to distinguish these various bases (unit cost, average cost, FIFO, LIFO, base stock, standard cost, etc.) from the method chosen to apply them in particular manufacturing situations (job costing, batch costing, process costing, etc).

From the point of view of *SSAP 9*, the relative merits of the different bases are determined by the extent to which the valuation of year-end stock they provide approximates to actual cost. Such a view precludes LIFO and base stock which are more concerned to charge against income the 'real' cost of stock consumed.

Considering both viewpoints, the relative merits of the bases in question can be summarised as follows:

(1) FIFO

Advantages:

(i) Most likely approximation to actual physical stock movements.
(ii) Easy to operate with or without perpetual inventory records.
(iii) Tends to give balance sheet values approaching replacement.

Disadvantages:

(i) If used for the purposes of price determination, may result in an unrealistic pricing structure.
(ii) In periods of high inflation may lead to significant overstatement of the 'real' profit.

(2) Other bases recognised under *SSAP 9:*

Unit cost:

Advantages:

(i) By definition gives actual cost of stock held at the year-end.
(ii) Enables exact profit in historic cost terms to be determined in respect of contracts completed during the year.

Disadvantages:

(i) Generally impracticable to operate because of the extent of detailed records required.
(ii) May give rise to problems similar to those for FIFO in a period of inflation.

Average cost:

Advantages:

(i) Smooths the effect of seasonal or other cost fluctuations.
(ii) Where a moving average is used, will tend to give balance sheet values approaching replacement cost.

(iii) In certain circumstances can be more quickly determined than any other method.
(iv) Most likely approximation to actual physical stock movements in dealing with raw materials which are continually delivered into and drawn from tanks, silos, etc.

Disadvantages:

(i) To be accurate generally requires very careful calculation and frequent updating.
(ii) If carelessly applied can result in either the distortions of FIFO or of LIFO without these being immediately apparent.

Standard cost
Advantages:

(i) Facilitates budgetary control.
(ii) Enables timely presentation of accounts.

Disadvantages:

(i) Needs frequent review to ensure that the standard costs in use bear a reasonable relationship to actual costs.
(ii) Requires a relatively sophisticated accounting and control system.

(3) LIFO

Advantages:

(i) Matches revenues with up to date costs and consequently gives a closer identication of 'real' profit.
(ii) Can provide a more realistic basis for determining price levels.

Disadvantages:

(i) In periods of significant price changes results in inaccurate balance sheet stock valuation.
(ii) Requires more detailed stock records than FIFO.

ANSWER E3. BYRON LTD

(a) *Calculation of profits and losses on uncompleted contracts*

	Contract Nos.		
	13	*17*	*21*
	£	£	£
Costs incurred to date	26,000	31,200	15,300
Further costs to be incurred	6,000	4,800	34,700
Estimate of final cost	32,000	36,000	50,000
Sales value	40,000	29,000	60,000
Estimated total profit (loss) on contract	8,000	(7,000)	10,000

(i) *Contract 13*

The job is well advanced, and it appears that a comfortable profit will be achieved. Using cost to date over estimated total cost as a reasonable indicator of progress, attributable profit is

$$\frac{£26{,}000}{£32{,}000} \times \text{estimated total profit of } £8{,}000$$

i.e. £6,500

(ii) *Contract 17*

This contract is clearly in major difficulties. The whole of the foreseeable loss of £7,000 should be provided for, and the contract should be valued at net realisable value of £24,200 (£31,200 less £7,000).

(iii) *Contract 21*

This contract is not sufficiently advanced to start taking profit.

				Contract Nos.				
		13		*17*		*21*		*Total*
Summary		£	£	£	£	£	£	£
Cost		26,000		31,200		15,300		72,500
Attributable profit		6,500		—		—		6,500
		32,500		31,200	—	15,300		79,000
Foreseeable loss	—		7,000		—		7,000	
Progress payments invoiced	30,000	30,000	19,200	26,200	12,000	12,000	61,200	68,200
Net balance sheet value		2,500		5,000		3,300		10,800

(b) The following general assumptions are particularly important:

(i) Total contract revenues to be received can be determined.
(ii) An adequate estimating process exists—in particular that it is possible to arrive at a realistic estimation of costs required to complete a contract and to assess realistically the degree of completion of a contract.
(iii) The actual contract is clearly defined so that costs can be clearly identified, thus enabling comparison of actual with estimates.

With regard to this particular question, these assumptions are crucial, for example:

(i) With contract 13, are the estimated future costs and degree of completion both realistic and prudent?
(ii) As regards contract 17, is £7,000 a realistic and prudent estimate of total loss?

(c) *Detailed trading and profit and loss account for the year ended 31 Dec. 19–6*

	£	£	£
Turnover			526,000
Cost of sales:			
Wages		230,000	
Materials consumed £(107,000 – 5,000)		102,000	
Depreciation—plant	10,000		
—vehicles	6,250		
		16,250	
Plant hire		8,000	
Direct expenses		19,000	
Plant running expenses		39,000	
		414,250	
Less: Net value of work-in-progress at 31.12.-6		10,800	
			403,450
Gross profit			122,550
Administrative expenses:			
Salaries		58,000	
Office and administration		21,000	
Auditors' remuneration		2,000	
Directors' remuneration		20,000	
Bank charges		4,000	
Depreciation—furniture		700	
			105,700
Profit on ordinary activities			16,850

(d) *Extract from accounting policies—long-term contract work-in-progress*

Long-term contract work-in-progress is valued at cost plus attributable profit or cost less any foreseeable losses. Payments received on account are deducted in arriving at the group balance sheet figure.

Profit is included on long-term contracts in accordance with *SSAP 9* and amounts to £6,500. The inclusion of such profit is a departure from the statutory valuation rules for current assets but is required, and allowed by *s.1 CA 1981*, to enable the accounts to give a true and fair view.

(e) *Balance sheet note: Long-term contract work-in-progress*

The balance sheet item amounts to £10,800.

The note would reveal:	£	£
Cost		72,500
Attributable profit		6,500
		79,000
Less: Foreseeable loss	7,000	
Progress payments received and receivable	61,200	
		68,200
Net balance sheet value		10,800

Progress payments received in cash amounted to £51,000.

Workings:

See part (a).

Tutorial note

For each balance sheet item of stock (i.e. materials and long-term contract work-in-progress) the difference if material, between the balance sheet amount and the replacement cost must be shown: Para. 27(3), Sch. 1, CA 1981.

ANSWER F1.

(a) (i)

Date	*Ref.*	*Details*	*Dr.* £	*Cr.* £
1.1.–0	1	Investment in P Ltd	225,000	
		Cash		225,000
		Purchase of 75,000 shares in P Ltd at £3 per share		
	2	Cash	22,500	
		Investment income		22,500
		Receipt of dividend from P Ltd		

			Dr. £	*Cr.* £
1.4.–0	3	Investment in R Ltd	300,000	
		Cash		300,000
		Purchase of 200,000 shares in R Ltd		
31.12.–0	4	Cash	25,000	
		Investment in R Ltd		6,250
		Investment income		18,750
		Receipt of dividend from R Ltd in respect of the year ended 31.12.–0. One quarter of dividend paid out of pre-acquisition profits.		

(ii)

Date	*Ref.*	*Details*	*Dr.* £	*Cr.* £
1.1.–0	1	Investment in P Ltd	225,000	
		Cash		225,000
		Purchase of 75,000 shares in P Ltd at £3 per share		
31.12.–0	2	Investment in P Ltd	45,000	
		Profit and loss account		45,000
		Group share of profits of P Ltd (75% × 60,000)		
	3	Cash	22,500	
		Investment in P Ltd		22,500
		Receipt of dividend from P Ltd already dealt with on equity method of accounting		
1.4.–0	4	Investment in R Ltd	300,000	
		Cash		300,000
		Purchase of 200,000 shares in R Ltd		
31.12.–0	5	Investment in R Ltd	46,875	
		Profit and loss account		46,875
		Group share of post-acquisition profits of R Ltd for year ended 31.12.–0 (25% × 9/12 × 250,000)		
31.12.–0	6	Cash	25,000	
		Investment in R Ltd (cost)		6,250
		Investment in R Ltd (reserves)		18,750
		Dividend from R Ltd, of which one quarter relates to pre-acquisition period		

(b) (i) The normal consolidation procedure involves allocating the share capital and reserves of a subsidiary between the holding company's share of share capital and minority interests. The holding company's share of capital and profits made prior to acquisition are set off against the cost of investment in an "adjustment account" and post-acquisition profits are transferred into group reserves.

If the equity method has been used in the holding company, then the reserves of the holding company are already equivalent to group reserves as the correct amount of retained profits of the subsidiary were added to the retained profits of the holding company. This means that in the consolidation procedure the holding company's share of the entire reserves of the subsidiary are transferred into the adjustment account.

Consolidation under traditional cost method

	Adjustment a/c			*P Ltd*		
	Dr.	*Cr.*		*Share capital*	*Reserves*	
	£	£		£	£	
Cost of investment	225,000			100,000	155,000	
				75,000	116,250	Group share (75%)
		168,750	=	75,000	+ 93,750	To Adjustment a/c
Goodwill		56,250				
	225,000	225,000				
					22,500	To group reserves
					116,250	

Consolidation under equity method

	Adjustment a/c			*P Ltd*		
	Dr.	*Cr.*		*Share capital*	*Reserves*	
	£	£		£	£	
Investment a/c	247,500			100,000	155,000	
		191,250	=	75,000	+ 116,250	Group share (75%) to Adjustment a/c
Goodwill		56,250				
	247,500	247,500				

Under the equity method the investment in subsidiary account has been increased by the group share of post-acquisition retained profits and this results in the group share of reserves in P Ltd being credited to the adjustment account.

In the profit and loss account the whole of the profit of the subsidiary would be included under the conventional approach to consolidation. The minority proportion of profits would be deducted separately. Under the equity method, only the group proportion of the profits of the subsidiary would be included;

	Conventional method	*Equity method*
	£	£
Profit of M Ltd	?	?
Profit of P Ltd	60,000	45,000
Profit after taxation	60,000	45,000
Minority interests	15,000	—
Profit attributable to M Ltd	45,000	45,000

(ii) If the traditional cost method were used, the equity method adjustments must be made for the purposes of the consolidation. Consolidated reserves would need to be credited with the group share of the post-acquisition reserves of the associated company ($25\% \times \frac{3}{4} \times 150{,}000$) of £28,125.
The consolidated balance sheet would include the investment in the associated company at a value representing the goodwill on acquisition plus share of net assets.

If the equity method were used in the holding company's own accounts, the adjustments have already been made and the reserves of M Ltd already include their share of the post-acquisition reserves of R Ltd.

ANSWER F2. ATLANTIC AND CROSSING

(i)

(a) *Consolidated balance sheet at 31 Jan. 19–6*

	£	£
Fixed assets		810,000
Current assets	x	
Creditors: Amounts falling due within one year	x	
Net current assets		520,000
Total assets *less* current liabilities		1,330,000
Creditors: Amounts falling due after more than one year. 8% debenture loans		120,000
		1,210,000
Capital and reserves		
Called up share capital		500,000
Share premium account		200,000
Profit and loss account		510,000
		1,210,000

(b) *Consolidated profit and loss account for the year ended 31 Jan. 19–6*

	£
Profit on ordinary activities after taxation	110,000
Minority interest	1,000
	109,000
Extraordinary profits on disposal	24,000
Profit for the financial year	133,000
Balance brought forward at 1.2.–5	377,000
Balance carried forward at 31.1.–6	510,000

Workings

(1) Profit after tax (before extraordinary item)	£
Atlantic (450–350)	100,000
Crossing 4/12 × (240–210)	10,000
	110,000

		£
(2) Minority interest		
10% × 4/12 × (240–210)		1,000
(3) Extraordinary profit on disposal		
Sale proceeds		360,000
Cost to Atlantic		300,000
Gain to Atlantic		60,000
Less: Attributable post acquisition reserves sold:		
—Brought forward at 1.2.–5		
90% × (210 – 180)	27,000	
—Arising in year of disposal		
90% × 4/12 × 30,000	9,000	
		36,000
Gain to group		24,000

(4) Revenue reserves at 1st Feb. 19–5

	£
Atlantic	350,000
Crossing 90% × (210 – 180)	27,000
	377,000

(5) Revenue reserves at 31st Jan. 19–6	
Per Atlantic accounts	450,000
Gain on disposal of shares	60,000
	510,000

F2. ATLANTIC AND CROSSING—PART 2

(ii)

(i) *Draft consolidation working papers*

Adjustment account

	£		£
Cost of remaining shares		Shares held	80,000
$\left(\frac{80}{90} \times £300{,}000\right)$	266,667	Pre acq. reserves 80%	
		× £180,000	144,000
		Goodwill c/d	42,667
	266,667		266,667

Minority interest

	£		£
Bal c/d	68,000	Shares	20,000
		Reserves	48,000
		(20% × £240,000)	
	68,000		68,000

Consolidated reserves

	£		£
Bal c/d	504,667	Atlantic Ltd	450,000
		Crossing Ltd (80% ×	
		£(240,000 – 180,000))	48,000
		Share disposal a/c	6,667
	504,667		504,667

Share disposal account

	£		£
Cost $\left(\frac{10}{90} \times £300{,}000\right)$	33,333	Proceeds	40,000
Reserves	6,667		
	40,000		40,000

(a) *Consolidated balance sheet at 31 Jan. 19–6*

	£	£
Fixed assets:		
Intangible assets		
Goodwill on consolidation		42,667
Tangible assets		1,100,000
£(810,000 + 290,000 + 42,667)		1,142,667
Current assets	x	
Creditors: Amounts falling due within one year	x	
Net current assets		250,000
Total assets *less* current liabilities		1,392,667
Creditors: Amounts falling due after more than one year.		
8% debenture loans	120,000	
Minority shareholders' interest	68,000	
		188,000
		1,204,667
Capital and reserves:		
Called up share capital		500,000
Share premium account		200,000
Profit and loss account		504,667
		1,204,667

(ii) *Calculation of profit on disposal of shares*

	Holding company	*Group*	
	£	£	£
Proceeds of sale	40,000		40,000
Cost (1/9 × £300,000)	33,333	33,333	
Attributable post-acquisition profits			
Attributable to disposal 10%		4,000	
			37,333
Extraordinary gain	6,667		2,667

	£000	*£000*
Reserves at acquisition		180
Reserves at disposal:		
At 1.2.–5	210	
1.2.–5 to 1.6.–5 4/12 × (240–210)	10	
		220
		40

Calculation of minority interest

	Total		*M1*
	£		£
1 Feb. to 31 May 19–5 10% ×	10,000	(4m)	1,000
1 Jun. 19–5 to 31 Jan. 19–6 20% ×	20,000	(8m)	4,000
	30,000		5,000

Reserves at 1 Feb. 19–5

	£	M*1*
		£
Atlantic		350,000
Crossing 90% × £(210,000—180,000)		27,000
		377,000

Retained profit for the year

Retained by Crossing (80% × £30,000)		24,000
Atlantic—as given	100,000	
—extraordinary item	2,667	
—earned by Crossing relating to shares sold (10% × £10,000)	1,000	
		103,667
		127,667

(b) *Consolidated profit and loss account for the year ended 31 Jan. 19–6*

	£
Profit on ordinary activities after taxation	130,000
Minority shareholders' interest	5,000
	125,000
Extraordinary profit on disposal	2,667
Profit for the financial year	127,667

Statement of retained profit

	£
Balance at 1 Feb. 19–5	377,000
Retained for year	127,667
Balance at 31 Jan. 19–6	504,667

Alternative calculation of group disposal surplus

		£	£
Proceeds of sale			40,000
Net assets disposed:			
OSC		100,000	
Reserves at 31.1.–5		210,000	
Profit to 1.6.–5 (4/12 × £30,000)		10,000	
		320,000	
Sold 10% of shares			32,000
			8,000
	£		
Goodwill sold:			
Cost		300,000	
OSC	100,000		
Pre-acq reserves	180,000		
	280,000		
Purchased 90%		252,000	
Goodwill acquired		48,000	
Sold 1/9			5,333
Extraordinary gain			2,667

ANSWER F2. ATLANTIC AND CROSSING—Part 3

(iii) *Consolidated balance sheet at 31 Jan. 19–6*

	£000	£000
Fixed assets:		
Tangible assets		810
Investments		
Related company		177
£(810,000 + 177,000)		987
Current assets	x	
Creditors: Amounts falling due within one year	x	
Net current assets		400
Total assets *less* current liabilities		1,387
Creditors: Amounts falling due after more than one year, 8% debenture loans		120
		1,267
Capital and reserves:		
Called up share capital		500
Share premium account		200
Profit and loss account		567
		1,267

Consolidated profit and loss account for the year ended 31 Jan. 19–6

	£000	£000
Profit on ordinary activities after taxation		119
Minority interests		1
		118
Extraordinary profit on disposal		72
Profit for the financial year		190
Retained by holding company	176.5	
Retained by associate	13.5	
	190	
Reserves:		
At 1 Feb. 19–5		377
Retained for year		190
At 31 Jan. 19–6		567

Workings:

Associated company

	£		£
Cost (45/90 × £300,000)	150,000		
Share of post-acq. res. 45% × £(240,000 – 180,000)	27,000		
	177,000		

Disposal account

	£		£
Cost (45/90 × £300,000)	150,000	Proceeds	240,000
Reserves	90,000		
	240,000		240,000

Consolidated reserves

	£		£
		Atlantic Ltd	450,000
		Disposal	90,000
		Associated Co	27,000
			567,000

Profit after tax:

Atlantic	100,000
Crossing (as subsidiary) 4/12 × £30,000	10,000
Crossing (as associate) 45% × 8/12 × £30,000	9,000
	119,000

Minority interest:

	£
Crossing 10% × 4/12 × £30,000	1,000

Extraordinary profit on disposal:

Proceeds	240,000
Assets sold 45% × £320,000	144,000
	96,000
Goodwill sold 45/90 × £48,000	24,000
	72,000

Retained profit for the year:	£
Associated company 45% × £30,000	13,500
Holding company:	
As given	100,000
Extraordinary gain	72,000
Profit of Crossing Ltd earned during year on shares sold 45% × £10,000	4,500
	176,500

ANSWER F3. HIYO, SILVER AND AWAY

(a) (i) In the case of material additions to or disposals from the group, the consolidated financial statements should contain sufficient information about the results of the subsidiaries acquired or sold to enable shareholders to appreciate the effect on the consolidated results (*para. 30 SSAP 14*). This might be done by disclosing the profit or loss of the subsidiary during the year of acquisition or disposal and by giving details of assets and liabilities at the date of purchase or sale.

(ii) Where there is a material disposal, the consolidated profit and loss account should include:

(1) the subsidiary's results up to the date of disposal;
(2) the gain or loss on the sale being the difference at the time of sale between;

(A) the proceeds; and
(B) the holding company's share of its net assets together with any premium (less any amounts written off) or discount on acquisition attributable to the shares sold (*para. 31 SSAP 14*).

(b) The effective date of acquisition or disposal is the earlier of:

(i) the date on which the consideration passes; and
(ii) the date on which an offer becomes or is declared unconditional.

This applies even if the acquiring company has the right under the agreement to share in the profits of the business acquired from an earlier date (*para. 32 SSAP 14*).

(c)

The Hiyo Group Ltd
Consolidated balance sheet at 31 Dec. 19–8

	£000	£000
Fixed assets		
Intangible assets		
Goodwill on consolidation		
Tangible assets		92.5
Investments		x
Related company (note 1)		407.7
		x
Current assets	x	
Creditors: Amounts falling due within one year	x	
Net current assets		x
Total assets *less* current liabilities (note 2)		2,435.2
Minority shareholders' interest		297.5
		2,137.7
		£000
Capital and reserves		
Called up share capital		1,000.0
Profit and loss account		1,137.7
		2,137.7

Consolidated profit and loss account
for the year ended 31 Dec. 19–8

	£000	*£000*
Turnover		13,600.0
Change in stocks of finished goods and work in progress		x
		x
Raw materials and comsumables	x	
Other external charges	x	
Staff costs	x	
Depreciation	x	
Other operational charges	x	
		x
Trading profit (note 3)		1,333.0
Income from shares in related company		40.5
Profit on ordinary activities before taxation		1,373.5
Taxation on profit on ordinary activities:		
Group taxation	568	
Taxation on related company profits	16.2	
		584.2
Profit on ordinary activities after taxation		789.3
Minority interests		57.4
Profit attributable to the members of Hiyo (note 4)		731.9
Extraordinary profit (note 5)		25.8
Profit for the financial year		757.7
Dividends		340.0
Amount added to retained profit		417.7
Retained by holding company		325.0
Retained by subsidiary company		22.5
Retained by related company		70.2
		417.7

Statement of movement on group reserves

	Group £000	*Associate* £000	*Total* £000
At 1 Jan. 19–8	720.0	—	720.0
Arising on disposal of shares	(140.4)	140.4	—
Retained for year	420.4	(2.7)	417.7
	1,000.0	137.7	1,137.7

Notes to the accounts

	£000	£000
1. *Related company*		
Share of net assets		385.2
Goodwill on acquisition		22.5
		407.7
2. *Total assets less current liabilities*		
Sundry assets as given		2,178
Dividend receivable from associated company		27
		2,205
Dividend payable by Hiyo Ltd	240	
Minority dividend of Silver Ltd	30	
		(270)
Goodwill on consolidation		92.5
Investment in related company		407.7
		2,435.2

3. *Group trading profit*
   This includes £160,000 relating to Silver Ltd, the newly acquired subsidiary and £270,000 of Away Ltd earned before its partial disposal during the year.
4. Of which £582,500 is dealt with in the separate accounts of the holding company. A separate profit and loss account for the holding company has not been presented.
5. This is the profit arising on the sale of 35% of the shares of Away Ltd during the year and consists of the proceeds less the assets of Away attributable to the shares sold at the date of sale.

(d) The publication of the revised *SSAP1* marks the start of a review of all accounting standards by the Accounting Standards Committee. The main reasons for its publication are:

(i) to clarify the definition of what constitutes an associated company;

(ii) to restate the disclosure requirements in a manner consistent with other accounting standards and, in particular, to require the use of the equity method of accounting in the manner stated in *SSAP 14;*

(iii) to clarify the treatment of related items, e.g. dividends receivable from associates, loans and current accounts receivable from or payable to associates, minority interests in associated companies.

The main differences between the old and the new SSAPs are:

(i) *Definition*
The old *SSAP 1* definition specifically mentions the holding of 20% or more of equity voting rights. The new definition concerns itself with substantial influence over policy decisions and the level of 20% is given only as guidance as to whether substantial influence exists.

(ii) *Holding of shares*
SSAP 1 (revised) specifically mentions that in deciding whether substantial influence exists a holding company should take account of its subsidiary company holdings in associates but not associates' holdings in associates.

(iii) *Balance sheet presentation*
In the revised SSAP the balance sheet value of the associate should be split between:

(1) share of net tangible assets;
(2) share of goodwill;
(3) share of goodwill arising on acquisition (or less discount on acquisition);

The original *SSAP 1* requires a split between:

(1) cost; and
(2) group share of post-acquisition reserves.

(iv) The revised SSAP requires current assets and liabilities owing between the group and the associate to be reflected as a current item in the consolidated balance sheet. No details were given specifically in the original *SSAP 1*

(v) An investment company with no subsidiaries may reflect a holding in an associate by publishing a separate balance sheet under the revised SSAP. In the original *SSAP 1* the details must be given by way of a note to the balance sheet.

Workings:

1. Shareholdings

Silver—75% acquired after 8 months (4/12 post-acquisition).
Away—80% for 9 months
35% sold
45% for last 3 months (associated company)

2. Reserves of Silver Ltd

	£000		*£000*
Adj (75% × 360)	270.00	Bal b/d	390.00
CR (75% × 30)	22.50		
Min (25% × 390)	97.50		
	390.00		390.00

3. Adjustment account

	£000		*£000*
Cost	1,000.0	Shares	600.00
		Reserves	270.00
		Con Res (pre-acq div)	37.50
			907.50
		Goodwill	92.50
	1,000.0		1,000.00

4. Consolidated reserves

	£000		*£000*
Adj (pre-acq div)	37.50	Hiyo	880.00
Balance c/d	1,137.70	Silver	22.50
		Disposal (working 8)	135.00
		Away (working 9)	137.70
	1,175.20		1,175.20

5. Minority interests (S only)

	£000		*£000*
		Shares	200.00
		Reserves	97.50
			297.50

6. *Reserves of Silver at acquisition*

	£000
At 1.1.19–8	300
To 31.8.19–8 (8/12 × 90)	60
	360

7. *Pre-acquisition dividend from Silver*

	£000
Dividend receivable by Hiyo (75% × 120)	90.00
Maximum post-acquisition dividend (75% × 4/12 × 210)	52.50
Pre-acquisition dividend	37.50

This dividend must be included in the reserves of Hiyo since dividends receivable have been accrued by the holding company but the cost of investment is still at its original £1 million. The adjustment is to take the pre-acquisition dividend out of the reserves of Hiyo and deduct it instead from the cost of investment.

8. Disposal of shares

	£000		£000
Cost of shares sold (35/80 × 480)	210	Proceeds	345
Consolidated reserves	135		
	345		345

Cost of original shares = £135,000 + £345,000
= £480,000.

9. *Value of associated company*
(a) *Following the old SSAP 1*

	£000
Cost (45/80 × 480)	270.0
Share of post-acquisition reserves 45% (356 – 50)	137.7
	407.7

(b) *Following SSAP 1 (revised)*

	£000	£000
Share of assets 45% × (916 – 60)		385.2
Share of goodwill:		
Cost	270.0	
Share of pre-acquisition assets 45% (500 + 50)	247.5	
		22.5
		407.7

10. Turnover = 8,000 + (4/12 × 6,000) + (9/12 × 4,800)
 = 13,600.

11. *Group profit*

	£000
H profit less group dividends (1,020 – 117)	903
S (4/12 × 480)	160
A (9/12 × 360)	270
	1,333

12. *Associated company*

	£000
Profit before tax 45% × 3/12 × 360	40.5
Tax 45% × 3/12 × 144	16.2

13. Group tax = 400 + (4/12 × 180) + (9/12 × 144) 568.0

14. *Minority interests*

	£000
S 25% × 4/12 × 300	25.0
A 20% × 9/12 × 216	32.4
	57.4

15. *Gain on sale of shares*

	£000	£000
Proceeds		345.0
Net assets at date of sale:		
Shares	500	
Reserves at 1.1.–8	200	
Profit to 30.9.–8 (9/12 × 216)	162	
Sold	35% × 862	
		301.7
c/f		43.3

	£000	£000	£000
		b/f	43.3
Goodwill on acquisition:			
Cost (135 + 345)		480	
Shares	500		
Reserves	50		
	80% × 550	440	
		40	
Goodwill sold = 35/80 × 40			17.5
			25.8

16. *Retained for the year*

	£000
Hiyo:	
As given (280) less pre-acquisition dividend (37.5)	242.5
Extraordinary gain	25.8
Earned by Away on shares sold (35% × 162)	56.7
	325.0
Silver:	
75% × 4/12 × 90	22.5
Away:	
45% × 156	70.2
	417.7

17. *Opening consolidated reserves*

	£000
Hiyo Ltd	600
Away Ltd 80% × (200 – 50)	120
	720

18. *Transfer of reserves on sale of shares*

	£000
Away Ltd:	
Reserves at sale (200 + 162)	362
At acquisition	50
	312

45% of shares remaining 45% × 312 = 140.4

	£000
Retained by associate for last three months:	
Share of profit 45% × 3/12 × 216	24.3
Dividend 45% × 60	27.0
Reduction in share of reserves	2.7

19. *Dealt with in accounts of Hiyo*

	£000
Profit after tax	620.0
Less: Pre-acquisition dividend	37.5
	582.5

ANSWER F4. METROPOLIS LTD

Group balance sheet at 31 Dec. 19–5

Notes:

Notes		£	£
	Fixed assets		
	Tangible assets		x
1.	Investments: Subsidiaries not consolidated (390,000 + 157,600)		157,000
			547,600
	Current assets		
	Stocks	x	
2.	Debtors	x	
2.	Investments	x	
	Cash at bank and in hand	x	
		107,000	
3.	Creditors: Amounts falling due within one year	178,000	
	Net current liabilities		(71,000)
	Total assets *less* current liabilities		476,600
	Capital and reserves		
	Called up share capital		100,000
	Profit and loss account		376,600
			476,600

Group profit and loss account for the year ended 31.12.–5

	£
Group profit	122,200
Share of profits of non consolidated subsidiaries	43,400
Profit on ordinary activities before taxation	165,600
Tax on profit on ordinary activities	49,600
Profit attributable to shareholders of Metropolis Ltd	116,000
Dividends	40,000
Retained profit for the year	76,000

Statement of group reserves	£
Reserves at 1.1.–5	300,600
Retained profit for the year	76,000
Reserves at 31.12.–5	376,600

Notes to the accounts

1. *Investment in subsidiaries not consolidated*

	£
Euston Ltd	
Your company holds 80% of the shares in Euston Ltd, an insurance company. The nature of the business of Euston Ltd is so different from the rest of the group that your directors feel that it would be misleading to consolidate Euston Ltd into the group results. The investment is, therefore, valued at cost plus the group proportion of the reserves of Euston Ltd since its acquisition.	66,000
Separate financial statements of Euston Ltd are set out in note 4.	
Marylebone Ltd	
A civil war in Utopia has caused severe restrictions in the group's ability to exercise control of this subsidiary. The investment is valued at cost plus the group proportion of reserves since acquisition and up to the date the restriction began (1 Jul. 19–5). Negotiations are proceeding with the new Utopian government to re-establish our control over Marylebone.	79,800
Premium on acquisition £3,000	
Waterloo Ltd	
Although your company owns 60% of the equity shares of Waterloo Ltd, it is unable to exercise control due to the existence of voting rights in non-equity shares. This investment is valued at cost plus the group proportion of the reserves of Waterloo since its acquisition due to the significant influence which your company is able to exert over the policies of Waterloo.	11,800
Premium on acquisition £1,000	157,600

2. *Current assets*

	£
(a) Investments include investment in Pancras Ltd at cost	31,000

This recently acquired subsidiary is due to be sold in Oct. 19–6 under the terms of the acquisition. The investment is therefore only a temporary one and thus the investment is valued at cost.
Premium on acquisition £1,000

(b) Debtors include amounts due to Metropolis from subsidiaries not consolidated:	£
Euston Ltd	32,000
Marylebone	4,000
Pancras Ltd	4,000
	40,000

3. *Creditors: Amounts falling due within one year*

These include the following amounts due to subsidiaries which have not been consolidated:	£
Pancras Ltd	8,000
Waterloo Ltd	10,000
	18,000

4. *Summarized financial statements of Euston Ltd*

Balance sheet at 31 Dec. 19–5:	£	£
Share capital		50,000
Reserves		30,000
		80,000
Fixed assets		108,000
Current assets		24,000
		132,000
Less: Current liabilities	20,000	
Amount due to Metropolis	32,000	
		52,000
		80,000

The intra-group balance with Metropolis has arisen due to a short term loan made by the holding company to Euston Ltd. The figures above may be reconciled to the group balance sheet as follows:

	£	£
Share of net assets (80% × 80,000)		64,000
Premium on acquisition		2,000
		66,000

5. *Group retained profit for the year*

	£
Dealt with in the separate accounts of Metropolis	70,000
Retained in subsidiary companies	6,000
	76,000

Workings
Balance Sheet

1. Euston—use equity method of accounting:

	£
Cost	58,000
Reserves (80% × 10,000)	8,000
	66,000

2. Marylebone—use equity method when restrictions began:

Cost	33,000
Reserves (60% × 78,000)	46,800
	79,800

3. Pancras—temporary investment:

Cost—current asset	31,000

4. Waterloo—equity method—significant influence:

Cost	10,000
Reserves (60% × 3,000)	1,800
	11,800

5. Victoria—consolidated:

	£
Cost	2
Shares	2
Goodwill	*NIL*

6. Consolidated reserves

	£		£
		Metropolis	320,000
		Euston (working 1)	8,000
		Marylebone (working 2)	46,800
		Waterloo (working 4)	1,800
			376,600

7. Premiums on acquisition of subsidiaries

	Euston	*Marylebone*	*Pancras*	*Waterloo*
	£	£	£	£
Cost	58,000	33,000	31,000	10,000
S/c acquired	(40,000)	(24,000)	(22,500)	(6,000)*
Reserves (pre acq.)	(16,000)	(6,000)	(7,500)	(3,000)
	2,000	3,000	1,000	1,000

*60% of O.S.C. (£10,000)

Profit and loss account

8. Dividends received by Metropolis

	£
Euston 80% × 20,000	16,000
Pancras—prior to acquisition	Nil
Waterloo—60% × 3,000	1,800
	17,800

9. Group profit

Metropolis 140,000 – 17,800	122,200

10. Share of profits of non-consolidated subsidiaries

		£
Euston 80% ×	46,000 =	36,800
Waterloo profit	12,000	
Less: payable to pref. shareholders	1,000	
60% ×	11,000	6,600
		43,400

11. Taxation

Metropolis	30,000
Euston 80% × 20,000	16,000
Waterloo 60% × 6,000	3,600
	49,600

12. Opening group reserves

	£
Metropolis	250,000
Euston 80% × (24,000 – 20,000)	3,200
Marylebone 60% × (88,000 – 10,000)	46,800
Waterloo 60% × (6,000 – 5,000)	600
	300,600

13. Split of retained profit for the year

		£
Metropolis		70,000
Euston 80% × 6,000	4,800	
Marylebone	Nil	
Waterloo 60% × 2,000	1,200	6,000
		76,000

ANSWER F5

1. Consolidated financial statements are a form of group accounts which present the information contained in the separate financial statements of a holding company and its subsidiaries as if they were the financial statements of a single entity (*SSAP 14, para. 12*).

   They consist normally of a consolidated balance sheet, profit and loss account and funds flow statement together with supporting notes.

   Under the Companies Acts, a company may produce group accounts in a form other than consolidated accounts. If any other form is used the group accounts should explain by way of note why such other form has been used in preference to consolidated accounts. The accounts would need to state to what extent results of subsidiaries have been dealt with in the accounts of the holding company (Sch. 1 CA 1981).

   Forms of group accounts which could be used, but which in practice are very rare, include:

   (a) Producing a full set of accounts for each company within the group.
   (b) Producing summarised accounts for each company.
   (c) Consolidating different groups of subsidiaries and therefore producing a number of sets of consolidated accounts.
   (d) Producing a set of consolidated accounts for some group companies and individual accounts for others.

   Subject to certain limited exceptions, none of the above comply with *SSAP 14.*

2. Under *SSAP 14* a subsidiary should be excluded from consolidation if:

   (a) Its activities are so dissimilar from those of other companies within the group that to consolidate would be misleading.
   (b) The holding company holds more than one-half of the equity shares of the subsidiary but either does not control half the votes or has contractual or other restrictions imposed on its ability to appoint the majority of the board of directors.
   (c) The subsidiary operates under severe restrictions which significantly impair control by the holding company.
   (d) Control is intended to be temporary.

3. (a) The existence of exchange control restrictions do not in themselves constitute severe long-term restrictions which impair control. Thus, Victoria Ltd should be consolidated in the normal way. The standard requires that if there are significant restrictions on the ability of the holding company to distribute profits, the extent of the restrictions should be indicated (*SSAP 14, para. 36*).
   (b) If a subsidiary does not prepare its own financial statements to the same date as the group, it should use special financial statements

to cover the period to the end of the accounting period of the group. In the case in question this is from 1 Jan. to 31 Mar. (*SSAP 14, para 17*).

If it is not possible to obtain such special financial statements appropriate adjustments should be made to the consolidated financial statements for any abnormal transactions in the intervening period. The accounts should disclose:

(i) The name of the subsidiary;
(ii) Its accounting date (and period, if different);
(iii) The reason for using different dates.

(*SSAP 14, para. 18*).

(c) Uniform accounting policies should be used in the consolidated financial statements. Where such policies are not adopted by a subsidiary, appropriate adjustments should be made. That would appear to be the case here. The accounts of London High Level Ltd should be adjusted to use the group's depreciation policy.

In exceptional cases where adjustment is impracticable different policies may be used provided that they are generally acceptable and there is disclosure of:

(a) the different types of policies used;
(b) an indication of the effect on group results;
(c) the reasons for the different treatment.

(*SSAP 14, para. 16*).

(d) It would appear that the business of Manvers Ltd is so different from the rest of the group that it should not be consolidated, as to do so would be misleading.

The group accounts of Carrington Ltd should include separate financial statements for Manvers Ltd. These statements should give:

(a) a note of the interests of Carrington Ltd;
(b) particulars of intra-group balances;
(c) the nature of transactions with the rest of the group;
(d) a reconciliation with the amounts included in the consolidated financial statements of Carrington Ltd which should be dealt with using the equity method of accounting.
(*SSAP 14, para. 23*).

(e) The accountant would need to determine the effective date of acquisition of Midland Ltd which should be the earlier of

(i) the date on which consideration passes; and
(ii) the date on which the offer became or was declared unconditional.
(*SSAP 14, para. 32*).

The cost of acquisition of Midland needs to be allocated between the underlying net tangible and intangible assets so that a goodwill or capital reserve figure can be calculated. This procedure may necessitate a revaluation of the assets of Midland at the date of acquisition. (*SSAP14, para. 29*).

The consolidated profit and loss account should include the results of Midland from the date of acquisition, and the statements should give sufficient information to enable the shareholders of Carrington to appreciate the effect of the acquisition of Midland (*SSAP 14, para. 30*).

ANSWER G1

Consolidated Balance Sheet
as at 31.12.–2

	£	£
Fixed assets		
Intangible assets—goodwill		3,500
Other		66,334
Current assets	32,500	
Creditors: amounts falling due within one year	24,167	
Net current assets		8,333
Total assets *less* current liabilities		78,167
Less: Creditors: amounts falling due after more than one year	32,667	
Minority interests	10,000	
		42,667
		35,500
Capital and reserves		
Called up share capital		10,000
Reserves		25,500
		35,500

Notes to balance sheet
Fixed asset

	Goodwill £	*Other* £
Cost—at 1.1.–2	3,500	87,444
Exchange adjustment—at 31.12.–2		5,556
	3,500	93,000
Depreciation—at 1.1.–2	—	19,852
Charge for the year		5,077
Exchange adjustment—at 31.12.–2		1,737
	—	26,666

H Ltd Group
Consolidated profit and loss account for the year ended 31.12.–2

	£
Profit on ordinary activities before taxation	9,846
Tax on profit on ordinary activities	3,538
	6,308
Minority interests	923
Profit for the financial year transferred to reserves	5,385

Statement of reserves

	Holding Co.	*Subsidiary*	*Total*
	£	£	£
Reserves	11,000	7,500	18,500
Profit for the year	4,000	1,385	5,385
Exchange gain		1,615	1,615
	15,000	10,500	25,500

Note to profit and loss account
Depreciation £5,077

Workings to Balance Sheet
(1) *Translation of balance sheet*

	$	*Rate*	£
Fixed assets:			
Cost	120,000	2.4	50,000
Depreciation	(40,000)	2.4	(16,666)
Debtors	30,000	2.4	12,500
	110,000		45,834
Creditors	10,000	2.4	4,167
Loan	40,000	2.4	16,667
Share capital	10,000	4.0	2,500
Reserves:			
Pre-acquisition	20,000	4.0	5,000
Post-acquisition	30,000	Bal.	17,500
	110,000		45,834

(2) Adjustment account

	£		£
Cost of investment	8,000	Share capital:	
		60% × 2,500	1,500
		Pre-acq reserves:	
		60% × 5,000	3,000
		Goodwill c/d	3,500
	8,000		8,000

(3) MI account

	£		£
Balance c/d	10,000	Share capital:	
		40% × 2,500	1,000
		Reserves:	
		40% × 22,500	9,000
	10,000		10,000

(4) CRR account

	£		£
Balance c/d	25,500	b/d H.	15,000
		Re: Subsidiary:	
		60% × 17,500	10,500
	25,500		25,500

(5) *Fixed asset disclosure*
Opening fixed assets

	S Ltd	*Rate at 1.1.–2*		*H Ltd*	*Total*
	$		£	£	£
Cost	120,000	2.7	44,444	43,000	87,444
Depreciation	32,000	2.7	11,852	8,000	19,852

Workings to the profit and loss account

(a) Translation of profit and loss account

	$	*Rate*	*£*
Profit before depreciation	18,000	2.6	6,923
Depreciation	8,000	2.6	3,077
	10,000	2.6	3,846
Tax	4,000	2.6	1,538
	6,000		2,308

(b) Calculation of exchange difference

(i) Reconstruction and translation of opening balance sheet

	$	*Last year's translation rate*	*£*	*This year's translation rate*	*£*	*Exchange difference*
Share capital	10,000	4.0	2,500	4.0	2,500	
Reserves						
Pre acq	20,000	4.0	5,000	4.0	5,000	
Post acq (30,000–6,000)	24,000	BAL.	12,500	BAL.	15,000	2,500
Net assets	54,000	2.7	20,000	2.4	22,500	2,500

(ii) Calculation of total exchange difference

	£
Sterling value of post-acquisition reserves at 1.1.–2	12,500
Sterling value of post-acquisition reserves at 31.12.–2	17,500
Increase	5,000
Sterling profit per profit and loss account translation	2,308
Gain on exchange	2,692

(c) *Consolidation working paper*

	H £	*S* £	*Total* £
Profit before depreciation	8,000	6,923	14,923
Depreciation	2,000	3,077	5,077
	6,000	3,846	9,846
Tax	2,000	1,538	3,538
	4,000	2,308	6,308
M.I. 40% × 2308		923	923
Retained profit for year	4,000	1,385	5,385
Reserves b/f 60% × 12,500	11,000	7,500	18,500
Exchange gain 60% × 2692		1,615	1,615
	15,000	10,500	25,500

ANSWER G2

Consolidated balance sheet as at 31.12.–2
(part of overall totals)

	£
Fixed assets	
Intangible assets:	
Goodwill on consolidation	3,500
Tangible assets	20,000
	23,500
Current assets	
Debtors	12,500
Creditors: Amounts falling due within one year	4,167
Net current assets	8,333
Total assets *less* current liabilities	31,833
Creditors: Amounts falling due after more than one year:	
Loan	(16,667)
Minority interest	(4,666)
	10,500

	£
Capital and reserves	
Called up share capital	x
Profit and loss account	2,500

Notes to accounts

Tangible fixed assets

Fixed assets:	
Cost at beginning of year	30,000
Exchange adjustment	—
Cost at end of year	30,000
Accumulated depreciation at beginning of year	8,000
Charge for year	2,000
Exchange adjustment	—
Accumulated depreciation at end of year	10,000
Net book value at beginning of year	22,000
Net book value at end of year	20,000

Consolidated profit and loss account
for year ended 31.12.–2
(part of overall totals)

	£
Profit on ordinary activities before taxation	3,926
Taxation on profit on ordinary activities	1,667
Profit on ordinary activities after taxation	2,259
Minority interests (40% × post tax profits)	904
Profit attributable to members of group	1,355
Exchange gain	—
Retained profit for year	1,355

Statement of reserves
(part of overall totals)

	£
Group reserves b/f (60% of post-acquisition translated reserves at beginning of year)	1,145
Retained profit for year	1,355
	2,500

Workings

(1) *Translation of balance sheet*

	$	Rate	£
Fixed assets:			
Cost	120,000	4.0	30,000
Depreciation	(40,000)	4.0	(10,000)
Debtors	30,000	2.4	12,500
	110,000		32,500
Creditors	10,000	2.4	4,167
Loan	40,000	2.4	16,667
Share capital	10,000	4.0	2,500
Reserves:			
Pre-acquisition	20,000	4.0	5,000
Post-acquisition	30,000	Bal.	4,166
	110,000		32,500

(2) Adjustment account

	£		£
Cost of investment	8,000	Share capital:	
		60% × 2,500	1,500
		Pre-acq reserves:	
		60% × 5,000	3,000
		Goodwill c/d	3,500
	8,000		8,000

(3) MI account

	£		£
Balance c/d	4,666	Share capital:	
		40% × 2,500	1,000
		Reserves:	
		40% × 9,166	3,666
	4,666		4,666

(4) CCR account

	£		£
		Re: Subsidiary:	
		60% × 4,166	2,500

(5) *Fixed asset disclosure*

Translated amount of opening fixed assets

	$	Rate	£
Cost	120,000	4.0	30,000
Depreciation	32,000	4.0	8,000

(6) *Translation of profit and loss account*

	Rate	£
Profit before depreciation	2.6	6,923
Depreciation	4.0	2,000
		4,923
Taxation	2.4	1,667
		3,256

(7) *Calculation of exchange difference*

The opening balance sheet is required to be known as far as the amounts of monetary and non-monetary items. Just one figure is required for monetary as they would have all been translated at the closing rate.

Reconstruction and translation of opening balance sheet

	$	Translation rate used last year	£
Fixed assets:			
Cost	120,000		
Depreciation	32,000		
	88,000	4.0	22,000
Monetary items (bal figure)	(34,000)	2.7	(12,593)
	54,000		9,407
Share capital	10,000	4.0	2,500
Reserves:			
Pre-acquisition	20,000	4.0	5,000
Post-acquisition (30,000–6,000)	24,000	Bal.	1,907
	54,000		9,407

	£
Sterling value of post-acquisition reserves at 1.1.–2	1,907
Sterling value of post-acquisition reserves at 31.12.–2	4,166
Increase	2,259
Sterling profit per profit and loss translation	3,256
Loss on exchange	997
To operating profit	(997)

ANSWER G3. TOWERS AND MANUEL

Closing rate method

Closing balance sheet as at 31 Dec. 19–7

	£000	£000
Fixed assets		
Intangible asset:		
Goodwill on consolidation		19.00
Tangible assets (1,659.26 – 587.78)		1,071.48
Investment		
Quoted equity shares		16.67
		1,107.15
Current assets		
Stocks	211.93	
Debtors	659.04	
Cash at bank and in hand	31.15	
	902.12	
Creditors: Amounts falling due within one year		
Trade creditors	257.74	
Proposed dividends		
Holding company shareholders	70.00	
Minority shareholders	1.34	
	329.08	
Net current assets		573.04
Total assets *less* current liabilities		1,680.19
Creditors: Amounts falling due after more than one year:		
Long term loan	149.63	
Minority shareholders interest	50.30	
		199.93
		1,480.26
Capital and reserves		
Called up share capital		800.00
Profit and loss account		680.26
		1,480.26

Consolidated profit and loss account for the year ended 31 Dec. 19–7 (closing rate method)

	£000	£000
Turnover		3,239.06
Change in stocks of finished goods and in work in progress		x
		x
Raw materials	x	
Other external charges	x	
Staff costs	x	
Depreciation	167.45	
Other operating charges	x	
		x
Profit on ordinary activities before taxation		492.93
Taxation on profit on ordinary activities		224.67
Profit on ordinary activities after taxation		268.26
Minority shareholders interest		6.44
Profit attributable to members of group		261.82
Dividends—paid	40	
proposed	70	
		110.00
Retained profit		151.82

Note to the accounts
Statement of retained profits

	£000
Balance at 1 Jan. 19–7	550.66
Retained profit	151.82
Exchange loss (80% × 27.77)	(22.22)
Balance at 31 Dec. 19–7	680.26

Workings

(1) *Balance sheet translation at 31.12.–7*

	P000	*Rate*	*£000*
OSC	400.00	4.0	100.00
Reserves:			
Pre-acquisition	30.00	4.0	7.50
Post-acquisition	249.00	Bal.	143.98
Loans	80.00		29.63
Creditors	125.00	2.7	46.30
Dividends	18.00		6.67
	902.00		334.08
Fixed assets:			
Cost	700.00	2.7	259.26
Depreciation	210.00	2.7	77.78
	490.00		181.48
Investment	45.00		16.67
Stock	151.00		55.93
Debtors	73.00	2.7	27.04
Current account	139.00		51.48
Cash	4.00		1.48
	902.00		334.08

(2) *Consolidation working papers* (all figures £000)

Adjustment account

	£		£
Cost	105.00	OSC	80.00
		Reserves	6.00
		Goodwill	19.00
	105.00		105.00

Reserves M

	£		£
Adjustment account		Balance b/d	
(80% × 7.5)	6.00	Pre-acquisition	7.50
MI (20%)	30.30	Post-acquisition	143.98
CRR (80% × 143.98)	115.18		
	151.48		151.48

MI account

	£		£
Balance	50.30	OSC	20.00
		Reserves	30.30
	50.30		50.30

CRR

	£		£
Balance c/d	680.26	Towers	565.08
		Manuel	115.18
	680.26		680.26

Dividend cancellation = 6.67 − 5.33
= 1.34 (MI)

(3) *Profit and loss account translation*

	P000	*Rate*	*£000*
Sales:			
External	1,347	2.55	528.24
Inter-company	422	Actual	162.78
	1,769		691.02
Cost of sales	1,411	2.55	553.33
	358		137.69
Depreciation	(70)	2.55	(27.45)
Sundry expenses	(131)	2.55	(51.37)
Taxation	(68)	2.55	(26.67)
	89		32.20
Dividends:			
Interim	(12)	2.6	(4.61)
Final	(18)	2.7	(6.67)
	59		20.92

(4) *Calculation of exchange difference*

(*a*) *Reconstruction and translation of opening balance sheet*

	P000	*Rate*	*£000*
OSC	400	4.0	100.00
Reserves:			
Pre-acquisition	30	4.0	7.50
Post-acquisition	190	Bal.	150.83
	620		258.33
Net assets	620	2.4	258.33

(b)

	£000
Sterling value of post-acquisition reserves at 1.1.–7	150.83
Sterling value of post-acquisition reserves at 31.12.–7	143.98
Decrease	6.85
Add: Sterling value of retained profit for year	20.92
Exchange loss	27.77

(5) *Consolidated profit and loss account workings*

	£000	*£000*
(a) *Sales* (2,710.82 + 528.24)		3,239.06
(b) *Profit before taxation:*		
Sales		3,239.06
Cost of sales (2,033.10 – 162.78 + 553.33)		2,423.65
		815.41
Expenses (104.56 + 51.37)	155.93	
Depreciation (140.00 + 27.45)	167.45	
Individual company translation gain	(0.90)	
		322.48
		492.93

(c) *Minority shareholders interest*

20% × 32.2	6.44

(6) *Group reserves at 1.1.–7*	*£000*
Towers balance b/f	430.00
Manuel 80% × 150.83	120.66
	550.66

ANSWER G4. ELTERWATER

Consolidated accounts of the Elterwater Group
(a) *Consolidated balance sheet (extracts)*

	£000
(i) Investment in associated company:	
Share of net assets	68.3
Premium on acquisition	4.7
	73.0
(ii) Consolidated reserves (part relating to that retained by associated company)	37.0
(iii) Dividend receivable from associated company (current asset)	2.7

(b) *Consolidated profit and loss account (extracts)*

	£000
(i) Share of profit of associated company	10.3
(ii) Share of tax charge of associated company	4.7
(iii) Profit retained by associated company	3.0

(c) *Statement of reserves*
Included within the overall totals are the following amounts relating to the associated company:

	£000
Balance at 1.1.–9	18.8
Retained profit	3.0
Exchange adjustment	15.2
Balance at 31.12.–9	37.0

Workings

Translation of balance sheet at 31 Dec. 19–9

	G000	*Rate*	*£000*
Ordinary share capital	400	4.3	93.0
Reserves:			
Pre-acquisition	49	4.3	11.4
Post-acquisition	188	Bal.	123.2
Proposed dividend	25	2.8	8.9
Sundry creditors	69	2.8	24.6
	731		261.1
Fixed assets:			
Cost	962	2.8	343.6
Depreciation	388	2.8	138.6
	574		205.0
Stock	76	2.8	27.1
Debtors	59	2.8	21.1
Cash	22	2.8	7.9
	731		261.1

Translation of profit and loss account for year ended 31 Dec. 19–9

	G000	*Rate*	*£000*
Gross profit	187		
Expenses	(43)		
Depreciation	(34)		
Profit before taxation	110	3.2	34.4
Taxation	(50)	3.2	(15.6)
	60		18.8
Proposed dividends	(25)	2.8	(8.9)
Retained profit	35		9.9

Reconstructed balance sheet at 31 Dec. 19–8

	G000	*Rate*	*£000*
Ordinary share capital	400	4.3	93.0
Reserves:			
Pre-acquisition	49	4.3	11.4
Post-acquisition	153	Bal.	62.8
	602		167.2
Net assets	602	3.6	167.2

Calculation of exchange differences

	£000
Post-acquisition reserves:	
At 1.1–9 (above)	62.8
At 31.12.–9	123.2
Increase	60.4
Retained profit (profit and loss account translation)	9.9
Gain on translation	50.5

(a) *Associated company investment*

	£000
(i) Share of net assets:	
Translated s/c + reserves 93.0 + 11.4 + 123.2	227.6
30% × 227.6	68.3
(ii) Premium on acquisition:	
Cost of investment	36.0
Less: 30% × s/c + reserves at acquisition 30% × (93.0 + 11.4)	31.3
	4.7
(iii) Current assets:	
Dividend receivable from associate 30% × 8.9	2.7
(iv) Consolidated reserves attributable to associated company, 30% × 123.2	37.0

Consolidated profit and loss account

	£000
(a) Group profit before tax, 30% × 34.4	10.3
(b) Group share of tax charge of Santana, 30% × 15.6	4.7
(c) Retained profit attributable to associated company:	
Profit and loss account translation, 30% × 9.9	3.0

Statement of reserves
Retained profits attributable to associated company at 1.1.–9

	£000
(a) 30% × 62.8	18.8
(b) Exchange difference: 30% × 50.5	15.2

ANSWER G5. MOORGATE PRODUCTIONS LTD AND TROPICAL ISLANDS DEVELOPMENTS LTD

Consolidated balance sheet of Moorgate Productions Ltd and its subsidiary as at 31 Oct. 19–9

Ref. to workings	£000	£000	£000
Fixed assets			371,287
Current assets			
Stocks		93,613	
Debtors		115,471	
Cash at bank and in hand		15,626	
		224,710	
(2) Creditors: Amounts falling due within one year:			
Trade creditors	104,428		
Dividend to MI	2,000		
Taxation	58,363		
Dividend	13,021	177,812	
Net current assets			46,898
Total assets *less* current liabilities			418,185
Creditors: Amounts falling due after more than one year:			
Long term loans	220,236		
(2) Minority shareholders interest	17,046		
			237,282
			180,903

	£000
Capital and reserves	
Called up share capital—ordinary shares of £1 each	
—Authorised	75,000
—Issued and fully paid	73,000
(2) Profit and loss account (note 1)	107,903
	180,903

Consolidated profit and loss account of Moorgate Productions Ltd and its subsidiaries for the year ended 31 Oct. 19–9

Ref. to workings

	£
Turnover	939,575
Cost of sales	671,123
Gross profit	268,452
Administrative and distributive costs	172,306
Profit on ordinary activities before taxation	96,146
Tax on profit on ordinary activities:	49,869
Profit on ordinary activities after taxation	46,277
(3) Minority interests	4,201
Profit attributable to the members of Moorgate Productions Ltd (of which £35,775 has been dealt with in the separate accounts of the holding company)	42,076
Dividends—proposed	13,021
Amount added to retained profit	29,055

Notes to the accounts	*£000*
1. *Reserves*	
At 1st November, 19–8 (working 6)	77,638
Profit retained for the year	29,055
Exchange adjustments (working 5)	1,210
	107,903

2. *Accounting policies*
(a statement of accounting policies, including those in the question relating to depreciation and foreign currency, would follow)

Workings (All calculations are to the nearest £000)

(1) Translation of final accounts of Tropical Islands Developments Ltd.

(a) Balance sheet at 31 Oct 19–9

	N000	*Rate*	*£000*
Ordinary share capital	20,000	5	4,000
Reserves—post acq	65,230	(Bal)	38,615
Loans	200,000	2.0	100,000
Creditors	45,698	2.0	22,849
Tax	20,232	2.0	10,116
Dividends	10,000	2.0	5,000
	361,160		180,580
Fixed assets (net)	220,000	2.0	110,000
Stock	52,734	2.0	26,367
Debtors	60,596	2.0	30,298
Cash	27,830	2.0	13,915
	361,160		180,580

(b) Profit and loss account for the year ended 31 Oct. 19–9

	N000	*Rate*	*£000*
Turnover	547,634	2.05	267,139
Cost of sales	410,857	2.05	200,418
	136,777		66,721
Admin. costs	95,017	2.05	46,350
Profit before tax	41,760	2.05	20,371
Taxation	20,232	2.05	9,869
	21,528		10,502
Dividends payable	10,000	2.0	5,000
Retained profit	11,528		5,502

(2) Consolidation working papers

Reserves—Tropical Islands Developments Ltd

	£000		£000
Minority interest		Balance b/d—pst acq.	38,615
(40% × 38,615)	15,446		
Consolidated reserves			
(60% × 38,615)	23,169		
	38,615		38,615

Dividend payable

	£000		£000
Consolidated reserves			
60% × 5,000	3,000	Balance b/d	5,000
Current liability c/d	2,000		
	5,000		5,000

Minority Interest (MI)

	£000		£000
Balance c/d	17,046	Share capital	
		40% × 4,000	1,600
		Reserves	15,446
	17,046		17,046

Consolidated reserves

	£000		£000
Balance c/d	107,903	Moorgate	81,734
		Inter co. dividend	3,000
		Reserves—	
		Tropical Islands	23,169
	107,903		107,903

(3) *Minority interests in the profits for the year*

	£000
40% × £10,502,000 =	4,201

(4) *Profits retained by subsidiary company*

60% × £5,502,000 =	3,301
Profits retained by holding company:	
Per question	22,754
Dividend receivable from subsidiary	3,000
	25,754

(5) *Translation difference*

(i) Reconstruction and translation of opening balance sheet

	N000	*Rate*	*£000*
OSC	20,000	5	4,000
Reserves			
65,230 – 11,528	53,702	Bal.	31,096
	73,702		35,096
Net assets	73,702	2.1	35,096

(ii) Translated opening post acq. reserves	31,096
Translated closing post acq. reserves	38,615
Increase	7,519
Less: Translated retained profit for year	5,502
Exchange gain	2,017
(iii) To reserves 60% × 2,017 =	1,210

(6) *Group reserves at 1.11.19–8*

	£000
Moorgate Productions (81,734 – 22,754)	58,980
Subsidiary	
60% of Translated opening reserves	
(see workings) 60% × 31,096	18,658
	77,638

Tutorial note concerning gain arising on the disposal of the shares
The extraordinary gain arising on the sale of the shares in 19–2 would have been 8 million shares at N0.50 = N4 million. This would have been included in the reserves of the holding company at the rate of exchange ruling at that date. It would not be affected by subsequent exchange rate changes. It is not possible (nor indeed necessary) to calculate the gain for the purpose of these consolidated accounts.

ANSWER H1. AVARICIOUS PLC

(a) *Parochial Ltd: investors ratios*

(i) Dividend per share $= \dfrac{\text{Dividend for the year}}{\text{No. of shares in issue and ranking for dividend}}$

19–4 $\dfrac{£27{,}000}{400{,}000} = 6.75\text{p}$

19–5 $\dfrac{£17{,}000}{400{,}000} = 4.25\text{p}$

19–6 $\dfrac{£22{,}000}{400{,}000} = 5.50\text{p}$

19–7 $\dfrac{£15{,}000}{400{,}000} = 3.75\text{p}$

19–8 $\dfrac{£20{,}000}{400{,}000} = 5.00\text{p}$

This is the actual amount paid to the shareholder by the company. The dividend carries a tax credit so that it is common for the accounts of public companies to also show the gross equivalent, including this credit. In this case, based on a basic rate of 30% the amount is

$5\text{p} \times \dfrac{100}{70} = 7.14\text{p}$

(ii) Dividend cover $= \dfrac{\text{Profit available to pay ordinary dividend}}{\text{Ordinary dividend}}$

19–4 $\dfrac{89{,}000}{27{,}000} = 3.30$

19–5 $\dfrac{95{,}000}{17{,}000} = 5.59$

19–6 $\dfrac{157{,}000}{22{,}000} = 7.14$

19–7 $\dfrac{185{,}000}{15{,}000} = 12.33$

19–8 $\dfrac{294{,}000}{20{,}000} = 14.70$

(b) *Valuation of Parochial Ltd*

For the purchase of the whole of the share capital, it would be usual to estimate a range of prices between two valuations, one based on earnings and the other on net assets.

A dividend yield basis would be more applicable to a minority holding and would be distorted in this case by the unusually high cover.

(1) *Earnings valuation*
The problem is essentially one of calculating a maintainable earnings figure at 19–8 prices attributable to the ordinary shareholders, and from that calculating a value for those shares by use of an expected P/E ratio.

(i) Maintainable earnings at 19–8 prices
The difficulty is to eliminate the effects of inflation and abnormal fluctuation. Profit after taxation has increased at the following annual rates:

19–5	6.7%
19–6	65.3%
19–7	17.8%
19–8	58.9%

This compares with other profit and loss account trends of:

	Sales growth	Trading profit growth	Profit before tax growth
19–5	25.8%	31.9%	39.6%
19–6	33.3%	45.3%	40.3%
19–7	50.6%	37.3%	44.7%
19–8	38.5%	37.7%	47.1%

These show a fairly steady upward movement, with the much greater fluctuation in profit after tax arising from a very variable percentage tax charge, presumably stemming from the omission from the deferred tax provision of any liability in respect of capital gains rolled over.

Taking account of the above the 19–8 profit before tax figure looks easily maintainable. The appropriate tax charge to make is discussed below.

(ii) Required P/E ratio
Here the difficulty relates to finding a quoted company in a similar trade, of a similar size and risk and with similar market prospects, to provide a guide to a reasonable P/E ratio.

The data from the *Financial Times* shows two companies very differently appraised by the market. L's earnings per share of 21.0p (340/16.2) exceeds that of K of 14.9p (103/6.9) by 41%, but its share price is more than three times higher.

Without knowing the reasons for this, and in the absence of information as to the comparability of Parochial Ltd with either of these companies, a fair P/E ratio for Parochial Ltd is taken to be a straight average of the two given,

i.e. $\dfrac{6.9 + 16.2}{2} = 11.6.$

It would perhaps be usual to discount this for the lack of marketability of the shares of an unquoted company, but since Parochial Ltd shows such strong growth potential, no adjustment will be made.

(iii) Application of P/E ratio to earnings figure
The P/E ratio is based on after tax figures which may have suffered varying amounts of deferred tax, calculated in accordance with SSAP 15.

An indication of the value of Parochial Ltd based on earnings is therefore:

	£
Profit before tax for 19–8	600,000
Less: Taxation at 52%	312,000
	288,000
Multiplied by expected P/E ratio of 11.6	£3,341,000

(2) *Net asset valuation*
Given the profitability of Parochial Ltd and the apparent scope for expansion, the net asset value indicates little more than a safety net.

Net book value of the net assets is stated at £1,297,000. It is difficult to assess the value of the components of the net assets figure, but the following assumptions seem reasonable:

(i) Since the freehold property is shown at cost, the figures taken are likely to be less than market value.
(ii) Given the nature of the trade, the stock is unlikely to be obsolete.
(iii) The figure for debtors is too small for errors in valuation to be material.
(iv) The company's apparent shortage of cash will not affect the going concern assumption.

On this basis, the minimum asset backing of the shares is around the book value.

(3) *Range of value*
Taking account of the above and subject to the limitations mentioned, a reasonable valuation of Parochial Ltd would be in the range £1.3 million to £3.3 million with a tendency towards the upper end of this range, depending on the prospects for further expansion.

(c) *Three additional topics in an accountant's report*

(i) *Accounting policies*
These are required to give the user an indication of how important items in the accounts have been treated, and whether or not any changes in the policies have taken place over the five years and have not been adjusted for by the reporting accountants.

(ii) *The split of the business between wholesale and retail*
A breakdown of sales, profits and assets employed, where available, between the major activities will help to give a better understanding of the trends identified in (b) above and enable a more accurate assessment of the strengths, weaknesses and future prospects of the business.

(iii) *Adjustments*
In order to show a true picture of the company's performance over the five years, the reporting accountants may find it necessary to make certain adjustments to the audited accounts. There is no statutory guidance to the nature of such adjustments, but they will include such items as material sources of revenue which are expected not to recur in the future or material changes in accounting policies.

ANSWER H2. HURD PLC

(i) *Hurd Plc*

(a) *Earnings per share*

	£
Profit after tax (before extraordinary items)	73,000
Less: Preference dividend	13,000
Attributable to ordinary shareholders	£60,000
Number of ordinary shares	600,000
Earnings per ordinary share	10p

(b) *Dividend yield*

	Ordinary	*Preference*
Net dividend per share	8.125p	6.5p
Add: ACT (30/70)	3.482	2.786
	11.607	9.286

Yield $\frac{11.6}{150p} \times 100 = 7.7\%$ $\frac{9.3p}{60p} \times 100 = 15.5\%$

(c) *Dividend cover*

$$\frac{\text{Earnings available}}{\text{Dividends paid and proposed}}$$

i.e. Preference $\frac{73,000}{13,000} = 5.6$ Ordinary $\frac{60,000}{48,750} = 1.23$

(d) *Price/earnings ratio*

$$\frac{\text{Price per share}}{\text{Earnings per share}} \quad \text{i.e.} \quad \frac{150p}{10p} = 15$$

(e) *Market capitalisation*

	£
Preference capital—200,000 shares at 60p	120,000
Ordinary capital—600,000 shares at 150p	900,000
	£1,020,000

Note: The market capitalisation of the ordinary capital could be arrived at alternatively:

i.e.	Equity earnings		PE ratio	
	60,000	×	15	= £900,000

(ii) *Factors affecting required dividend yield on minority holding of ordinary shares in a private company*

(a) Comparable market yield
(b) Transferability
(c) Management
(d) Size of holding
(e) History and prospects
(f) Security of income
(g) Disposition of other shareholdings

(iii) *Jim*

The value of a share may be computed using DCF techniques:

(a) Present value of future dividend stream	x
Plus	
(b) Present value of ultimate sale proceeds	x
Present value per share	£x

Thus

(a) Dividend stream—25p discounted using an annuity of 12% for 3 years i.e. 25p × 2.4018	60p
(b) Sale proceeds—net present value (balance)	190p
Current share price (per question)	250p

If 190p represents the present value, the ultimate sale proceeds may be computed using the net present value tables for 12% at the end of 3 years:

$$\text{i.e.} \quad \frac{190\text{p}}{0.7118} = 267\text{p}$$

(iv) *Goldie*

Yield to redemption

(a) *Simple (non-discounted) basis*

(i) Flat income yield

$$9\% \times \frac{100}{75} = 12\%$$

(ii) Simple yield to redemption

$$\frac{\text{Profit on redemption}}{\text{Current price}} \times 100 \text{ i.e. } \frac{25}{75} \times 100 = 33\tfrac{1}{3}\%$$

Over 6 years this represents an annual profit of

$$\frac{33\frac{1}{3}\%}{6} = 5.5\%$$

∴ Overall yield to redemption (non-discounted) is $12\% + 5.5\% = 17.5\%$

(b) *Discounted basis*

Stage 1 *Summarise cash flows and apply trial rates*

Year	Cash flow	First trial 15% Factor rate	First trial 15% Present value	Second trial 18% Factor rate	Second trial 18% Present value
	£		£		£
1–6	9 pa	Annuity for 6 years 3.7845	34.06	3.4976	31.48
6	100	0.4323	43.23	0.3704	37.04
			£77.29		£68.52

Stage 2 *Interpolate present values*

	(i) *Trial 1*	(ii) *Initial Investment*	(iii) *Trial 2*
(i) DCF factors	15%	?	18%
(ii) Present values	77.29	75	68.52
(iii) Range of present values	← 8.77 →		
(iv) Trial 1 minus initial investment	← 2.29 →		

Time adjusted rate of return

$$15\% + \left\{\frac{2.29}{8.77} \times (18 - 15)\%\right\}$$

i.e. $15\% + 0.8\% = 15.8\%$

∴ Yield to redemption (on a discounted basis) is 15.8%.

ANSWER H3. HOMES PLC

Terms of offer for Gardens Plc	Nominal value £	Market value £
(a) to acquire 1m 8% preference shares:		
6% preference shares at 75p	1,400,000	1,050,000
(b) to acquire 4m ordinary shares:		
(i) Ordinary shares at £4	600,000	2,400,000
(ii) 8% Unsecured Loan stock 19.19/24 at par	1,309,513	1,309,513
(c) to acquire 8m 'A' ordinary shares		
(i) Ordinary shares at £4	1,050,000	4,200,000
(ii) 8% Unsecured Loan stock 19.19/24	2,886,913	2,886,913
		£11,846,426

Workings

(a) *Preference shares*

	£
Present income £1m at 8%	80,000
5% increase	4,000
	£84,000
Capitalised at 6%	£1,400,000

(b) *Ordinary shares*

PE ratios	*H Plc* £	*G Plc* £
Profit after tax	3,060,000	680,000
Preference dividend at 6%/8%	60,000	80,000
Earnings attributable to equity	3,000,000	600,000
Shares in issue	12,000,000	12,000,000
Earnings per share (EPS)	25p	5p
PE ratio Homes Plc $\frac{400p}{25}$	16	

(c) *Valuation of Gardens Plc using required PE ratio*

Ordinary—16 × 75% = 12   5p × 12 = 60p

'A' ordinary 16 × 75% × 35/40 = 10.5   5p × 10.5 = 52.5p

(d) *Issue of Homes Plc shares*

To acquire (i) Ordinary 4m at 60p = £2.4m

Issue by Homes Plc at £4 = $\frac{2.4\text{m}}{4}$ = 600,000 shares

(ii) 'A' ordinary 8m at 52.5p = £4.2m

Issue by Homes Plc at £4 = $\frac{4.2\text{m}}{4}$ = 1,050,000 shares

(e) *Loan stock issue*	*Ordinary*	*'A' ordinary*
	£	£
Present income (Gardens Plc dividends)	160,000	320,000
Future income (Homes Plc dividend)		
12% × £600,000	72,000	
12% × £1,050,000		126,000
Loss of income	88,000	194,000
5/6 thereof	73,333	161,667
Add: Tax credit (30/70)	31,428	69,286
	104,761	230,953
Capitalised at 8%	£1,309,513	£2,886,913

ANSWER H4. STRANGHUM LTD

Messrs Maxus and Minus
Stranghum Ltd
Tabernacle Street
London

Dear Sirs

Valuation of shares in Stranghum Ltd
In accordance with your instructions we have prepared the following valuations of your shareholdings in the above company. It is understood that the holdings are to be offered separately to independent buyers.

(a) *Shares held by Maxus*
Since these shares comprise 95% of the issued capital, a range of prices must be computed using the following alternative bases:

. . . assets—based on attributed values of the underlying net tangible assets.
. . . assets—based on the capacity of the assets to generate earnings using a target rate of return of 16%.
. . . earnings—based on suitably discounted PE ratio of a similar quoted company, but taking into account a control premium.

	£	£
(i) Assets—attributed values		
Net assets at book values		300,000
Add: Freehold revaluation		60,000
		360,000
Less: Goodwill		50,000
Net tangible assets		310,000
Per share (200,000) (ex div)		£1.55
Add: Proposed dividend		0.15
Per share (cum div)		£1.70
(ii) Assets—earnings capacity		
Capital employed		
Net assets		300,000
Less: Freehold	100,000	
Goodwill	50,000	
		150,000
Operating assets		£150,000

	£
Return	
Profit before tax	70,000
Less: Notional rent	14,000
	56,000
Add: Excess directors' emoluments	8,000
	64,000
Less: Tax (at 50%)	32,000
Return on operating assets	£32,000
Required return on capital employed	16%
	£
Capitalised value of operating profit	200,000
Add: Freehold (at valuation)	160,000
	£360,000
Per share (ex div)	£1.80

(iii) PE ratio basis
Since Stranghum Ltd is unquoted, a suitable PE ratio to be used for valuation would be (say) 75% of PE ratio of similar quoted company (i.e. 75% × 8 = 6).

	£
Profit after tax (per question)	35,000
Add: Excess remuneration (less tax)	4,000
	£39,000
Earnings per share (200,000)	19.5p
Value per share (19.5p × 6) (ex div)	117p

To this value must be added a control premium which will be dependent, to a large extent, on the willingness (and need) of Maxus to sell and on the intentions of an intending purchaser.

(iv) Summary
The range of prices (ex div) within which the shares might be offered for sale are as follows:

Assets—attributed values	£1.55
—earnings capacity	£1.80
PE ratio—minimum price	£1.17

Clearly Maxus should offer the shares for sale at £1.80, but may be prepared to accept a lower figure—probably not less than £1.55.

(b) *Shares held by Minus*
In view of the fact that Minus has no control over the financial policy of the company, we feel his shares should be valued on a dividend yield basis. We consider that, in view of his insecure position, a yield of at least 20% would be required on these shares. The dividend for the year ended 31 Mar 19–0 was, in fact, 21.4% (i.e. 15% plus tax credit at 30/70) and we would suggest that a reasonable value would be:

$£1 \times \frac{21.4}{20}$	£1.07 per share
To which must be added the proposed dividend	15
Giving a total value per share (cum div) of	£1.22

We would point out that on the purchase of Maxus' holding, which amounts to 95% of the issued share capital of the company, the provisions of s.209, Companies Act 1948, could come into operation. This would mean that Minus would be entitled to have his shares acquired either on terms similar to those offered to Maxus, or on such other terms as may be agreed or the Court may order. The purchaser of Minus' holding would therefore be taking a calculated risk.

Yours faithfully . . .

Tutorial note:

In this answer two assumptions have been made in areas where considerable difference of opinion arise. These assumptions are:

(*a*) *Price/earnings ratio of 6 taken as factor to capitalise earnings in* (*a*) (*i*). *The ratio of 8 given in the question relates to a larger quoted company and it would appear reasonable to reduce the ratio to approximately 6 for Stranghum Ltd.*

(*b*) *In part* (*b*) (*valuation of Minus' holding*) *a required dividend yield of 20% is taken, which is a reasonable increase on the 10% given in the question having regard to the smaller size of the company and the vulnerability of Minus as a minority shareholder in a company in which a single individual holds 95% of the issued share capital.*

ANSWER H5. GRAPES LTD

The Directors
Grapes Ltd

Gentlemen

Proposed acquisition of entire share capital of Pip Ltd

Further to your recent request, we give below a detailed explanation of three of the methods adopted for the valuation of shares.

1. *Assets basis*
Under this method shares are valued by reference to the value of the underlying net assets of the company. Depending on the purpose of the acquisition the assets may be valued on one of the following bases:

(a) *Break-up value basis*
The method assumes that some or all of the assets will be immediately realised and will not continue to be used in the business. This method might be appropriate, for instance, where the company has valuable freehold property which may not be essential to the particular activities of the company being acquired, or which as a result of rationalisations may be superfluous to the needs of the new enlarged group.

(b) *Going concern basis*
Under this method the assets are valued on the presumption that they will be retained for use in the business. In addition to valuing the tangible assets (freehold, plant, stock, etc.) it will be necessary to arrive at a valuation of the goodwill of the company—that is its ability to earn profits in excess of those expected from the capital employed in that particular type of business.

There are no precise bases which can be adopted in valuing goodwill, although one of the most suitable methods is to value the entire undertaking by capitalising the profits earned at the rate of return which would be expected from an investment in that particular company. This has the indirect effect of valuing the goodwill on the basis of the capitalised value of the super profits of the company to be acquired.

From the total value of the assets to be acquired there will be deducted the liabilities of the company in order to arrive at the value of the *net* assets and thus the price to be paid for the issued share capital.

It is a basis which is suitable for the valuation of a 100% interest in a company.

2. *Price/earnings ratio*
This ratio relates the earnings per share to the price paid for each share and thus indicates the number of years it will take to recoup the purchase price of the shares in terms of the current level of earnings.

The price/earnings ratio will therefore indicate, based on the current level of earnings, the return which will be made on your company's investment in Pip Ltd. Assuming that the shares in this company are not quoted the shareholders of the vending company will require a bid price which will give an 'exit' price/earnings ratio similar to that of a comparable quoted company.

If the shares in Pip Ltd were quoted, the price offered must be sufficiently above the current price to reflect the 'control premium' payable for a 100% interest. The amount of this premium will be determined to a certain extent by the spread of shareholdings in Pip Ltd. The more closely these are controlled by family interests the higher will be the price which must be offered in order to persuade all the existing shareholders to sell.

From the viewpoint of your own company it will be necessary to determine the earnings yield which is expected and required from this particular investment and thus the price/earnings ratio on which the shares are to be acquired. Having done this, the price/earnings ratio is a suitable method to use in relation to a 100% acquisition of shares.

3. *Gross dividend yield*
This percentage relates the dividend per share to the price per share and will therefore vary according to the dividend policy of the company. Since you are to acquire control of Pip Ltd you will be able to dictate the level of distribution to be made. Since you are concerned with the underlying earnings and not the amount of the distributed profit, this method would *not* be appropriate in valuing a 100% acquisition of shares.

4. *Conclusion*
It must be appreciated that there is no precise basis which can be adopted in valuing a holding of shares. Both the assets and the price/earnings ratio basis will give an indication of the range of prices within which a bid should be made. In the end result it will be necessary to offer a price at which it is anticipated there will be a 100% acceptance. If this price is in excess of those computed on an assets basis or on a price/earnings ratio basis, the amount of the excess or premium must depend on the value of the new company in the group as a whole.

We shall be pleased to offer any further information or explanations you may require.

Yours faithfully

Snoggins & Co
Accountants

ANSWER H6. FRAIL PLC

The Directors
Frail Plc

Gentlemen
Offer for the ordinary stock of Hale Plc
Having examined the information given regarding Frail Plc, Hale Plc, and the facts leading up to the present proposals for an offer for the ordinary stock of Hale Plc I am now able to reply to your enquiries as follows:

1. *The offer could be improved upon without putting the existing shareholders of Frail Plc to any disadvantage*
This opinion has been arrived at after consideration of the following circumstances:

(i) *Value of bid*

	£
For every 5 shares in Hale Plc	
11 Ordinary at £1.50	16.50
2 Preference at 50p	1.00
	£17.50

i.e. £3.50 per share (against present price of £3)

(ii) *Comparison of return*
Existing income on holding of 50 ordinary shares in Hale Plc

	£	£
Dividend 15% on 50 shares		7.50
Future income on shares in Frail Plc		
Dividend—ordinary—6% on 110 shares	6.60	
preference—$4\frac{1}{2}$% on 20 shares	0.90	
		7.50

(iii) *Present investment ratios*

	Frail Plc	*Hale Plc*
Share price—ordinary	150p	300p
Dividend per share	6p	15p
Dividend yield (grossed at 30%)	5.71%	7.14%
Earnings per share	15p	60p
Dividend cover	2.5 times	4 times
PE ratio	10	5

(iv) *Flow of funds*
Of the surplus cash of £200,000, £150,000 ought to be invested in the warehouse of Hale Plc in order to reduce the costs of rental finance now advised.

(v) *Savings due to merger*

	£
Present rent of warehouse of Hale Plc	12,000
Less: Interest formerly received by Frail Plc (£150,000 at 6% pa)	9,000
	3,000
Overheads and management	52,000
	55,000
Less: Corporation tax (50%)	27,500
	£27,500

(vi) *Combined profits*

	£
Frail Plc 15p on 10m shares	1,500,000
Hale Plc	900,000
	2,400,000
Savings due to merger	27,500
	2,427,500
Less: Additional preference dividend £600,000 at $4\frac{1}{2}$%	27,000
Available for equity	2,400,500

(vii) *Equity capital*

	£m
Frail Plc—existing	10
—additional 11 for 5	3.3
	13.3

(viii) *Revised earnings per share*
With projected earnings of £2,400,500 and 13.3m shares in issue EPS would be 18p (previously 15p) giving a PE ratio of 8.3 (previously 10) on a share price of 150p.

2. *Conclusion*
It can therefore be seen that the majority of the benefit accrues to the shareholders of Frail Plc, since earnings per share increase with a compensating reduction in the PE ratio. Under the present scheme the shareholders of Hale Plc receive a capital gain of 50p per share but no increase in income.

Since the rate of growth of profits of Hale Plc is expected to be materially in excess of those expected from the Frail group, the shareholders of Hale Plc are being asked to forego their interest in this growth potential in return for a capital gain of 50p per share.

Some advance in the offer terms is therefore needed in order that the benefits arising from the merger may be more fairly shared between the shareholders of both companies.

Yours faithfully
Bloggs & Snodgrass
Accountants

ANSWER H7. JAMES LTD AND CHARLES LTD

(a) *Basis of acquisition of issued capital by Jamchar Ltd*
(i) *Issue of 9% loan stock 19.33 for net assets*

	James Ltd		*Charles Ltd*	
	£	£	£	£
Furniture		12,000		16,000
Less: Depreciation at 15% pa		3,600		4,800
		8,400		11,200
Investments (at market value)		14,000		30,000
Stock	31,200		35,200	
Debtors $(39{,}600 \times \frac{100}{99} + 800)$	40,800		43,200	
		72,000		78,400
		94,400		119,600
Current liabilities		49,500		56,400
		£44,900		£63,200
Total loan stock issued		£108,100		

(ii) *Issue of Ordinary shares*

	James Ltd	*Charles Ltd*
	£	£
Profit—year to 30 Jun. 19.–2	11,850	13,900
30 Jun. 19.–3 (×2)	40,000	32,600
	£51,850	£46,500
Two years' purchase of average weighted profit (i.e. 2/3)	£34,567	£31,000
Total ordinary shares issued	£65,567	

(b) *Jamchar Ltd*
Balance sheet (immediately after acquisition)

	£
Fixed assets	
Investments: Subsidiary	173,667
Provisions for liabilities and charges	
9% loan stock 19.33	108,100
	65,567
Capital and reserves	
Called up share capital	65,567

Workings
(a) *Computation of adjusted profit—James Ltd*

	19.–2 £ –	*19.–2* £ +	*19.–3* £ –	*19.–3* £ +
Net profit per accounts		12,800		14,200
Stock—conversion to LIFO—19.–2		400		
—19.–3				1,250
Depreciation—increase in rate from 10% to 15%	600		600	
Debtors—general provision for bad debts not required—1/99 × £24,750		250	250	
—1/99 × £39,600				400
Advertising—written off in year ended 30 Jun. 19.–2	4,000			2,000
Excess directors' remuneration		3,000		3,000
	4,600	16,450	850	20,850
		4,600		850
Adjusted profit		£11,850		£20,000

(b) *Stock*

	FIFO basis Units	Price £	Value £	*LIFO basis* Units	Price £	Value £
At 30 Jun 19.–2						
Purchased 1 Jun.–30 Jun. 19.–2	1,000	11	11,000	200	11	2,200
pre 1 Jun. 19.–2 (bal)	1,500	10	15,000	2,300	10	23,000
	2,500		£26,000	2,500		£25,200
At 30 Jun. 19.–3						
Purchased 1 May–30 Jun. 19.–3	1,500	12	18,000	500	12	6,000
pre 1 May 19.–3 (bal)	1,500	11	16,500			
(i) pre 1 Jun. 19.–2 (as above)				2,300	10	23,000
(ii) 1 Jun. 19.–2–1 May 19.–3	(bal)			200	11	2,200
	3,000		£34,500	3,000		£31,200

Note:
It is assumed that at no stage during the year ended 30 Jun. 19.–3 did the stock in hand fall below 2,300 units.

(c) *Sales*	*19.–2*	*19.–3*
	£	£
Reduction in closing/opening stock £(26,000–25,200)	800	800
Reduction in closing stock £(34,500–31,200)		3,300
Increase in cost of goods sold	800	2,500
Profit loading—50%	400	1,250
∴ Increase in sales value	£1,200	£3,750
∴ Increase in profit arising from change in basis of stock valuation	£400	£1,250

(d) *Depreciation*

	James	Charles
Cost—19.–1	£12,000	£16,000
Depreciation—year ended 30 Jun. 19.–2	1,200	2,400
∴ Rate (straight line)	10%	15%

Tutorial notes

(*a*) *Stock—in this case the student was required to revise the basis of stock valuation from*

(*i*) *FIFO—the earliest goods purchased are sold leaving the latest purchases in stock to*

(*ii*) *LIFO—the latest goods purchased are sold leaving the earliest purchases in stock.*

The purpose of the LIFO basis is to charge the trading account with goods purchased at current prices, so that sales and purchases are both shown in terms of current values. The side effect of this basis, however, is to value stock at the cost of the earliest purchases (i.e. at out-of-date prices). Over a period of years, if the stock in hand is never completely sold out, the closing stock could be valued at prices ruling when the business commenced. It is for this reason that the Institute have recommended that LIFO is not normally a suitable basis to be used for stock valuation—surprising, therefore, that James Ltd is changing to that basis!

The first stage in the conversion to LIFO is to identify the units in stock (on a FIFO basis) at 30 Jun. 19.–2:

	Units	Price	Value
		£	£
Purchased 1–30 Jun. 19.–2	*1,000*	*11*	*11,000 (given)*
Total stock value (per balance sheet)			*26,000*
∴ Stock purchased pre 1 June 19.–3			*£15,000*
At a unit price of		*10*	
∴ Units in stock $\frac{15,000}{10}$	*1,500*		
	2,500		

On a LIFO basis, the 800 units sold in Jun. 19.–2 must be matched with the 1,000 units purchased in that period, leaving 200 units in stock. Since it is known that there were 2,500 units in stock, the balance of 2,300 units would be valued at pre 1 Jun 19.–2 prices.

A similar computation must be made at 30 Jun 19.–3 with the added complication that under the LIFO basis it must be assumed that part of the stock relates to units purchased prior to 1 Jun 19.–2 (to the extent of the units in stock at 30 Jun. 19.2—2,300 units). Thus the effect of the LIFO basis in valuing stock at out-of-date prices is clearly shown.

(b) Sales

Having revised the stock valuation it would be easy to overlook the fact that all goods are sold at cost + 50%. Not only does the change to LIFO affect the stock valuation—it also affects the cost of goods deemed to have been sold. This may be easily illustrated if it is assumed that total purchases for the year ended 30 Jun. 19.–2 amounted to £100,000.

	FIFO basis	LIFO basis
	£	£
Purchases	*100,000*	*100,000*
Less: *Closing stock*	*26,000*	*25,200*
	74,000	*74,800*
Gross profit 50%	*37,000*	*37,400*
Sales	*111,000*	*112,200*

Thus the overall effect of the change to LIFO is to increase profit by £400. A similar effect arises in 19.–3 but in this case the change in both opening and closing stock valuations must be considered.

(c) Provision for bad debts

Care must be taken to ensure that in the second year, only the increase in the general provision is adjusted.

(d) Advertising

Having written off the whole of the advertising cost in the first year, the amount originally charged in the second year must be written back.

The moral in most of the adjustments is clear—do they affect more than one year?

ANSWER H8. WALNUT CASTINGS LTD

27 Queen Street
Ryde
30 Nov. 19.–4

The Directors
Walnut Castings Ltd

Gentlemen,

Proposed offer of £2.50 per share for entire Ordinary Share Capital of Cashew Industrials Ltd

We have now considered your proposals for the acquisition of the whole ordinary share capital of Cashew Industrials Ltd, a company which is also engaged in the manufacture of light engineering products for the export market.

We regret that we do not consider that the form of your offer will suit the existing shareholders of Cashew Industrials Ltd, as their investment income is likely to be reduced after the merger due to the imposition of capital gains tax on their capital proceeds. Such a tax would not arise in the event of the offer of £2.50 per share in cash being expressed in some form of share exchange for shares in your own company. The value of your offer, at £2.50 does, however, appear to be adequate.

Due to your intention to dispose of surplus property of Cashew Industrials, the capital effectively employed by that company in trading is £179,000, as shown in Appendix 1. The future maintainable profits of that company would amount to £59,000 gross after the merger, as shown in Appendix 2, so that the rate of return, as shown in Appendix 3, would be 33% compared with 27.4% at present. Such rates of return indicate good profitability generally, and such is borne out, after providing for taxation and preference dividend in Appendix 4, where the earnings for the ordinary shares are shown as at present at 21.5p, and after merger at 26.5p. On the offer value of £2.50 per share, or £250,000 for the entire ordinary capital, the earnings yields indicated are 8.6% at present, and 10.6% in future.

The present earnings yield of 8.6% is a reasonably good selling level, having regard to the size of the company, its growth rating, the type of activity and competitive risks, etc. The proposed or planned earnings yield after the merger of 10.6% would, however, also appear to be attractive to your own company, but such earnings yields should be compared with your own existing profit plan. The cost of control and the cost of acquiring a potential or future competitor do not appear to be excessive in that the whole offer may be carried through at the price or value of £2.50 per share.

Yours faithfully
Axe & Co
Accountants

APPENDIX 1

Capital employed	£	£	£
Property at cost	87,500		
at valuation		120,000	
Less: Part due to be sold		60,000	
			60,000
Plant and machinery, at cost, less depreciation			40,500
			100,500
Net current assets			100,550
			201,050
Less: Loan			22,050
			£179,000

APPENDIX 2

Future Maintainable Profits, etc		
Profit after all charges except taxation	49,000	
Add back—Savings in directors' remuneration	7,500	
—Further economies due to merger	2,500	
Future maintainable profits		59,000
Less: Corporation tax at 50%	29,500	
Preference dividend	3,000	
		32,500
Net earnings for ordinary shares		£26,500

APPENDIX 3

Rate of Return on Capital Employed			
Future maintainable profits—as at present		£49,000	
—after merger			£59,000
Capital employed	£179,000		
Rate of return—as at present		27.4%	
—after merger			33.0%

APPENDIX 4

Earnings for Ordinary Shares		
Net earnings for ordinary shares—at present, per accounts	£21,500	
—after merger		£26,500
Earnings per share on present ordinary shares	21.5p	26.5p
Earnings yield (at £2.50 per share)	8.6%	10.6%

ANSWER H9. ENGINEERING PRODUCTS LTD

(a) *Summarised information for the five years to 31 Dec. 19.14*

Earnings per share	—current	4.50p
	average 19.10–19.14	3.80p (working a)
Price per share	—current	unquoted
	range 19.10–19.14	unquoted
Dividend per share	—current	2.00p
	average 19.10–19.14	1.40p (working b)
Book value of net assets per share		
	—using all book values	22.00p
	—valuing land at current use value	24.00p (working d)
	—valuing land at development value	26.00p (working d)

(b) *Recommended price for sale of two million shares to the public*

(i) General observations

The offer for sale of two million shares would represent the disposal of a minority interest and would leave the family interest with voting control of the company. The terms of issue would normally be based on the dividend yield and PE ratio of comparable quoted companies. In order to attract investors it would be usual to offer the shares on a higher dividend yield and lower PE ratio than those of the comparable quoted companies.

(ii) Machine Components Plc

Machine Components Ltd (MC Ltd) is assumed to represent a comparable quoted company which has a current dividend yield of 8.9% (gross) and a PE ratio of 8 and with the current dividend covered 2 times by earnings.

(iii) Method of issue

In the present state of the market, it is unlikely that the sponsoring brokers would contemplate a general offer for sale to the public. It is more likely that they would recommend a private placing of shares with selected clients. If a general offer for sale is to be made, the terms will have to compare very favourably with a similar quoted company.

(iv) Engineering Products Ltd

While Engineering Products Ltd (EP Ltd) shows steadily increasing profits over the five years 19–10–19–14, the growth rate is not indicative of a highly dynamic company. If the results were adjusted for inflation it might well be found that profits had not increased in real terms at all.

Against this, it is relevant to note that the return on capital employed of EP Ltd (excluding the development land) is 20% compared with 15% for MC Plc.

(v) Recommended range of prices
Based on dividend yield (19–14) of MC Plc

$$\left(2p \times \frac{100}{70}\right) \times \frac{100}{8.9} = 32p \text{ per share}$$

Based on average dividend yield (19–10–14) of MC Plc and average dividend per share

$$\left(1.4p \times \frac{100}{70}\right) \times \frac{100}{6.9} = 29p \text{ per share}$$

The second value indicates that dividends have been increasing and tends to undervalue the shares on a current basis.

Based on PE ratio (19.14) of MC Plc $\left(\text{i.e. } \frac{24}{3p} = 8\right)$

4.5p × 8 = 36p per share
Given the present state of the market, a discount is considered appropriate and a range of 29p to 35p is suggested.

(vi) Summary
On the range of prices indicated, the dividend yields and PE ratios (on current earnings and dividends) would be as follows:

Price	Dividend yield (gross)		PE ratio
29p	$\frac{2p}{29p} \times 100 \times \frac{100}{70}$	9.9%	$\frac{29p}{4.5p} = 6.4$
35p	$\frac{2p}{35p} \times 100 \times \frac{100}{70}$	8.2%	$\frac{35p}{4.5p} = 7.8$
MC Plc		8.9%	8.0

(c) *Recommended price for sale of three million shares to a single buyer*

(i) General observations
Three million shares represent a controlling interest. Since a buyer would be able to control the company's dividend policy, valuation on a dividend yield basis would not be appropriate.
Appropriate bases of valuation would be:

—PE ratio basis
—asset basis.

(ii) PE ratio basis
This would be based on the PE ratio of MC Plc suitably discounted to reflect the fact that EP Ltd would continue as an unquoted company. Since MC Plc is quoted on a PE ratio of 8 it would be suitable to use something like 6 for EP Ltd. To the price thus computed would be added a control premium to reflect the added value attaching to a controlling interest.

Current earnings per share of EP Ltd	4.5p
Capitalised using PE ratio of (say) 6	27p
Add: Control premium (say)	9p
	36p

(iii) Asset basis valuation

An asset basis valuation would be based on the value of

(a) The net tangible assets.

(b) The total capital employed determined by capitalising the maintainable earnings at a required rate of return.

(a) Net tangible assets

Net assets at book values (as represented by share capital and reserves)	1,100
Add: Revaluation of freehold £(250,000–50,000)	200
	1,300
Per share	26p

(b) Capitalised value of earnings

(Applying ROCE of Machine Components Plc to operating earnings of Engineering Products Ltd)

MC Plc	
Earnings per share (per question)	3p
Net assets per share	20p
Return	15%
EP Ltd	*£000*
Earnings	225
Less: Rent of alternative premises	15
Operating earnings	210
Capitalised at 15%	1,400
Add: Land at development value	250
	1,650
Per share	33p

(iv) Summary

PE ratio basis	36p
Assets—net tangible	26p
capitalised value	33p

Since the price of 36p includes an arbitrary control premium of 9p the bid price for the sale of a controlling interest is likely to be within the range of 26p to 36p.

Workings

(a) *Average earnings per share (EP Ltd)*

Total earnings 19.10–19.14	£950,000
Average earnings 19.10–19.14	£190,000
EPS (5,000,000 shares)	3.80p

(b) *Average dividend per share (EP Ltd)*

Total dividends 19.10–19.14	£350,000
Average dividends 19.10–19.14	£70,000
Per share (5,000,000 shares)	1.40p

(c) *Average dividend yield (MC Plc)*

Average dividends per share	1.2p
Average share price	25p

Average dividend yield $\frac{1.2\text{p}}{25\text{p}} \times 100 \times \frac{100}{70}$ 6.9%

(d) *Revaluation of net assets*

	Basis of revaluation	
	Current use	*Development*
	£000	*£000*
Share capital and reserves	1,100	1,100
Surplus on revaluation of land	100	200
	1,200	1,300
Per share	24p	26p

Dividend yield, price/earnings ratio and dividend cover of Machine Components Plc

$$\text{Dividend yield} \quad \frac{1.50}{24.00} \times 100 \times \frac{100}{70.00} = 8.9\%\ \text{(gross)}$$

$$\text{Price/earnings ratio} = \frac{24.00}{3.00} = 8\ \text{times}$$

$$\text{Dividend cover} = \frac{3.00}{1.50} = 2\ \text{times}$$

(e) *Return on capital employed (EP Ltd)*

$$\text{ROCE} = \frac{\text{Operating earnings}}{\text{Capital employed less land}} \times 100\%$$

$$= \frac{210{,}000}{(1{,}100{,}000\text{–}50{,}000)} \times 100\%$$

$$= 20\%$$

ANSWER H10. MASSIVE LIMITED

(a) *Issue of Loan stock and ordinary shares*

	North Ltd		*South Ltd*		*West Ltd*	
	£000	*£000*	*£000*	*£000*	*£000*	*£000*
Tangible fixed assets		620		480		360
Other assets		35		280		85
		655		760		445
Less: Liabilities	80		130		35	
10% loan stock	70		—		40	
		150		130		75
Net tangible assets		505		630		370
Average annual profits		90		120		50
Less: Loan stock interest (10%)		7		—		4
		83		120		46
Capitalised at 10%		830		1,200		460
Less: Net tangible assets		505		630		370
Goodwill		325		570		90
Issue of:						
12% loan stock at par	(1,505)	505		630		370
£1 ordinary shares	(985)	325		570		90
	2,490					

(b) *Effect on 1,000 shares in South Ltd*

(i) *Exchange of securities*

South Ltd shares valued at $\frac{1,200}{500}$ = 240p each

1,000 South Ltd at 240p = £2,400

Exchanged for:

12% Loan stock	$\frac{630}{1,200} \times £2,400$	1,260
Massive Ltd £1 ordinary shares	$\frac{570}{1,200} \times £2,400$	1,140
		£2,400

(ii) *Equity earnings*

		South Ltd	Massive Ltd (i)	Massive Ltd (ii)
		£000	£000	£000
Profit before loan interest		120	520	230
Less: Loan interest:				
12% × 1,505	180.6			
10% × 110	11			
	191.6		191.6	191.6
Equity earnings		120	328.4	38.4
Equity shares in issue		500	985	985
Earnings per share		24p	33.34p	3.9p
Value per share on the basis of a required price/earnings ratio of 10		240p	333p	39p

(iii) *Investment values*

	South Ltd	Massive Ltd	
	£	£	£
1,000 South Ltd at 240p	2,400		
1,140 Massive Ltd at 333p/39p		3,796	445
£1,260 12% Loan stock at par		1,260	1,260
	2,400	5,056	1,705
Gain (loss) in value		£2,656	£(695)

(c) *Alternative Scheme*

The proposed scheme contains two major disadvantages:

(i) The capital structure of Massive Ltd is too highly geared. The content of fixed interest capital of the group would be £(1,505,000 + 110,000) = £1,615,000 against equity capital of £985,000.

(ii) By making Massive Ltd the holding company with three wholly owned subsidiaries, the present reserves of those subsidiaries would, using generally accepted accounting principles, be regarded as pre-acquisition profits and thus non-distributable.

An alternative scheme would have to overcome these points.

Capital Gearing

It is usual to find that a debenture trust deed incorporates provisions whereby the maximum loan stock (or debentures) which a company is permitted to issue is restricted by reference to asset cover and interest cover. As a *general* rule (which may be varied in particular circumstances) the following restrictions apply:

(i) Asset cover—overall borrowings are restricted to share capital plus reserves.
(ii) Interest cover—overall interest payable is restricted so that it is covered 4 times by the average profits (before interest) of the previous 3 years.

Using these criteria, the maximum issue of loan stock would be:

(i) Asset cover
The assets of the new undertaking amount to £2,490,000 and thus, to be covered, say, twice, the loan stock issue would be restricted £1,245,000. With existing loan stock of £110,000, the new issue would be limited to £1,135,000. If, as is likely, intangible assets are ignored, the maximum issue would be restricted to one-half of £1,505,000 = £752,500 (less existing issue).

(ii) Interest cover

	£
The average historic earnings amount to	260,000
The maximum interest payable if covered 4 times would be $\frac{260,000}{4}$	65,000
Less: Existing interest—10% × £110,000	11,000
	£54,000
Maximum issue at coupon rate of 12% £54,000 × $\frac{100}{12}$	£450,000

Thus the new issue would be restricted to £450,000. This figure would be increased to the extent that the average profits for the last 3 years exceeded £260,000 (these are average profits for the last 5 years).

Distributable reserves
In accordance with generally accepted accounting principles, the pre-acquisition profits of a subsidiary company are not available for distribution by the holding company. This means that the existing reserve balances of North Ltd, South Ltd and West Ltd would be frozen.

There is an argument that where a *merger* occurs (basically the acquisition of 90% of the equity voting share capital, settled by the issue of equity voting share capital in the bidding company) the pre-acquisition profits of the subsidiary are *not* frozen. This view was expressed in the original ED 3 and again in ED 31 and is known as *merger accounting* ("pooling" in America). This treatment has not, however, gained full support in the United Kingdom. In any event, the desire to settle the bid by the issue of a substantial block of loan capital would mean that the criteria for applying merger accounting principles would not have been fulfilled.

If it were considered desirable to maintain a fund of existing retained earnings within the new group it would be necessary for one of the existing companies to bid for the shares in the other companies. After the revaluations South Ltd is the largest single company in the new group, and it is probably most suitable to make this company the new holding company.

Summary
The alternative scheme would involve a bid by South Ltd settled by the issue of £450,000 12% loan stock and the balance in shares.

The disadvantage of this scheme from the view point of the shareholders of North Ltd and West Ltd would arise from the fact that part of the consideration for their shares would be settled by the issue of non-equity loan stock. This would compare with the situation as regards the shareholders of South Ltd who would continue to own only equity shares in the enlarged holding company. On this basis they would own a greater proportion of the equity of South Ltd than they would have held in Massive Company Ltd.

ANSWER H11. CRUMBLE LTD

(a) Price/earnings ratio

This ratio relates the earnings per share to the price paid for each share and thus indicates the number of years it will take to recoup the purchase price of the shares in terms of the current level of earnings.

Here the difficulty relates to finding a quoted company in a similar trade, of a similar size and risk and with similar market prospects, to provide a guide to a reasonable P/E ratio.

The data for the three public companies indicate average P/E ratios in the range 8 to 10. In the absence of information as to the comparability of Crumble Ltd with any of these companies, a fair P/E ratio would be around 9.

However, to take account of the lack of marketability of the shares of an unquoted company the P/E ratio should be reduced to, say, 75% of the P/E ratio of a similar quoted company i.e. to 75% × 9 = 6.75.

As the P/E ratio reflects what the market believes will be the company's future earnings, it would appear sensible to apply the ratio to the average of future profits over the next five years, calculated as follows:

		£
Year 1		85,000
Year 2	1.05 × Year 1	89,250
Year 3	1.05 × Year 2	93,713
Year 4	1.05 × Year 3	98,399
Year 5	1.05 × Year 4	103,319
		469,681
Average		93,936

$$\text{Earnings per share} = \frac{93{,}936}{200{,}000} = \qquad 46.97\text{p}$$

$$\begin{aligned}\text{Value of ordinary share} &= \text{P/E ratio} \times \text{EPS} \\ &= 6.75 \times 46.97\text{p} \\ &= £3.17\end{aligned}$$

(b) *Dividend yield*

The dividend yield relates the dividend per share to the price per share and will therefore vary according to the dividend policy of the company. Where a majority shareholding is being acquired or where a whole business is being bought or sold then this method will not be appropriate in valuing the shares. In these cases the purchaser will acquire overall control and will be more concerned with the underlying earnings and not the amount of distributed profit.

The average dividend yields of the three public companies operating in the same market are all about 17%. It is assumed that this figure is the gross dividend yield and has been calculated using dividends grossed up at the ACT rate of 30/70. The value of an ordinary share can then be calculated by applying the rate of 17% to the gross dividend paid by Crumble Ltd.

Assuming the level of dividend paid in the past will continue into the future, the future dividend per share will be

$$\frac{£30{,}000}{200{,}000} = 15\text{p}$$

This is equivalent to a gross dividend of $15 \times \frac{100}{70} = 21.4\text{p}$

The value of an ordinary share is then $21.4 \times \frac{100}{17} = £1.26$

(c) *Balance sheet values*

A calculation of the net assets per share based on the net book values of assets appearing in the balance sheet, provides a quick and simple method of valuing a company's shares. However, such a valuation is likely to give poor results. The balance sheet may include items such as formation or preliminary expenses, which although included in net assets have no real value to the business. (However, the student should note that para. 3 (2) Sch. 1 CA 1981 now prohibits such expenses being shown as assets.) But the main reason for the failure of this method results from fixed assets being included in the balance sheet on an historic cost accounting basis. Where such assets were bought several years ago, their current value may as a result of inflation, greatly exceed the balance sheet figure and consequently the share valuation will be depressed.

Net assets per balance sheet:	£
Share capital	200,000
Reserves	595,000
	795,000

$$\text{Net assets per share} = \frac{£795,000}{200,000} = £3.98$$

(d) *Net assets valuation*

As in the previous method, a net assets valuation values shares by reference to the underlying net assets of the company. However, it represents an improvement on the previous method as the assets are now included at their current values. It is assumed that the business is to be sold as a going concern. The assets can then be valued on the presumption that they will be retained for use in the business rather than on a liquidation basis.

A disadvantage of this valuation basis, is that it ignores the company's future earnings prospects.

	£	£
Fixed assets at valuation		
Land and buildings		610,000
Plant and equipment		288,000
Motor vehicles		102,000
		1,000,000
Current assets—as per balance sheet		293,000
		1,293,000
Less: Current liabilities	180,000	
Loan	150,000	
		330,000
		963,000

$$\text{Net assets per share} = \frac{£963,000}{200,000} = £4.82$$

Notes:

1. Preliminary expenses have been ignored as having no real value to the business.
2. It has been assumed that the balance sheet figures for debtors and stock are equal to the current market values of these assets.

(e) *Super profits valuation*

The previous method failed to take into account the future earnings potential of the business. The super profits or dual capitalisation method overcomes this problem by attempting to arrive at a valuation of the goodwill of the company. Goodwill represents the ability to earn profits in excess of those expected from the tangible assets employed in that particular type of business.

	£
Average future profits (see (a))	93,936
Less: Expected profits on tangible assets 12.5% × £963,000	120,375
Super profits	(26,439)

Capitalise at a rate equal to the expected return on non-tangible assets i.e. $17\frac{1}{2}\%$

$$\text{Goodwill } £(26,439) \times \frac{100}{17.5} = £(151,080)$$

Net tangible assets	963,000
Add: Goodwill	(151,080)
	811,920

$$\text{Value per share} = \frac{£811,920}{200,000}$$

$$= £4.06$$

Note

As can be seen from the above calculation the goodwill figure is negative and thus must throw doubt on whether such a calculation is relevant in this particular case. The company is, therefore, not achieving its target rate of return on its tangible assets or capital employed.

(f) *Present value of future cash flows*

This method differs from those dealt with above, in that it attempts to produce a share valuation by looking at future cash flows rather than future profits. The argument in favour of future cash flows assumes that a shareholder's willingness to invest in a company will depend on the future stream of dividends, such dividends being paid out of future cash flows.

Calculation of present value of future cash flows:

Year	*Cash flow* £	*Discount factor at* $17\frac{1}{2}\%$	*PV* £
1	100,000	0.85	85,000
2	120,000	0.72	86,400
3	140,000	0.62	86,800
4	10,000	0.52	5,200
5	150,000	0.45	67,500
Present value of company			330,900

$$\text{Value per share} = \frac{£330,900}{200,000} = £1.65$$

Note

The above calculation is only approximate as it ignores all cash flows beyond year 5.

Assuming that all annual cash flows beyond year 5 are equal to year 5 profits of £103,319 (see (a)), then the calculation could be improved as follows:

The cash flows after year 5 can be treated as a perpetuity beginning at the end of year 5.

PV of perpetuity at

$$\text{end of year 5} = 103,319 \times \frac{100}{17.5} = £590,394$$

PV of perpetuity at

$$\text{beginning of year 1} = 590,394 \times 0.45 = £265,677$$

$$\text{Total PV of company} = 330,900 + 265,677 = £596,577$$

$$\text{Value per share} = \frac{£596,577}{200,000} = £2.98$$

ANSWER H12. PUBLIC COMPANY

Analysis of results from point of view of a potential investor in the ordinary shares

Working		*Current*	*Next year*
1	(i) Basic EPS	7.3p	8.2p
1	(ii) Fully diluted EPS	8.1p	8.8p
2	Dividend per share	5.0p	5.2p
3	Dividend cover	1.46	1.58
4	Gross dividend yield	5.7%	5.9%
5	P/E ratio	17.1	15.2
6	(i) Income gearing (no loan stock conversion)	38.8%	36.0%
	(ii) Income gearing (all loan stock converted)	9.2%	8.6%

A potential investor in ordinary shares will be concerned principally with the return on his investment. This return will come in the form of:

(i) income from dividends and
(ii) capital growth as reflected in the share price.

The dividend income from the public company does not appear to be particularly outstanding. The current dividend yield of 5.7% is expected to increase to 5.9% next year, however these figures do not compare favourably with the 13.8% return currently being paid to the 11% convertible loan stock holders. In fact the figures for fully diluted earnings per share show an improvement on those for basic earnings per share, indicating that, from the point of view of an ordinary shareholder, an early conversion of the loan stock would be advantageous.

The comparatively high costs of servicing the convertible loan stock and the preference shares accounts for the appreciable level of income gearing (38.8% for the current year and 36.0% next year) being experienced by the company. However, this should not threaten the security of an ordinary shareholder's investment as the current dividend cover of 1.46 appears to be adequate and is expected to increase to 1.58 next year. With the conversion of the loan stock, the dividend cover and the earnings attributable to the ordinary shareholders will both be expected to show a further increase.

The price/earnings ratio, currently standing at 17.1 would appear to be high indicating good growth prospects for the company. This is borne out by the fact that next years profits after tax and preference dividend are expected to show an increase of 12.4%. It has been assumed in the calculations of accounting ratios that the current market price of an ordinary share, i.e. 125p will not change. On this basis, next years P/E ratio will drop to 15.2. In practice, however, the P/E ratio will probably remain fairly constant and the market price of an ordinary share will rise to around

$$\frac{17.1}{15.2} \times 125 = 141\text{p}$$

to reflect the growth in earnings.

However, in order to properly assess the results of the public company, it would be necessary also to compare the above accounting ratios with those of companies operating in a similar type of business or industry.

Workings

1. *Earnings per share*

	Current	*Next year*
(i) *Basic EPS*	£	£
Profit after tax	30,240	33,500
Less: Preference dividend	3,960	3,960
Earnings	26,280	29,540
Equity shares in issue	360,000	360,000
Basic EPS	7.3p	8.2p

	Current		*Next year*	
(ii) *Fully diluted EPS*	£	£	£	£
Earnings (as above)		26,280		29,540
Add: Interest on 11% convertible loan stock (11% × £240,000)	26,400		26,400	
Less: Corporation tax at 52%	13,728		13,728	
		12,672		12,672
		38,952		42,212
Equity shares in issue		360,000		360,000
Maximum no of new shares on conversion ($\frac{1}{2}$ × 240,000)		120,000		120,000
		480,000		480,000
Fully diluted EPS		8.1p		8.8p

2. *Dividend per share*

	Current	*Next year*
	£	£
Ordinary dividend	17,820	18,711*
Equity shares in issue	360,000	360,000
Dividend per share	5.0p	5.2p

*The expected value of next year's dividend is calculated as follows:

	Dividend	*Probability*	*Expected value*
	£		£
Zero growth	17,820	×0.5	8,910
10% growth	19,602	×0.5	9,801
			18,711

3. *Dividend cover*

	Current	*Next year*
Basic EPS (working 1)	7.3p	8.2p
Dividend per share (working 2)	5.0p	5.2p
Dividend cover	1.46	1.58

4. *Gross dividend yield*

	Current	*Next year*
Net dividend per share (working 2)	5.0p	5.2p
Gross dividend per share (net dividend × 100/70)	7.1p	7.4p
Market price of ordinary share	125p	125p
Gross dividend yield	5.7%	5.9%

5. *Price earnings ratio*

	Current	*Next year*
Market price of ordinary share	125p	125p
Basic EPS (working 1)	7.3p	8.2p
P/E ratio	17.1	15.2

6. *Income gearing*
Income gearing can be defined as:

$$\frac{\text{Debt interest + Preference dividend}}{\text{Profit before debt interest and tax}} \times 100\%$$

(i) *No loan stock conversion*

	Current		*Next Year*	
	£	£	£	£
Debt interest		26,400		26,400
Preference dividend	3,960		3,960	
Add: Corporation tax (×52/48)	4,290		4,290	
		8,250		8,250
		34,650		34,650

	Current	*Next year*
	£	£
Profit after tax	30,240	33,500
Add: Corporation tax		
(× 52/48)	32,760	36,292
	63,000	69,792
Add: Interest on 11% convertible loan stock	26,400	26,400
	89,400	96,192
Incoming gearing	38.8%	36.0%

(ii) *All loan stock converted*

	Current	*Next year*
	£	£
Preference dividend	8,250	8,250
Profit before tax	89,400	96,192
Income gearing	9.2%	8.6%

Note
As the preference dividend has to be paid out of profits which have suffered coporation tax, the preference dividend has been grossed up at a corporation tax rate of 52%. Thus, £8,250 of pre-tax profits will have to be earned to cover a preference dividend of £3,960.

7. *Yield on loan stock*

	£
Interest 11% × 240,000	26,400
Market value 240,000 × 80p	192,000
Yield to loan stock holders	13.8%
Cost to company after tax 13.8% × (100–52)%	6.6%

8. *Premium on conversion of loan stock*
The terms of conversion are 1 ordinary share for each £2 of loan stock.

	£
Market value of £2 of loan stock (£2 × 0.80)	1.60
Market value of 1 ordinary share	1.25
Premium on conversion	0.35
Premium as a percentage of the value of 1 ordinary share	28%

9. *Growth in profits*

	Current £	*Next year* £	*Increase*
Profits after tax	30,240	33,500	10.8%
Profits after tax and preference dividend	26,280	29,540	12.4%

ANSWER H13. CLAYBORN LTD

Earnings data of Nigerian company (N)

	End of year 1	2	3	4	5	
Sales	1,000,000	1,250,000	1,500,000	1,750,000	2,000,000	
Fixed costs	100,000	100,000	100,000	100,000	100,000	
Variable costs	750,000	937,500	1,125,000	1,312,500	1,500,000	
	150,000	212,500	275,000	337,500	400,000	
Tax (Nigeria)	45,000	63,750	82,500	101,250	120,000	
Profits after tax	105,000	148,750	192,500	236,250	280,000	
Distributed dividends	52,500	74,375	96,250	118,125	140,000	
Retained earnings	52,500	74,375	96,250	118,125	140,000	
Cash flow data						
Retained earnings	52,500	74,375	96,250	118,125	140,000	
Depreciation	50,000	50,000	50,000	50,000	50,000	
Dividends withheld (40%)	21,000	29,750	−50,750			
Additional Working Capital Investment	−50,000	−50,000	−50,000	−50,000	−50,000	
Return of Working Capital						+250,000
	+73,500	+104,125	+45,500	+118,125	+140,000	+250,000

Terminal value of Nigerian company (in five years' time)

	250,000	= Working capital return
$73{,}500\,(1.10)^4$ =	107,611	= Net Cash Flow Year 1, reinvested for 4 years
$104{,}125\,(1.10)^3$ =	138,590	= Net Cash Flow Year 2, reinvested
$45{,}500\,(1.10)^2$ =	55,055	= Net Cash Flow Year 3, reinvested
$118{,}125\,(1.10)$ =	129,938	= Net Cash Flow Year 4, reinvested
	140,000	= Net Cash Flow Year 5
	821,194	Total

of which 40% belongs to Clayborn = £328,478

Rates of exchange

now	N2.00 = £1	i.e.	N1 = £0.50000
End year 1	2.20 = £1		N1 = 0.4545
2	2.40 = £1		N1 = 0.4167
3	2.60 = £1		N1 = 0.3846
4	2.80 = £1		N1 = 0.3571
5	3.00 = £1		N1 = 0.3333

Cash flow–return to Clayborn in UK

Year				Exchange rate	£
3	(Back Dividends	N	50,750	0.3846	19,518
	(Current Dividends	N	38,500	0.3846	14,807
4	Current Dividends	N	47,250	0.3571	16,872
5	(Current Dividends	N	56,000	0.3333	18,665
	(Value of Investment	N	328,478	0.3333	109,482

One can use the above data to make an investment decision in one of two ways. One approach is to discount the cash flow to be received by Clayborn to obtain its present value and compare this with the value in sterling of the present offer from Nigeria. The second approach is to convert the offer from Nigeria into sterling and allowing for the investment possibilities in the UK, compound this up to obtain the terminal value of the sum at the end of year 5, which can be compared with the terminal value of the Nigerian investment plus the terminal value of the dividends received and reinvested in the UK. The answer will determine the first approach.

	Cash flow in UK	Discount factor at 15%	Present value
Year 3	£34,325	0.6575	£22,569
4	16,872	0.5718	9,647
5	128,147	0.4972	63,715
Present value of investment if do not sell			£95,931

Present value of offer N150,000 = £75,000
Decision based on figures—do not sell.

Note

This question should be seen as being more concerned with the problem of cash flows arising from joint ventures, than as a problem of overseas investment. The only aspect really concerned with foreign investment is the fluctuating exchange rate. The withholding of dividends could arise in a domestic joint venture.

It has been assumed the 'cash flow data' related to an even flow throughout a year, with the exception of the return of the working capital which is at the end of the five years. For reinvestment purposes the flow has been assumed not to start earning returns until the end of the year in which it is received. Different assumptions, with respect to timing, are equally acceptable.

ANSWER H14. LAFAYETTE LTD

Valuation method

		£000	£000
(a) (i) Asset basis	Goodwill	5,000	
Revalued $\left(£1.5\,m \times \frac{100}{8}\right)$	Property	18,750	
	Plant	20,000	
	Investments	7,500	
	Debtors	5,000	
	Stock	3,000	
	Cash	1,000	
			60,250
Less:			
Debenture payment		−7,500	
Creditors		−6,000	
Assets of Preference shareholders		−4,000	−17,500
			42,750
Number of equity shareholders			20,000,000
			=£2.14 per share

(ii) P/E ratio
Earnings per share (19–2)

$$= \frac{\text{Earnings after tax \& preference dividends (before extraordinary items)}}{\text{Number of shares}}$$

$$= \frac{£2{,}800}{20{,}000} = £0.14$$

Average P/E ratio for X and Y = 9.75
Suggested price = £0.14 × 9.75 = £1.365

(iii) Dividend Yield

$$\frac{\text{Dividend Net (19–2)}}{\text{No. of shares}} \qquad \frac{£1{,}000}{20{,}000} = £0.05$$

$$\text{Times covered} \qquad \frac{£0.14}{£0.05} = 2.8 \text{ times}$$

$$\text{Dividend gross} \qquad £0.05 + \left(\frac{30}{70} \times £0.05\right)$$

$$= £0.0714$$

Average gross dividend yield for X and Y = 4.5%

$$\text{Suggested price} = x \left(\text{where } \frac{£0.0714}{x} = 4.5\%\right)$$

$$= £1.59$$

There is clearly a big difference between the value per share arrived at on an asset basis and one based on earnings. The highest price is the £2.14, but the purchaser may not be willing to accept this. It is based on the market value of the freehold property, which presumably, is needed by Lafayette in order to continue in business. It also includes a valuation for Goodwill, an intangible asset. If the Goodwill valuation is excluded, which might well be justified as the profits of Lafayette are falling and the Property is kept at its balance sheet value, the asset basis shows the following valuation:

	£000
Property	10,000
Plant	20,000
Investments	7,500
Current Assets	9,000
	46,500
Outgoing	17,500
	29,000

This is £1.45 per share, which is near to the prices arrived at by the P/E ratio and dividend yield methods. A price of £1.60 or £1.50 would appear to be a reasonable price, but in the negotiations Lafayette should start by asking for a higher figure, nearer to the £2 per share based on asset values under one set of assumptions, namely asset stripping and a move to other premises without loss of profits.

(b) Lafayette directors should be reluctant to drop below the £1.45. The buyer can, however, point to the falling profits over the last three years. The price should be based on future earnings. We are not told about these, but the indications from the last three years are not good.

Another argument why the £1.45 based on market ratios might be high is that the P/E ratio and dividend yields are based on the average values for two companies that are larger than Lafayette, and who already have a market quotation. These two other companies are, therefore, presumably safer than the smaller Lafayette, and higher yields and lower P/E ratios should therefore be used in calculating Lafayette's price.

ANSWER H15. BARRINGTON PLC AND HUNT PLC

(a) *Offer price*

(i) To find the maximum price that Barrington Plc should pay for Hunt Plc, it is necessary to value the combined company after the takeover and deduct from that value the current value of Barrington Plc.

Current value of Barrington Plc

Shareholders interest rate is given by $i = \frac{d(1+g)}{Vo} + g$

Where d = Current dividends
Vo = current ex-div price
g = growth rate

$$\therefore i = \frac{0.40(1+0.05)}{4.20} + 0.05$$

$= 0.10 + 0.05 = 0.15$ or 15%
∴ Return demanded by shareholders in Barrington Plc is 15%.
This will fall to 14% if Hunt Plc is taken over.
Market capitalisation of Barrington Plc is 5,000,000 shares × £4.20 = £21 m

Value of combined company
Initial net profit of the combined company will be:
£4,000,000 + £800,000 + £1,200,000 = £6,000,000
∴ Initial dividend is £3,000,000
Market capitalisation of the combined company is given by

$$Vo = \frac{d(1+g)}{(i-g)}$$

Using i = 14%
g = 5%
d = £3,000,000

$$Vo = \frac{3{,}000{,}000\,(1+0.05)}{0.14\text{–}0.05} = \frac{3{,}150{,}000}{0.09}$$

$$= £35\text{ m}$$

Increase in value of company is £35,000,000 − £21,000,000 = £14,000,000
∴ The maximum that Barrington Plc could pay for Hunt Plc is £14 m or £5.60 per share.

Note: It has been assumed that the £1 million received from sale of Hunt Plc assets has been used to help generate the additional profit and therefore should not be taken into account in the price to be paid.

(ii) The minimum price that shareholders in Hunt Plc should be willing to accept is the current market value, i.e. £2 per share.

(b) *Issue of Barrington Plc shares*

Let the number of shares to be allocated be n.
Let the share price after the deal be V_T
Shareholders in Hunt Plc will receive £2 × 2,500,000 = £5,000,000
∴ Value of the new shares after the takeover must equal £5 million

i.e. $nV_T = 5{,}000{,}000$

$$\therefore V_T = \frac{5{,}000{,}000}{n}$$

From a(i), market capitalisation of combined company will be £35,000,000
$\therefore (5{,}000{,}000 + n)V_T = 35{,}000{,}000$
Substituting for V_T

$$(5{,}000{,}000 + n) \times \frac{5{,}000{,}000}{n} = 35{,}000{,}000$$

$$= \frac{25 \times 10^{12}}{n} + 5{,}000{,}000 = 35{,}000{,}000$$

$$\therefore (30 \times 10^6)n = 25 \times 10^{12}$$

$$\therefore n = \frac{25}{30} \times 10^6 = 833{,}333$$

∴ No. of shares to be issued 833,333
Total number of shares in issue will be 5,833,333

$$\therefore \text{Share price } V_T \text{ will be } \frac{35{,}000{,}000}{5{,}833{,}333} = £6 \text{ per share}$$

Existing shareholders in Barrington Plc

	£
Market value of their existing holding 5,000,000 × £4.20	21,000,000
Market value of their holding after the takeover 5,000,000 × £6.00	30,000,000
Gain to existing shareholders	9,000,000

New shareholders in Barrington Plc

	£
Market value of existing holding in Hunt Plc 2,500,000 × £2	5,000,000
Market value of new shares in Barrington Plc 833,333 × £6	5,000,000
Gain to new shareholders	Nil

(c) *Other factors affecting the desirability of the proposed takeover*

Takeovers frequently fail to achieve all that is expected of them. There are many reasons for this, but the key factor must be the inability of managements to realise and follow through the rationalisation and integration of the two companies. This historical experience must be borne in mind in evaluating the proposed acquisition.

Furthermore, in practice, many acquisitions are made for non-financial factors, for example, to increase market share, to achieve market domination, because of a desire to diversify, to obtain vertical intergration, and so on. Clearly, in this example an important objective must be to increase the extent of the market share by acquiring another company making a similar product.

No explanation is given of the way in which the profit is suddenly going to increase by £1.2 million. From the data given there appears no logical reason why this should be so. If it is to be achieved by rationalisation, then has the impact of this on sales revenue been adequately considered? If it is to be achieved by staff reductions then has the cost of redundancies and of potential union opposition been taken into account?

The information at the moment gives no indication of the policy to be followed in obtaining the improvement in profit. It is likely that the shareholders of both companies would want to know exactly who is going to be responsible for pushing through the necessary changes. In addition, if the shareholders of Hunt Plc are also managers of the business they will be particularly concerned about their own positions.

The presumption in the question is that this would be an uncontested bid. If the directors of Hunt Plc resist the bid or if there are other potential buyers in the market this could considerably increase the actual costs of making the takeover. In fact these costs have been completely ignored in the analysis, but could prove to be quite substantial. In considering this it should be borne in mind that the position of the shareholders of Hunt Plc will change dramatically. For example, a 50% shareholder of Hunt Plc would find himself owning only 7% of the shares in Barrington Plc.

The attitudes of both the unions and the government will need to be taken into account. In particular, whether there is a risk that a monopoly situation will be created and an investigation made.

Finally, it should be noted that the analysis has been carried out in terms of maximising the market value of the equity investment in the companies. It has been presumed that this hinges on a relation between anticipated future dividends and the rate of return currently required by investors in the companies—the dividend valuation model. In practice the value of shares will also be affected by such traditional measures as price earnings ratio, impact on reported profits and by changes in the level of risk associated with investment in the combined company as compared to investments in the individual companies. It may be concluded that whilst from the data provided the acquisition looks extremely attractive, and one from which shareholders in both companies could benefit substantially, a great deal more detailed information should be obtained before a final decision is taken. The information obtained should be such as to answer the points raised above.

ANSWER H16. MR CANARIO

To: Mr Canario
From: A N Advisor

Report on the valuation of the consultancy practice of Mr Puskas.

1. *Terms of reference*
   To suggest a suitable offer price for the consultancy business of Mr Puskas based on the data collected at our meeting on 30 Jun. 19–10.

2. *Conclusion*

   On the basis of the available data, the most likely acceptable price is in the region of £110,000. Additional information which would be useful before a final decision is made is summarised in para 10.

3. *Bases of valuation*

   There are two main types of approach to valuing a business. A valuation of the tangible net assets of a business will give a minimum value of the business. This is described in paragraph 4. It is more realistic to value the business in terms of its income generating capacity, as described in paragraphs 5 to 8. However, this involves more subjective estimates.

4. *Valuation of the tangible net assets of the business*

   This involves more than just adding up the balance sheet figures. These figures will be stated at historical cost, that is the cost of the assets when they were acquired, and are likely to be out of date because of inflation.

If the business is to be acquired as a going concern, that is for continued operation, it is useful to know how much it would cost to set up a similar business by purchase of the assets individually. This can be determined by examining the replacement costs of the assets.

Estimates for Mr Puskas business are as follows:

Replacement cost	£92,800
Realisable value	£81,600

Details are given in Appendix 1.

Neither of these two figures are necessarily very useful on their own. Since the business is to be acquired as a going concern, the fixed assets will not be realised. The realisable value is therefore probably irrelevant, but it is useful as a figure which gives a minimum value to the business.

5. *Valuation in terms of income generating capacity*

This approach overcomes the problems of asset valuation. The purchaser of the business is seen as paying a sum of money now (the purchase price) in order to acquire the rights to the profits, and hence cash surpluses, generated by the business in the future.

Three methods will be considered:

—Discounted cash flow	(paragraph 6)
—Price earnings ratio	(paragraph 7)
—Return on capital employed	(paragraph 8)

6. *Discounted cash flow valuation*

The aim of this calculation is to show the maximum sum of money which it would be worthwhile paying for the business. The alternative to buying the business is to invest the purchase price, earning an annual interest rate of 10%. The consultancy business must therefore do at least this well.

The present value of a stream of cash receipts is the sum of money which when invested at a given interest rate will grow to exactly the same amount as the sum of the cash receipts if each receipt is also invested at the same interest rate.

The maximum purchase price of the business can therefore be taken as the present value of the stream of cash surpluses generated by the business. For ease of valuation, these cash surpluses are assumed to occur once per year and are calculated as the profit for the year less the proprietor's salary, which has not been taken into consideration in this profit figure.

The life of the business is taken to be to perpetuity. In practical terms this means at least twenty years. Using standard perpetuity formulae, two possible valuations have been calculated in appendix 2.

These represent a range of possible valuations from as low as the tangible asset valuation (£80,000) to higher than the maximum amount of money which you could spend (£270,000).

The profits from 19–5 to 19–9 have been fairly steady. The fluctuations in profit make a trend difficult to follow, but it appears that on average profits have not kept pace with inflation.

The results of most businesses will be significantly worse in 19–10 than in preceding years as the world moves into a deep recession.

The pessimistic assumption, therefore, is that profits and proprietors salary will remain constant at about £16,000 and £8,000 respectively, leading to a valuation of £80,000. Note that it is possible to be even more pessimistic, and to assume that while profits of the business will remain constant, your salary in your present employment will rise. This would lead to a lower valuation still. In the long run, however, it is felt that salary and business profits will probably rise at the same rate.

The optimistic assumption assumes that profits of the business will rise at about 7% per annum in line with the expected long term rate of inflation. If the interest rate obtainable on your investments remains at 10%, this leads to a high valuation of £266,667.

The third calculation in the appendix recognises that it is not really valid to compare an investment in the consultancy, which produces fluctuating profits, with a relatively risk-free investment in a deposit account. A valid comparison would be with an investment in equity shares, which earned an equivalent interest rate of, say 14% per annum. This produces a valuation of £114,286.

The valuation figure is in fact extremely sensitive to the estimate of $r - g$ in the formula given, that is the difference between the expected rate obtainable on alternative investments and the expected growth rate of earnings in the business. Inflation makes these two figures extremely difficult to estimate, and in practice it is sometimes easier to look at price earnings ratios.

Despite these difficulties, the discounted cash flow approach is the valuation method with the soundest theoretical basis.

7. *Price earnings ratio valuation*

The PE ratio can be calculated for a quoted share as the ratio between the current market price and the latest reported earnings per share.

Thus market price = earnings per share × PE ratio.

This formula can be applied to the valuation of the consultancy business. A suitable PE ratio is agreed. This should be based on the average ratio for a quoted business in a similar risk class. The figure is reduced somewhat to allow for the fact that the unquoted business is less marketable.

A PE ratio of 10 applied to a profit after proprietors salary of £10,000 gives a valuation of £100,000 (Appendix 3).

The PE ratio takes the place of $\frac{1}{r-g}$ in the previous paragraph.

The problem is that the price earnings ratio for any company is affected by the expected growth rate of that company. An 'average PE ratio for a type of business' is therefore theoretically invalid.

The advantage of using PE ratios is that they are based on prices determined by market forces. They therefore reflect what price people are prepared to pay rather than indicating a maximum sum which it would be worthwhile paying. The method is also less subjective and easier to use than the method in the previous paragraph.

However, the approach is naive and feasible primarily because the real problems are ignored.

PE ratios are also subject to the criticism that they should really be based on current cost earnings if valid comparisons between companies are to be made. The same criticism applies to the return on capital employed method which is described next.

8. *Return on capital employed*

The return produced by the net assets used in the business should be as good as that produced by similar businesses. Return on capital employed is most meaningful when expressed in current cost figures. An example of the form of calculation is given in appendix 4.

A more detailed estimate cannot be made without examination of current cost accounts. However, in essence the calculation is just another version of those in paragraphs 6 and 7.

9. *Summary of results*

Method	*Valuation (£)*
Asset valuation, replacement cost	92,800
realisable value	81,600
Present value cash surpluses —best estimate	114,286
PE ratios	100,000
ROCE	120,000

On the basis of the information given, it is unlikely that a sum much below £110,000 would be acceptable to Mr Puskas.

10. *Other information which would be useful before making the final decision*

1. Detailed profit and loss accounts and balance sheets for the last five years, including current cost figures if possible. This would indicate whether the business has grown in size, e.g. the ratio of profit to turnover, etc.

2. Details of any assets not shown in the books, e.g. work in progress.
3. Further details of the freehold property. Could the business be purchased without it? Is it fully utilised? At the moment, most of the proposed purchase price appears to be for this property.
4. Further details about the nature of the consultancy business. Is it technically up to date? What are your plans for development of the business?
5. Details of the major clients, if any, of the business. Do they provide returning business or are most jobs single assignments?
6. Does Mr Puskas intend to practice after sale of the business? Will it be necessary to enter into a contract in restraint of trade?
7. To what extent will business drop away if not personally supervised by Mr Puskas?

Appendix 1

Valuation of tangible net assets

	Net replacement cost	*Realisable value*
	£	£
Freehold premises	80,000	76,000
Office equipment	7,600	2,000
Motor car	4,600	3,000
Debtors (less bad debts written off)	6,600	6,600
	98,800	87,600
Less: Current liabilities	6,000	6,000
	92,800	81,600

Appendix 2

Possible valuations based on estimated distributable cash

(i) *Pessimistic assumption*

19–10 profits will probably be down—say £16,000—assuming no growth in profits, and interest rate staying at 10%.

Consultancy profit less current salary = £(16,000 − 8,000) = £8,000.

Present value of a stream of annual receipts of £8,000 to perpetuity

$$= \frac{£8,000}{0.1} = \underline{\underline{£80,000}}$$

(ii) *Optimistic assumption*

Present value of a stream of receipts starting at A and increasing at a compound rate of g per annum where r is the discount rate

$$= \frac{A}{r - g}$$

Assume r remains at 0.10 (10%)
g is 0.07 (7%)
A is £8,000 (as in (i))

$$\text{Present value} = £\frac{8,000}{0.10 - 0.07} = \underline{\underline{£266,667}}$$

(iii) *Comparison with more risky investments*

Assume g is 0.07
A is £8,000
r is 0.14 that is 14%

made up of a risk free rate of interest of 10% and risk premium of 4%.

$$\text{Present value} = £\frac{8,000}{0.14 - 0.07} = \underline{\underline{£114,286}}$$

Appendix 3

Valuation by agreed price earnings ratio

Latest reported earnings	18,200	
Less: Proprietor's salary	8,000	
	10,200	say £10,000
Agreed PE ratio	10	
Agreed price £10,000 × 10 =	£100,000	

Appendix 4

Valuation by ROCE

	£
Expected historical cost profit in 19–10, after deducting proprietor's salary	8,000
Less: Current cost adjustments	
Depreciation and monetary working capital (debtors only), say	2,000
Expected current cost profit	6,000

Required current cost ROCE, say 5%

$$\text{Value of assets employed} = \frac{£6,000}{5\%} = \underline{\underline{£120,000}}$$

ANSWER N1. RESTART LTD

(a)

Capital reduction account

		£			£
19–7			19–7		
1 Oct.	Patents and trade marks	10,000	1 Oct.	8% Cum pref. shares	80,000
	Provision for doubtful debts	30,000		Ordinary share capital	240,000
	Plant and machinery	50,000		Freehold properties*	120,000
	Shares in subsidiary	20,000			
	Deferred revenue expenditure	24,000			
	Profit and loss account	220,000			
	Balance transferred to Capital reserve	86,000			
		440,000			440,000

*Alternatively credited direct to capital reserve

Ordinary share capital account

		£			£
19–7			19–7		
1 Oct.	Capital reduction a/c	240,000	30 Sep.	Balance	240,000
	Balance c/d	330,000	1 Oct.	Bank	80,000
				Directors' loans	30,000
				Bank	220,000
		570,000			570,000
			1 Oct.	Balance b/d	330,000

Bank account

19–7			19–7		
1 Oct.	Ordinary share capital	80,000	30 Sep.	Balance	104,000
	Ordinary share capital	220,000	1 Oct.	Balance c/d	256,000
	Cum. pref. share capital	60,000			
		360,000			360,000
	Balance b/d	256,000			

Cumulative preference share capital account

		£			£
19–7			19–7		
1 Oct.	Capital reduction a/c	80,000	30 Sep.	Balance	320,000
	Balance c/d	300,000	1 Oct.	Bank	60,000
		380,000			380,000
			1 Oct.	Balance b/d	300,000

Patents and trade marks

		£			£
19–7			19–7		
30 Sep.	Balance	34,000	1 Oct.	Capital reduction a/c	10,000
				Balance c/d	24,000
		34,000			34,000
1 Oct.	Balance b/d	24,000			

Plant and machinery

	£		£
19–7		19–7	
30 Sep. Balance	120,000	1 Oct. Capital reduction a/c	50,000
		Balance c/d	70,000
	120,000		120,000
1 Oct. Balance b/d	70,000		

Shares in subsidiary

	£		£
19–7		19–7	
30 Sep. Balance	120,000	1 Oct. Capital reduction a/c	20,000
		Balance c/d	100,000
	120,000		120,000
1. Oct. Balance b/d	100,000		

Freehold properties

	£		£
19–7			
30 Sep. Balance	70,000		
1 Oct. Capital reduction a/c	120,000	Balance c/d	190,000
	190,000		190,000

Loan from directors

	£		£
19–7		19–7	
1 Oct. Ordinary share capital, 120,000 shares @ 25p each	30,000	30 Sep. Balance	30,000

(b) *Restart Ltd*

Balance sheet as at 1 Oct. 19–7

	£	£
Fixed assets		
Intangible assets: Patents and trade marks		24,000
Tangible assets:		
Freehold properties	190,000	
Plant and machinery	70,000	
		260,000
Investments: Shares in subsidiary at cost *less* amount written off		100,000
		384,000
Current assets		
Stocks	124,000	
Debtors: Trade debtors	130,000	
Amounts owed by subsidiary	42,000	
Cash at bank and in hand	256,000	
	552,000	
Creditors: Amounts falling due within one year: Trade creditors	220,000	
Net current assets		332,000
Total assets *less* current liabilities		716,000
Capital and reserves		
Called up share capital (note)		630,000
Other reserves: Capital reserve on reconstruction		86,000
		716,000

Note to the accounts

Share capital

	£
Authorised	700,000
Issued 1,320,000 ordinary shares of 25p each fully paid	330,000
400,000 10% cumulative preference shares of 75p each fully paid	300,000
	630,000

(c) *Division of profit*

	Expected profit without reconstruction £		*Expected profit with reconstruction* £
	60,000		100,000
Preference shareholders, 320,000 × 8%	25,600	300,000 × 10%	30,000
Ordinary shareholders, balance	34,400	$\frac{960}{1,320} \times 70,000$	50,909
Directors	—	$\frac{360}{1,320} \times 70,000$	19,091
	60,000		100,000

ANSWER N2. REJUVENATED

Allocation of profit	(*a*) *Rejuvenated* (*19–4*)	(*b*) *Rejuvenated* (*19–10*)
	£	£
10% Loan, 19–12	100,000	
15% Loan, 19–22		150,000
5% Preference shares	50,000	
8% Preference shares		40,000
Ordinary shares (balance)	150,000	
20% dividend (20% × £200,000)		40,000
		230,000
Split of remaining profit on a per share basis		
Ordinary shares (see working)		6,364
Deferred shares (see working)		63,636
	300,000	300,000

Working

No. of ordinary shares	200,000
No. of deferred shares, £100,000 × 20	2,000,000
	2,200,000

Profit to:

Ordinary shareholders

$$\frac{200}{2{,}200} \times 70{,}000 = 6{,}364$$

Deferred shareholders

$$\frac{2{,}000}{2{,}200} \times 70{,}000 = 63{,}636$$

(c) *Amounts available to interested parties*	£	£
Debenture holders:		
Interest	150,000	
Dividends $\frac{1}{4}$ (40,000 + 6,364)	11,591	
		161,591
Preference shareholders:		
Preference dividend	40,000	
Ordinary dividend $\frac{1}{4}$ (40,000 + 6,364)	11,591	
		51,591
Ordinary shareholders:		
Ordinary dividend $\frac{1}{2}$ (46,364)	23,182	
Deferred dividend	63,636	
		86,818
		300,000

(d) *Gearing—based on book values*
Reflecting capital position:

$$\frac{\text{Long term loans} + \text{preference shares}}{\text{Share capital} + \text{reserves} + \text{long term loans}}$$

Rejuvenated (19–4)	*Rejuvenated (19–10)*
$\frac{1,000 + 1,000}{3,350}$	$\frac{1,000 + 500}{1,850}$
= 0.60	= 0.81

Reflecting income position assuming £300,000 is total profits:

$$\frac{\text{Interest on long term debt} + \text{preference dividends}}{\text{Profit before interest and dividends}}$$

Rejuvenated (19–4)	*Rejuvenated (19–10)*
$\frac{100,000 + 50,000}{300,000}$	$\frac{150,000 + 40,000}{300,000}$
= 0.50	= 0.63

ANSWER N3. THE SHIRES PROPERTY CONSTRUCTION COMPANY LTD

(a) *Journal entries*

		Dr. £	*Cr.* £
(1)	Ordinary shares of £1 each	200,000	
	Ordinary shares of 25p each		50,000
	Reconstruction Account		150,000
	Redesignation of issued share capital as 25p shares (formerly £1 shares) and transferring excess nominal value to Reconstruction Account.		
(2)	5% Cumulative preference shares of £1 each	70,000	
	8% Cumulative preference shares of £1 each		35,000
	Ordinary shares of 25p each		35,000
	Exchange of 5% preference shares for 8% preference shares and 25p ordinary shares		

		Dr. £	Cr. £
(3)	Cash	60,000	
	Ordinary shares of 25p each-200,000		50,000
	Share Premium Account 5p-200,000		10,000
	Issue of 200,000 25p ordinary shares at a premium of 5p to present ordinary shareholders.		
(4)	Interest payable on debentures	12,800	
	Ordinary shares of 25p each-20,000		5,000
	Reconstruction Account-Difference		7,800
	Capitalization of unpaid debenture interest		
	8% Debentures 19–12	80,000	
	$9\frac{1}{2}$% Debentures 19–12		80,000
	Increase of interest rate on 19–12 Debenture to $9\frac{1}{2}$%		
	Cash	8,100	
	Reconstruction Account	900	
	$9\frac{1}{2}$% Debenture 19–12		9,000
	Issue of £9,000 Debentures at a discount of 10%		
(5)	Loans from directors	16,000	
	Ordinary shares of 25p each (10,000)		2,500
	Share premium		7,500
	Reconstruction Account (amount of loans cancelled)		6,000
	Capitalisation and writing off of director's loans		
(6)	Reconstruction Account	99,821	
	Goodwill		60,000
	Profit and Loss Account		39,821
	Writing off of goodwill and debit balance on P & L Account.		
(7)	Cash	60,000	
	Investment in shares quoted		27,000
	Reconstruction Account		33,000
	Sale of shares at a profit of £33,000		
(8)	No journal entry required.		

		Dr £	Cr £
(9)	Trade creditors	46,000	
	Cash		46,000
	Payment to trade creditors on account		
(10)	Reconstruction Account	7,069	
	Debtors		7,069
	Writing off of bad debts		
(11)	Land		66,000
	Building	52,754	
	Equipment		754
	Stock and work in progress		70,247
	Reconstruction Account	84,247	
	Revaluation of fixed assets	137,001	137,001

(b) *The Shires Property Construction Co. Ltd*
Balance sheet at 1 Jan. 19–10 (after reconstruction)

	£	£
Fixed assets		
Tangible assets		
Land at valuation		90,000
Building at valuation		80,000
Equipment at valuation		10,000
		180,000
Current assets		
Stock at valuation	50,000	
Debtors	63,623	
Cash at bank and in hand	45,387	
	159,010	
Creditors: Amounts falling due within one year		
Trade creditors	50,247	
Net current assets		108,763
Total assets less current liabilities		288,763
Creditors: Amounts falling due after more than one year		
$9\frac{1}{2}\%$ Debenture loans 19–12		89,000
		199,763

Capital and reserves	£
Called up share capital (note)	177,500
Share premium account	17,500
Other reserves: Capital reconstruction account	4,763
	199,763

Note to the accounts
Share capital

	Authorised £	*Issued and fully paid* £
Ordinary shares of 25p each	200,000	142,500
8% Cumulative preference shares of £1 each	100,000	35,000
	300,000	177,500

(c) *Division of pre tax profit*

Interested parties	*Working*	*Before reconstruction* £	*After reconstruction* £	£
Debenture holders				
Gross interest	2	6,400		8,455
20,000 Ords + ACT	4	—		1,317
		6,400		9,772
Preference shareholders				
Dividend + ACT	3	5,000	4,000	
140,000 Ords. + ACT	4	—	9,221	
				13,221
Directors	4	—		659
Ordinary shareholders				
Balance including ACT	4	38,600		26,348
		50,000		50,000

(d) *Comments on the capital structure*

Gearing is $\dfrac{£35,000 + £89,000}{£199,763 + £89,000} = 43\%$

This is a bit high for a UK building company. It will reduce when the large debenture is paid off in 19–12. Indeed dividends on ordinary shares will have to be very restrained if cash is to be available to redeem the debentures. Alternatively debenture holders might agree to exchange them for ordinary shares.

The shareholders funds cover the cost of the fixed assets. The capital structure is reasonably satisfactory.

The debenture holders have done very well. Their interest has been increased by $1\frac{1}{2}\%$ but the redemption date has not been changed. The 10% capital gain over a period of less than three years is another advantage.

Workings

(1) Trial balance after reconstruction.

	Dr. £	*Cr.* £
Land	90,000	
Building	80,000	
Equipment	10,000	
Stock	50,000	
Debtors	63,623	
Cash	45,387	
Ordinary shares of 25p		142,500
8% cumulative preference shares of £1		35,000
$9\frac{1}{2}\%$ Debenture 19–12		89,000
Trade creditors		50,247
Share Premium Account		17,500
Reconstruction Account		4,763
	339,010	339,010

(2) Debenture interest gross: Before 8% × £80,000 = £6,400

: After $9\frac{1}{2}\%$ × £89,000 = £8,455

This does of course include interest on capitalized interest.

(3) Preference dividends must include the related advance corporation tax (ACT) as there is no franked investment income or mainstream corporation tax to allow relief by set off.

Dividend gross: Before 5% × £70,000 × 10/7 = £5,000

: After 8% × £35,000 × 10/7 = £4,000

(4) The balance of the profits of £50,000 belongs to the ordinary shareholders.

	£	£		£	£
Before:		50,000	After:		50,000
Less: Debenture interest	6,400			8,455	
Preference divi.	5,000	11,400		4,000	12,455
Available for ordinary shareholders		38,600			37,545

After:

Issued share capital	*Shares*
	£
Debenture holders	20,000
Preference shareholders	140,000
Directors shares	10,000
Other shareholders	400,000
	570,000

Profits available to pay dividend and ACT.

Debenture holders	20,000/570,000 × £37,545 =	1,317
Preferred shareholders	140,000/570,000 × £37,545 =	9,221
Directors	10,000/570,000 × £37,545 =	659
Others	400,000/570,000 × £37,545 =	26,348
		37,545

ANSWER N4. HEAVY PLC

(a) *Consolidated balance sheet following the acquisition of Small Ltd*

	£000	*£000*
Fixed assets (working 3)		
Intangible assets		
Goodwill on consolidation (working 1)		80
Tangible assets		x
		1,180
Current assets (working 4)	400	
Creditors: Amounts falling due within one year	400	
Net current assets		–
Total assets *less* current liabilities		1,180
Creditors: Amounts falling due after more than one year	300	
Minority interest (working 2)	60	
		360
		820

	£000
Capital and reserves	
Called up share capital	660
Share premium account	160
	820

Workings

1. *Adjustment account*

	£000		£000
Cost (2 × 160 × £1.00)	320	Shares (80% × 200)	160
		Group share of surplus on revaluation of assets (80% × (200 – 100))	80
		Goodwill on consolidation	80
	320		320

2. *Minority interest*

	£000		£000
Consolidated balance sheet	60	Shares (20% × 200)	40
		Share of surplus on revaluation (20% × (200 – 100)	20
	60		60

3. *Fixed assets*

	£000	£000
Heavy Plc		500
Small Ltd—per accounts	400	
Add: Revaluation surplus	200	
		600
Goodwill on consolidation		80
		1,180

4. *Current assets*

	£000	*£*
Heavy Plc		300
Small Ltd—per accounts	200	
Less: Revaluation deficit	100	
		100
		400

(b) *Period of write-off of goodwill*
The main arguments in favour of the EEC approach which limits the period of write-off to a maximum of five years are as follows:

(i) Goodwill arises out of accounting entries and is an intangible asset which unlike say, plant and machinery cannot exist separately from the business.
(ii) There are two types of goodwill: that arising on the acquisition of a business, i.e. purchased goodwill and inherent goodwill which is built up by a business over several years and reflects the fact that as a going concern the business is worth more than the value of its net tangible assets. Balance sheets show only the former, partly due to the difficulties of valuing inherent goodwill. The inconsistent treatment of carrying only purchased goodwill and the belief that purchased goodwill ultimately reverts to inherent goodwill provide strong reasons for an early write-off.
(iii) Unless specifically allowed for, goodwill can distort the calculation of important accounting ratios such as 'return on capital employed'. Further, it may make the balance sheet appear untidy and may hinder a layman's appreciation of the accounts especially if he does not understand the true nature of goodwill.
(iv) The economic life of an intangible asset like goodwill is both difficult to define and to measure.

Arguments in favour of writing-off goodwill over its economic life, include:

(i) The purchaser of a business expects the assets of that business including its goodwill to continue to generate profits for a number of years into the future. It was for this reason that he was prepared to pay a price for the business in excess of the value of its net tangible assets, and thus create goodwill in the first place. Therefore, goodwill should be written off over its economic life defined as the number of years for which the purchased profits are anticipated.
(ii) Such a policy complies with the provisions of the Companies Acts which require goodwill to be written off over a period not exceeding the useful economic life of the goodwill: para. 21(3) Sch. 1 1981. It should be noted, however, that this rule applies only to goodwill which is recognised as an asset in an individual company's accounts.

It does not relate to goodwill arising on consolidation which need not, therefore, be written off.

(iii) The choice of a writing off period of five years appears arbitrary. It can be argued that this period should be varied to suit different kinds of enterprises.

(iv) The write-off of goodwill over a short period would, at a time of recession, make companies profit and loss accounts appear even worse.

(c) *Merger accounting*

The features of merger accounting that differentiate it from the acquisition method are:

(i) The accumulated profits of the subsidiary at the date of the merger are not regarded as pre-acquisition profits. Such profits are therefore, still available for distribution and are not frozen as in the situation where acquisition accounting is used. As a result, the accumulated profits in the consolidated balance sheet will usually be calculated simply by adding together the accumulated profits for both companies.

(ii) No share premium arises on the shares issued by the holding company in exchange for shares in the subsidiary. This results from the practice of recording the cost of the subsidiary company's shares in the books of the holding company at the nominal value of the shares issued by the holding company. Under the acquisition method if the value of the subsidiary company's net assets exceeds the nominal value of the shares issued by the holding company, then the excess must be transferred to a share premium account, the balance on which will not be available to pay a dividend.

(iii) The assets and liabilities of each company are included in the consolidated accounts at their net book values as per the individual company's accounts. However, these values may be adjusted to achieve uniform accounting practice. Under the acquisition method the subsidiary's assets will usually be revalued at the date of acquisition.

(iv) The only difference to be accounted for on a consolidation will be the difference between the nominal value of the shares issued by the holding company and the nominal value of the shares acquired in the subsidiary. Where the nominal value of the shares issued exceeds that of the shares acquired, then the difference should be treated as reducing reserves. (Unrealised surpluses before revenue profits or realised surpluses.) On the other hand if the nominal value of the shares issued is less than that of the shares acquired then the difference should be treated as a capital reserve.

(v) As a consequence of (i) to (iv) above, goodwill on acquisition will rarely arise.

ANSWER N5. DOWN LTD

(a) *Capital reduction account*

		£		£
Ordinary stock account—allotment of ordinary stock in satisfaction of arrears of dividend		3,000	Preference share Capital account—reduction of 15p per share on 50,000 shares	7,500
Cash-discharge of contingent liability		1,200	Ordinary share capital account—reduction of 80p per share on 100,000 shares	80,000
Cash-costs		2,000	Property—profit on transfer to debenture holders	2,250
Amounts written off:			Shares in associated company—profit on sale	27,450
Goodwill	12,000			
Patents	5,000			
Deferred expenditure	12,500			
Stock	15,500			
Bad debts	9,750			
Profit & loss account	45,000	99,750		
		105,950		
Non-distributable reserve		11,250		
		117,200		117,200

(b) *Balance sheet* (*after capital reduction*)

Notes:

	£	£
Fixed assets		
Tangible assets		
Land and buildings at cost		31,000
Plant and machinery at cost *Less:* depreciation		42,000
		73,000
Current assets		
Stocks	22,000	
Debtors	35,000	
Cash at bank and in hand (see working)	47,250	
	104,250	
Creditors: Amounts falling due within one year	42,500	
Net current assets		61,750
Total assets *less* current liabilities		134,750
Creditors: Amounts falling due after more than one year		
5% Debenture loans (secured)	10,000	
12% Debenture loans (secured)	8,000	
		18,000
		116,750

	£
Capital and reserves	
Called up share capital (note)	105,500
Other reserves: Capital reserve arising on scheme of capital reduction	11,250
	116,750

Note to the accounts
Share capital

	Authorised £	*Issued and fully paid* £
Ordinary stock of £1 each	100,000	63,000
6% Cumulative preference stock of £1 each	50,000	42,500
	150,000	105,500

Working

Cash account

	£		£
Sale of associated company shares	42,450	Balance b/d	28,000
New issue of 12% debentures	8,000	Contingent liability	1,200
Ord. shares taken up by directors (balance due 40,000–12,000)	28,000	Costs of reduction	2,000
		Bal c/d	47,250
	78,450		78,450

ANSWER N6

The Directors
Harvey Ltd

Gentlemen

Scheme of Capital Reduction

In accordance with your instructions we have prepared a scheme of capital reduction which we consider will be acceptable to the creditors, members, and to the Court.

Firstly it is necessary to consider the basic principles which should be followed in drafting such a scheme. These are as follows:

(a) The majority of any loss arising should be borne by the ordinary shareholders.
(b) Some part of the loss may be borne by the preference shareholders. There would normally be a compensating adjustment to the rate of dividend.
(c) Arrears of preference dividend would be cancelled, ordinary shares for part being issued in compensation.
(d) Any balance on the share premium account should be utilised.
(e) The amount made available under the scheme should be used:
   (i) to write off the debit balance on profit and loss account
   (ii) to write off fictitious assets
   (iii) to write down other assets to estimated realisable value
   (iv) to provide for costs and other losses arising under the scheme.
(f) Additional working capital must be provided. The majority of such finance should be provided by the class which will suffer the greatest loss upon a liquidation, i.e. the ordinary shareholders.

   Additional working capital could be provided by the sale and leaseback of the freehold property although if this were done, the debentures, being secured by a fixed charge, would have to be redeemed.

   Alternatively, the debenture holders might be induced to provide funds by the issue of a further debenture carrying an attractive interest rate (say 18%) secured by a 2nd charge on the freehold and a floating charge on all other assets. The debenture might also carry conversion or subscription rights into equity capital.
(g) In order to placate the creditors it would be usual:
   (i) to pay off the preferential creditors
   (ii) to pay an immediate dividend to the unsecured creditors.

   It would also be necessary to pay the arrears of debenture interest.

   Our detailed proposals are as follows:
   (i) The ordinary shares should be reduced to 10p shares and then consolidated into £1 shares.
   (ii) The preference shares should be reduced to 80p shares and then consolidated into £1 shares. The rate of dividend should be increased to 8%.
   (iii) The arrears of preference dividend should be cancelled in consideration of the issue of one new £1 ordinary share for every £9 arrears.
   (iv) The balance on share premium account should be utilised.
   (v) The quoted investments should be sold to provide working capital.
   (vi) The amount made available under the scheme should be used as in paragraph (e) above.
   (vii) The debenture interest and preferential creditors should be paid.

(viii) A payment of 25p in £ should be made at once to all other creditors.

(ix) The directors should provide additional working capital in the form of 50,000 new £1 ordinary shares.

The balance sheet as it would appear after the scheme has been put into operation is attached.

We shall be pleased to supply any further information you may require.

Tweed & Co

Balance sheet (after capital reduction)

	£	£
Fixed Assets at valuation		
Tangible assets:		
Freehold		80,000
Plant and machinery		17,000
		97,000
Current Assets		
Stocks	49,000	
Debtors: Trade debtors	21,000	
Bills receivable	3,000	
Cash at bank and in hand (5,400 + 50)	5,450	
	78,450	
Creditors: Amounts falling due within one year	33,000	
		45,450
Net current assets		
Total assets *less* current liabilities		142,450
Creditors: Amounts falling due after more than one year		
5% Debenture loans (secured)		40,000
		102,450
Capital and reserves		
Called up share capital (note)		101,000
Other reserves: Capital reserve arising on scheme of capital reduction		1,450
		102,450

Note to the accounts
Share capital

	Authorised £	*Issued and fully paid* £
Ordinary shares of £1 each	200,000	61,000
8% preference shares of £1 each	50,000	40,000
	250,000	101,000

Workings

Capital Reduction Account

	£		£
Ordinary shares issued in compensation for arrears of preference dividend	1,000	Amounts written off:	
Contingent liability	1,800	Ordinary share capital	90,000
Costs	1,200	Preference share capital	10,000
Profit and loss account	59,300	Share premium account	10,000
Formation expenses	2,450	Freehold revaluation	20,000
Deferred expenditure	7,800		130,000
Amounts written off:		Profit on sale of quoted investments	7,500
Plant	21,000		
Goodwill	20,000		
Stock	13,000		
Debtors	7,500		
Bills receivable	1,000		
Balance transferred to non-distributable reserve	1,450		
	£137,500		£137,500

Bank Account (projected)

	£		£
Sale of investments	17,500	Balance b/f	42,400
Ordinary shares—subscribed by directors	50,000	Contingent liability	1,800
		Costs	1,200
		Debenture interest	1,000
		Preferential creditors	4,700
		Unsecured creditors—dividend 25p in the £	11,000
		Balance c/f	5,400
	£67,500		£67,500

ANSWER N7. SHATTERHOPES LTD

The Board of Directors
Shatterhopes Ltd
78 Green Street
Manchester 7

4 Nov. 19.07

Gentlemen

Proposed capital reorganisation scheme

(1) *Terms of reference*
This report deals with the proposed capital reorganisation scheme of your company, prepared in such a manner as to be acceptable to all parties concerned in the reorganisation.

(2) *Information*
This has been limited to the summarised balance sheet as at 30 Sep. 19.07 together with further information amplifying this balance sheet.

(3) *General considerations*
The objects of the proposed scheme are as follows:

(a) to bring the net assets of the company in line with share capital and therefore with the earning capacity of the company;
(b) to adjust the capital gearing of the company in such a manner as to make the company more financially efficient, bearing in mind that the reorganisation of share capital must be acceptable to *both* the ordinary and preference shareholders;
(c) to improve both the liquidity and working capital of the company.

(4) *Details of the proposed scheme*
Particulars of the proposed reorganisation scheme are as follows:

(a) The ordinary shares are to be written down to 25p each.
(b) The preference shareholders are to waive their rights to the arrears of dividend, and in return are to choose whether they wish to convert their holdings to a new issue of 9% cumulative preference shares, or ordinary shares of 25p each on a 4 for 1 basis. The balance sheet of your company after the proposed reorganisation scheme and the comments on the financial position of the company after the scheme have been prepared on the assumption that 50% of the preference shareholders will elect to take this latter alternative.
(c) The Lendem Bank Ltd should be persuaded to convert their existing debentures to a new issue with an interest rate of 10% and to take up a further £10,000 of these debentures in view of the increased value of the collateral.
(d) The bank overdraft is to be repaid in full, and amounts totalling £20,000 are to be paid to trade creditors at once.
(e) It is noted that the directors have agreed to waive half the loans owed to them. It is suggested that the balance of these loans is to be met by the issue to them of ordinary shares of 25p each.

(f) Goodwill, deferred development expenditure and the balance on the profit and loss account are to be written off in full, whilst plant is to be revalued at £16,000.
(g) The Land and Buildings are to be revalued at £55,000 and the quoted investment is to be sold for £50,000.
(h) £16,166 is to be written off the stocks and a provision of 10% for doubtful debts is to be made.
(i) The balance made available under the scheme to be set aside for costs of the scheme.

(5) *Effect of the proposed scheme on the balance sheet of the company*
Assuming that the Court and the parties concerned accept the proposed scheme, the balance sheet of the company would be as follows:

Fixed Assets	£	£
Tangible assets:		
Land and buildings, at valuation		55,000
Plant at valuation		16,000
Fixtures and fittings at cost	3,855	
Less: Depreciation	1,225	2,630
		73,630
Current Assets		
Stocks	24,000	
Debtors £(35,802 – 3,580)	32,222	
Cash at bank and in hand	20,591	
	76,813	
Creditors: Amounts falling due within one year:		
Trade creditors	43,420	
Net Current Assets		33,393
Total assets less *current liabilities*		107,023
Creditors: Amounts falling due after more than one year		
10% Debenture loans (secured)		40,000
		67,023

Capital and reserves	£
Called up share capital (note)	65,000
Other reserves: Capital reserve arising under capital reorganisation	2,023
	67,023

Note to the accounts
Share capital

	Authorised	*Issued and fully paid*
	£	£
Ordinary shares of 25p each	100,000	45,000
9% Cumulative preference shares of £1 each	40,000	20,000
	140,000	65,000

(6) *Comments on the financial position of the company, assuming the proposed scheme is accepted.*

(i) *Liquidity*—the position has improved from a potentially dangerous situation to one of relative comfort, as disclosed by comparison of the quick assets, or "acid test" ratios before and after reorganisation respectively.

	Debtors plus cash:*Current liabilities*
Original	£35,802:£88,629
	or
	0.4:1
Revised	£52,813:£43,420
	or
	1.2:1

Ostensibly, sufficient quick assets now exist with which to meet the claims of creditors—should they demand payment simultaneously. Moreover, after reorganisation, the company has the cash to defray running expenses and/or the costs of expansions.

Although debtors have been included as a quick asset, some of these may, in fact, prove to be bad, while others may not be realised expeditiously.

(ii) *Working Capital*—this again shows a marked improvement; the company relying far less upon finance from outsiders for its working capital. Greater security may now be offered to potential creditors, while it may be possible to negotiate more favourable terms with suppliers. The relevant ratios, before and after reorganisation respectively,

	Tangible current assets:*Current liabilities*
Original	£75,968:£88,629
	or
	0.86:1
Revised	£76,813:£43,420
	or
	1.77:1

It should be noted that deferred development expenditure (a fictitious asset) prior to reorganisation must be excluded from current assets.

(iii) Capital gearing—consequent upon reorganisation, the company is more highly geared i.e. there is a greater proportion of fixed interest capital. Furthermore, the sum required to service the preference shares and debentures has risen by £900 per annum. The higher gearing will tend to make the ordinary shares more speculative, especially if profits are subject to violent fluctuation. However, having regard to the improved overall financial position, coupled with the fact that the preference dividends were three years in arrear, the ordinary shareholders would appear to have an improved prospect of a dividend in subsequent years. The reduction in the amount of equity capital may also result in a higher percentage return, either in the form of dividends or retained funds than was potentially possible before reorganisation.

The relevant ratios, before and after reorganisation respectively are as follows:

	Ordinary shares:Fixed return capital
Original	£80,000:£70,000 or 1.14:1
Revised	£45,000:£60,000 0.75 or 1

Note: this ratio may, alternatively, be expressed as a percentage of ordinary shares or fixed return capital to total capital.

(7) *Conclusions*

It is suggested that the attached scheme will be acceptable to the parties concerned and it is therefore recommended that this scheme is adopted by the Board of your company and put before the shareholders of the company for their approval.

If you should require any further information or have any queries relating to the above please do not hesitate to contact us.

Yours faithfully...

Working

(1) *Capital reduction account*

	£		£
Amounts written off		Revaluation-land	15,000
Goodwill	20,000	Profit on sale of investment	5,000
Plant	1,031	Loans waived	5,000
Stock	16,166	Balance c/d – amount required under scheme	57,977
Debtors	3,580		
Development expenditure	15,000		
P & L A/c	27,200		
	£82,977		£82,977
Balance b/d	57,977	Amount written off ordinary capital	60,000
Transfer to non-distributable reserve (to cover costs?)	2,023		
	£60,000		£60,000

(2) *Cash account*

	£		£
New debenture issue	10,000	Balance b/d	15,209
Sale of quoted investment	50,000	Arrears of debenture interest repaid	4,200
		Payment to trade creditors	20,000
		Balance c/d	20,591
	60,000		60,000

ANSWER N8. CONVERTIT PLC

(a) *Journal*

	£	£
8% Redeemable preference shares A/c	2,000,000	
Profit and loss account (or other distributable reserve)	200,000	
Cash		1,100,000
Ordinary share capital A/c		343,750
Share premium A/c		756,250
	£2,200,000	£2,200,000
Redemption of 8% preference shares at a premium of 10% satisfied 50% in cash and 50% by the issue of 25p ordinary shares at mid-market price of 80p per share, on 1 July 19.06 and writing off redemption premium under s.45 CA 1981		
Profit and Loss A/c (or other distributable reserve)	900,000	
Capital Redemption Reserve Fund A/c		900,000
Transfer required under s.53 CA 1981 in respect of preference shares not replaced by the proceeds of a fresh issue of shares (2,000,000 – 1,100,000)		
9% Convertible loan stock A/c	1,500,000	
Share premium A/c	120,000	
Ordinary share capital A/c		506,250
Share premium A/c		1,113,750
	£1,620,000	£1,620,000
Conversion of 9% loan stock at a premium of 8% into 25p ordinary shares at mid-market price 1 Jul. 19.06 of 80p each and writing off conversion premium under s. 56 Companies Act 1948		
Cash—	6,400	
Cash		6,400
Sale of fractional allotments of ordinary shares to preference and loan stock holders (8,000 @ 80p) and distribution pro-rata of sales proceeds.		

Tutorial note

It has been assumed that the redeemable preference shares were not originally issued at a premium. Any premium payable on redemption must then be written off against the company's distributable profits.

If the above shares had been issued at a premium then part of the redemption premium may be written off against the share premium account. The amount to be written off in this way is the lesser of:

(a) the original premium received on the issue of the redeemable shares, and

(b) the current balance on the share premium account.

However, in order for this exception to apply the premium payable on the redemption must be paid out of the proceeds of a fresh issue of shares made for the purpose of redemption *s.45 CA 1981.*

(b) *Effect on present holder of 1,000 25p ordinary shares*

	Anticipated 19.07	*19.06*
(i) P/E ratio – 19.06 $\frac{80p}{7.8p}$ (to be maintained for 19.07)	10.3	10.3
(ii) EPS	9.6p	7.8p
(iii) Market value – 19.07 (anticipated EPS × Required P/E ratio) 9.6p × 10.3	99p	80p
(iv) Dividend yield:		
Anticipated dividend 19.07 (net)	4.8p	
Tax credit 30/70	2.06	
	6.86p	
Percentage of market value 99p = Dividend yield	6.93%	6.96%

Workings

(a) *Redemption of preference shares*

		£	£
Nominal value			2,000,000
Redemption premium 10%			200,000
			2,200,000
Settled by—cash 50%			1,100,000
—issue of shares at 80p (100/80 × £1,100,000 = 1,375,000)			
Nominal value	1,375,000 @ 25p	343,750	
Premium	1,375,000 @ 55p	756,250	1,100,000
	80p		2,200,000

(b) *Conversion of loan stock*

	£
Nominal value	1,500,000
Premium 8%	120,000
	1,620,000

Settled by issue of shares at 80p (100/80 × £1,620,000 = 2,025,000)

		£
Nominal value	2,025,000 @ 25p	506,250
Premium	2,025,000 @ 55p	1,113,750
		1,620,000

(c) *Present profits and forecast profit*

	p
Dividend (gross) based on 6.96% yield on 80p value	5.57
Less: Tax @ 30%	1.67
	3.9
EPS (dividend × dividend cover)	7.8p

	£	£
Equity profit after tax 10,000,000 × 7.8p		780,000
Add: Preference dividend (£2,000,000 × 8%)		160,000
Profit after taxation (19.06)		940,000
Add: anticipated increase (30%)		282,000
Projected 19.07 profit (on present capital structure)		1,222,000
Add: Debenture interest (9% × £1,500,000)	135,000	
Less: Corporation tax @ 52%	70,200	64,800
Projected equity earnings for 19.07		£1,286,800

(d) *Dividends and EPS for 19.07*

Revised equity capital:

Original number of 25p shares	10,000,000
Issued to preference shareholders	1,375,000
Issued to loan stock holders	2,025,000
	13,400,000

Maximum dividend 19.07 to maintain present cover ($\frac{1}{2}$ × 1,286,800) £643,400

Dividend per share $\frac{£643,400}{13,400,000}$ 4.8p

EPS 2 × 4.8p 9.6p

ANSWER P1

The Directors,
Life & Line Ltd

Gentlemen

We have examined the audited accounts of Life and Line Ltd and its subsidiary companies for the periods relevant to this report.

The summarised combined profit and loss account and balance sheets set out below are after making such adjustments as we consider appropriate. In our opinion these summaries, together with the notes thereon, give respectively a true and fair view of the profits of the group for the periods stated and of the state of affairs of the group at the date(s) stated.

Profit and Loss Accounts

	Note	19.00	19.01	19.02	19.03	19.04
		£000	*£000*	*£000*	*£000*	*£000*
Sales	1	16,081	18,049	21,364	29,425	32,869
Cost of sales	2	11,290	12,304	11,449	15,683	20,279
Profit before taxation		4,791	5,745	9,915	13,742	12,590
Taxation		1,541	2,095	3,311	5,123	5,390
Profit after taxation	3	3,250	3,650	6,604	8,619	7,200
Minority interests		(x)	(x)	(x)	(x)	(x)
Extraordinary items	4	1,112	(540)	(458)	(1,411)	(3,429)
Profit attributable to ordinary shareholders		4,362	3,110	6,146	7,208	3,771
Ordinary dividends	5	2,300	2,300	4,200	5,100	5,100
		2,062	810	1,946	2,108	(1,329)

Balance sheet

	Note		19.04
			£000
Fixed Assets	6		
Ships Ships under construction		} no details of depreciation adjustment ∴ for each asset	
		per B/S	247,568
Properties Plant & equipment		} Add: reduced depreciation	3,100
			250,668
Trade investments (at cost less provision)	7		22,635
			£273,303

	Note	£000	£000
Current Assets			b/f 273,303
Stocks		23,105	
Debtors		42,081	
Cash		27,020	
		£92,206	
Current Liabilities			
Creditors		42,860	
Bank overdraft		4,025	
Taxation		8,741	
Dividend		5,100	
		60,726	
Net Current Assets			31,480
			304,783
Less: Loans and debentures	8	(69,717)	
Investment grants		(18,433)	
Minority shareholders		(10,840)	
			(98,990)
Net Assets			205,793
Representing:			
Issued share capital			36,428
Reserves	9		169,365
			£205,793

Notes

Accounting Policies

1. The principal accounting policies of the group which have been applied in the foregoing summaries consistently throughout the period under review are

 (a) *Depreciation*

 During the period to 31 Dec. 19.04 the company reassessed the expected lives and rates of depreciation of most of its fixed assets. The following bases now apply in writing down assets to their estimated residual value:

Oil rig servicing vessels	10.00%
Container ships, tankers, oil/bulk/ore carriers	6.67%
Other ships	5.00%
Properties	?
Plant and equipment	?

 No depreciation is provided on ships under construction. For the purposes of the prospectus profits have been adjusted for depreciation in all five years under the new basis. The depreciation charge for 19.04 on the new basis was £8,308,000 compared with £9,208,000 on the old basis.

(b) *Stocks and work in progress* are valued at lower of cost and net realisable value.
Tutorial Note: *Details of bases of ascertaining cost, etc should be included if material to the understanding of the accounts.*
(c) *Sales* represents sales to third parties excluding inter-group sales
(d) *Company law disclosure requirements*
The company has taken advantage of s.17 CA 1981, which provides that the accounts of shipping companies may be prepared under the requirements of the previous Sch.8 CA 1948, as unamended by CA 1981.

2. *Cost of sales* includes

	Years ended 31 Dec.				
	19.00	*19.01*	*19.02*	*19.03*	*19.04*
	£000	*£000*	*£000*	*£000*	*£000*
Depreciation (note 1a)	6,271	7,569	6,986	6,662	8,308
Interest payable	2,095	3,500	4,200	4,900	6,500
Profit on sale of short-term investments		310	94		

3. *Taxation* comprises UK corporation tax based on profits for the five years (at ?%)

4. *Extraordinary items*

	Years ended 31 Dec.				
	19.00	*19.01*	*19.02*	*19.03*	*19.04*
	£000	£000	£000	£000	£000
Profit/(loss) on sale of ships	972	934	(458)	(1,172)	740
Profit on sale of investments	140	26			
Provision for reduction in value of trade investments		(1,500)		(239)	(4,169)
	£1,112	£(540)	£(458)	£(1,411)	£(3,429)

Tutorial notes:
(i) Since ships are sold every year it could be argued, quite reasonably, that the profits/losses arising on disposal occur in the normal course of trade and should be dealt with as exceptional items above the line.
(ii) It is arguable whether the profit on sale of investments of £26,000 in 19.01 is sufficiently material to be classed as extraordinary.

5. Dividends paid during the periods under review were at the following rates per share 10% 10% 12% 14% 14%

Tutorial note; If share capital has changed *within* two years of date of prospectus then details of issue required
capital changes in 19.02 or 19.03 –

19.02 dividend £4,200,000 = 12% – capital = £4.2m $\times \frac{100}{12}$ = £35m

19.03 capital £36.428m
No date or details of change given.

6. *Fixed Assets* at 31 Dec. 19.04 comprise

	At valuation £000	*At cost* £000	*Depreciation* £000	*Book value* £000
Ships				
Ships under construction		(Details are unknown)		
Properties				
Plant and equipment				
				250,668

7. *Trade Investments*
   The directors' valuation of the unquoted investments at 31 Dec. 19.04 was £23 million.
8. *Loans and debentures* are all repayable within 5 years
9. *Movements on reserves*—these were as follows:

	Years ended 31 December				
	19.00 £000	*19.01* £000	*19.02* £000	*19.03* £000	*19.04* £000
At beginning of period	163,768	165,830	166,640	168,586	170,694
Retained profits	2,062	810	1,946	2,108	(1,329)
At end of period	165,830	166,640	168,586	170,694	169,365

10. There were no capital commitments at 31 Dec. 19.04.

Yours faithfully,
Bloggs and Co
Chartered Accountants

Workings

(a) *Adjustment of profit figures:*

	19.00 £000	*19.01* £000	*19.02* £000	*19.03* £000	*19.04* £000	*Further adjustment required* £000
Profits before tax	4,041	5,495	8,915	12,642	12,590	
Adjustments: reduction in depreciation	750	250	1,000	1,100	—	£(3,100)
	4,791	5,745	9,915	13,742	12,590	
Turnover per question	16,081	18,049	21,364	29,425	32,869	
Cost of sales	£11,290	12,304	11,449	15,683	20,279	

(b) *Proof of retained profits*

	19.00 *£000*	*19.01* *£000*	*19.02* *£000*	*19.03* *£000*	*19.04* *£000*
Retained per question	200	1,100	1,404	2,419	(1,329)
Profit (loss) —ship	972	934	(458)	(1,172)	
—investments	140	26			
	1,312	2,060	946	1,247	(1,329)
Provision— Investments		(1,500)		(239)	
	1,312	560	946	1,008	(1,329)
Depreciation— reduction	750	250	1,000	1,100	—
	2,062	810	1,946	2,108	(1,329)

Tutorial notes

(*i*) *The new disclosure requirements in the Companies Act 1981, relating to the form and content of company accounts may be followed by banking, insurance or shipping companies, if they so wish. However, these companies can choose to continue to prepare their accounts under the previous requirements provided that their accounts state this fact. The solution has been prepared on the basis of the old requirements.*

(*ii*) *Note that no information is given in the question as to minority interest, although a figure does appear in the balance sheet. An appropriate indication of this has been made in the profits statement.*

(*iii*) *Profit before tax for each year is adjusted* only *for*

... extraordinary items (per SSAP6) charged or credited 'above the line' incorrectly

... prior year adjustments (per SSAP6)

Adjustment is not made for subsequent revision of accounting estimates correctly made on the basis of information available at the balance sheet date. Adjustment would not *therefore be made in respect of the provision for surveys.*

ANSWER P2. X LTD

The actions which would be taken in preparation of the report are as follows:

1. *Acquisition of shares*
   The post-acquisition profits or losses of Y Ltd would be included in the five-year table of results from the date of acquisition. No adjustment would be made for profits or losses prior to acquisition. Since the report shows six funds flow statements, the issue of shares will be

reflected. However, if it appears appropriate, the results of the acquired subsidiary might be shown in a separate tabulation.

Mention would be made of the constituent companies on which the report is based in the introductory section of the report. Details of the share issue would not be necessary in the report, since the change in share capital did not take place within the last two periods covered in the prospectus.

2. *Goodwill*
The reporting accountant is required to deal throughly with accounting policies adopted by the company in dealing with items considered to be material or critical to the determination of results and of net assets reported on and to include a statement of policies in his report. This might be included as a separate statement or in the notes to the balance sheet summaries. However, para.21 (4) Sch.1 CA 1981 *will* require the period chosen for writing off goodwill and the reasons for choosing that period to be disclosed in a note to the accounts. The reporting accountant should ensure that the write off period of 5 years does not exceed the useful economic life of the goodwill in order to comply with para.21 (3) Sch.1 CA 1981. It is not clear from the question when the goodwill arose—however, the tables given in the report should be on a consistent basis—i.e. the new policy of writing off goodwill at the rate of 20% per annum should be applied over the period of existence of that goodwill. Prior year adjustments would therefore have to be made, where applicable, in compliance with SSAP 6. This means that adjustments would be made to reserves brought forward in the relevant periods.

3. *Sale of factory*
The sale of one of X Ltd's factories would be shown as an extraordinary item in the table of profits, i.e. below the line. The amount would not be stated after the relevant corporation tax on the chargeable gain which has been deferred by roll over as this potential tax liability would only be disclosed in a note to the accounts per *SSAP 15* (as this company has not decided, in principle, to dispose of the replacement unit).

4. *Cost of moving plant and machinery*
Since such costs are considered to be 'outside the normal activities of the business' they would also be treated as an extraordinary item.

   The amount of £65,000 would be shown net of tax, if it is an allowable expense for taxation purposes. Adjustments would, therefore, be necessary in relation to the corporation tax shown in the accounts on 'normal' profits or losses for that year. The reporting accountant would also need to ascertain that these costs had not been included in the overhead absorption in the valuation of stock.

5. *Professional fees*
Since the three charges mentioned are material and are within the normal activities of the company, they would be disclosed separately as abnormal items in the accounts. The normal accounts presentation would be to include these charges in the note on profit before

taxation—thus these would be shown separately in the cost of sales note (in addition to depreciation and financial charges as required by the Stock Exchange's Yellow Book).

6. *Interest-free loans by directors*
No adjustment would be necessary to the accounts for these loans. The accounts should show the prospective investors exactly what has happened over the period under review. However, the reporting accountant is required to include notes on 'any other material matters' in his report and since the availability of working capital will be of obvious importance to the company's future prospects full details of these arrangements should be given.

7. *Government grants*
Where the accounting policy of the company has changed during the period under review, the results and balance sheets would be adjusted, so that all the accounts were presented on the new basis. Adjustment would therefore have to be made to the periods prior to 19.03. These would involve prior year adjustments to the figures for reserves (assuming the grants were not treated as deferred credits) and to the notes on movements in fixed assets. It is not clear how depreciation was charged over the period, but this should be calculated on the net cost of the assets. Thus adjustment may be necessary in this respect and hence to deferred tax provisions.
Again, the accounting policy would have to be stated within the body of the report and the figures for depreciation shown in the notes to the table of profits i.e. in the cost of sales note.

8. *VAT points*
The correction of fundamental accounting errors would normally necessitate a prior year adjustment on reserves brought forward; however, the errors mentioned have occurred in the last financial period to be covered in the report, thus adjustments will simply be made to figures shown in the summarised tables. In accordance with *SSAP 5* turnover should be stated exclusive of VAT (unless irrecoverable)—thus the figure for sales in the table of profits would be adjusted accordingly and the note would indicate this basis of calculation. The amount due *to* Customs and Excise would thus become £29,000 (£45,000 less £16,000) in the last balance sheet.
VAT charged on the purchase of cars is irrecoverable and would be included with the assets to which it relates. Thus £12,500 would be deducted from works overhead and added to the cost of motor vehicles in the balance sheet. Further adjustments would then be necessary to take into account (i) capital allowances not claimed—since these should be calculated on the gross figure; (ii) depreciation—since the charge for the year should be based on the full amount; and (iii) taxation adjustments, both to corporation tax and deferred tax. Since the charge of £12,500 was originally included in work's overhead, the reporting accountant would have to ensure that the stock valuation at the year-end did not include a proportion of the amount involved—again this will depend on the company's policy as regards stock.

ANSWER P3. DIONYSUS LTD

Statement setting out adjustments made to profits for the 5 years ended 31 December

SECTION A	*Years ended* 31 *December*				
	19.01	*19.02*	*19.03*	*19.04*	*19.05*
	£000	*£000*	*£000*	*£000*	*£000*
Revenue reserves					
At end of year	94	134	198	235	261
At beginning of year	83	94	134	198	235
Net increase	11	40	64	37	26
Adjustments to retained profits					
Deferred taxation			38		
Under/overprovision for					
Corporation tax	3	(2)			
Change in basis of stock valuation		(15)			
Profit of associated company			(76)		
Dividends	15	25	20	20	40
Tax	8	12	49	55	61
Associated company	–	–	(27)	(30)	(32)
Investment income	(10)	(9)	–	–	–
Profit on sale of freehold	–	(15)	–	–	–
Items required to be shown separately	45	44	80	62	66
Carried to Section B	72	80	148	144	161

SECTION B	*19.01*	*19.02*	*19.03*	*19.04*	*19.05*
	£000	*£000*	*£000*	*£000*	*£000*
Transferred from Section A	72	80	148	144	161
Items in Section A regarded as proper (i) charges (ii) credits					
in arriving at the profit of each period (19.03 (80,000–25,000))	(45)	(44)	(55)	(62)	(66)
	27	36	93	82	95
Adjustments					
Share of associated company	22	24	27	30	32
Stock adjustment (15,000 – 11,000)	4				
	53	60	120	112	127

		19.01	*19.02*	*19.03*	*19.04*	*19.05*
		£000	*£000*	*£000*	*£000*	*£000*
	b/f	53	60	120	112	127
Taxation						
In audited accounts		8	12	49	55	61
Associated company		11	12	–	–	–
Under/overprovisions		3	(2)	–	–	–
Applicable to extra-ordinary item		–	–	10	–	–
Deferred taxation		7	5	–	–	–
		29	27	59	55	61
Profit after tax		24	33	61	57	66
Extraordinary items						
Profit on sale of freehold (less tax) (15,000 – 4,000)		–	11	–	–	–
Sequestration of assets abroad (25,000 – 10,000)		–		(15)		
		24	44	46	57	66
Dividends		15	25	20	20	40
Retained profit for year		9	19	26	37	26

ANSWER P4

		A £000	*B* £000
(a)	Share exchange:		
	Sundry net assets (book value)	170	110
	Revaluation surplus	10	5
	Unrecorded goodwill	20	5
		200	120
	Number of shares	100	80
	Value per share	£2.00	£1.50

A will offer 3 shares for every 4 held by B shareholders.
Number of shares issued by A = 80,000 × $\frac{3}{4}$
= 60,000

A Ltd: Consolidated balance sheet	*£000*
Fixed assets	
Intangible assets	
Goodwill	5
Tangible assets	X
	X
Net current assets	X
Total assets less Current liabilities (170 + 115 + 5)	290
Capital and reserves	
Called up share capital	160
Share premium account	60
Profit and loss account	70
	290

Note: It has been assumed that there are no long term liabilities.

Adjustment account

	£000		£000
Cost of shares—	120	Nominal value of Shares in B	80
		Pre-acquisition reserves:	
		Reserves	30
		Revaluation Surplus on assets	5
		Goodwill c/d	5
	120		120

A Ltd Balance sheet

	£000
Fixed assets	
Tangible assets	X
Investment	
Shares in (B) at cost	120
	X
Net current assets	X
Total assets less Current liabilities (170 + 120)	290
Capital and reserves	
Called up share capital	160
Share premium account	60
Profit and loss account	70
	290

(b) Valuation of shares:

	A £000	B £000	C £000
Net asset value per (a)	200	120	320
Number of shares	100	80	200
Value per share	£2	£1.50	£1.60

C Ltd Shares issued to A Ltd $100{,}000 \times \frac{£2}{£1.60} = 125{,}000$

C Ltd Shares issued to B Ltd $80{,}000 \times \frac{£1.50}{£1.60} = 75{,}000$

Total 200,000

C Ltd balance sheet

	£000
Fixed assets	
Investments:	
Shares in A Ltd at cost (100 × £2)	200
Shares in B Ltd at cost (80 × £1.50)	120
Total assets	320
Capital and reserves	
Called up share capital	200
Share premium	120
	320

C Ltd Consolidated balance sheet

	£000
Fixed assets	
Intangible assets	
Goodwill	25
Tangible assets	X
	X
Net current assets	X
Total assets less Current liabilities (170 + 110 + 15 + 25)	320
Capital and reserves	
Called up share capital	200
Share premium account	120
	320

Adjustment account

	£000				£000
Cost of shares in		Nominal value of shares			
A Ltd	200	A Ltd			100
B Ltd	120	B Ltd			80
		Pre-acquisition reserves			
			A	*B*	
		Reserves	70	30	100
		Revaluation	10	5	15
		Goodwill c/d	20	5	25
	320				320

	A	*B*
(c) Value of shares (as in (a) above)	£2	£1.50

A will offer 3 of its shares for every 4 held, as before.

A Ltd Balance Sheet

	£000
Fixed assets	
Tangible assets	X
Investment	
shares in B at cost	60
	X
Net current assets	X
Total assets less Current liabilities (170 + 60)	230
Capital and reserves	
Called up share capital	160
Profit and loss account	70
	230

A *Ltd Consolidated balance sheet*

	£000
Fixed assets	
Tangible assets	X
Net current assets	X
Total assets less Current liabilities (170 + 110)	280
Capital and reserves	
Called up share capital	160
Other reserves: Capital reserve on consolidation	20
Profit and loss account (70 + 30)	100
	280

Adjustment account

	£000		*£000*
Cost of shares (nominal value)	60	Nominal value of shares acquired	80
Reserve on consolidation (non-distributable).	20		
	80		80

(d) Valuation of shares (as in (b) above); shares issued by C Ltd to:

	A	*B*	*C*
Valuation of shares (as in (b) above)	£2	£1.50	£1.60
Shares issued by C Ltd to	125,000	75,000	

C Ltd balance sheet

	£000
Fixed assets	
Investments:	
Shares in A Ltd at cost	125
Shares in B Ltd at cost	75
Total assets	200
Capital and reserves	
Called up share capital	200

C Ltd consolidated balance sheet

	£000
Total assets *less* current liabilities (170 + 110 + 15)	295
Capital and reserves	
Called up share capital	200
Unrealised reserve	5
Revaluation reserve	5
Profit and loss account	85
	295

Workings

Adjustment account

	A Ltd £000	*B Ltd £000*		*A Ltd £000*	*B Ltd £000*
Cost of investments	125	75	N.V. of shares acquired	100	80
Unrealised reserve		5	Written off reserves		
			Revaluation reserve	10	
			Profit and loss account	15	
	125	80		125	80

Reserves:

	A £000	*B £000*	*Adjustment £000*	*Consolidated £000*
Profit and loss	70	30	(15)	85
Revaluation	10	5	(10)	5
Unrealised reserve			5	5

(*e*)	*A* £000	*B* £000	*C* £000
Sundry net assets (at valuation)	180	115	
Goodwill	20	5	
	200	120	320
10% Synergy-apportioned 200:120	20	12	32
	220	132	352
No. of shares	100	80	200
Value of one share	£2.20	£1.65	£1.76
Shares issued	$100{,}000 \times \frac{£2.20}{1.76}$	$80{,}000 \times \frac{£1.65}{1.76}$	
	= 125,000	= 75,000	

N.B. So long as the synergy is apportioned in the ratio of asset market values there is no change in the number of shares issued to each company.

ANSWER P5

The Directors,
Sellit Plc

Gentlemen

PROPOSED SCHEME OF AMALGAMATION

This report considers the values of the shares of your company and those of Go Plc on the basis that an exchange of ordinary shares will take place resulting in your company acquiring the whole of the issued ordinary shares of Go Plc as a means of achieving a merging of interests.

Valuation of Go Plc
The acquisition of such a majority holding requires the valuation of shares based on the value of the underlying assets. The assets can be valued, individually, on a going concern basis or in total by reference to the requirements of the investor as to equity earnings, normally expressed in the light of a required price/earnings ratio. It is usual to base the required P/E ratio on that of a similar quoted company and we have based our calculations therefore on your own P/E ratio adjusted to reflect

the smaller size of Go Plc and the consequent anticipated higher earnings per share.

Schedule 1 attached calculates the values on these alternative bases as follows:

Underlying asset values	122p
P/E ratio (based on 75% of the P/E ratio of the midpoint of your highest and lowest prices)	96p
Present quotation (based on minority holding)	76p

Since the goodwill valuation is based upon an estimation of the required yield on net tangible assets and in view of the economies of scale and the advantage that you will acquire in terms of suitable sites for expansion we feel that the bid should be pitched in the region of 125p which would give a price sufficiently above the current quotation to attract the Go Plc shareholders. This price is based on assets after dividends and is therefore 'ex dividend'. Should the bid be 'cum dividend' the price must be increased by the dividend of 2.5p per share. We have assumed an 'ex dividend' bid for the remainder of this report.

Valuation of your company

Schedule 1 shows the asset value of your shares (valuing goodwill at a required return on net tangible assets of 10%) as 145p compared with your current quotation of 70p. However, it should be possible to convince the Go Plc shareholders of a higher share value when it is considered that the market quotation is based on a minority holding. We therefore suggest that to allow for the estimated rate of return employed in valuing your goodwill the shares be valued for the scheme at 140p. This is, of course, an 'ex dividend' price.

Basis of exchange

To acquire Go Plc @ 125p per share by issue of Sellit Plc shares at 140p. The exchange will be at the rate of

	100 Sellit Plc	at 140p =	140
for	112 Go Plc	at 125p =	140

This values the goodwill of Go Plc as the difference between the total acquisition cost:

6,800 @ 125p	8,500,000
Less: Value of net tangible assets	7,135,000
	1,365,000

Should you require any further information in relation to the bid please do not hesitate to contact us.

Yours faithfully,

Higgins & Snow
Accountants

Schedule 1 *Valuation of shares*	*£000*	*Sellit Plc* *£000*	*£000*	*Go Plc* *£000*
(a) *Values of underlying net assets*				
Assets at revalued amounts				
Land & Buildings		24,100		5,300
Equipment		8,000		2,300
Vehicles		4,200		1,400
Current assets		27,865		7,175
		64,165		16,175
Less: Liabilities				
Current	19,610		6,810	
Taxation	5,260		1,630	
Loan stock	—		600	
		24,870		9,040
Net tangible assets		39,295		7,135
Goodwill based on super-profits				
Profit after tax		4,885		1,500
Less: Return on net tangible assets at say 10% (after tax)		3,930		714
Super profit		955		786
Goodwill say $1\frac{1}{2}$ years purchase		1,433		1,179
Net tangible assets (after proposed dividends)		39,295		7,135
		40,728		8,314
Number of shares (25p each)		28,000		6,800
Value per share (ex dividend)		145p		122p
(b) *Using required P/E ratio*				
(1) *Present P/E ratio*				
Profit after taxation		4,885		1,500
Number of shares		28,000		6,800
E.P.S.		17.4p		22p
P/E ratio based on average of high and low prices				
Sellit	101p	5.8		
Go	107.5p			4.89

The normal requirement would be to base the required P/E on 70% to 80% of that applicable to Sellit Plc i.e. 75% × 5.8 = 4.35, valuing Go Plc shares at 22p × 4.35 = 96p (based on P/E ratio of Sellit Plc computed on average of high and low prices).

(b) *Consolidated balance sheet after scheme*

	£000	£000
Fixed assets		
Intangible assets		
Goodwill on consolidation (working 1)		1,365
Tangible assets		
Land and buildings	29,400	
Equipment and fittings	10,300	
Vehicles	5,600	
		45,300
		46,665
Current assets		
Stocks	19,540	
Debtors	3,350	
Cash at bank and in hand	12,150	
	35,040	
Creditors: Amounts falling due within one year		
Bank overdraft	1,000	
Trade creditors	21,770	
Taxation	2,080	
Dividends	1,570	
	26,420	
Net current assets		8,620
Total assets: *Less: Current liabilities*		55,285
Creditors: Amounts falling due after more than one year 5%, unsecured loan 19.20	600	
Taxation	6,890	7,490
		47,795
Capital and reserves		
Called up share capital (working 2)		8,518
Share premium account (working 3)		6,982
Revaluation reserve (working 4)		8,000
Other reserves: Capital reserve		8,050
Profit and loss account		16,245
		47,795

Workings

1. *Goodwill on consolidation*

	£000	£000
Cost of shares in Go Plc (6,800 × £1.25)		8,500
Less: Share capital and reserves of Go Plc	5,155	
Asset revaluations (9,000 – 7,020)	1,980	
		7,135
		1,365

2. *Share capital*

	£000
Original	7,000
Issued to Go Plc	
$6{,}800 \times \frac{125}{140} = 6{,}071$ shares @ 25p	1,518
	8,518

3. *Share premium*

	£000
Value of shares issued	
6,071 × 140p	8,500
Less: Nominal value	
6,071 × 25p	1,518
	6,982

4. *Revaluation reserve*

	£000
Fixed assets of Sellit Plc at revalued amounts	
(24,100 + 8,000 + 4,200)	36,300
Less: Original book value	28,300
	8,000

(c) *Merger accounting*

The merger principles regard a scheme as a pure 'pooling' of interests without there being any acquisition of assets by one shareholder group. The accounts thus try to reflect the total assets shown in the separate books of all the member companies. This is achieved by recognising both shares issued and acquired under the scheme at nominal value. Thus the goodwill of the acquired company and, if desired, asset revaluations, are not reflected in view of the fact that no 'purchase' of assets takes place, nor can a share premium arise.

The other major important effect of merger accounting is the treatment of the distributable profits of the 'acquired' company. Since the shareholders are the same persons, owning effectively the same assets, the reserves that were distributable prior to the scheme remain so after its implementation. This is perhaps the most controversial aspect of merger accounting, however, the Companies Act 1981 now contains provisions which have the effect of allowing the use of merger accounting. *ED31* has been issued since this change in legislation giving details of the circumstances in which merger accounting can be applied, and giving the method.

ANSWER P6. HOPE LTD

(a) Alternative treatment of goodwill arising on consolidation

(i) The Accounting Standards Committee set up in 1974 two working parties in order to reflect the significant differences in approach to the problem of accounting for goodwill:

Working Party A (the Pinkney Party) took the view that money (or money's worth) has been expended in acquiring goodwill, and therefore the cost should be capitalised and written off through profit and loss account over the period of its expected useful life (not exceeding 40 years). Clearly 40 years is an arbitrary period, but it happens to coincide with proposals in the USA!

Working Party B (the Davison Party) took the view that most British bankers, investment analysts and financial journalists leave goodwill out of their calculations when reckoning up the worth of a company, recognising that it is, at best, a very peculiar asset since it cannot be separated from the business and sold. The committee expressed the view that goodwill should either be written off immediately or shown as a permanent deduction from shareholders capital and reserves (the dangling debit). On balance they were against writing off the asset, since good money had been paid for the asset and writing if off at once caused the asset to disappear.

The 'dangling debit approach' is said to have two advantages:

... it has the effect of doing exactly what any wise analyst does when reviewing a company's balance sheet;

... it puts companies with purchased goodwill on the same footing as those whose goodwill, although it may exist, has been generated internally and is not, therefore, valued in the balance sheet.

(ii) *Companies Act 1981*

Para.21 Sch.1 CA 1981 requires goodwill to be written off through the profit and loss account over its useful economic life. However, this rule relates only to goodwill shown as an asset in an individual company's accounts and does not apply to goodwill on consolidation.

(iii) *ED30*

Exposure draft 'Accounting for Goodwill' was issued in 1982. Two methods of accounting for goodwill are given which apply to both purchased goodwill and goodwill arising on consolidation. They are:

(1) Amortise goodwill through the profit and loss account, before profit or loss on ordinary activities, over its estimated useful life.

or

(2) Write goodwill off immediately against reserves representing realised profits.

The choice of one of these two methods is left to the individual company, but once the choice is made it should apply to all acquisitions.

(b) Two methods of reflecting the acquisition of Prey Ltd in the consolidated balance sheet of the group are the 'Acquisition' and the 'Merger' methods.

Consolidated Accounts using both methods are given below.

Consolidated balance sheet—Acquisition method

	£000	*£000*
Fixed assets		
Intangible assets		
Goodwill on consolidation		84
Tangible assets (540 + 210)		750
		834
Current assets	1,860	
Creditors: Amounts falling due within one year	675	
Net current assets		1,185
Total assets: *Less:* Current liabilities		2,019
Capital and reserves		
Called up share capital (3,420 × 25p)		855
Share premium account (480 × 55p)		264
Profit and loss account		900
		2,019

Consolidated balance sheet—Merger method	*£000*	*£000*
Fixed assets		
Tangible assets (540 + 120)		660
Current assets	1,860	
Creditors: Amounts falling due within one year	675	
Net current assets		1,185
Total assets: *Less:* Current liabilities		1,845
Capital and reserves		
Called up share capital		855
Profit and loss account (see working)		990
		1,845

Workings

Profit and loss account:	
Reserves: Hope Ltd	900
Prey Ltd	150
	1,050
Less: Excess purchase price over nominal value	60
	990

Using the acquisition method the purchase price of Prey Ltd is the market value of shares issued, whereas under the merger method the shares are issued at nominal value. Additionally, under the acquisition method fair values must be attributed to the underlying net assets acquired. The set-offs necessary under each method as a preliminary to consolidation are:

	Acquisition *£000*			*Merger* *£000*
Investment in Prey Ltd			Investment in Prey Ltd	
480,000 shares at 80p		384	480,000 shares at 25p	120
Less: Shareholders funds acquired			*Less:* Share capital of Prey Ltd	60
Share capital of Prey Ltd	60			
Reserves of Prey Ltd	150			
Revaluation of fixed assets	90	300		
Excess purchase price over book value of assets acquired		84	Excess purchase price over nominal value of shares acquired	60

Advantages of merger accounting

Proponents of the merger would argue that if the two companies were to continue as separate entities:

(i) the total revenue reserves would be available for dividend
(ii) assets would be valued at historic cost.

Merely because the companies continue in a different form, merger proponents would ask, 'Why should assets of one company be valued at historic cost but of the acquired company at current value?' This argument would clearly not be valid if current cost accounting principles were adopted by both companies.

Weaknesses of merger accounting

(i) Return on capital employed
Since assets are shown at historic cost, the value of the capital employed disclosed under the merger method is lower than that which would arise under the acquisition method. Thus, directors wishing to show the highest possible return on capital employed would use the merger method wherever possible.

(ii) In America, where merger accounting (or 'pooling') has been extensively used, abuses have occurred where the pre-acquisition profits of an acquired subsidiary have been used by the new holding company to boost dividend payments, resulting in a consequent increase in share price.

(iii) Considerable difficulty has been experienced, both in the USA and in the UK, in defining precisely when a merger has taken place. The Jenkins Committee on Company Law Reform accepted that the application of acquisition accounting principles could operate unreasonably on a reconstruction. The Committee's view, however, was that it would be dangerous to extend merger principles beyond a true reconstruction, since to do so would enable companies to 'buy profits' and use them for payment of dividends.

ANSWER P7. OLDFASHIONED PLC

SSAP 3 (*Earnings per share*) is intended to apply to the audited accounts of listed companies. It is assumed that this is the case here.

(a) (1) Calculation of earnings per share

(i) Basic EPS	*Oldfashioned Plc*	*Sixties Plc*
Earnings	£1,000,000	£800,000
No. of shares	4,000,000	800,000
Basic EPS	25p	100p

(ii) Fully diluted EPS	*Oldfashioned Plc*		*Sixties Plc*	
	£	£	£	£
Profit after tax		1,000,000		800,000
Interest on 8% convertible loan stock	80,000		160,000	
Less: Corporation tax	41,600		83,200	
		38,400		76,800
Earnings		1,038,400		876,800
No. of shares in issue		4,000,000		800,000
Maximum no. of new shares on conversion		1,000,000		4,000,000
		5,000,000		4,800,000
Fully diluted EPS		20.8p		18.3p

(2) Presentation in the profit and loss accounts

Oldfashioned Plc	*Year ended 30 Sep.*	
	19–9	*19–8*
Basic earnings per ordinary share of 50p	25p	?p
Fully diluted earnings per ordinary share of 50p	20.8p	?p

Note to accounts

The calculation of basic earnings per ordinary share is based on earnings of £1 million (19–8?) and 4 million shares in issue throughout the two years ended 30 Sep. 19–9.

The fully diluted earnings per share is based on adjusted earnings of £1,038,400 (19–8?) after adding back interest net of corporation tax on the 8% convertible unsecured loan stock. The maximum number of shares into which this stock becomes convertible on 31 Mar. 19–10 is 1 million making a total of 5 million ordinary shares issued and issuable (19–8?).

Sixties Plc	*Year ended 30 Sep.* 19–9	19–8
Basic earnings per ordinary share of 50p	100p	?p
Fully diluted earnings per ordinary share of 50p	18.3p	?p

Note to accounts
The calculation of basic earnings per ordinary share is based on earnings of £800,000 (19–8?) and 800,000 ordinary shares in issue throughout the two years ended 30 Sep. 19–9.

The fully diluted earnings per share is based on adjusted earnings of £876,800 (19–8?) after adding back interest net of corporation tax on the 8% convertible unsecured loan stock. The maximum number of shares into which this stock becomes convertible on 31 Mar. 19–10 is 4 million shares, making a total of 4,800,000 ordinary shares issued and issuable (19–8?).

Tutorial note
Comparative figures for fully diluted earnings per share would only be shown if the assumptions in 19–8 still apply in 19–9. This would be so, for example, if 31 Mar. 19–10 were the first date on which conversion could have taken place.

Corporation tax has been taken as 52%.

(b) Calculation of earnings per share after merger
Estimated earnings for year ended 30 Sep. 19–10

	Oldfashioned £	*Sixties* £	*Eighties* £
Profit after tax	1,000,000	1,000,000	2,000,000
Interest on 8% convertible loan stock net of corporation tax (6 months)	19,200	38,400	57,600

Number of shares in Eighties

	Oldfashioned (000)	*Sixties* (000)	*Eighties* (000)
Ordinary shares	4,000	800	4,800
Conversion of loan stock	1,000	4,000	5,000
			9,800

(i) Basic EPS
Weighted average number of shares in issue during the year £4.8 million + $\frac{1}{2}$ × £5.0 million = £7.3 million.

$$\text{Basic EPS} = \frac{£2{,}000{,}000}{7{,}300{,}000}$$

$$= 27.4\text{p}$$

$$\text{(ii) Fully diluted EPS} = \frac{£2{,}057{,}600}{9{,}800{,}000}$$

$$= 21.0\text{p}$$

Tutorial note
The calculation of a fully diluted earnings per share figure in this situation is not specifically covered by *SSAP 3*. However in order to give a true and fair view of the current EPS so as to be able to compare it with the EPS which shareholders can expect to achieve in the year to 30 Sep. 19–11 (when there will be no loan stock outstanding at any time during the year), a fully diluted EPS should be shown.

(c) (i) *Proforma balance sheet of Eighties Plc at 1 Oct. 19–9*

	£000
Fixed assets	11,500
Net current assets	3,000
Total assets *less* current liabilities	14,500
Creditors: Amounts falling due after more than one year 10% Debenture loans 19–25/29	7,000
	7,500
Capital and reserves	
Called up share capital	4,900
Unrealised reserve	2,600
	7,500

Workings

Balance sheets of individual companies assuming full conversion of convertible unsecured loan stock.

	Oldfashioned	*Sixties*
	£000	*£000*
Ordinary shares (50p)	2,500	2,400
Reserves and unappropriated profit	1,500	600
Share premium	500	—
10% debentures	4,000	3,000
	8,500	6,000
Fixed assets (at value)	6,000	5,500
Net current assets	2,500	500
	8,500	6,000

Conversion of loan stock in Oldfashioned Plc

	£
Nominal value of con. unsec. loan stock	1,000,000
Nominal value of ordinary shares to be issued	500,000
Share premium	500,000

Assuming the new shares in Eighties Plc are issued at par, the number of 50p shares issued = 9.8 million.

Fair value of shares issued by Eighties

	£000
Ordinary shares issued	4,900
Fair value of net tangible assets *less* liabilities (4.5 million + 3.0 million)	7,500
Unrealised reserve (required by *ED 31*)	2,600

Tutorial note

The pro forma balance sheet of Eighties Plc does not reflect the actual position at 1 Oct. 19–9. Instead, it indicates what the position at 1 Oct. 19–9 would have looked like had the effects of the merger been taken into account.

Pro forma balance sheets are often a useful way of reflecting the impact of significant non-adjusting post balance sheet events such as acquisitions and disposals of subsidiaries.

(ii) *Pro forma consolidated balance sheet at 1 Oct. 19–9 on merger accounting basis*

	£000
Fixed assets	11,500
Net current assets	3,000
Total assets less current liabilities	14,500
Creditor: amount falling due after more than one year	
10% Debentures 19–25/29	7,000
	7,500
Capital and reserves	
Called up share capital	4,900
Share premium	500
Revenue reserves	2,100
	7,500

Tutorial note
The main point of note is that in the above balance sheet, the distributability of the £2.1 million reserves is preserved. This is not so under acquisition accounting.

Merger accounting is allowed by *ED31* provided certain conditions are satisfied. In the case of Eighties, the conditions are satisfied and thus acquisition accounting is inappropriate.

(d) ED31 requires the following conditions to be met in order for a business combination to be accounted for as a merger: (paragraph 17).

(*i*) *the business combination should result from an offer to the holders of all equity shares and the holders of all voting shares which are not already held by the offeror; the offer should be approved by the holders of the voting shares of the company making the offer; and*

(*ii*) *the offer should be accepted by holders of at least 90% of all equity shares and of the shares carrying at least 90% of all votes of the offeree company; for this purpose, any convertible stock is not to be regarded as equity except to the extent that it is converted into equity as a result of the business combination; and*

(*iii*) *not less than 90% of the fair value of the total consideration given for the equity share capital (including that given for shares already held) should be in the form of equity capital; not less than 90% of the fair value of the consideration given for voting non-equity share capital (including that given for shares already held) should be in the form of equity and/or voting non-equity share capital.*

All business combinations are acquisitions except those which satisfy the above conditions.

(e) There are some business combinations for which acquisition accounting is held not to produce satisfactory results, in particular when two companies or groups combine by means of a share for share exchange as in the above example. In such circumstances, it may be more accurate to speak of two groups of shareholders pooling their interests or merging.

It was to deal with such situations that merger accounting was originally developed. In commenting on the accounting treatment adopted for combinations effected by means of share for share exchanges (including certain group re-organisations), some have objected to the workings of acquisition accounting which gave rise to:

(i) the pre-acquisition reserves of the acquired company being frozen so that they cannot be distributed even though the shareholders immediately before and after the combination are the same;
(ii) the creation of a share premium account or other form of unrealised reserve;
(iii) the recognition of goodwill; and
(iv) an increase in the charge for depreciation of the acquired company's fixed assets (this is only significant in historical cost accounting).

Merger accounting was developed so that those four disadvantages did not arise. When the shareholders of two companies pool their interests, the combined financial statements do not differ from the aggregate of the financial statements of the two previously separate companies. More specifically:

(i) because the shares issued as consideration by the holding company are recorded at nominal value instead of fair value, no share premium or undistributable reserve arises and pre-acquisition profits are not frozen; (to the extent that they are not required to eliminate differences between nominal values of shares issued and shares acquired). In the above example £600,000 of the reserves of Sixties are regarded as available for distribution.
(ii) goodwill is not recognised because it too only arises as a product of the use of the fair value (i.e. market value) of the shares issued;
(iii) merger accounting does not in general involve any change in the carrying value of the net assets of either of the combining companies and so no increased depreciation charge arises.

ANSWER P8

(a) *Journal entries*

	Dr.	*Cr.*
	£000	*£000*
(i) Dr Cash account	3,000	
Cr Application & allotment account		3,000
Being the receipt of cash on application for shares.		
(ii) Dr Application & allotment account	750	
Cr Share capital account		750
Being the recording of issue of 1,000,000 ordinary shares of 75p nominal value.		
(iii) Dr Application & allotment account	2,250	
Cr Cash account		2,250
Being return of cash to unsuccessful applicants, first applied monies to balance due on allotment.		
(iv) Dr Call account	500	
Cr Share premium account		500
Being the recording of the balance due by 31 Dec. 1981		
(v) Dr Cash account	500	
Cr Call account		500
Being the receipt of cash due following allotment		

(b) The main matters to which attention should be directed in the preparation of a published profit forecast are as follows:

(i) Consideration of the general economic climate, including possible changes in exchange rates and interest rates.
(ii) Likely demand for the company's products having regard both to the general economic climate and the company's likely market share.
(iii) The likely outcome of wage negotiations and the possibility of industrial action.
(iv) The ways in which capital raised is to be applied and the effect on production capacity and direct and fixed costs.
(v) The reliability of interim and management accounts and previous budgets.
(vi) Full disclosure of all material accounting policies.
(vii) Full disclosure of all the assumptions on which the forecast is based.
(viii) Whether the forecast is consistent with forecast balance sheets.
(ix) Whether sufficient working capital is available, and in particular whether proper cash flow forecasts are to be prepared to support the forecast.
(x) Proper checks on the arithmetical accuracy of the forecast.

Working
Number of shares to be issued

	£
Capital in issue	
500,000 7% preference shares of £1	500,000
1,000,000 ordinary shares of 75p	750,000
	1,250,000
Authorised capital	2,000,000
Total of new issue	750,000

$$\text{Number of shares to be issued} = \frac{750,000}{0.75} = \underline{1,000,000}$$

ANSWER P9. COMBINED ENGINEERING PLC

Rex Garages Ltd
Pro forma balance sheet at 31 Jul. 19–2

	£000	£000
Fixed assets—Tangible assets		
Properties (W1)		302
Plant and machinery		462
Vehicles		437
		1,201
Current assets		
Stocks (W2)	2,368	
Debtors and prepayments	1,675	
Cash	8	
	4,051	
Creditors: Amounts falling due within one year		
Bank overdraft (W4)	1,217	
Trade creditors and accruals	1,486	
	2,703	
Net current assets		1,348
Total assets less current liabilities		2,549
Creditors: Amounts falling due after more than one year		
Loans		1,700
		849

	£000
Capital and reserves	
Called up share capital	500
Reserves	349
	849

Combined Engineering plc
Pro forma balance sheet at 31 Jul. 19–2

	£000	£000
Fixed assets:		
Tangible assets		
Properties	3,646	
Plant and machinery	4,201	
Vehicles	2,948	
		10,795
Investments		
Shares in group companies (W7)	1,050	
Loans to group companies (W8)	1,000	
		2,050
		12,845
Current assets		
Stocks	12,529	
Debtors and prepayments	11,620	
Cash	25	
	24,174	
Creditors: Amounts falling due within one year		
Bank overdraft (W9)	16,084	
Trade creditors and accruals	11,206	
	27,290	
Net current liabilities		(3,116)
Total assets less current liabilities		9,729
Creditors: Amounts falling due after more than one year		
Loans		5,000
		4,729
Capital and Reserves		
Called up share capital		2,000
Reserves (W11)		2,729
		4,729

Workings

1. *Properties*

	£000
Properties per balance sheet	1,352
Book value of properties sold	(950)
Amounts written off	(100)
	302

2. *Stocks*

	£000
Stocks per balance sheet	3,368
Cost of stocks sold (W3)	(1,000)
	2,368

3. *Cost of stocks sold*

	£000
Loan from Combined Engineering plc	1,000
Temporary advance	150
	1,150
Balance of proceeds of sale of properties (1,200 – 750)	(450)
Proceeds from sale of stock	700
Cost of stocks sold $700 \times \frac{100}{70} =$	1,000

4. *Bank overdraft*

	£000
Bank overdraft per balance sheet	1,817
Loan from Management Venture Capital Ltd	(600)
	1,217

5. *Reserves*

	£000
Reserves per balance sheet	499
Profit on sale of property (1,200 – 950)	250
	749
Write down of remaining property	(100)
Loss on sale of stock	(300)
	349

6. *Loan capital*

	£000
Loan capital per balance sheet	3,000
Repayment of loans secured on property	(900)
Repayment of loan from Combined Engineering plc	(1,000)
	1,100
Loan from Management Venture Capital Ltd	600
	1,700

7. *Shares in subsidiaries at cost*

	£000
Per balance sheet	1,550
Cost of shares in Rex	(500)
	1,050

8. *Loans to subsidiaries*

	£000
Per balance sheet	2,000
Loan to Rex repaid	(1,000)
	1,000

9. *Bank overdraft*

	£000
Bank overdraft per balance sheet	17,483
Redundancy payments	450
Proceeds of sale of Rex (W10)	(849)
Loan to Rex repaid	(1,000)
	16,084

10. *Proceeds of sale of Rex*

	£000
Net asset value at 30 Apr. 19–2:	
Share capital	500
Reserves as adjusted (W5)	349
	849

11. *Reserves*

	£000
Reserves per balance sheet	2,830
Redundancy payments	(450)
Profit on sale of Rex (W12)	349
	2,729

12. *Profits on sale of Rex*

	£000
Proceeds	849
Cost of shares sold	(500)
	349

ANSWER P10. CAPITAL REORGANISATION

(a) *Journal Entries*
(1) Books of the proposer

Adjustment journal

Date	*Particulars*	*£000*	*£000*
	Share premium account	178,326.9	
	Capital Shares capital account		178,326.9
	Scrip issue of new Capital Shares to ordinary shareholders under the provisions of s. 56(2) CA 1948 in accordance with resolutions passed on . . . in company meeting.		
	Capital Shares capital account	178,326.9	
	Capital reduction account		178,326.9
	Capital reduction account	178,326.9	
	12% Capital Notes 1986 account		178,326.9
	Reduction of share capital by cancellation of all Capital Shares and issue of 12% Capital Notes 1986 in lieu under the provisions of s. 66 CA 1948 in accordance with the resolutions passed on . . . in company meeting and a Court Order dated . . .		
	Cash	2,700.0	
	Capital Noteholders' suspense account		2,700.0
	Capital Noteholders' suspense account	2,700.0	
	Cash—to Capital Noteholders		2,700.0
	Sale of £3m fractional entitlements 12% Capital Noteholders and distribution of net proceeds to the owners per Appendix A of the proposal of 11 February 1977.	5,400.0	5,400.0

(2) Books of the offeror

Adjustment Journal

Date	*Particulars*	*£000*	*£000*
	7.5% Convertible Unsecured Loan Stock	8,117.7	
	Stockholders' account		8,117.7
	Stockholders' account	8,117.7	
	Ordinary share capital account-shares of 25p	(see workings)	2,333.8
	Share premium account		5,783.9
		16,235.4	16,235.4
	Cancellation of 7.5% Convertible Unsecured Loan Stock 1984–89 and issue of 115 new ordinary shares of 25p at a premium under the provision of ss. 56 & 61 CA 1948 in accordance with the resolutions passed on . . . . . in company meeting.		

Working
Nominal value of ordinary shares of 25p is

$$\frac{8,117,700}{100} \times 115 \times \frac{25}{100} = \underline{£2,333,839}$$

(b) Calculation of effect of proposal and offer on original holdings
(1) Proposal to holder of 100 ordinary shares of 25p

(i) Retains his ordinary shares as before and has a scrip issue of £32.50 12% Capital Notes 1986

(ii) Capital Value	£
After proposal:	
100 shares @ 160p	160.00
£32.50 Capital Notes @ Par	32.50
	192.50
Before proposal:	
100 shares @ 160p	160.00
Gain to holder of 100 shares	32.50

Tutorial note:
The assumption that market prices of existing securities will not change is extremely optimistic.

	£
(iii) Annual income (gross)	
After proposal	
100 shares @ 3.595p × $\frac{100}{65}$	5.53
£32.50 notes @ 12%	3.90
	9.43
Before proposal:	
100 shares @ 3.595p × $\frac{100}{65}$	5.53
Increase in gross income	3.90

Note:
Since Capital Notes 1986 were issued in units of £100, a person holding 100 shares only would receive cash of £29.25. For comparison purposes this has been ignored.
(£32.50 × $\frac{2.7}{3}$ = £29.25—Fractions sold for £2.7m)

(2) *Offer to holder of £100 7.5% Convertible Unsecured Loan Stock 1984/89 (CULS)*

(i) Losses whole of loan stock in exchange for 115 new ordinary shares of 25p each

	£
(ii) Capital value	
After offer:	
115 shares @ 67p	77.05
Before offer:	
£100 7.5% CULS	70.00
(Conversion option value £23.2862 × 4 @ 67p = £62.41)	—
Gain to holder of £100 7.5% CULS	7.05
(iii) Annual income (gross)	
After offer:	
115 shares @ 4.493p × $\frac{100}{65}$	7.95
Before offer:	
£100 @ 7.5%	7.50
Increase in gross income	0.45

ANSWER Q1

(a) It is invariably necessary for a company's accounts to be adjusted prior to their inclusion in a prospectus report since the purpose of such a report is quite different from that of the company's published accounts presented to its shareholders.

Published accounts are prepared by a company's directors for presentation to committed investors, i.e. shareholders, in order to acquaint them with the results of the company's activities during the latest complete year of stewardship. Information included in prospectus reports is addressed to potential investors in such a way as to enable them to form an opinion on the likely prospects of the company in question under future trading conditions, so far as the latter may be assessed. Since the accountant's report usually relates to a five year period, it is important to ensure that the results over the five years can be compared in a meaningful way.

It will therefore, be necessary for the information in published accounts to be represented so as to facilitate the above purposes.

(b) The instances in which a company's accounts need to be adjusted prior to their inclusion in an accountant's report fall into three types:

(i) Where there have been any changes in accounting policies during the five years reported upon, it would be necessary to adjust profits and assets of earlier years in such a way that the results of all five years were based on current accounting policies. Such adjustments are also required where accepted accounting principles have not been applied.
Example: Changes in the basis of treatment of research and development expenditure, depreciation, or the basis of valuation of stock and work-in-progress.

(ii) When information of a material nature becomes available after the accounts have been prepared, and the accounts would otherwise have reflected this information had it been available earlier.
Example: Although adjustments would not normally be made to bad debt provisions, exceptional situations might arise where material amounts were involved and adjustment was required in the light of new information.

(iii) Where there have been material sources of revenue or categories of expenditure of a non-recurring nature.
Example: Where a separate section of the business has been discontinued or sold, then not only would the profit or loss on discontinuance or sale be eliminated, but also the profits of the business as a whole would need to be adjusted to ensure comparability of profit figures.

Tutorial notes to part (b)

(1) Before the arrival of *SSAP 6*, some companies used 'reserve accounting' whereby certain items of a revenue nature were put direct to reserves rather than through the profit and loss account. Since an accountants' report covers a five year period, it may, therefore, be necessary to adjust the results of earlier years so that the profit and loss accounts were drawn up on an *SSAP 6* basis in terms of extraordinary items and exceptional items.
(2) It is important to note that items such as expropriation of assets or discontinuance of a significant part of the business should be reported as extraordinary items and not eliminated from the five year summary
(3) As regards subsidiaries purchased or sold during the five year period, adjustment should normally be made. The 'Yellow Book' (p. 58 para 9) states that 'There should be included in the body of the prospectus, when appropriate, an explanation of the trend of profits as shown in the accountants' report, dealing in particular with the effects of changes in the financing of the company, and of the acquisition of subsidiaries, etc.'
(c) *Checklist of matters required by the Stock Exchange to be covered by an accountant's report relating to a prospectus of a private company seeking a quotation for its shares*

(1) *Profits and losses*

For each of the past five years (or if the company has been carrying on business for less than five years, the years for which accounts have been made up) state:

(a) Sales to third parties (specifying also the method of calculation)
(b) Cost of goods sold, stating separately:

(i) Amortisation, depreciation and obsolescence charges;
(ii) Financial expenses—interest and discounts

(c) Other income—investment income and rents
(d) Share of profits of associated companies
(e) Profit before tax and extraordinary items
(f) Taxation
(g) Extraordinary items less taxation
(h) Profit attributable to shareholders
(i) Preference dividends (with details)
(j) Profit attributable to ordinary shareholders
(k) Ordinary dividends (with details)
(l) Retained profits
(m) Earnings per share

Note
It is assumed that the private company does not have any subsidiaries, nor has it agreed to acquire another company subsequent to the latest balance sheet date.

(2) *Disclosure of assets and liabilities*
Draw up a balance sheet as at the end of the last accounting period in full compliance with the disclosure requirements of the 1948 and 1981 Companies Acts for annual accounts.

(3) *Age of figures reported upon*
Ensure that the date of the prospectus is within six months of the latest period reported upon.

(4) *Source and application of funds statements*
Draw up summarised source and application of funds statements for the five years (if applicable) covered by the report.

(5) *Disclosure of accounting policies*
Disclose a statement of accounting policies for all material or critical areas.

(6) *Any other matters which are relevant for the purposes of the report*
This may include several possibilities. For example, profit trends may be materially affected by the refinancing of loan capital with further equity. The accountant should refer to this in his report. Another possibility would be restrictions on remittances of overseas earnings, although this point is now covered by paragraph 36 of *SSAP 14* (Group Accounts).

ANSWER Q2

The main points which an accountant would wish to consider in carrying out an examination of the accounting policies and calculations for a profit forecast in connection with a client's application for the admission of its securities for a listing on the Stock Exchange include the following:

(1) Whether the profit forecast under review is based on forecasts regularly prepared for the purpose of management, or whether it has been separately and specifically prepared for the immediate purpose;
(2) Where profit forecasts are regularly prepared for management purposes, the degree of accuracy and reliability previously achieved, and the frequency and thoroughness with which estimates are revised.
(3) Whether the profit forecast under review represents the management's best estimate of results which they reasonably believe can and will be achieved as distinct from targets which the management have set as desirable;
(4) The extent to which profit forecast results for expired periods are supported by reliable interim accounts;
(5) The details of the procedures followed to generate the profit forecast and the extent to which it is built up from detailed forecasts of activity and cash flow;
(6) The extent to which profits are derived from activities having a proved and consistent trend and those of a more irregular, volatile or unproved nature;

(7) How the profit forecast takes account of any material extraordinary items and prior year adjustments, their nature, and how they are presented;
(8) Whether adequate provision is made for foreseeable losses and contingencies and how the profit forecast takes account of factors which may cause it to be subject to a high degree of risk, or which may invalidate the assumptions;
(9) Whether working capital appears adequate for requirements; normally this would require the availability of properly prepared cash-flow statements; and where short-term or long-term finance is to be relied on, whether the necessary arrangements have been made and confirmed;
(10) The arithmetical accuracy of the profit forecast and the supporting information and whether forecast balance sheets and sources and applications of funds statements have been prepared—these help to highlight arithmetical inacccuracies and inconsistent assumptions.

ANSWER Q3

(a) A report is required by qualified accountants in respect of the following matters relating to B Ltd:

(i) the profits or losses of B Ltd for each of the completed financial years immediately before publication of the prospectus. (If B Ltd has been incorporated for less than five years, for the years since incorporation).
(ii) a statement that no accounts have been made up to within three months of the publication date, if this is the case.
(iii) the assets and liabilities of B Ltd at the most recent balance sheet date.
(iv) the statement of accounting policies.
(v) any other matters considered to be relevant for the purposes of the report.

It should be noted that the 'Yellow Book' does not require the six balance sheets in this situation, although in practice these are often given.

(b) The duties of the reporting accountant (in the prospectus situation here, this would be either the auditor or the auditor joined with another accountant) in relation to a profit forecast, are to examine and report upon the accounting bases and calculations used for the forecast.

(c) (i) The overall effect of the Listing Agreement on the company is to bind the company to observe certain rules and procedures regarding its status as a listed company.
(ii) The Listing Agreement takes the form of a resolution to be passed by the board of directors.
(iii) The Listing Agreement requires the company to notify the Quotations Department of the Stock Exchange of any

preliminary profit announcements, immediately after the relevant board meeting has been held. The company is also required to prepare a half-yearly or interim report which must either be sent to security holders or inserted in two leading daily newspapers.

(iv) The minimum contents of a preliminary profit announcement are:

(1) Group turnover
(2) Group profit (or loss) after all charges including taxation
(3) United Kingdom and, where material, overseas taxation
(4) Profit attributable to members of the holding company (i.e. after deduction of outside interests)
(5) If material, the extent to which profit has been affected by extraordinary items
(6) Rates and amounts of dividends paid and proposed
(7) Earnings per share (in respect of a year)
(8) Comparative figures for the corresponding previous periods in respect of all of the above items.
(9) Any supplementary information which the directors consider necessary for a reasonable appreciation of the results.

(d) The rule (effective from 1 Sep. 1977) is that 25% of the equity capital of a company should normally be in the hands of the public at the time of admission to listing. The 'public' means persons not associated with the directors or major shareholders

(e) A Class I transaction is a transaction considered sufficiently material to call not only for an announcement to be made to the Quotations Department of the Stock Exchange and the Press, but also to require a circular (A 'Class I circular') to be sent to shareholders. There are four possible criteria and if any of them apply, the transaction is considered class I (the Council may relax this rule in certain cases):

(i) the value of the assets acquired or disposed of amounts to more than 15% of the assets of the acquiring or disposing company,
(ii) the net profit before tax attributable to the assets acquired or disposed of amounts to more than 15% of the profits of the acquiring or disposing company,
(iii) the aggregate value of the consideration given or received amounts to more than 15% of the assets of the acquiring or disposing company,
(iv) the equity capital issued by an acquiring company as consideration amounts to more than 15% of the equity capital previously in issue.

Where a Class I circular relates to the acquisition of a company which is not listed, and therefore where no published information such as Extel cards is available, an accountants' report is required. This will report, among other matters, on five years profits and the most recent balance sheet.

(f) (i) An accountant's report containing any significant qualification or reservation as to any of the five years reported upon, would not normally be regarded by the Quotations Department as acceptable.
(ii) Where a qualified report appears in an acquisition circular, the Council of the Stock Exchange may require that the company seeks approval for the acquisition from the shareholders in general meeting. (It should be noted that the Listing Agreement requires the company to notify the Quotations Department without delay of particulars of any material acquisitions or realisations of assets.)

(g) In the absence of detailed stock records, accountants should:

(i) Review the system of controls and stocktaking procedures applying during the period.
(ii) Examine stock summaries and such other supporting records as are available.
(iii) Review the auditors' working papers and discuss with them the work carried out year by year.
(iv) Compare the detailed profit and loss accounts and obtain satisfactory explanations for unusual variations.
(v) Consider various key ratios such as gross profit/sales and stock/cost of sales.
(vi) Ensure that any apparent discrepancies which have arisen during the period have been properly investigated and explained.

As a result of these procedures, accountants will have to use their judgement as to whether:

(i) they are satisfied as to the valuation of the stock, or
(ii) they are unable to form a satisfactory opinion, or
(iii) they believe the stock to be incorrectly valued.

(h) *Enforcement of the City Code*
The City Code on Takeovers and Mergers is a statement of 14 Principles, 39 Rules and some Practice Notes published by a Panel representing the principal categories of financial institutions in the City of London. It is an expression of the code of conduct and practice which the City considers should guide companies in takeovers. It does not have the force of law.

The Code is intended to apply to companies listed on the Stock Exchange and to a lesser degree, to other public companies. It does not apply to offers to acquire the shares of private companies or of companies not resident in UK for exchange control purposes (except in special cases *Practice Note 1*). It is considered impracticable to impose on take-overs rules in such detail that they could be uniformly and compulsorily applied to many different takeovers. Companies which make takeover bids and their advisers are expected as a matter of good conduct to observe the spirit as well as the letter of the Code and to submit to the Panel for adjudication and guidance any novel or debatable issues which they may encounter in observing the Code. A company which flagrantly infringed the Code or defied a ruling of the Panel might lose the Stock Exchange listing of its shares. The merchant bank which advised a client company to persist in such conduct might have to withdraw from the Issuing Houses Association. But these sanctions in their full rigour have never been invoked.

(i) *Standards of care and legal liabilities*

(i) In drafting takeover documents the same standard of care is required as the *CA 1948* demands in the preparation of a prospectus: *Principal 12.*

(ii) In any offer the directors of the company which make the offer must formally declare that all reasonable care has been taken to ensure that facts stated and opinions expressed are fair and accurate, that no material facts have been omitted and that the directors jointly and severally accept responsibility accordingly: *Rule 14*. If that declaration proved to be unfounded there might be legal liability under the Misrepresentation Act 1967 or for common law negligence or on specific points under s.438 CA 1948 or the Prevention of Fraud (Investments) Act 1958 by which takeover bids are regulated. But the legal position is obscure.

(iii) An auditor as auditor has no obligation to report on profit forecasts. His duties as auditor are limited to reporting on the accounts: s.14 CA 1967. However, the Code requires that where a profit forecast is made, whether by the board of the offerer or of the offeree company, the auditors or consultant accountants (as well as any financial adviser such as a merchant bank named in the offer document) will (i) examine and (ii) report on the accounting bases and calculations from which the profit forecast is derived. The report together with the consent of the auditors and others must be included in any documents issued in connection with an offer: *Rule 16.* Specific notes of guidance are given in Practice Note 3 on profit forecasts. Although it would be unusual for an auditor to decline to report on any profit forecasts in an offer document he can and indeed he would have to carry out a proper investigation. There have been a number of instances where auditors have been given insufficient time to carry out a proper enquiry into profit forecasts. They would lay themselves open to substantial claims for professional negligence if they reported in such circumstances. When adequate facilities are provided it would be against the spirit of the Code to decline to report.

ANSWER R1. BAFFLE LTD

Consolidated Statement of Source and Application of Funds for the year ended 31 Jul. 19–7	*£000*	*£000*
Group profit before tax		850
Add: Depreciation		1,950
Sources generated from operations		2,800
Other sources		
Issue of shares	1,750	
Minority interest at date of acquisition	600	
Increase in debenture stock	500	2,850
		5,650
Applications		
Additions to fixed assets	5,920	
Dividends paid—Baffle Ltd	450	
—minority shareholders	50	
Purchase of goodwill	200	
		6,620
		970
Decrease in working capital		
Increase in stock	400	
Increase in debtors	800	
Increase in creditors	(1,300)	(100)
Decrease in net liquid assets		870
Decrease in cash balances		600
Increase in bank overdraft		270
		870

Summary of the effects of the acquisition of New Ltd	*£000*
Purchase of fixed assets	2,500
goodwill	200
stock	300
debtors	400
cash	500
debentures	(500)
creditors	(800)
	2,600
Less: minority interest	600
	2,000

	£000
Financed by issue of shares	1,750
Cash	250
	2,000

Workings

			£000
1. Profit before tax			
Increase in group reserves (4700–3400)			1,300
Less: Share premium (1750 – 700)			1,050
Increase in revenue reserves			250
Add: dividends—holding company			450
			700
Add: Minority interests			
At 31 Jul. 19–7		700	
At acquisition			
assets	3,700		
liabilities	1,300		
	2,400 × 25%	600	
Increase in post-acq period		100	
Add: Share of dividend (25% × 200)		50	150
			850
Tax			–
			850

2. Fixed Assets	
Increase in WDV (9070–5100)	3,970
Add: Depreciation	1,950
Additions	5,920

ANSWER R2. GREAT EASTERN LTD

Statement of Source and Application of Funds for the year ended 31 Dec. 19–8

		£
Group Profit before tax		83,000
Adjustment for items not involving a movement of funds		
Depreciation		62,000
Sources generated from operations		145,000
Other sources		
Proceeds of share issue	25,000	
Loan stock issue	5,000	
		30,000
		175,000
Applications		
Purchase of fixed assets	95,000	
Tax paid	27,000	
Dividends paid by Great Eastern Ltd	20,000	
Dividends paid to minority shareholders	7,000	
		149,000
Changes in working capital		26,000
Increase in stock	5,000	
Increase in debtors	26,000	
Increase in creditors	(1,000)	
		30,000
		4,000
Increase in bank overdrafts		10,000
Increase in cash balances		6,000
		4,000

Workings:

1. Profit before tax	
GE (91–38)	53,000
Y (54–24)	30,000
	83,000
2. Depreciation (GE 38 + Y 24)	62,000

		GE		*Y*
3. Fixed Assets		£		£
Increase in WDV		22,000		11,000
Add: Depreciation		38,000		24,000
		60,000		35,000
	Total		95,000	
4. Tax				
Balance b/fwd		18,000		3,000
Profit and loss		23,000		11,000
		41,000		14,000
Balance c/fwd		20,000		8,000
Paid		21,000		6,000
	Total		27,000	
5. Dividends				
Balance b/fwd		10,000		10,000
P & L a/c—ordinary divs		15,000		12,000
		25,000		22,000
Balance c/fwd		5,000		12,000
Ordinary divs paid		20,000		10,000
Minority proportion 20%				2,000
Minority preference dividend				5,000
				7,000

ANSWER R3. SPIXWORTH PLC

(a) *Statement of value added for the year ended 30 Jun. 19–8*

		£000	%
Turnover		31,311	
Bought-in materials and services		12,818	
		18,493	
Dividends received from associated company		40	
Value added		18,533	100
Applied as follows:			
To pay employees' wages, salaries and pensions		12,123	65.4
To pay providers of capital:	£000		
Interest on loans	120		
Dividend to shareholders	900		
Dividends to minority interests	13		
		1,033	5.6
To pay government:			
Corporation tax £(2,600 – 100)		2,500	13.5
To provide for maintenance and expansion:			
Depreciation	1,056		
Transfer to replacement reserve	300		
Retained profits	1,521		
		2,877	15.5
		18,533	100.0

Workings

	£000
1. Bought-in materials, etc.:	
Purchases	7,192
Direct overheads	3,520
Indirect overheads	2,106
	12,818

2. To pay employees:

	£000
Wages	8,306
Salaries	2,941
Pension contributions	840
Directors' remuneration	36
	12,123

3. Dividends to MI:

		£000
Preferential 70% × £10,000	=	7,000
Ordinary 40% × £15,000	=	6,000
		13,000

4. Retained profits:

Group retained profit	1,657
Less: Group share of retained profit of associate 40% × £350,000	140
	1,517
Add: Minority interest's share in retained profit 40% × £10,000	4
	1,521

(b) The making of profit has been and always will be a very important element in the objectives of any organisation in a capitalistic economy. Although profit making may not be the most important aim of business enterprises and will certainly not be the only aim, it is difficult to see business enterprises continuing in existence in the long-term unless profits are made

Published reports of business enterprises certainly lay great stress on the profit figure and it is without doubt the keynote figure in the profit and loss account. The idea that profit is the sole aim of business enterprises also tends to be supported by articles in the financial press and indeed the media as a whole.

Despite this, published reports are tending to become more comprehensive than previously although it may be that a downturn in the economy may force companies to reduce the volume, and hence the cost of their reports. Thus a modern report deals not merely with a profit and loss account but with such matters as:

(a) a balance sheet, giving the financial position of the company at a particular date;
(b) a statement of source and application of funds showing how liquidity of the company has changed;

(c) a director's report giving details required by statute, little of which relates directly to profitability;
(d) a chairman's report dealing with the general progress of the firm and possibly with future prospects.

Additional objectives of business enterprises include the following:

(i) To create wealth for differing groups in a stable manner over the long-term.
The corporate report could therefore perhaps give details of a value added statement, showing how the wealth of the organisation has been allocated between the various groups within the concern over a ten-year period.
(ii) To create stable employment
The report could contain an employment report dealing with the number of employees during the year, how this has changed, and the distribution between sex, age, locality, etc.
(iii) Continued existence
In some cases a company may have done well merely to survive. This might be outlined in a chairman's report (and often will be if profits are very low!).

ANSWER R4. THE DUNCAN MANUFACTURING CO.

(a) *Statement of value added for the year ended . . .*

	£000	£000	%
Turnover (working 1)		1,250	
Bought-in materials (working 2)		500	
		750	
Duncan's share of associated companies earnings		100	
Value added		850	100.0
Applied as follows:			
To pay employees:			
Wages, PAYE, and pensions (working 3)		300	35.3
To pay providers of capital:			
Interest on loans	120		
Dividend to shareholders	65	185	21.8
To pay government:			
Corporation tax		165	19.4
To provide for maintenance and expansion:			
Depreciation	100		
Retained profits	100	200	23.5
		850	100.0

Workings

1. *Turnover*

	£000
Sales (net of VAT)	1,200
Royalties received	50
	1,250

2. *Bought in materials*

	£000
Opening stock	200
Purchases	800
	1,000
Less: Closing stock	500
	500

3. *Wages, PAYE and Pensions*

	£000
Wages (net)	200
PAYE	50
Pensions	50
	300

Note

The figure of £100,000 for associated companies earnings shown in the annual accounts represents Duncan's share of the total associated companies earnings for the period. This item has been included in the value added statement by showing the figure of £100,000 as being an addition to value added. Retained profits then include the whole of the earnings retained as per the P & L A/c of Duncan, i.e. £100,000.

Alternatively, it is possible to treat only the associated companies dividends received of £50,000 as being an addition to value added. The retained profits will then be calculated as follows:

	£000	£000
Earnings retained as per P & L A/c of Duncan		100
Less: Duncan's share of retained profits of associates:		
Associated companies earnings	100	
Less: Dividends received	50	50
Retained profits		50

(b) *To Managing Director* *1 Jun. 19—*
From A. N. Accountant
Treatment of depreciation and taxation in value added statements
With reference to your query on the above, the following points should be made.

(i) *Depreciation*
The annual depreciation charge can be viewed in two ways. First, it can be considered to represent the value of fixed assets consumed during the year in the process of earning profits. Depreciation is then treated as an external cost. Second, it can be viewed as being a reinvestment of funds in the business, to provide for the maintenance and replacement of fixed assets. This leads to depreciation being treated as a distribution of value added.

(1) *Treatment as external cost*
Under this method, depreciation is regarded as an expense and will be treated in the same way as materials bought-in. It will, therefore, be deducted from sales and will reduce the value the business adds to its goods. However, the Corporate

Report suggests that depreciation should not be treated as an external cost, but as a distribution of value added.

(2) *Treatment as distribution of value added*

This method views depreciation as a means of ploughing profits back into the business. It follows that depreciation should be treated as an application or distribution of the value the business adds to its goods, rather than as a deduction in arriving at value added. The argument for this method is based on the idea that management control the financial resources of the firm, and that by charging depreciation they are merely reinvesting funds in the business.

Either of the above methods can be used to display depreciation in the value added statement. The Corporate Report, however, recommends that depreciation be treated as a distribution of value added, and it is therefore suggested that this method is followed.

(ii) *Taxation*

The treatment of taxation in value added statements will depend on the tax involved, the main taxes being VAT, PAYE and corporation tax. These three taxes will be looked at in turn.

(1) *VAT*

In most instances a company will not suffer VAT on either its purchases or its sales, and the firm can therefore be considered to be acting merely as a tax collector for the government. It follows, that the most appropriate method of treating VAT, is to leave it out of the value added statement, altogether. (This is the treatment used in part (a) of the question).

As the company does not actually suffer VAT, it would be wrong to regard VAT as an external cost. It would be possible to treat VAT as a distribution of value added and the effect of such treatment is outlined in appendix 1.

Appendix 1

Treatment of VAT and PAYE as a distribution of value added

If VAT and PAYE are treated on this basis then the figures appearing in the value added statement for turnover, payments to employees and payments to government will be adjusted as follows;

	£000
Turnover: As per statement in (a)	1,250
Add: VAT on sales	180
	1,430
To pay employees: As per statement	300
Less: PAYE	50
	250

	£000
To pay government: As per statement	165
Add: VAT	180
PAYE	50
	395

(2) *PAYE*

In paying the PAYE the company is again merely acting as a tax collector for the government. The remarks made for VAT therefore apply here, with one exception. Since, PAYE represents a deduction from an employee's wages, it cannot be left out of the value added statement altogether. It must be added back to wages in order to arrive at the gross wages figure paid to employees.

The treatment of PAYE as a distribution of value added is outlined in Appendix 1.

(3) *Corporation tax*

Corporation tax is the only one of the three taxes mentioned which represents a real transfer between the company and the government. Unlike, the previous cases it should therefore be included in the value added statement either as an external cost or as an allocation of company funds. It appears sensible to treat the government, in the same way as employees and providers of capital and thus include corporation tax as a distribution of value added.

There is no accounting standard on the subject of value added statements, and therefore companies are free to adopt the treatment they wish. However, as outlined above, it would appear appropriate to regard the company as a collecting agent for the government, when dealing with VAT and PAYE, and to treat corporation tax as a distribution of value added.

ANSWER R5. SAUCES LTD

(a) *Statement of source and application of funds for the year-ended 30 Sep. 19–6*

Ref. to workings		*£m*	*£m*
	Source of funds		
	Profit before tax and extraordinary items		87.3
	Extraordinary items		22.3
			109.6
	Adjustment for items not involving the movement of funds or dealt with as a separate application of funds:		
(3)	Depreciation	77.1	
(4)	Preproduction expenses written off	8.6	
(5)	Exploration and development expenses written off	22.2	
(6)	Profits retained in associated companies	(1.6)	
			106.3
	Total generated from operations		215.9
	Funds from other sources		
	Proceeds of share issue	34.0	
	Increase in long-term indebtedness	118.8	
			152.8
			368.7
	Application of funds		
	Expenses of share issue	0.9	
(1)	Tax paid	58.1	
(2)	Dividends paid	10.1	
(3)	Additions to property, plant and equipment	164.3	
(4)	Preproduction expenses	21.3	
(5)	Exploration and development costs	17.0	
			271.7
			97.0

Increase (decrease) in working capital		£m
Increase in stock		71.4
Increase in debtors		26.5
Increase in creditors		(21.0)
Movement in net liquid funds:		
Increase in bank balance	42.1	
Increase in short-term borrowings	(22.0)	
		20.1
		97.0

Workings:

(1) Taxation account

	£m		£m
Cash paid (bal fig)	58.1	Balances b/d:	
Balances c/d:		Corporation tax	93.9
Corporation tax	68.2	Deferred tax	116.6
Deferred tax	132.9	P & L account (see note (1))	48.7
	259.2		259.2

(2) Dividends account

	£m		£m
Cash paid (bal fig, see note (2))	10.1	Balance b/d	9.9
Balance c/d	13.1	P & L account	13.3
	23.2		23.2

(3) Plant and machinery account (NBV)

	£m		£m
Balance b/d	695.7	Depreciation charge	77.1
Cash paid	164.3	Balance c/d	782.9
	860.0		860.0

(4) *Preproduction expenses*

	£m
Charged in the profit and loss account	8.6
Increase in balance £m (53.5 – 40.8)	12.7
Expenditure incurred	21.3

(5) *Exploration and development costs*

	£m
Charged in the profit and loss account	22.2
Decrease in balance £m(10.0 – 4.8)	5.2
Expenditure incurred	17.0

(6) *Associated company investment*

	£m
Balance at 1.10.–5	86.1
Investing company's share of post-acquisition retained profits	1.6
Surplus on revaluation	14.1
Balance at 30.9.–6	101.8

Notes:

(1) It is assumed that the tax charge of £48.7m does not include an amount in respect of the associated company. This is extremely unlikely but no information is given in the question on this particular point.
(2) It is difficult to reconcile the dividends paid of £10.1m. The only possibility is that this figure consists of the proposed dividend of £9.9m together with half this year's preference dividend, (£0.2m). This would then mean that proposed dividends this year relate to both the ordinary dividends (£12.9m) and the second half of the preference dividend (£0.2m). This conflicts with the descriptions given in the profit and loss account and is unlikely in practice.
(3) It is assumed that there have been no disposals of fixed assets during the year.
(4) The share issue expenses have been shown as a separate application. Some companies might net this amount off against the gross proceeds of issue on the grounds that the amount involved was not material.

(b) *Reasons for SSAP 10*
Statement of Standard Accounting Practice Number 10 entitled *Statement of Source and Application of Funds* was issued in Jul. 1975. Its issue recognised two principal points:

(1) there was a need for such a statement showing the movement of funds within a company or group as part of the annual published report of the entity concerned; and
(2) that given the need for such a statement there was a desire for minimum standards of disclosure and if possible for a standardised format.

It is under these two main headings that the reasons for *SSAP 10* can be summarised.

(1) *The usefulness of a statement of source and application of funds*
The profit and loss account and the balance sheet of a company

show, *inter alia*, the amount of profit which the company has made during a period and the allocation of its resources at the beginning and end of that period. It is argued, however, that they fail to highlight the cause or effect of the movement of a company's resources during a particular period. For a fuller understanding of a company's affairs, therefore, the statement of source and application of funds will perform three main tasks:

(i) First, it will provide a link between the balance sheet and the profit and loss account of the organization.
(ii) Second, it will underline the difference between profitability and liquidity and help interested parties to appreciate that although historical cost profits may be at record levels it may still be necessary to find additional finance, raise prices, or keep dividends or wage increases down to a minimum.
(iii) Third, the statement will highlight the importance of the levels of liquid funds within the organisation and the effect of the profitability and investment policies of management on these liquid funds.

(2) *The necessity for minimum disclosure requirements and standardisation of format*

The principle of the funds statement is very simple and its layout has a large number of variations. It can, for instance, merely be a list of the changes in the balance sheet items from one year to the next or, on the other hand, be a multi-column statement showing much more detail of balance sheet changes together with funds arising from profits.

The other main problem is that the funds statement can be prepared using different concepts. It can, for instance, be treated merely as a cash account. Alternatively, funds can be treated as working capital, or, under the 'total funds concept', all changes can be accounted for including, for instance, the revaluation of assets.

SSAP 10 lays down minimum disclosure requirements and its appendix includes suggested layouts which have been followed in the first part of this answer.

ANSWER R6. FURNITURE AND CHAIRS

(a) *Furniture Ltd and subsidiary*

Consolidated statement of source and application of funds for the year ended 31 May 19–9.

Source of funds	*£000*	£000
Profit before taxation		3,200
Adjustment for item not involving the movement of funds: Depreciation		1,150
Total generated from operations		4,350
Funds from other sources		
Issue of shares in Furniture Ltd for cash	2,000	
Issue of shares in subsidiary for cash to outside shareholders	10	
Issue of 10% debentures	1,500	
		3,510
		7,860
Application of funds		
Purchase of fixed assets	3,450	
Taxation paid	1,260	
Dividends paid to members of Furniture Ltd	1,010	
Dividends paid to outside shareholders in subsidiaries	28	
		5,748
		2,112
Increase (decrease) in working capital		
Increase in stocks		350
Increase in debtors		750
Increase in trade creditors		(250)
		850
Movement in net liquid funds:		
Increase in cash	1,350	
Increase in overdrafts	(88)	
		1,262
		2,112

Workings:

(1) *Profit before taxation*

	£000	£000
Trading profit Furniture Ltd		3,500
Chairs Ltd		300
		3,800
Less: Debenture interest Furniture Ltd	500	
Chairs Ltd	100	
		600
		3,200

(2) *Issue of shares in subsidiary*

	£000
Total value of issue	50
Less: Amount taken up by holding company	40
	10

(3) *Purchase of fixed assets*

	£000	£000
Balance at 31 May 19–8 Furniture Ltd		10,000
Chairs Ltd		1,400
		11,400
Additions (balancing figure)		3,450
		14,850
Depreciation for year Furniture Ltd	1,000	
Chairs Ltd	150	
		1,150
Balance at 31 May 19–9 Furniture Ltd	12,000	
Chairs Ltd	1,700	
		13,700

(4) *Taxation paid*

Taxation account (combined)

	£000		£000
Balance b/f		Balance b/f	
ACT recoverable:		Current taxation:	
Furniture Ltd	497	Furniture Ltd	1,446
Chairs Ltd	14	Chairs Ltd	60
Taxation paid (diff)	1,260	Charges to P & L in year	
		Furniture Ltd	1,400
		Chairs Ltd	100
Balances c/f		Balances c/f	
Current taxation:		ACT recoverable:	
Furniture Ltd	1,695	Furniture Ltd	546
Chairs Ltd	127	Chairs Ltd	41
	3,593		3,593

(5) *Dividends paid to members of Furniture Ltd*

Furniture Ltd—dividends payable account

	£000		£000
Dividends paid (diff)	1,010	Balance b/f	500
Balance c/f	600	Charges to P & L in year	1,110
	1,610		1,610

(6) *Dividends paid to outside shareholders in subsidiaries*

Chairs Ltd—dividends payable to minorities

	£000		£000
Dividends paid (diff)	28	Charges to P & L in year:	
		Preference (All)	28
Balance c/f	11	Ordinary (20%)	11
	39		39

Tutorial note

The statement above follows the lines of that given in the appendix (which was non-mandatory) to *SSAP 10* except that minorities are dealt with on a dividend payment basis because this is considered to be more straightforward and less likely to confuse non-accountant readers of funds flow statements.

The alternative presentation would be to deduct minority interest in the profit after tax (£42,400) from the group profit before tax and add back the minority share of unpaid dividends and profit retained for the year (£14,400) under adjustments for items not involving the movement of funds.

(b) *Result of changing acquisition date to 1 Jun. 19–8*

Had Chairs Ltd been acquired on 1 Jun. 19–8 it would have amounted to an acquisition in the year. This could have been dealt with in two ways:

(i) The detailed breakdown method.
(ii) The net outlay method.

Assuming that the acquisition was made for cash, the balance sheet of Furniture Ltd at 31 May 19–8 would have shown a cash and bank balance £400,000 higher (the cost of the shares acquired on 1 Jun.).

Taking the different methods in turn, the following adjustments would be required to the statement of source and application of funds:

(1) *Detailed breakdown*	*£000*
Funds from other sources	
Capital reserve arising on purchase of Chairs Ltd	80
Debentures in issue by Chairs Ltd at acquisition	500
Taxation owed by Chairs Ltd at acquisition	46
Interest of outside shareholders in Chairs Ltd at acquisition	520
	1,146
Application of funds	
Purchase of fixed assets (*increased by*)	1,400
	(254)

Increase (decrease) in working capital	*£000*	*£000*
Increase in stocks (*increased by*)		400
Increase in debtors (*increased by*)		1,250
Increase in trade creditors (*increased by*)		(250)
		1,400
Movement in net liquid funds:		
Increases in cash (*decreased by*)	(350)	
Increase in overdraft (*increased by*)	(1,304)	
		(1,654)
		(254)

(2) *Net outlay*

Application of funds	*£000*
Acquisition of Chairs Ltd	400
	(400)
Increase (decrease) in working capital	
Movement in net liquid funds:	
Increase in net cash (*decreased by*)	(400)
	(400)

In both cases the items above would be referred to the following note: *Summary* (detailed breakdown method)/*Analysis* (net outlay method) *of the effects of acquisition of Subsidiary Ltd.*

	£000		*£000*
Net assets acquired:		Discharged by:	
Fixed assets	1,400	Cash paid	400
Stocks	400	Capital reserve	
Debtors	1,250	arising on consolidation	80
Cash and bank balances	50		
Debentures	(500)		
Trade creditors	(250)		
Taxation	(46)		
Overdraft	(1,304)		
	1,000		
Less: Minority interest	520		
	480		480

Workings:

(1) *Taxation owed by Chairs Ltd*

	£000
Current taxation at 31 May 19–8	60
Less: ACT recoverable at 31 May 19–8	14
	46

(2) *Minority interest at date of acquisition*

In ordinary shares:	
Total net assets acquired	1,000
Less: Preference shares not purchased	400
	600
Attributable to minority – 20%	120
In preference shares—All	400
	520

(3) *Decrease in cash (detailed breakdown)*

	£000
Used by Furniture Ltd to acquire Chairs Ltd	400
Less: Acquired on purchase of Chairs Ltd	50
	350

ANSWER R7. HALSALL LTD

(a) *Halsall Ltd*

Statement of source and application of funds
for the year ended 31 Oct. 19–8

(Based on the accounts of the group and showing the effects of the acquisition of Ormskirk Ltd on the separate assets and liabilities of the group).

	£	£
Source of funds		
Profit before tax		267,420
Adjustments for items not involving the movement of funds—depreciation		40,700
Total generated from operations		308,120
Funds from other sources		
Ordinary shares issued*	37,500	
Corporation tax on acquisition of Ormskirk Ltd	17,400	
Minority interest in Ormskirk Ltd at acquisition	12,675	
		67,575
Total sources		375,695
Application of funds		
Dividends paid	37,500	
Tax paid	49,700	
Purchase of goodwill*	15,675	
Purchase of plant*	269,750	
		372,625
		3,070
Increase (decrease) in working capital		
Increase in stocks*	63,200	
Increase in debtors*	20,678	
Increase in creditors—excluding tax and proposed dividends*	(30,470)	
Movement in net liquid funds—Decrease in cash balance	(50,338)	
		3,070

**Summary of the effects of the acquisition of Ormskirk Ltd*

Net assets acquired:	£	Discharged by:	£
Fixed assets	83,750	Shares issued	37,500
Goodwill	15,675	Cash paid	50,000
Stock	20,000	Minority interest	12,675
Debtors	16,500		
Cash	2,700		
Creditors	(21,050)		
Taxation	(17,400)		
	100,175		100,175

Workings

(1) Dividend paid:

	£
Last year proposed final	25,000
This year interim	12,500
	37,500

(2) Minority interest reconciliation:

	£
MI at acquisition 15% × £84,500	12,675
Consolidated P & L account	4,320
MI at 31 Oct. 19–8	16,995

(from this it can be deduced that no dividend was paid to minority shareholders between 1 Jul. 19–8 and 31 Oct. 19–8).

Tutorial note

The above method is often referred to as the *detailed breakdown approach.*

(b) If the source and application of funds statement was prepared with the aim of showing the effect of the acquisition of the subsidiary as a separate item (i.e. the *net outlay approach*), the following items would change:

(i) Corporation tax on acquisition of Ormskirk, minority interest at acquisition, and purchase of goodwill, would no longer appear.

(ii) Under application of funds would appear: *Purchase of shares in Ormskirk Ltd—£87,500.*

(iii) The following items would change:

	£
Acquisition of plant	186,000
Stock	43,200
Debtors	4,178
Cash	(53,038)
Creditors	(9,420)

(c) The survey of Published Accounts indicates that both approaches are widely used by leading quoted companies. *SSAP 10* permits the use of either approach.

The main problem with the detailed breakdown approach is that it does not highlight, as a separate item, the effect of the acquisition of a subsidiary. Furthermore, items such as *minority interest at the date of acquisition* may appear confusing to a reader of financial statements. From a presentation point of view the net outlay approach does appear to have advantages

Some companies have adopted a multi-column approach, using separate columns to highlight the effect of acquisitions and disposals of subsidiaries.

ANSWER R8. GRASMERE GROUP

(a) Value added may be defined as a measure of the wealth created by a company and its employees. It is essentially the difference between the revenue earned by their efforts, and the cost of materials, fuel and services consumed in earning that revenue.

(b) *Grasmere Ltd Group*

Statement of value added for the year ended 31 Dec. 19–8

	£000	£000	%
Sales to customers outside the group		4,168	
Less: Bought in materials and services		3,014	
Value added by the group		1,154	
Profits of associated company		63	
Value added available for retention or sharing		1,217	100
Applied as follows:			
To employees:			
Wages, pensions and other benefits		487	40
To providers of capital:			
Interest on borrowing	44		
Dividends to Grassmere shareholders	120		
Dividends to outside shareholders in subsidiaries	5		
		169	14
To government as taxation on profits		250	20
Retained in associated company		24	2
Reinvested in the business:			
Depreciation	155		
Retained profit	132		
		287	24
		1,217	100

Workings:

(1) *Bought in materials and services*

This is effectively a balancing figure:

	£000	£000
Sales		4,168
Profit before tax		468
∴ Overheads and expenses		3,700
Less: Items to be disclosed separately:		
Interest	44	
Wages and salaries	487	
Depreciation	155	
		686
		3,014

(2) *Dividends to outside shareholders*

	£
10% × £(20,000 + 30,000)	5

(3) *Retained in associated company*

	£
30% × £80,000	24

(4) *Retained profit*

	£	
Holding company	102	
Subsidiary (100% × retained)	30	
		132

(c) (i) *Minority interest*

The minority share of the profit of Easedale Ltd has been dealt with in two places:

(1) Dividends paid and proposed have been dealt with as applied to providers of capital

(2) Minority share of retained profit (10% × £30,000) has been added to Grasmere's share of retained profit of Easedale (£27,000) and the total of £30,000 included in retained profit of £132,000.

A less preferable alternative would be to show retained profits as £129,000 (agreeing with the consolidated profit and loss account) and to show applied to providers of capital—minority shareholders £5,000 + £3,000 = £8,000. It is suggested that this would show a misleading picture since a large proportion of this total has been retained by the subsidiary.

(ii) *Associated company*
Grasmere's share of the profit before tax has been shown separately. Attributable tax has been included in the total of £250,000, and the share of retentions has been shown separately.

A less preferable alternative would be to include merely the group's share of the dividend received (£12,000) in the consolidated value added statement. This would appear to go against the spirit of *SSAP 1* on associated companies.

ANSWER R9. ACCOUNTING RATIOS

(a) *The solvency factors in years to 30 Apr.*

	Go-go Products Ltd		*Numerous Inventions Ltd*	
	19–7	*19–6*	*19–7*	*19–6*
	£	£	£	£
(1) Profit before tax / Current liabilities	1,400 / 7,930 = 0.18	935 / 9,970 = 0.09	1,090 / 4,357 = 0.25	1,278 / 2,467 = 0.52
	Better ←		Worse →	
(2) Current assets / Total liabilities	10,801 / 9,339 = 1.16	11,537 / 11,138 = 1.04	6,798 / 4,412 = 1.54	4,859 / 2,505 = 1.94
	Better ←		Worse →	
(3) Current liabilities / Total tangible assets	7,930 / 15,445 = 0.51	9,970 / 16,765 = 0.59	4,357 / 8,748 = 0.50	2,467 / 6,389 = 0.39
	Better →		Worse ←	
(4) No credit interval: Net current assets / Operating costs less depn (decimals of a year)	2,871 / 28,356 = 0.10	1,567 / 24,198 = 0.06	2,441 / 8,313 = 0.29	2,392 / 6,571 = 0.36
	Better ←		Worse →	

	Go-go Products Ltd 19–7	*Go-go Products Ltd* 19–6	*Numerous Inventions Ltd* 19–7	*Numerous Inventions Ltd* 19–6
(5) Acid test	£	£	£	£
Current assets less stock / Current liabilities	4,558 / 7,930 = 0.57	4,764 / 9,970 = 0.48	5,812 / 4,357 = 1.33	3,602 / 2,467 = 1.46
	Better ←		Worse →	
(6) Long term solvency				
Liabilities and loans / Total tangible assets	9,339 / 15,445 = 0.60	11,138 / 16,765 = 0.66	4,412 / 8,748 = 0.50	2,505 / 6,389 = 0.39
	Better →		Worse ←	

(b) *Comparison of the two companies*
In each of the six ratios Numerous Inventions Ltd (NI) is shown to be in a sounder financial position than Go-go Products Ltd (GG). In each of the six ratios GG has improved its solvency and NI has suffered a reverse

Both companies have increased their sales by some 20% but for NI this has meant a drop of 4.69% in the ratio of net profit to sales and for GG an increase of 0.98%. On the assumption that the two companies are in the same trade it would appear that GG might be able to increase its prices so as to improve its profitability and thus its solvency (ratio (1)). The *acid test* (ratio (5)) shows the discomfort of GG. This ratio ought to be about unity. Attempting to fend off creditors of £5,261 with only £516 in the bank cannot be much fun. However, the company should be able to borrow by means of an overdraft. It has had quite a good year. NI must improve its cost control whilst it still has time. In the long-term both companies seem sound (ratios (2), (3) and (6)).

The *no credit interval* (ratio (4)) is an unusual ratio. It shows the length of time (as a proportion of a year) that the company could continue trading if all credit facilities were withdrawn by suppliers etc. GG would barely last a month. NI could survive for about three months.

(c) *Ratio analysis as a predictor of failure*
For many years, ratio analysis has been used extensively by a wide range of users of financial statements (bankers, investment analysts, auditors and management) for many different purposes. Comparisons may be made over a period of time (intra-firm) or between one business and another similar business (inter-firm)

More recently an extended use of ratio analysis is being considered, namely whether on the basis of historically prepared accounts it is possible to say whether or not a particular business may be viewed as

ANSWER R10

(a) *Definition of earnings per share*

The earnings per share is the profit in pence attributable to each equity share. Earnings is defined as profit after tax, minority interest and preference dividend but before taking account of extraordinary items. To arrive at the figure of earnings per share, earnings are divided by the number of equity shares in issue and ranking for dividend.

(b) (i) *Earnings per share for 19–8*

$$\text{Earnings per share} = \frac{£600{,}000}{3{,}589{,}490} \times 100 = \underline{16.7}\text{p}$$

(ii) *Earnings per share for 19–7*

Earnings per share reported in 19–7

$$= \frac{£453{,}000}{3{,}200{,}000} \times 100 = \underline{14.156}\text{p}$$

$$\text{Adjustment for rights issue} = 14.156\text{p} \times \frac{76.67}{80} = \underline{13.6}\text{p}$$

Workings—part (b):

(i)

	19–8	*19–7*
	£	£
Profit after tax	612,000	465,000
Preference dividend	12,000	12,000
Earnings	600,000	453,000

(ii) Adjustment for rights issue:

	No. of shares	£
Holder of 100 shares before rights issue —value	100 × 80p	80.00
Rights subscription	20 × 60p	12.00
	120	92.00

$$\therefore \text{Ex-rights (theoretical price)} = \frac{£92}{120} = 76.67\text{p}$$

(iii) Number of shares—current year:

(Cum) 3,200,000 × 6/12 × 80/76.67 (ex)	= 1,669,490
3,840,000 × 6/12	= 1,920,000
Adjusted number of shares	3,589,490

a going-concern. The technique, linear discriminant analysis, is used in the USA but is new to this country. If the technique proves successful it will be of great assistance to the auditor.

(c) *Disclosure in published accounts*

(i) Profit and loss account (extract)

	Year ended 30 Sep.	
	19–8	*19–7*
Earnings per ordinary share of 25p	16.7	13.6p

(ii) *Note*

The calculation of earnings per share is based on earnings of £600,000 (19–7: £453,000) and on the weighted average of 3,589,490 ordinary shares after adjustment of the number of shares in issue prior to the rights issue on 31 Mar. 19–8. The earnings per share for 19–7 have been adjusted accordingly.

(d) The fully diluted earnings per share should be shown on the face of the profit and loss account of quoted companies in the following three circumstances:

(i) where the company has issued a separate class of equity shares which do not rank for dividend in the period under review, but which will do so in the future;
(ii) where the company has issued debentures, loan stock or preference shares convertible into equity shares of the company;
(iii) where the company has granted options or issued warrants to subscribe for equity shares of the company

(e) Certain recent accounting standards and exposure drafts have caused problems as regards measurement, evaluation and comparison of earnings per share. These include:

(i) Deferred taxation (*SSAP 15*)—during the changeover period to *SSAP 15*, different companies have adopted varying criteria for the calculation of the tax charge. It is hoped standardization will be achieved once all companies adopt a consistent approach towards *SSAP 15*
(ii) Depreciation (*SSAP 12*)—some companies revalue fixed assets and base their depreciation on the new figure (as required by *SSAP 12*). The problem arises because the historical cost convention allows the inclusion of revaluation figures in the final accounts. This causes problems of comparability of earnings.
(iii) Inflation itself affects different companies in different ways and thus distorts the profit figure on which earnings per share is based.
(iv) Problems may also be caused by accounting standards which have been in issue for some time, e.g. *SSAP 6* on prior year adjustments and extraordinary items.

ANSWER R11

(a) *Benefits of accepting the new cash offer*

Middle market quotation of Madame Tussaud shares on 21 Nov. 1977	$30\frac{1}{2}$p
Cash offer	65p
Increase (representing 113%)	$34\frac{1}{2}$p

This increase is subject to capital gains tax.

Note that this was the comparison made in the actual offer document for the new recommended offer. (This comparison with the market price on 17 Jan. 1978, the day preceding the announcement of the new offer, would show an increase of 65p – $59\frac{1}{2}$p which is equivalent to 9%.)

(b) *Benefits of accepting the convertible alternative*
In the light of the information given, the benefits can be looked at from two viewpoints:

(i) *Capital*

	£
Middle market quotation of 100 Madame Tussaud shares on 21 Nov. 1977	30.50
£65 nominal of Pearson convertible (per Cazenove letter) £65 × 98%	63.70
Increase (representing 109%)	33.20

(ii) *Income*

	£
For a holder of 100 Madame Tussaud shares:	
Forecast dividend (including tax credit) for the year ending 31 Dec. 1978	4.83
Interest on £65 nominal of Pearson convertible	6.82
Increase (representing 41%)	1.99

ANSWER R12. NORTHERN MANUFACTURING PLC

(*a*) *Calculation of earnings per share as disclosed in the accounts of 19–8 and 19–9.*

	19–8 £	*19–9* £
Share numbers:		
Per question	600,000	
Rights issue at full market price		
4/12 × £600,000 =		200,000
8/12 × 1,000,000 =		666,667
		866,667
On conversion of 8% loan	500,000	500,000
	1,100,000	1,366,667

	19–8 £	*19–9* £
Earnings:		
Per question	67,000	140,000
Loan interest net of corporation tax (see note) per question	40,000	40,000
Irrecoverable advance corporation tax	33,000	60,000
Net basis: Undiluted	67,000	140,000
Add: Loan interest	40,000	40,000
Diluted	107,000	180,000
Nil basis: Undiluted	67,000	140,000
Add: Irrecoverable ACT	33,000	60,000
	100,000	200,000
Diluted	67,000	140,000
	40,000	40,000
	33,000	60,000
	140,000	240,000

Earnings per share:

		19–8	*19–9*
Net basis:	Undiluted	$\frac{£67,000}{£600,000} = 11.17p$	$\frac{£140,000}{£866,667} = 16.15p$
	Diluted	$\frac{£107,000}{£1,100,000} = 9.73p$	$\frac{£180,000}{£1,366,667} = 13.17p$
Nil basis:	Undiluted	$\frac{£100,000}{£600,000} = 16.67p$	$\frac{£200,000}{£866,667} = 23.08p$
	Diluted	$\frac{£140,000}{£1,100,000} = 12.73p$	$\frac{£240,000}{£1,366,667} = 17.56p$

Notes:
1. The disclosure on a Nil basis would be advisable although it is discretionary: *Para. 9 SSAP 3.*
2. Loan interest is allowable for corporation tax and should therefore be added back net of corporation tax to arrive at earnings available to ordinary shareholders. As the question states that no corporation tax is payable in the foreseeable future it has been ignored: *Para. 30 App. 1 SSAP 3.*

(*b*) *PE ratios with earnings per share on a net basis*

	Undiluted	*Diluted*
Current price	$\frac{180p}{16.15p} = 11.1$	$\frac{180p}{13.17p} = 13.7$
Range—lowest	$\frac{110p}{16.15p} = 6.8$	$\frac{110p}{13.17p} = 8.4$
—highest	$\frac{200p}{16.15p} = 12.4$	$\frac{200p}{13.17p} = 15.2$

(*c*) *Liquidity ratios*

		19–8	*19–9*
Current ratio Current assets:	Current liabilities	1,140:540 2.1	1,800:1,000 1.8
Liquidity ratio Liquid assets:	Current liabilities	540:540 1.0	800:1,000 0.8
Period of debt collection (assume all sales on credit) (Debtors/Turnover) × 365 days		500/5,000 × 365 = 37 days	800/7,000 × 365 = 42 days

Overdraft must be renewed every three months. It is therefore treated as a current liability.

(*d*) *The liquidity position*

There is a general worsening of the liquidity position between 19–8 and 19–9. The current and liquidity ratios show some slippage and it is proving a little more difficult to collect in the debtors. The funds flow statement confirms the picture. However, partly as a result of the share issue the company is living comfortably within its overdraft position and should not need to go beyond the £750,000 maximum previously negotiated. The following comments might be made.

	19–8	*19–9*
(1) Gearing	1,100/2,000 = 55%	1,100/2,700 = 41%

This is a very high gearing. The percentage has fallen as a result of the share issue but the past performance of distributing all profits in dividends and a 'planned expansion of activities' may necessitate further loan or share issues shortly. The conversion of the 8% loan on 31 Dec. 19–15 will reduce the gearing substantially.

(2) Stocks:

	19–8	*19–9*
Stock/turnover	600/5,000 = 12%	1,000/7,000 = 14%

Stocks have increased at a greater rate than sales.
If stock levels can be reduced without losing sales the liquidity position can be improved.

(3) Creditors and debtors:

	19–8	*19–9*
Creditors/turnover	350/5,000 = 7%	700/7,000 = 10%

Little information is available about purchases so that no very meaningful ratios can be examined. The above rather crude comparison shows that there has been a possible slowing up of payments to creditors. This might be extended still further.

Collection of debts within 42 days is quite good and it seems unlikely this can be much improved.

Conclusion

The directors must plan their proposed expansion of business with care. The company's present liquidity position is not unsatisfactory but they must be careful not to jeopardise the situation by going too quickly. They should consider whether:

(a) Stock levels can be reduced without unduly depressing sales and efficiency.
(b) Debtors can be brought back to an average of 37 days as in 19–8.

(c) Creditors can be pushed to provide more credit without causing disruption of deliveries or withdrawal of credit facilities.

In the light of the above, the directors should determine what proportion of the necessary finance is to be provided by equity, either by retention of profits, or further share issues and then ensure that the remaining money will be available from lenders as it is required. At the same time they might consider converting the non-fluctuating portion of the overdraft into a medium or long-term loan.

ANSWER R13.

(a) Effects of conversion on capital and income values.

(i) Number of shares offered: $\frac{832}{0.832} \times 1 = 1{,}000$

(ii) Capital gain:

Market value of shares:	£
Cum. dividend 1,000 × 98p	980.00
Gross value of dividend 1,000 × 2.6p × 100/67	38.81
Ex. dividend	941.19
Less: Market value of loan stock: £832 × 81.27/100	676.17
Gain	265.02

Tutorial note
The dividend has been deducted gross in the manner of the actual Grand Metropolitan offer document. However, this is an over-simplification because of the differential tax position of a seller of a capital asset and the recipient of a dividend.

(iii) Income loss:

	£
Interest on loan stock: £832 × 10/100	83.20
Expected gross dividend: £1,000 × 4.6p × 100/67	68.66
Loss	14.54

This calculation assumes that the maximum dividend will be paid for the current year and puts no value on that earlier receipt of income obtained by the investment in loan stock.

(b) Expected additional information:

(i) Details of liability, if any, to capital gains tax.
(ii) Recommendation to convert where beneficial.
(iii) Action required by the holder of the loan stock.
(iv) Date on which it is expected that dealings will commence in the shares taken up in the conversion.
(v) Procedure for coping with fractional entitlements.

The company would also enclose a copy of its most recent published accounts.

(c) Journal entries for conversion.

Date	*Details*	*Dr.*	*Cr.*
19 Mar. 1979	10% Convertible Unsecured Loan Stock	16,640,000	
	Ordinary Share Capital		10,000,000
	Share premium		6,640,000
	Being conversion of the whole of the outstanding Convertible Loan Stock 1991/96 into 20,000,000 50p ordinary shares in accordance with the offer document 6 Feb. 1979		

(d) Reasons for proposal that the company should convert for all stockholders.

The calculation in (a) above shows the capital benefit of conversion.

The income loss is, in fact, notional because a holder of loan stock would obtain a larger income than at present by converting into ordinary shares, selling them and purchasing loan stock in another company.

This is demonstrated by the following calculations:

	£
Capital value of shares offered	941.19
Nominal value of 10% loan stock able to be purchased for this amount in another company per question: £941.19/£81.27 × 100	1,158.10
Annual interest at 10% £1,158.10 × 10/100	115.81
Current interest	83.20
Increase	32.61

A holder of loan stock who took this action would find some of the gain eliminated by dealing costs and perhaps capital gains tax, but generally it would be beneficial converting even if he did not wish to accept the risk associated with ordinary shares.

Consequently, it could be argued that it is only the indolent or the ignorant who would fail to take up the offer. To protect the latter, if not the former, it would be fair for conversion to be made automatic where it is beneficial.

However, if the share and/or loan stock prices were to change so that the conversion was no longer beneficial before dealing in the new shares was possible, or even after that date for those who had not liquidated their investment, there would be ample scope for disputes.

ANSWER R14. TOR LTD

To: The Board of Directors
X Ltd
From: A N Adviser
Subject: Report on Tor Ltd

1. *Introduction*
This report examines the performance and position of Tor Ltd with a view to a takeover bid, and is based on limited financial data.
N.B. Policy changes may be implemented after a takeover which could alter the capital structure, the asset structure and the trading performance as outlined below.
2. *Performance*
The performance ratios given in Appendix A show a considerable improvement during 19–2 which can be attributed to increased margin

on sales rather than efficiency in the use of assets, which has remained poor. Even a capital intensive company could be expected to turn over its assets more than once.

Current cost results are considerably poorer than those on an historic cost basis and, although the 19–2 results are better than those for 19–1, they are well below the current rate of interest on borrowings and provide an extremely poor return on capital invested.

3. *Flow of funds*
The company appears to be implementing an expansion programme which involved acquisitions of fixed assets £910,000 (19–2) and £270,000 (19–1). This is being financed largely from internal sources although the company did make a share issue of £297,000 in 19–2. Relatively small amounts were also raised in both years from long-term loans and sales of fixed assets. Although the company has not used short-term funds to any great extent, the policy of using internal finance has placed substantial strains on working capital. The liquidity ratio has suffered as a result.

4. *Position*
A detailed breakdown of the current cost value of the assets is not available so this analysis is restricted to the historic cost information. The company is extremely capital intensive as one would expect in the petroleum industry with fixed assets being turned over less than once in either year.

Other asset usage is reasonable, and constant. Stock turnover is what one might expect in such an industry while credit control and payment of creditors place no strains on liquidity nor give cause for concern about the efficiency of management in these areas. The liquidity position is poor and worsening, and the position is not helped by using retentions to finance long-term asset acquisition and stock holdings rather than using long-term capital sources; this policy starves working capital of sufficient funds. The company is not insolvent but is not in a good position to withstand commercial shocks.

The capital gearing of the company and the interest cover appears to have potential for considerable expansion with consequent tax advantages. There is no apparent risk of non-payment of interest or capital. However, bearing in mind earlier comments on liquidity, an injection of short-term borrowed funds is not advisable.

5. *Conclusion*
There is a lack of information concerning the future prospects of this company and the petroleum industry in general. A decision to make a takeover bid should be based on information concerning the future; an analysis of past performance is at best a poor guide to the wisdom of an investment in Tor Ltd.

It can be seen that the company has considerably improved its trading performance in the past year. However, unless the return on capital of 8.4% (on a current cost basis) can be improved upon, an investment is unlikely to give a sufficient return.

The liquidity of the company is also a problem area and would require an injection of funds immediately. The gearing potential may provide the answer to this and for further expansion, provided the funds are of a long-term nature.

Unless funds are available, and unless an improved return on capital can be obtained to cover the cost of such funds and the required rate of return of our [the bidder's] company, an investment is not recommended.

Appendix A

Ratios	*Historic cost basis*		*Current cost basis*	
	19–2	*19–1*	*19–2*	*19–1*
*Return on capital employed (Earnings before interest and tax/year end capital including short-term loans)	824 / 3,058 = 26.9%	262 / 2,207 = 11.9%	359 / 4,276 = 8.4%	110 / 3,012 = 3.7%
*Earnings before interest and tax/sales	824 / 2,591 = 31.8%	262 / 1,774 = 14.8%	359 / 2,591 = 13.9%	110 / 1,774 = 6.2%
*Asset turnover	2,591 / 3,058 = 0.85 times	1,774 / 2,207 = 0.80 times	2,591 / 4,276 = 0.61 times	1,774 / 3,012 = 0.59 times

Ratios	*Historic cost basis* 19–2	19–1	*Current cost basis* 19–2	19–1
Gross profit/Sales	1,271/2,591 = 49.1%	644/1,774 = 36.3%	—	—
Operating expenses/sales	447/2,591 = 17.3%	382/1,774 = 21.5%	—	—
Return on equity capital (profit after tax, minority interests and preference dividend/ ordinary shares plus reserves)	514/2,395 = 21.5%	149/1,708 = 8.7%	—	—
*Current ratio	886:680 = 1.30:1	587:363 = 1.62:1	—	—
*Liquidity ratio	(886–554): 680 = 0.49:1	(587–388): 363 = 0.55:1	as HC	
*Stock turnover (stock/cost of sales × 365)	554/1,320 × 365 = 153	388/1,130 × 365 = 125	as HC	
*Debtor turnover	330/2,591 × 365 = 46 days	191/1,774 × 365 = 39 days	as HC	
*Credit turnover (Creditors/cost of sales × 365)	306/1,320 × 365 = 85	201/1,130 × 365 = 65	as HC	
Fixed asset turnover	2,302/2,591 = 0.9 times	1,493/1,774 = 0.8 times	—	—
*Gearing (debt/total capital)	308/3,058 = 10%	228/2,207 = 10.3%	308/4,276 = 7.2%	228/3,012 = 7.6%
*Interest cover (earnings before interest and tax/ interest)	824/48 = 17.2 times	262/34 = 7.7 times		

Note: These ratios are only intended as a guide to the areas to be covered. Alternative calculations are possible in many cases and therefore workings should always be given.

ANSWER R15. UNSATIABLE APPETITES PLC

(a) The purpose of presenting the earnings per share statistic in the annual accounts is to assist users of the financial statements in the calculation of the price–earnings ratio which is an important stock market indicator.

In addition, it helps users compare the profitability of the company from one period to another where there have been rights issues or issues of shares to acquire other businesses which may make comparison of aggregate earnings misleading. Comparison of earnings on a 'per share' basis after making allowance for share issues will be more meaningful. It also enables comparisons of past performance to be made between companies on a basis independent of changes in capital.

Another purpose of presenting the statistic is to assist users in appreciating the potential effect of the conversion of securities or the exercise of options at some future date on the earnings attributable to existing shareholders. This potential dilution is reflected in the fully diluted earnings per share figure disclosed in the accounts.

Lastly, disclosure of earnings per share may assist users in calculating dividend cover by comparing earnings per share with dividends per share. Although this could be done on an aggregate basis, it may be simpler to calculate on a 'per share' basis especially in view of the fact that the earnings figure used in the calculation of earnings per share will be standardised from one company to another as required by SSAP 3.

(b) The following earnings per share figures will be disclosed in the published accounts for the year ended 31 Dec. 19–9:

	19–9	*19–8*
Basic	24.8p *(W5)*	16.6p *(W3)*
Fully diluted	15.5p *(W8)*	

Fully diluted earnings per share for the corresponding previous period has not been shown since the assumptions on which it would have been based have changed during the current period.

Workings

1. *Bonus fraction for rights issue*

	Shares		£
Existing holding	4	@ 70p	2.80
Rights	1	@ 60p	0.60
New holding	5		3.40

Theoretical ex rights price $\frac{3.40}{5}$ 68p

Bonus fraction for rights issue $\frac{\text{Actual cum rights price}}{\text{Theoretical ex rights price}}$ $\frac{70}{68}$

	£
2. *Shares in issue (19–8)*	
At 1 Jan. 19–8	160,000
Bonus issue: (1 Apr. 19–8) 1 for 4	40,000
	200,000
Bonus effect of rights issue *(W1)* 2 for 68	5,882
	205,882

3. *Earnings per share (19–8)* £

EPS $\frac{39{,}590 - 5{,}400}{205{,}882\ (W2)}$ 16.6p

4. *Shares in issue (19–9)*	
At 1 Jan. 19–9 (including rights issue)	250,000
Shares issued on exercise of option (only included for 1 month) 1/12 × 20,400	1,700
	251,700

5. *Earnings per share (19–9)*

EPS $\frac{67{,}820 - 5{,}400}{251{,}700\ (W4)}$ 24.8p

6. *Fully diluted shares (19–9 only)*	
At 1 Jan. 19–9 (before any dilution)	250,000
Exercise of options from 1 Jan. 19–9 (100,000 × 70/68*)	102,941
Conversion of loan stock from 1 Jul. 19–9 6/12 × 300,000	150,000
	502,941

*Optionholders' entitlements have been adjusted for the bonus element, of the rights issue.

7. *Earnings for fully diluted basis only (19–9)*

	£
Basic earnings (67,820 – 5,400)	62,420
Interest on proceeds of exercise of options	
Options exercised during year	
$20{,}400 \times £0.75 \times \frac{68^*}{70} \times 14\% \times 0.48 \times \frac{11}{12}$	916
Options not exercised during year	
$(102{,}941 - 20{,}400) \times £0.75 \times \frac{68^*}{70} \times 14\% \times 0.48$	4,041
Interest saved on loan stock	
$£300{,}000 \times 15\% \times 0.48 \times \frac{6}{12}$	10,800
	78,177

*The exercise price of the options has been adjusted for the bonus effect of the rights issue.

8. *Fully diluted earnings per share (19–9)*

EPS $\frac{78{,}177\ (W7)}{502{,}941\ (W6)}$ 15.5p

Assumption
It has been assumed that there are no variable elements in the tax charge and therefore earnings per share on a 'nil' basis has not been calculated.
Tutorial note
No information is given in the question about the effect of the rights issue on the entitlements of the optionholders but it is normal practice for the terms of issue of options to include a provision to make allowance for the bonus effects of subsequent scrip and rights issues. Therefore, in the answer above, adjustments have been made to both the number of shares to which the optionholders would be entitled and to the exercise price of the options using the bonus fraction calculated for the rights issue which is the most logical fraction to use from the information given.

In practice, it is more normal for adjustments to be made on the basis of the actual price ruling for the 'nil' paid rights compared to the amount payable per share for the rights. A typical extract from the terms of issue of options is as follows:

'If the Company, on a date on or before the subscription date, makes any offer of ordinary share capital by way of rights to holders of its ordinary share capital (the ordinary shares so offered being hereinafter referred to as 'the new shares'), then on the occasion of each such offer the subscription price shall be adjusted so that the number of ordinary shares to be issued in respect of every £100 subscribed (and pro rata for any other amount) shall be increased by a number equal to:

$$\frac{A \times C}{B + C}$$

where:

(1) A equals the number of the new shares (including any fraction of a new share) which would have been offered to an option holder had he exercised his right to subscribe £100 on the day immediately preceding the record date for such offer on the basis then applicable;
(2) B equals the price per share at which the new shares are being offered to the holders of the Company's ordinary share capital; and
(3) C equals the average of the middle market quotations on the Stock Exchange, (based on the Daily Official List) for the new shares 'nil' paid during the period in which the new shares are dealt in on the Stock Exchange, 'nil' paid;

and the number of options shall be increased appropriately.'

ANSWER R16. VALUE ADDED STATEMENTS

(a) (i) Differences and similarities between the concept of value added and application of group sales revenue.

Differences

The principal difference between the concept of added value and that of application of group sales revenue is in the treatment of amounts paid to outside suppliers of goods and services.

Underlying the value added concept is the assumption that suppliers have no fundamental interest in the business entity and that their payment is merely a necessary expense.

On the other hand, the attitude underlying the application of sales revenue approach is that suppliers do have an interest in the business entity and that the long term health and success of the entity is not only dependent upon the employees and providers of capital (and indirectly the government), but also on the efforts of and good relationships with suppliers. This is an attitude that is reflected in the Japanese style of business where great emphasis is placed on the long-term continuity and quality of suppliers rather than short term price benefits. It is also a philosophy followed by certain forward-looking UK companies such as Marks and Spencer.

Similarities

Although there is a different emphasis under the two concepts, there are many similarities.

For example, the main elements of the statements are identical. These elements are sales and amounts paid to suppliers, employees, the Government and providers of capital and finally amounts retained in the business. Because of these common elements, one statement can be prepared (in general terms) from the information available in the other.

Another important similarity is that both statements move away from the traditional concept of profit and the view that a business entity exists solely for the benefit of the owners. Thus, although the two concepts differ with respect to the treatment of suppliers, they both are based on a much broader view of the role of a business entity within the economy and society in general.

(ii) Amounts allocated to employees.
Company A discloses 'wages, pensions and benefits to employees' as a single figure, with no breakdown of costs. This figure will almost certainly include the *gross* pay of employees for, while there is no standard on the subject, it is widely felt that this is best practice. Company B gives a more detailed breakdown of the application to employees and having deducted income tax and national insurance, shows employees' pay *net*, a relatively unusual practice.

Company A thus takes the common view that what is relevant in a statement of this kind is the full amount payable to employees, since it is gross pay which is the subject of company wage negotiations and additionally the company cannot be held responsible for government taxation policy. A company's gross payroll costs generally move consistently from year to year, whereas take-home pay can vary considerably, depending on changes in taxation policy and in an individual's personal circumstances (marriage, etc). Company B is more concerned with the application of funds, however, and its statement reflects the fact that much of an employee's nominal pay goes straight to the Inland Revenue. From the employee's point of view take-home pay is probably more important than gross pay and this treatment may be appropriate since many such statements are prepared primarily for employees.

(iii) Amounts allocated to providers of capital
There are two obvious differences in the amounts allocated to providers of capital. The first is that Company B regards income tax deducted from loan interest as an application to Government rather than to the providers of capital, again taking the view that the recipient is primarily interested in the net rather than the gross return. Company A however deals with the gross payment. Under the imputation scheme of corporation tax dividends are shown in the profit and loss account (and in the value added statement) at their net amounts without addition of the related tax credit. Thus Company B is attempting to show both interest and dividends on a comparable basis.

The second difference is that Company B has specifically included the overdraft as part of capital, since it takes the view that the overdraft is a permanent source of finance. Company A does not specifically indicate the treatment of overdraft interest, but it appears that it may have been included in bought-in goods and services.

Finally, neither company gives details of dividends to the minority shareholders in subsidiaries, but Company B appears to have adjusted for these within the retained profit figure while Company A gives no indication of the treatment of minority interests.

(b) Analysis, comparison and comment on information provided
In order to compare the information provided by the two statements it is necessary first to restate them on to a common basis as far as the information is available. Adjusting Company B's statement to reallocate the taxation, produces the following analysis in percentage terms.

	Company A		Company B	
	19–8	19–7	19–8	19–7
	%	%	%	%
Suppliers	67.6	66.6	69.6	69.7
Employees	26.9	26.8	10.0 *(W1)*	9.9 *(W1)*
Government	0.7	1.0	13.6 *(W2)*	13.5 *(W2)*
Interest	1.9	1.3	0.8 *(W3)*	0.7 *(W3)*
Dividends	0.8	0.9	2.4 *(W3)*	2.4 *(W3)*
Retained	2.1	3.4	3.6	3.8
Total sales	100.0	100.0	100.0	100.0

The most meaningful analysis is a comparison of the figures from year to year. For Company B, the percentage shares are very stable from 19–7 to 19–8. There were slight increases in the shares applied to employees, government and interest and a fall in the retention.

For Company A, the trends are more noticeable. As for Company B, the share of revenue applied to employees has risen and this trend is even more marked if amounts applied to employees are expressed as a percentage of value added which shows that employees received 82.9% of value added in 19–8 against 80.1% in 19–7. This probably indicates the effect of wage claims which were not fully passed on in higher prices or matched by productivity gains.

Other noticeable trends in Company A's figures are the sharp increase in interest payments and the drop in retentions. It appears that Company A is suffering from the effects of the recession and the high interest rates more severely than Company B. The drop in retentions at Company A is likely to be the result of a squeeze on profit margins with increased costs from suppliers, employees and interest charges not being fully reflected in selling prices.

A comparison of Company A with Company B is more difficult since, even after the adjustments made, the two sets of figures are not on a common basis. For example, Company B's total revenue includes sales taxes whereas it would appear that this is not the case for Company A. Other differences are the treatment of rates (these are likely to be included under amounts applied to local government for Company B but bought-in services for Company A) and the treatment of employer's national insurance (which appears to have been included under amounts applied to government for Company B but amounts to employees for Company A).

However, despite these different treatments some features stand out in a comparison of the two companies. Firstly, amounts applied to employees are much larger in Company A than Company B, even allowing for the differing treatment of employer's national insurance. This would seem to suggest that the two companies operate in different industries with Company B in a higher volume and less labour intensive industry than Company A. It has already been noted that the more labour intensive Company A felt the effects of wage claims more than Company B and this helps to explain that difference. A further illustration of the difference can be shown by calculating sales generated per £ of employee cost. The 19–8 figures show:

	Company A	*Company B*
Sales per £ of employee cost	£3.72	£10.03

A second noticeable difference between the two companies is the relationship between interest and dividends. The ratio of interest to dividends (a form of gearing measure) gives the following:

	Company A		*Company B*	
	19–8	19–7	19–8	19–7
Interest to dividends	2.2	1.4	0.3	0.3

This shows Company A to be more dependent on borrowed capital and the sharp rise in the burden of interest between the two years shows that either Company A suffered a deterioration in cash flow and gearing or that much of its debt is variable rate borrowing and it suffered from the effects of higher interest rates. Company B seems to have controlled its cash flow and level of interest charges much better.

The third difference between the two companies is in the amount applied to Government. In this case, however, interpretation is less precise since Company B's much larger percentage going to the Government has been swelled by sales taxes, local government rates and employer's National Insurance. Tentatively, the figures again point to different industries with the lower tax figure for Company A being the result of either lower profitability or lower taxable profits which may be due to heavy capital investment.

In summary, the analysis and comparison of the information provided by the two statements highlights some particular trends and differences but more information would be desirable before drawing firm conclusions.

Workings

1. *Applied to employees (Company B)*

	19–9	19–8
	£m	£m
Per statement	170.8	150.3
Add: Income tax and NI	33.0	27.9
	203.8	178.2

2. *Applied to government (Company B)*

		19–9		19–8
	£m	£m	£m	£m
Per statement		311.3		273.8
Less: Income tax and NI	33.0		27.9	
Income tax on loan interest	1.0		1.0	
		34.0		28.9
		277.3		244.9

3. *Applied to providers of capital (Company B)*

	19–9	19–8
	£m	£m
Per statement	64.5	55.4
Add: Income tax deducted	1.0	1.0
	65.5	56.4
Consisting of:		
Interest	15.8	12.0
Dividends	49.7	44.4
	65.5	56.4

ANSWER R17. NEW IDEAS PLC

	19–6 £	*19–5* £
(a) (i) *Creditors ratios*		
Current ratio = $\frac{\text{current assets}}{\text{current liabilities}}$	$\frac{50,199}{21,404}$	$\frac{46,589}{18,578}$
	= 2.34:1	= 2.51:1
Liquidity ratio = $\frac{\text{liquid assets}}{\text{current liabilities}}$	$\frac{24,773}{21,404}$	$\frac{26,358}{18,578}$
	= 1.16:1	= 1.42:1
(ii) *Management ratios*		
Return on capital employed = $\frac{\text{operating profit (before tax and interest)}}{\text{operating assets (net of trade creditors)}}$	$\frac{9,380}{37,838} \times 100$	$\frac{8,362}{32,677} \times 100$
	= 24.8%	= 25.6%
Operating profit on sales = $\frac{\text{operating profit}}{\text{sale}}$	$\frac{9,380}{264,626} \times 100$	$\frac{8,362}{220,393} \times 100$
	= 3.54%	= 3.79%
(iii) *Shareholder ratios*		
Dividend yield = $\frac{\text{dividend (gross)}}{\text{share price}}$	$\frac{1,500 \times 10/7 \times 100}{10,000 \times 1.2}$	$\frac{1,400 \times 10/7 \times 100}{10,000 \times 1.2}$
	= 17.9%	= 16.7%
Earnings per share = $\frac{\text{total earnings}}{\text{number of ordinary shares}}$	$\frac{4,000}{10,000}$	$\frac{3,720}{10,000}$
	= 40p p/s	= 37p p/s

(b) *Comments on changes indicated above*

(i) *Creditors' ratios*

Although there has been a fall in the current ratio, it still stands at a satisfactory level. The fall in the liquidity ratio has been fairly marked and is now only just satisfactory. A further reduction in this ratio could place the company in a vulnerable position. The main problem seems to be that cash resources have had to be used to finance the additional cost of stocks.

(ii) *Management ratios*

Although both the ratios show a deterioration compared with the previous year, the change involved is not unduly significant. Nevertheless, it might be argued that with inflation running at a very high rate, the real return on investment is not particularly attractive.

(iii) *Shareholder ratios*

The increase in the dividend yield merely reflects an increase in dividend per share. In order for meaningful comparisons to be made, the yield should be compared with that which could be obtained in similar companies offering a comparable degree of risk.

(c) *Balance sheet extracts at 30.4.–6 adjusted for the effects of the three possible schemes*

	£000	£000	£000	£000
	At present	*Alternative schemes*		
		(i)	(ii)	(iii)
Ordinary share capital	5,000	5,000	15,000	5,000
Reserves (inc. share premium)	14,763	14,763	20,763	14,763
Deferred tax (inclusion is optional)	5,433	5,433	5,433	5,433
Debenture stock 19–15/–19	10,000	10,000	10,000	10,000
Convertible stock 19–10	—	16,000	—	—
Debenture stock 19–10/19–20	—		—	16,000
Total	35,196	51,196	51,196	51,196
Gearing	10,000 / 35,196 = 0.28	26,000 / 51,196 = 0.51	10,000 / 51,196 = 0.19	26,000 / 51,196 = 0.51

(d) *Effect of three schemes on earnings per share*

	£000	£000	£000	£000
	At present	*Alternative proposals*		
Trading profit	9,380	9,380	9,380	9,380
Additional profits	—	3,500	3,500	3,500
	9,380	12,880	12,880	12,880
Interest payable:				
existing	(1,000)	(1,000)	(1,000)	(1,000)
additional		(1,600)	—	(2,080)
Profit before tax	8,380	10,280	11,880	9,800
Taxation—existing	(4,380)	(4,380)	(4,380)	(4,380)
adjustment		(950)	(1,750)	(710)
Earnings	4,000	4,950	5,750	4,710
Number of ord. shares (M)	10	10	30	10

Summary	*Present*	Schemes (i)	(ii)	(iii)
Earnings per share (pence per ordinary share)	40p	49.5p	19.2p	47.1p

The present earnings per share of 40p given above does not however represent a valid figure of comparison in the case of scheme (i) or scheme (ii).

In scheme (i) a fully diluted earnings per share shows that, once conversion takes place, a large fall in EPS occurs.

	£000	£000
Profit after tax as calculated		4,950
Add: debenture interest saved	1,600	
less tax at 50%	800	800
		5,750

Number of shares
10m at present + 16m from conversion = 26 million
Fully diluted EPS = 22.1p

In scheme (ii) the previous EPS should be adjusted for the bonus element in the rights issue.

	Number	*Value*	£
Before issue	10,000,000	£1.20	12,000,000
Rights	20,000,000	80p	16,000,000
	30,000,000	93.3p	28,000,000

$$\text{Adjusted EPS} = 40\text{p} \times \frac{\text{ex-rights price}}{\text{cum-rights price}} = 40\text{p} \times \frac{93.3}{120} = 31.1$$

(e) *The appropriate method of finance*
At present the earnings per share is 40p. With a share price of only £1.20 the shares seem very low in price (a PE ratio of only 3) and hence an earnings yield of a massive 33.3%. The proposed new scheme seems reasonably profitable with an expected return of almost 22% (3.5m ÷ 16m) but this is still considerably below the earnings yield.

It would seem unwise for the company to issue further shares on a rights basis when these shares seem so low in value. A rights issue will cause a big fall in earnings per share. Surely soon the share price will rise and a future share issue will be much more economic.

The issuing of convertible debenture stock to current shareholders has the merit of producing a short term cash advantage with an interest rate of 10%. Nevertheless the future conversion will cause a rapid fall in earnings per share. It will involve our shareholders with a further capital outlay in a non-equity security which may be of little interest to them. Also, on the assumption that our share price will rise quickly in the near future the conversion rate seems very generous and will presumably cause an increase in the price of the debenture.

It would thus seem best to issue 13% debentures at par. The gearing ratio would be high but not unacceptable. The 22% return from the investment would allow the interest to be paid and still provide an increase in earnings per share without requiring additional investment from our present shareholders.

ANSWER R18

(a) *Detailed breakdown approach*
Bristol Ltd—Source and application of funds statement for the year ended 31st December 19–6 (based on the accounts of the Group and showing the effects of disposing of a subsidiary on the separate assets and liabilities of the group)

	£000	£000
Profit before tax		781.5
Extraordinary item—surplus on sale of subsidiary		24.8
Adjustment for items not involving the movement of funds:		
Depreciation		164.0
Total generated from operations		970.3
Funds from other sources		
Sale of fixed assets*	293.0	
Sale of goodwill*	71.0	
		364.0
		1,334.3
Application of funds		
Dividends paid—holding company	105.0	
Minority shareholders	23.0	
Minority interest on disposal of subsidiary*	149.5	
Tax relating to disposal of subsidiary*	60.8	
Tax paid	506.0	
		844.3
		490.0
Increase in working capital		
Increase in stock*	43.0	
(Decrease) in debtors*	(90.0)	
(Increase) in creditors*	(12.0)	
	(59.0)	
Movement in liquid funds:		
Increase in cash balance*	549.0	
		490.0

**Summary of the effects of the disposal of Swindon Ltd.*

Net assets disposed of	*£000*	*Discharged by*	*£000*
Fixed assets	293.0	Cash received	320.0
Goodwill	71.0	Minority interest	149.5
Surplus on sale	24.8		
Stock	41.0		
Debtors	132.8		
Cash	26.7		
Creditors	(59.0)		
Taxation	(60.8)		
	469.5		469.5

(b) *Net outlay approach*

Statement of Source and application of funds (based on the accounts of the Group and showing the disposal of the subsidiary as a separate item)

	£000	*£000*
Profit before tax		781.5
Adjustments for items not involving the movement of funds—depreciation		164.0
		945.5
Funds from other sources		
proceeds of sale of subsidiary*		320.0
		1,265.5
Application of funds:		
Dividend paid—holding company	105.0	
minority shareholders	23.0	
Tax paid	506.0	
		634.0
		631.5
Increase in working capital		
Increase in stocks	84.0	
Increase in debtors	42.8	
(Increase) in creditors	(71.0)	
	55.8	
Movement in liquid funds		
Cash at bank	575.7	
		631.5

**Summary of the effects of the disposal of Swindon Ltd*

Net assets disposed of	*£000*	*Discharged by*	*£000*
Fixed assets	293.0	Cash received	320.0
Goodwill	71.0	Minority interest	149.5
Surplus on sale	24.8		
Stock	41.0		
Debtors	132.8		
Cash	26.7		
Creditors	(59.0)		
Taxation	(60.8)		
	469.5		469.5

Index